HOW ARBITRATION WORKS

Fourth Edition

1985-89 Cumulative Supplement

BROWN, ANDREW, HALLENBECK,
SIGNORELLI & ZALLAR, P.A.
300 Alworth Building
Duluth, MN 55802

1985-89 Cumulative Supplement

to

Elkouri & Elkouri

HOW ARBITRATION WORKS

Fourth Edition

Co-Editors

Marlin M. Volz
Professor of Law Emeritus
University of Louisville

Edward P. Goggin
Professor of Law
Northern Kentucky University

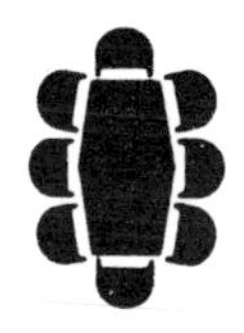

American Bar Association
Section of Labor and Employment Law

The Bureau of National Affairs, Inc., Washington, D.C.

Copyright © 1991
The Bureau of National Affairs, Inc.
Washington, D.C.
American Bar Association
Chicago, Illinois

Library of Congress Cataloging-in-Publication Data
(Revised for 1985-89 Cumulative Supplement)

1985-7 supplement to Elkouri & Elkouri How arbitration works/co-editors, Marlin M. Volz, Edward P. Goggin.
4th ed.
p. cm.
Includes bibliographical references.
ISBN 0-87179-587-6
1. Arbitration, Industrial—United States. I. Volz, Marlin M., 1917. II. Goggin, Edward P. III. Elkouri, Frank. How arbitration works.
KF3424.E53 1985 Suppl.
344.73′0189143 dc 19
[347.304189143] 88-7754
CIP

International Standard Book Number: 0-87179-673-2
Printed in the United States of America

® GCIU 302-L

This Supplement is dedicated to
Frank and Edna Asper Elkouri

Foreword

The Section of Labor and Employment Law of the American Bar Association is pleased to add this 1985–89 Cumulative Supplement to its outstanding series of treatises in the field of labor and employment law. *How Arbitration Works* by Frank and Edna Asper Elkouri has become the hallmark of publications in the field of labor arbitration.

The Supplement was conceived and prepared entirely by members of the Section's Committee on Labor Arbitration and the Law of Collective Bargaining Agreements. The planning, drafting, and initial editing of the manuscript for this volume was accomplished by more than 100 lawyers. This is not an easy task. All members of the Committee who participated in the extensive research, writing, and editing required to produce the draft manuscript, including the co-editors, did so without compensation motivated solely by their desire as professionals to maintain *How Arbitration Works* as a current and comprehensive exposition of labor arbitration.

Marlin M. Volz and Edward P. Goggin, co-editors of the Supplement, deserve special recognition. Without their dedication to the project and their willingness to contribute time from their busy schedules as professors and arbitrators to complete it, the volume could not have been published. All of us who use and rely upon *How Arbitration Works* are especially indebted to them.

With the publication of this Supplement, *How Arbitration Works* is assured of retaining its stature as the most authoritative and current treatise in its field.

Robert K. McCalla, Chairman
Section of Labor and Employment Law
American Bar Association

Donald J. Capuano, Chairman-Elect
Section of Labor and Employment Law
American Bar Association

Preface

This 1985-1989 Cumulative Supplement to the Fourth Edition of *How Arbitration Works* was conceived, planned, authored, and edited by members of the Committee on Labor Arbitration and the Law of Collective Bargaining Agreements, a standing committee of the Section of Labor and Employment Law of the American Bar Association. The Committee was also responsible for the publication in 1988 of the 1985-1987 Supplement, the first supplement to the Fourth Edition of the Elkouris' well-known treatise.

The concept of periodic supplements to *How Arbitration Works* was first suggested to the Committee in 1985 by Sara Adler of Los Angeles, an arbitrator and long-standing member of the Committee. During 1985 and 1986 Sara Adler and the then co-chairs of the Committee, William Dolson of Louisville, Harris Jacobs of Atlanta, and Anthony Oliver of Los Angeles, with the approval of the Section, approached the publisher, BNA, and through the publisher, the Elkouris, and obtained the consent and approval of both for the project. In 1986 a subcommittee was established to spearhead the project and final approval of the project was given by the Section Council. Committee members Marlin Volz of the University of Louisville School of Law and Edward Goggin of Salmon P. Chase College of Law, Northern Kentucky University, agreed to serve as co-editors of the first Supplement. With the overwhelming support of over 100 Committee members as chapter editors or topic authors, the projected publication date of early 1988 was met and the 1985-1987 Supplement went to press.

The resounding success of the 1985-1987 Supplement led to a decision by the Committee to undertake the preparation of a second cumulative Supplement to be published in late 1990 or early 1991 with the approval of the Section Council. The co-chairs of the subcommittee selected to oversee the project were Sara Adler, Anthony Oliver, and Donald Cohen of Chicago. Marlin Volz, a Committee co-chair, and Edward Goggin agreed once more to serve as co-editors of the Supplement and as members of the subcommittee. The subcommittee also included Nancy Sedmak and Ruth West, both of BNA and both active members of the Committee, along with the other Committee co-chairs, Charles Werner of St. Louis and William Nulton of Kansas City.

Work on the new Supplement commenced almost immediately following publication of the 1985-1987 Supplement. Once again the assistance of all Committee members was solicited to serve as chapter editors or topic authors and once again the members responded in overwhelming numbers. In all, 18 Committee members served as Chapter editors (12 of whom had also worked on the first Supplement); and 60 Committee members served as topic authors (43 had also worked on the first Supplement). All manuscripts were submitted to the co-editors in sufficient time to meet the projected publication date. As in the case of the first Supplement, the Elkouris gave their consent to but did not participate in the preparation of the 1985-1989 Supplement.

This Supplement has been prepared so that it dovetails and correlates directly with the text of the Fourth Edition of *How Arbitration Works*. It updates only the volume's material and does not add new chapters to it. However, some new subtopics reflecting new developments have been added in the Supplement. The Supplement text has its own footnotes, but uses the same topic headings as are found in the parent volume. The material for each chapter in the Supplement follows the same order and topic sequence as in the original text, although not every topic or subtopic is necessarily updated. Thus, for example, topics where no significant developments occurred are not treated in the Supplement. For the convenience of the reader, parallel page numbers of the Fourth Edition where topics and subtopics begin have been listed in parentheses in the Supplement's Table of Contents. The Supplement covers arbitration awards found in Volumes 82 through 93 of the BNA Labor Arbitration Reports.

Professor Goggin wishes to acknowledge the valuable contribution made by his research assistants James D. Allen, Jonathan P. Dameron, and Austin Price. Professor Volz wishes to acknowledge the valuable contribution of Lee Netherton, a graduate of the University of Louisville School of Law.

Obviously the publication of the 1985-1989 Cumulative Supplement could not have occurred without the assistance and cooperation of the Elkouris, the publisher, and the Section. However, the personal effort of all Committee members who participated in the planning, the drafting, and the editing of the Supplement is entitled to special acknowledgment. Most important, the Supplement would not have been possible without the commitment and dedication of Marlin M. Volz and Edward P. Goggin, the co-editors, who willingly and gratuitously contributed time from their busy schedules as professors and arbitrators. To them and to all of those contributors whose names are listed here and elsewhere in this volume we extend our heartfelt gratitude and appreciation.

William C. Nulton, Management Co-Chair
Helen M. Witt, Neutral Co-Chair
Nathan S. Paven, Union Co-Chair
Committee on Labor Arbitration and the
Law of Collective Bargaining Agreements

Contributors

Co-Editors

Marlin M. Volz
Professor of Law
University of Louisville
School of Law

Edward P. Goggin
Professor of Law
Salmon P. Chase College of Law
Northern Kentucky University

Chapter Editors

Thomas G. Bearden
Roger W. Benko
Richard R. Boisseau
Joseph C. D'Arrigo
Carrie G. Donald
William M. Earnest
Joseph F. Gentile
Richard E. Gombert
Edwin S. Hopson
Richard C. Hunt
Anita Christine Knowlton
Harvey Letter
Eugenia B. Maxwell
Frederick A. Morgan
Frances Asher Penn
Alfred C. Phillips
Julius Mel Reich
Edwin R. Render
Donald A. Romano
William F. Schoeberlein
Roland Strasshofer
A.W. VanderMeer, Jr.
A. Randall Vogelzang
Charles A. Werner

Topic Authors

Joel M. Alam
Louis Aronin
Donald A. Banta
Julia I. Baute
Jeffrey A. Blevins
John R. Bode
Richard R. Boisseau
Frederick J. Bosch
Laura Buckley
Lee Melville Burkey
Chris Burrows
Arthur T. Carter
Lawrence J. Casazza
James P. Casey
Gail Ann Chaney
Richard S. Cleary
Hal F.S. Clements
Donald Congress
Thomas S. Crabb
James J. Cronin

J. Bruce Cross
John H. Curley
Joseph C. D'Arrigo
Glenn E. Dawson
Alexander Dranov
John D. Dunbar
Theodore M. Eisenberg
R. Wayne Estes
James Fett
B. Frank Flaherty
Phyllis E. Florman
Darrell W. Foell
S. Joseph Forunato
Edna E.J. Francis
Angelo J. Genova
Joel C. Glanstein
Jerold E. Glassman
Patricia A. Greene
Lyle J. Guilbeau
David C. Hagaman
Melva Harmon
Eugene J. Hayman
Michael F. Hoellering
Amy B. Hubschman
Richard C. Hunt
Joshua M. Javits
Mark P. Johnson
Harold D. Jones, Jr.
John Kagel
Alan Karlan
I. Michael Kessel
Robert W. Kilroy
Anita Christine Knowlton
C. Randolph Light
Michael C. Lynch
Patrick J. Madden
Carol A. Mager
Thomas Y. Mandler
Michael F. Marino
Arthur J. Martin
Patrick J. McCarthy
John J. McGirl
Condon A. McGlothlen
John P. McGury
Alvin J. McKenna
Catherine J. Minuse
Abigail Modjeska
Thomas J. Munger
Lee Netherton
Terrence F. Nieman
Clifford R. Oviatt, Jr.
Edward A. Pereles
Bruce N. Petterson
Alfred C. Phillips
Maureen M. Rayborn
Cynthia D. Reich
Diane C. Reichwein
Michael T. Reynvaan
Leo P. Rock, Jr.
Jon Howard Rosen
Robert T. Rosenfeld
Arthur D. Rutkowski
Russell H. Rybolt
Ira Sandron
John F. Sass
Jeffrey A. Savarise
John S. Schauer
Gregory J. Schroedter
Kirk C. Shaw
Norman J. Slawsky
Barry R. Smith
Leslie R. Stein
Henry G. Stewart
Emanuel Tabachnick
David Leo Uelmen
Michael J. Underwood
George W. Van Pelt
A.W. VanderMeer, Jr.
Carl E. VerBeek
Bart Waldman
Keith E. White
Joseph E. Wiley
David P. Wood
George E. Yund

Table of Contents

---

*Page numbers where chapters, topics, and subtopics begin in the Fourth Edition are listed in parentheses in this Table.

Chapter 1

Arbitration and Its Setting

Collective Bargaining, Mediation, Fact-Finding, and Arbitration

A hybrid variation involving a cross between mediation and arbitration has been advanced in recent years as a response to situations in which arbitration is perceived to have become excessively delayed, expensive, or formalistic.[1] Labeled as grievance mediation, it proposes that after the final step of the internal grievance procedure, unresolved grievances will be referred to mediation rather than directly to arbitration, with arbitration reserved for those grievances which cannot be resolved through mediation. The mediator may not act as the arbitrator, and nothing which has been said or done in the grievance mediation proceedings is admissible in the arbitration.[2] The device was tested with significant positive results in the bituminous coal industry during an experiment lasting two and one-half years.[3]

The success of the arbitration process in resolving disputes within the collective bargaining relationship has led to numerous recommendations that the process be extended to protect unorganized employees.[4] The National Conference of Commissioners on Uniform State

---

[1]Simkin & Fidandis, Mediation and the Dynamics of Collective Bargaining, 2d ed., 178-179 (BNA Books, 1986); Brett & Goldberg, "Grievance Mediation in the Coal Industry: A Field Experiment," 37 Indus. & Lab. Rel. Rev. 49 (1983).

[2]Goldberg, "Mediation of Grievances Under a Collective Bargaining Agreement," 77 Nw. U.L. Rev. 270, 281 (1982). Also see Chapter 5, topic entitled "Grievance Mediation."

[3]Of 300 coal industry grievances and 25 grievances from other industries, 275 (85%) were reported resolved without arbitration, 50% by compromise. In 25% of the cases the mediator gave an advisory opinion, which was accepted by the parties 50% of the time. When grievances went to formal arbitration after mediation, the award was the same as the advisory opinion in 75% of the disputes. The average cost for the mediation of a grievance was $200. See Goldberg, "Grievance Mediation," Proceedings of the 36th Annual Meeting of NAA, 128, 131 (BNA Books, 1984).

[4]Experience with the arbitration of grievances of unorganized employees is described in Hepple, "Arbitration of Job Security and Other Employment-Related Issues for the Unorganized Worker," Proceedings of the 34th Annual Meeting of NAA, 18-76 (BNA Books, 1982); see also 3 Bornstein & Gosline, "Labor and Employment Arbitration," Ch. 72, §72.02(b) et seq. (1989) (discussing the use and effect of nonunion arbitration procedures and awards); Morris,

Laws has recently drafted a proposed Uniform Employment Termination Act which provides that a nonunion employee can demand arbitration of his discharge.[5]

The arbitration process has also found a place in public-sector bargaining. With the expansion of collective bargaining in the public sector, state statutes authorizing such bargaining frequently make provision for the use of interest arbitration as a means for resolving impasses that arise during contract negotiations.[6] However, the constitutionality of such statutes has been challenged with limited success.[7] Furthermore, such statutes generally provide constraints on the arbitrator's power to determine economic issues.[8]

"EGAPS—Arbitration Plans for Nonunion Employees," 14 Pepperdine L. Rev. 827 (1987); "Employment at Will," West's Federal Practice Manual, Vol. 1A, Ch. 21.16 §§1475.9.

[5]See "Draft Employment Termination Act," 138 Daily Lab. Rep. (BNA), at D-1 (August 30, 1989).

[6]Anderson & Krause, "Interest Arbitration: The Alternative to the Strike," 56 Fordham L. Rev. 153, 155 nn. 16–17 (1987); Rehmus, "Report of the Committee on Public Employment Disputes Settlement," Proceedings of the 39th Annual Meeting of NAA, 174 (BNA Books, 1987).

[7]Anderson & Krause, "Interest Arbitration: The Alternative to the Strike," 56 Fordham L. Rev. 153, 169 (1987). See also Aaron, Najita & Stern, Public-Sector Bargaining, 2d ed., 252-261 (BNA Books, 1988).

[8]For an analysis of the impact of "cap" and "lid" laws and other statutory constraints on interest arbitration, see Minami, "Interest Arbitration: Can the Public Sector Afford It? Developing Limitations on the Process," Proceedings of the 34th Annual Meeting of NAA, 241-272 (BNA Books, 1982).

Chapter 2

Legal Status of Arbitration

Federal Law: Private Sector

Post-Trilogy: *Lower Court Enforcement of Agreement to Arbitrate and Review of Award*

In many instances, courts have ordered arbitration where the arbitrability of the dispute is challenged. One court, for example, found that both the employee's underlying grievance and the employer's arbitration defenses were arbitrable, and affirmed a lower court's refusal to rule on the employer's defenses.[1] Another court held that the issue of timely compliance with grievance procedures is arbitrable.[2]

In an effort to discourage frivolous litigation, some courts have imposed sanctions for the bringing of claims that were previously decided at an arbitration proceeding. In one such case,[3] a union was awarded attorney fees where the employer's suit to vacate an arbitration award was without merit, was not based on customary statutory grounds, and was barred by the statute of limitations. The court emphasized that an employer that includes an arbitration clause in its collective bargaining agreement "will not be permitted to nullify the advantages to the union by spinning out the arbitral process unconscionably through the filing of meritless suits and appeals."[4]

Although the scope of reviewing an arbitration award is narrow, courts will vacate an award which does not draw its essence from the collective bargaining agreement.[5]

---

[1]Bechtel Constr. v. Laborers, 812 F.2d 750, 124 LRRM 2785 (CA 1, 1987). See also National R.R. Passenger Corp. v. Boston & Maine Corp., 850 F.2d 756 (D.C. Cir., 1988); and Ryan v. Liss, Tenner & Goldberg Sec. Corp., 683 F. Supp. 480 (D.N.J., 1988).

[2]Oil Workers Local 4-447 v. Chevron Chem. Co., 815 F.2d 338, 125 LRRM 2232 (CA 5, 1987).

[3]Dreis & Krump Mfg. Co. v. Machinists Dist. 8, 802 F.2d 247, 123 LRRM 2654 (CA 7, 1986).

[4]123 LRRM at 2661.

[5]Steelworkers v. Enterprise Wheel & Car Corp., 80 S.Ct. 1358, 46 LRRM 2423 (1960).

Thus a court of appeals relied on the essence standard in refusing to enforce an arbitrator's decision that the employer's "no-beards" policy was an unreasonable standard of appearance.[6] In another case, however, the same court found that an arbitration award reinstating an employee without back pay did draw its essence from the collective agreement,[7] reasoning that the award was an "obviously well-considered attempt to balance the conduct of the parties in light of the terms of the existing labor contract."[8]

Asserting that the arbitrator's award violates the clear language of the agreement remains one of the most often cited explanations for a court's refusal to uphold an award. A court of appeals affirmed the decision of a district court on this basis.[9] The agreement between the union and the company required the employer to pay damages to the aggrieved employees or the union if the employer failed to properly man its compressors. The arbitrator found such a violation and ordered the employer to man the particular set of compressors in the future, but refused to award past damages to the union. The district court remanded the case to the arbitrator for a calculation of past damages. The court of appeals affirmed, reasoning that since the arbitrator found that the employer had violated the agreement, he was compelled by the express terms of the agreement to award past damages for the violation.

The Fourth Circuit, U.S. Court of Appeals, in particular, uses the "essence" standard of *Enterprise Wheel*[10] as the legal means to set aside awards with which it disagrees.[11] In addition to vacating an award which is utterly unsupported by the evidence[12] or is contrary to the express language of the agreement,[13] the *Clinchfield* decisions[14] also reveal the court's willingness to scrutinize both the arbitrator's treatment of the evidence and his reasoning, and arguably imposed on him novel requirements that his decision be "reasonable" and that he explain his stance on the issues crucial to resolving the dispute before him.[15]

---

[6]Trailways Lines v. Trailways Joint Council, 807 F.2d 1416, 124 LRRM 2217 (CA 8, 1986).

[7]Walsh v. Union Pacific R.R., 803 F.2d 412, 123 LRRM 2789 (CA 8, 1986).

[8]803 F.2d at 414, 123 LRRM at 2791. For a fuller overview of Eighth Circuit cases, see Note, "Judicial Review of Labor Arbitration Awards: Refining the Standard of Review," 11 Wm. Mitchell L. Rev. 993 (1985).

[9]Operating Eng'rs Local 9 vs. Shauk-Artukovich, 751 F.2d 364, 118 LRRM 2157 (CA 10, 1985); see also Morgan Servs. v. Local 323, 724 F.2d 1217, 115 LRRM 2368 (CA 6, 1984) (arbitrator erred in ordering reinstatement of employee after finding insubordination where contract permitted employer to discharge employee for insubordination).

[10]Steelworkers v. Enterprise Wheel & Car Corp., 80 S.Ct. 1358, 46 LRRM 2423 (1960).

[11]See Woody, "Clinchfield Coal Co. v. District 28, United Mine Workers: A New Standard for Judicial Review of Labor Arbitration Awards?" 88 W. Va. L. Rev. 605 (1986). For a discussion of Sixth and Tenth Circuit cases on the issue, see Note, "Judicial Intervention in Arbitration Enforcement Cases—The Tenth Circuit Expands upon the Limited Judicial Review Standard of Enterprise Wheel," 62 Den. U.L. Rev. 593 (1985).

[12]Clinchfield Coal Co. v. Mine Workers Dist. 28, 720 F.2d 1365, 1371, 114 LRRM 3053 (CA 4, 1983) (Sprouse, J., concurring).

[13]720 F.2d at 1372.

[14]Clinchfield Coal Co. v. Mine Workers Dist. 28, 720 F.2d 1365, 114 LRRM 3053 (CA 4, 1983) (Clinchfield I); Clinchfield Coal Co. v. Mine Workers Dist. 28, 736 F.2d 998, 116 LRRM 2884 (CA 4, 1984) (Clinchfield II).

[15]Clinchfield Coal Co. v. Mine Workers Dist. 28, 720 F.2d at 1369. See also Woody, "Clinchfield Coal Co. v. District 28, United Mine Workers: A New Standard for Judicial Review of Labor Arbitration Awards?" 88 W. Va. L. Rev. 605, 608-610 (1986).

Clinchfield II represents yet another interference with finality of an arbitrator's award inasmuch as it holds that, even though the award is reasonable, it will still be reversed if the court has already ruled on the issue and the facts the arbitrator is called on to consider.[16]

Other courts of appeals have construed the essence standard more narrowly, however. The Third Circuit, for example, refused to vacate an award despite the employer's argument that the arbitrator ignored the clear language of the collective bargaining agreement.[17] Confirming the award, the court explained: "[A]lthough we have doubts about the correctness of the arbitrator's decision, the courts are not free to set it aside."[18] In a similar ruling, the Ninth Circuit held that a lower court erred in vacating an award which was a plausible interpretation of the collective bargaining agreement.[19]

The courts often note that an arbitrator has failed to follow the express, unambiguous terms of the contract. In many cases, the focus is on the arbitrator's authority to convert a greater penalty into a lesser one once a grievant has been found to have committed a violation. In two cases decided in 1988, the First Circuit upheld the employer's assertion that once a violation is proven the express language of the contract gives the employer the exclusive right to determine the penalty.[20] While it has been held that the interpretation of the contract is up to the arbitrator, in the *Warren* cases the court overruled the arbitrators' conclusions that the language on penalty was ambiguous, finding that the work rules had been incorporated into the contract.

The concept that the parties may limit the discretion of arbitrators in the area of fashioning a remedy is supported by the statement in *Misco* that the contract may vest unreviewable discretion in management to discharge an employee once a violation has occurred.[21] A Tenth Circuit decision declared that an arbitrator had departed from the contract by grafting principles of progressive discipline onto perfectly unambiguous language which vested total discretion over remedies in the employer.[22] The Eleventh Circuit ruled that the award cannot simply reflect the arbitrator's own notions of indus-

---

[16]For a critical analysis of the Clinchfield decisions, see Woody, "Clinchfield Coal Co. v. District 28, United Mine Workers: A New Standard for Judicial Review of Labor Arbitration Awards?" 88 W. Va. L. Rev. 605, 612 (1986) ("The industry may be saddled with judicial stare decisis which could, in the long term, be more onerous than the isolated arbitration decision"); Trumka, "Keeping Miners Out of Work: Cost of Judicial Revision of Arbitration Awards," 86 W. Va. L. Rev. 705 (1984).

[17]Roberts & Schaefer Co. v. Mine Workers Local 1846, 812 F.2d 883, 124 LRRM 2794 (CA 3, 1987).

[18]124 LRRM at 2796.

[19]Hughes Aircraft Co. v. Electronic & Space Technicians Local 1553, 809 F.2d 1442, 124 LRRM 2711 (CA 9, 1987).

[20]S.D. Warren Co. v. Paperworkers Local 1069, 845 F.2d 3, 128 LRRM 2175 (CA 1), cert. denied, 109 S.Ct. 555, 129 LRRM 3072 (1988); S.D. Warren Co. v. Paperworkers Local 1069, 846 F.2d 827, 128 LRRM 2432 (CA 1, 1988). See also Paperworkers Local 369 v. Georgia Pac. Corp., 841 F.2d 243, 127 LRRM 3112 (CA 8, 1988).

[21]Paperworkers v. Misco, Inc., 108 S.Ct. 364, 126 LRRM 3113, 3118 (1987). See discussion in text beginning at note 53 infra.

[22]Mistletoe Express Serv. v. Motor Expressmen's Union, 566 F.2d 692, 96 LRRM 3320 (CA 10, 1977).

trial justice.[23] The Fifth Circuit approved the vacation of an award of reinstatement of a riverboat captain whose carelessness almost caused a riverboat collision, reasoning that the arbitrator lacked authority under the contract to modify the employer's disciplinary decision.[24]

Attorney fees assessed by an arbitrator were upheld in a Second Circuit case. The court noted that while attorney fees are not routinely awarded in labor disputes, they were justified in this case and that, while an arbitrator is not authorized to award punitive damages as a matter of public policy under New York law, "We are not convinced that the award was punitive."[25] The Fourth Circuit also awarded attorney fees caused by an unjustified attempt by the company to overturn an arbitration decision.[26]

An award was vacated because an arbitrator relied on previous interpretations of agreements by a federal judge instead of making his own interpretation.[27] An award was also vacated because it was based on provisions of the NLRA. In vacating the award, the court stated that the arbitrator's decision must be based on the contract, even if the decision conflicts with federal statutory law.[28] A 1988 case held an award to be final and binding to the extent it resolves questions of contractual rights, but not with respect to discrimination issues.[29] A court held that any award regarding a discrimination claim would be against public policy. The mandate of Title VII and the underlying state discrimination claim could be thwarted by arbitration.[30]

A court may not substitute its interpretation of the agreement for that of an arbitrator. A railroad case held that the arbitrator's interpretation is conclusive even if it is in gross error.[31] In another case it was ruled that the award will not be vacated if grounds can be inferred from facts.[32]

A case that goes far in upholding the arbitrator's function was decided by the Tenth Circuit in 1989. The award had rescinded the discharge of an employee, with 23 years of service, who was discharged for failure to perform a duty. The arbitrator had found the employee's carelessness, laziness, and neglect did not result in the

---

[23]Bruno's, Inc. v. Food & Commercial Workers, 858 F.2d 1529, 129 LRRM 2815 (CA 11, 1988). See also Pennsylvania Power Co. v. Electrical Workers (IBEW) Local 271, 886 F.2d 46, 132 LRRM 2388 (CA 3, 1989); In re Marine Pollution Serv., 857 F.2d 91, 129 LRRM 2472 (CA 2, 1988).

[24]Delta Queen Steamboat Co. v. Marine Eng'rs, 889 F.2d 599, 133 LRRM 2077 (CA 5, 1989).

[25]Synergy Gas Co. v. Sasso, 853 F.2d 59, 129 LRRM 2041 (CA 2), cert. denied, 109 S.Ct. 559, 129 LRRM 3072 (1988). See also Gilling v. Eastern Airlines, 680 F. Supp. 169 (D.N.J., 1988) and Ultracashmere House, Ltd. v. Nordstrom, Inc., 123 F.R.D. 435 (S.D.N.Y., 1988).

[26]Food & Commercial Workers Local 400 v. Marval Poultry Co., 876 F.2d 346, 131 LRRM 2465 (CA 4, 1989).

[27]Union Appointed Trustees Funds v. Employer Appointed Trustees of Tapers Indus., 714 F.Supp. 104 (S.D.N.Y., 1989).

[28]Roadmaster Corp. v. Production & Maintenance Employees Local 504, 851 F.2d 886, 129 LRRM 2449 (CA 7, 1988).

[29]Owens v. Texaco, 857 F.2d 262, 129 LRRM 2925 (CA 5, 1988), cert. denied, 109 S.Ct. 1954, 131 LRRM 2200 (1989).

[30]Swenson v. Management Recruiters Int'l, 872 F.2d 264, 49 FEP 760 (CA 8), cert. denied, 110 S.Ct. 143, 50 FEP 1496 (1989).

[31]Hill v. Norfolk & Western Ry., 814 F.2d 1192, 124 LRRM 3057 (CA 7, 1987).

[32]Concorse Beauty School v. Polakov, 685 F. Supp. 1311 (S.D.N.Y., 1988).

required "just and sufficient cause" to terminate, since these terms were not specifically mentioned in the agreement. The arbitrator stated that if he had found dereliction of duty involving extreme carelessness and resulting in serious economic damage, that would have justified discharge. The arbitrator found, however, that the grievant was not "negligent" within the meaning of the contract. The court held that the findings and conclusions of the arbitrator, "correct or not," were rooted in the agreement and the court could not substitute its interpretation.[33]

Another Tenth Circuit decision established a novel remedial precedent in awarding the lion's share of the back pay against the union, where the employer had failed to properly recall an employee under the labor agreement.[34] The arbitrator held the union responsible for a two-year delay in bringing the case to arbitration. The award was premised on the breadth of the parties' issue stipulation.

A circuit court held that a district court exceeded its jurisdiction in reviewing the merits of a dispute involving a question of shift differential pay and overlapping hours. The employer had substantially admitted an ambiguity in the contract, which is a "classical" case for arbitration.[35] Several cases have upheld an arbitrator's action as being interpretation rather than modification.[36] An arbitrator properly considered past practice and negotiating history and other extrinsic evidence where the arbitrator determined that the contract was ambiguous.[37]

The Seventh Circuit, U.S. Court of Appeals, has also demonstrated a reluctance to review the merits of arbitration awards. In one case for example, it reinstated an award vacated by a lower court.[38] The contract stated that employees had to work a full calendar year at the company before being entitled to vacation benefits. The company subsequently closed the plant and those employees who were unable to complete their year with the company demanded vacation benefits. The arbitrator ordered payment of benefits, but the district court vacated the award as not drawing its essence from the agreement. The Seventh Circuit reinstated the award, holding that the arbitrator was not obliged to read the contract literally, and that the award should be upheld as long as the arbitrator's activity could plausibly be classified as interpreting the contract. The court further stated that the only time the arbitrator can be reversed is when he "must have based his

---

[33]Litvak Packing Co. v. Food & Commercial Workers Local 7, 886 F.2d 275, 132 LRRM 2383 (CA 10, 1989). See also Clean Coverall Supply Co. v. Construction, Bldg. Material, Ice & Coal Local 682, 688 F. Supp. 1364 (E.D. Mo., 1988).

[34]Food & Commercial Workers Local 7R v. Safeway Stores, 889 F.2d 940, 132 LRRM 3090 (CA 10, 1989).

[35]Bayamon Can Co. v. Congreso de Uniones Industriales de Puerto Rico, 843 F.2d 65, 128 LRRM 2130 (CA 1, 1988).

[36]Winery, Distillery & Allied Workers Local 186 v. E.J. Gallo Winery, 847 F.2d 1384, 128 LRRM 2631 (CA 9, 1988). See also New England Joint B. RWDSU v. Decatur & Hopkins Co., 677 F. Supp. 657, 125 LRRM 2959 (D. Mass., 1987).

[37]Manville Forest Prods. Corp. v. Paperworkers, 831 F.2d 72, 126 LRRM 2895 (CA 5, 1987).

[38]Ethyl Corp. v. Steelworkers, 768 F.2d 180, 119 LRRM 3566 (CA 7, 1985).

award on some body of thought, or feeling or policy or law that is outside the contract."[39]

Several courts have analyzed the scope of an arbitration agreement. In discussing whether disability benefits are arbitrable, the District of Columbia Circuit emphasized that this issue was to be decided by the court, not the arbitrator.[40] The question of a superintendent being assigned to do production work where the superintendent was not covered by the agreement was held to be arbitrable.[41] An arbitrator's interpretation of the nature of the issue is entitled to the same deference as his interpretation of the contract.[42] Presumption of arbitrability is extended to a situation where there may be concurrent jurisdiction with the NLRB.[43]

A court of appeals ruled that the NLRB was not required to defer to the decision of an arbitration panel upholding an employee's discharge, where the arbitration proceedings addressed only the issue of whether the employer had good cause to discharge the employee under the collective bargaining agreement and did not consider whether the employee was discharged for his grievance-filing activity.[44]

Another court set forth guidelines outlining when the NLRB should defer to the judgment of an arbitrator on matters involving unfair labor practices.[45] Deferral is appropriate where (1) the proceedings are fair and regular; (2) the parties agreed to be bound; (3) the decision is not repugnant to the purposes and policies of the act; (4) the contractual issue was factually parallel to the unfair labor practice issue; and (5) the arbitrator was presented generally with the facts relevant to resolving the unfair labor practice.[46]

---

[39]119 LRRM at 3568. For similar developments in the Eleventh Circuit, see Electrical Workers (IBEW) Local 199 v. United Tel. Co., 738 F.2d 1564, 117 LRRM 2094 (CA 11, 1984) (arbitrator was not constrained to read ambiguous language of contract literally and could reach a different conclusion if it were based on past bargaining of parties and/or on common law of shop).

[40]Air Line Pilots v. Delta Air Lines, 863 F.2d 87, 130 LRRM 2165 (D.C. Cir., 1988).

[41]Service Employees Local 106 v. Evergreen Cemetery, 708 F. Supp. 917, 133 LRRM 2336 (N.D. Ill., 1989).

[42]Pack Concrete v. Cunningham & Teamsters Local 162, 866 F.2d 283, 130 LRRM 2490 (CA 9, 1989).

[43]Communications Workers v. U.S. West Direct, 847 F.2d 1475, 128 LRRM 2698 (CA 10, 1988).

[44]NLRB v. Ryder/P.I.E. Nationwide, 810 F.2d 502, 124 LRRM 3024 (CA 5, 1987).

[45]Garcia v. NLRB, 785 F.2d 807, 121 LRRM 3349 (CA 9, 1986).

[46]121 LRRM at 3351; see also Olin Corp., 268 NLRB 573, 115 LRRM 1056 (1984) (Board will not engage in de novo examination of arbitrator's findings and will defer to arbitrator's judgment so long as conditions reiterated in *Garcia* are met); Chevron U.S.A., 275 NLRB 949, 119 LRRM 1238 (1985); Bakery Workers Local 25 v. NLRB, 730 F.2d 812, 115 LRRM 3390 (D.C. Cir., 1984) (approves *Olin* standard); but see NLRB v. Babcock & Wilcox Co., 736 F.2d 1410, 116 LRRM 2748 (CA 10, 1984) (where unfair labor practice issue was put before arbitrator but he expressly refused to rule on it, NLRB was right in declining to defer the award). For deferral to the arbitration process see United Technologies, 268 NLRB 557, 115 LRRM 1049 (1984) (where agreement contains a broad arbitration clause, and there are reasons to believe dispute can be successfully handled by arbitrator, NLRB will let arbitrator decide); Spann Bldg. Maintenance Co., 275 NLRB 971, 119 LRRM 1209 (1985) (deferral to arbitration mechanism appropriate even where hearing had not been scheduled and it appeared that union was not pursuing grievance). For a fuller treatment of the NLRB's policy of deferring to both arbitral awards and the arbitral process in general, and of the court's review of the Board's power to defer, see Comment, "The National Labor Relations Board's Policy of Deferring to Arbitration," 13 Fla. St. U.L. Rev. 1141 (1986).

On procedural issues arbitration awards are generally sustained. Inconsistent rulings on evidence are not fatal, and an arbitrator's decision is not invalid because of preliminary interim evidentiary determinations.[47] Where the same arbitrator, under the same contract and similar facts, rendered a different decision in a subsequent award, the award was upheld since the reasons were explained and the courts have a narrow scope of review.[48] An award was confirmed where it was issued three days late and no reply was made to a request for an extension. The court also discussed elements of waiver and lack of prejudice to the losing party.[49] An arbitrator may issue an award after his term has expired where he had concluded all of the hearing prior to the expiration of the term.[50] An arbitrator cannot award reinstatement and back pay to an employee beyond the expiration date of the contract.[51] A Tenth Circuit, U.S. Court of Appeals, case found this question to be jurisdictional.[52]

The public policy exception to the enforcement of arbitration awards was given a narrow construction by the Supreme Court in *Paperworkers v. Misco, Inc.*[53] The Court held, as it did in *Enterprise Wheel,*[54] that the courts are not authorized to reconsider the merits of an award, even if the parties allege that the award rests on errors of fact or on misinterpretation of the contract. In moving to vacate the arbitrator's award, the company had charged that the arbitrator had committed grievous error in finding that the evidence was insufficient to prove that the grievant had possessed or used marijuana on company property.[55] The evidence in question, which was relied upon by the company and the court of appeals, was information about marijuana in the grievant's car that was not available at the time the company made its decision to terminate the employee. The arbitrator refused to consider such evidence in formulating his award. In its decision, the court of appeals held that the evidence of marijuana in the grievant's car required that the award be set aside on public policy grounds.[56] The Supreme Court ruled that the formulation of public policy set out by the court of appeals did not comply with its *Grace* standard:[57]

> [A] court's refusal to enforce an arbitrator's interpretation of such contracts is limited to situations where the contract as interpreted would violate "some explicit public policy" that is "well defined and dominant,

---

[47]Mutual Redevelopment House v. SEIU Local 32 B–32 J, 700 F. Supp. 774 (S.D.N.Y., 1988).
[48]Hotel & Restaurant Employees Local 54 v. Adamar, Inc., 682 F. Supp. 795, 126 LRRM 3029 (D.N.J., 1987).
[49]McMahon v. RMS Elecs., 695 F. Supp. 1557 (S.D.N.Y., 1988).
[50]Pelham Parkway Nursing Home v. Service Employees Local 144, 132 LRRM 2744 (S.D.N.Y., 1989).
[51]Laborers Local 1273 v. Deaton Hosp., 671 F. Supp. 1049, 125 LRRM 2964 (D. Md., 1986).
[52]Barnard v. Commercial Carriers, 863 F.2d 694, 130 LRRM 2073 (CA 10, 1988).
[53]108 S.Ct. 364, 126 LRRM 3113 (1987).
[54]80 S.Ct. 1358 (1960).
[55]Paperworkers v. Misco, Inc., 125 LRRM at 3115.
[56]Misco, Inc. v. Paperworkers, 768 F.2d 739, 120 LRRM 2119 (CA 5, 1985).
[57]W.R. Grace & Co. v. Rubber Workers Local 759, 103 S.Ct. 2177, 113 LRRM 2641 (1983).

and is to be ascertained by reference to the laws and legal precedents and not from general considerations of supposed public interests."[58]

In essence, the Supreme Court has clearly indicated that for a court to vacate an arbitrator's award for public policy reasons, its decision must be based on a public policy that is ascertained by reference to laws and legal precedents and not some general considerations of supposed public interests.

In the *Stead Motors* case[59] the Ninth Circuit, U.S. Court of Appeals, followed and perhaps expanded *Misco,* while also emphasizing the extremely narrow scope of judicial review. In *Stead* the arbitrator had reinstated an employee who had been found negligent in maintaining vehicles on several occasions. The court held there was no violation of public policy; that state statutes prohibiting the operating of unsafe vehicles and providing for the inspection and certification of auto repair facilities were insufficient to establish the existence of an explicit well-defined and dominant public policy that would be contravened by reinstatement of the employee. The court went on to hold that to overturn the award, the public policy would have to go beyond merely determining public policy against certain kinds of careless behavior and bar reinstatement of the employee in question. Thus, the asserted public policy to prevail must specifically militate against the relief order of the arbitrator. The *Stead* court states that *Misco* recognized an arbitral judgment of an employee's amenability to discipline as a factual determination which cannot be questioned or rejected by the court.[60] The Ninth Circuit in *Stead* acknowledged that it was not following the *Delta Air Lines*[61] and *Iowa Electric Light & Power*[62] cases, which are described as "hard" cases involving, respectively, Federal Aviation Administration rules and the Nuclear Regulatory Commission. The court in *Stead* concluded that there was no legal proscription against the reinstatement of persons such as the grievant in this case and that the award did not otherwise have the effect of mandating any illegal conduct.

In other cases the *Misco* requirements as applied to public policy were not met, resulting in the arbitrator's award being upheld. An employee was arrested on drug charges away from the plant, and although he worked in a sensitive position he was reinstated.[63] An employee who had fired gunshots into his supervisor's unoccupied vehicle also was reinstated. In this case the court of appeals criticized the district court for second-guessing the arbitrator's evidentiary con-

---

[58]Paperworkers v. Misco, Inc., 108 S.Ct. 364, 126 LRRM 3113, 3119 (1987).

[59]Stead Motors of Walnut Creek v. Automotive Machinists Lodge 1173, 843 F.2d 357, 127 LRRM 3213 (CA 9, 1988), reh'g en banc, 886 F.2d 1200, 132 LRRM 2689 (CA 9, 1989), cert. denied, 58 U.S.L.W. 3739 (1990).

[60]886 F.2d at 1216, 132 LRRM at 2701.

[61]Delta Air Lines v. Air Line Pilots Ass'n, 861 F.2d 665, 130 LRRM 2014 (CA 11, 1988), cert. denied, 110 S.Ct. 201, 132 LRRM 2623 (1989).

[62]Iowa Elec. Light & Power v. Electrical Workers (IBEW) Local 204, 834 F.2d 1424, 127 LRRM 2049 (CA 8, 1987).

[63]Florida Power Corp. v. Electrical Workers (IBEW) Local 433, 847 F.2d 680, 128 LRRM 2762 (CA 11, 1988).

clusions and construction of the contract.[64] No violation of public policy was found where back pay was ordered in the case of employees who were discharged in violation of a project agreement for failing an invalid test, despite the claim that the Nuclear Regulatory Commission should have decided whether the safety plan was consistent with regulatory standards.[65] An extended sick leave for a police officer resulting in decreased police protection was held not to be a violation of public policy.[66]

The Eleventh Circuit held that *Misco* standards were met where a pilot operated an aircraft while intoxicated. The court observed that every state, as well as the federal government, made driving while intoxicated illegal.[67] Reinstatement was rejected when there was jeopardy to a nuclear reactor safety system because an employee had left for lunch too early. The court cited a well-defined national policy requiring strict adherence to nuclear safety rules.[68] Where an employee operated potentially hazardous electrical equipment, the district court vacated the arbitrator's decision to reinstate the employee even though the arbitrator had found that the employee in question was a chronic heavy drug user and testing showed him to be in a state of intoxication at the time of his drug screening. The court distinguished *Misco,* which involved smoking in a car in a parking lot. The court also observed that if the employer permitted this activity it would be an accessory to the wrongdoing.[69]

De Novo Litigation Following Arbitration

Courts have reached different results in determining whether state wrongful discharge actions are preempted by federal labor law.[70]

In the *Lueck v. Aetna Life Insurance Co.* case, the Supreme Court made it clear that a claim is preempted by LMRA § 301 if it involves interpretation of the employee's contractual rights.[71] Nevertheless, *Lueck* does state that an employee's claim might not be preempted if it is based on a state rule that "proscribes conduct or establishes rights

---

[64]U.S. Postal Serv. v. Letter Carriers, 839 F.2d 146, 127 LRRM 2593 (CA 3, 1988).

[65]Daniel Int'l Corp. v. Electrical Workers (IBEW) Local 257, 856 F.2d 1174, 129 LRRM 2429 (CA 8, 1988), cert. denied, 109 S.Ct. 1140, 130 LRRM 2656 (1989).

[66]City of Stamford v. Stamford Police Ass'n, 540 A.2d 400, 130 LRRM 2999 (Conn. App., 1988).

[67]Delta Air Lines v. Air Line Pilots, 861 F.2d 665, 130 LRRM 2014 (CA 11, 1988), cert. denied, 110 S.Ct. 201, 132 LRRM 2623 (1989).

[68]Iowa Elec. Light & Power v. Electrical Workers (IBEW) Local 204, 834 F.2d 1424, 127 LRRM 2049 (CA 8, 1987).

[69]Georgia Power Co. v. Electrical Workers (IBEW) Local 84, 707 F. Supp. 531, 130 LRRM 2419 (N.D. Ga., 1989).

[70]See generally AAA, "Implications of State Wrongful Discharge Actions on the Grievance Arbitration Remedy," Lawyers' Arbitration Letter (June, 1987); Lindau, Crawford, Hathaway & Hyde, "Arbitral Awards Versus Public Policy: The Continuing Conflict," 39 N.Y.U. Nat'l Conference on Labor §§ 13.01-13.04 (1986); Jauvtis, "The Impact of Wrongful Discharge Suits on Grievance-Arbitration Procedures in Collective Bargaining Agreements," 36 Lab. L.J. 307 (1985); Murphy, "Labor Arbitration and the State Public Policy: Garibaldi v. Lucky Food Stores," 38 N.Y.U. Nat'l Conference on Labor, §§ 13.01-13.06 (1985).

[71]105 S.Ct. 1904, 118 LRRM 3345 (1985).

and obligations independent of a labor contract."[72] The Supreme Court followed this rationale in *Lingle v. Norge Division of Magic Chef,* and allowed an employee to maintain a claim of retaliatory discharge by her employer for exercising her rights under the Illinois workers' compensation laws.[73] The Court reasoned that the state law remedy did not require construing the collective bargaining agreement for § 301 preemption purposes.[74] In other cases decided by the Supreme Court, actions based upon state law were held to be preempted by § 301 when any interpretation of the terms of the collective bargaining agreement was required.[75]

Such rationale was used, for example, by a court of appeals to also allow an action based upon a Connecticut statute that prohibited employers from discharging an employee in retaliation for filing a workers' compensation claim.[76]

Another exception to the federal preemption of state wrongful discharge claims occurs where an employee's discharge involves a violation of a clearly defined state public policy. This public policy exception was recognized in a case where an employee was fired after reporting a shipment of spoiled milk to health authorities.[77] He grieved his discharge, but an arbitrator ruled that he had been discharged for cause. The employee then filed a state action claiming that his termination was prompted by his "whistle-blowing," in violation of California public policy. The court ruled that the arbitration award did not estop the employee from raising his statutory claim under California law, reasoning that such a claim "poses no significant threat to the collective bargaining process" where it furthers a state interest in protecting the general public which transcends the employment relationship.[78]

The same court has limited *Garibaldi* in subsequent decisions, however. In one case for example, it ruled that the employee's claim was preempted by federal labor law,[79] stating that the employee "was

[72]105 S.Ct. at 1912.

[73]108 S.Ct. 1877, 128 LRRM 2521 (1988).

[74]108 S.Ct. at 1882, 128 LRRM at 2525. See also Miller v. AT&T Network Sys., 850 F.2d 543, 128 LRRM 2987 (CA 9, 1988) (wrongful discharge case based on Oregon statute prohibiting firing of employee for physical handicap created mandatory and independent state right not preempted by § 301).

[75]Electrical Workers (IBEW) v. Hechler, 107 S.Ct. 2161, 125 LRRM 2353 (1987).

[76]Baldracchi v. Pratt & Whitney Aircraft Div., United Technologies Corp., 814 F.2d 102, 125 LRRM 3363 (CA 2, 1987).

[77]Garibaldi v. Lucky Food Stores, 726 F.2d 1367, 115 LRRM 3089 (CA 9, 1984), cert. denied, 105 S.Ct. 2319 (1985). See also Garcia v. NLRB, 785 F.2d 807, 121 LRRM 3349 (CA 9, 1986) (court refused to uphold NLRB's decision enforcing arbitral committee's order to suspend an employee for declining to honk his horn in violation of state traffic laws).

[78]Garibaldi v. Lucky Food Stores, 726 F.2d at 1375. See also Vincent v. Trend W. Tech. Corp., 828 F.2d 563, 126 LRRM 2451 (CA 9, 1987) (wrongful discharge case of employee fired in retaliation for reporting perceived illegalities stemming from sources other than collective bargaining agreement and thus was not preempted by § 301); Paige v. Henry J. Kaiser Co., 826 F.2d 857, 126 LRRM 2145 (CA 9, 1987), cert. denied, 108 S.Ct. 2819, 128 LRRM 2664 (1988) (wrongful discharge claim based on violation of a state public policy is not preempted because it is a nonnegotiable independent state law right).

[79]DeSoto v. Yellow Freight Sys., 811 F.2d 1333, 124 LRRM 3070 (CA 9, 1987). See also Garcia v. NLRB, 785 F.2d 807, 121 LRRM 3349 (CA 9, 1986) (termination of employee who refuses to act contrary to law constitutes retaliatory discharge); Olguin v. Inspiration Consolidated Copper Co.,

not acting in defense of a public policy * * *, but incorrectly asserting his own interpretation of the law."[80]

The Supreme Court carved out another exception concerning preemption by federal labor law in *Caterpillar, Inc. v. Williams,* where former employees who moved to management and other positions outside the bargaining unit were downgraded to unionized positions and assured that their downgrades were temporary. The employer allegedly assured the employees that if the plant were ever closed they would be employed at other facilities. However, the company later notified them that they would be laid off. The employees then filed an action based solely on state law alleging that the company had breached their individual employment contracts. The Court held that employees covered by a collective bargaining agreement were permitted to assert their legal rights, including state law contract rights, as long as the contracts relied upon were not dependent upon interpretation of the collective bargaining agreement.[81]

State courts have disagreed on whether employees must plead exhaustion of the grievance arbitration procedure to state a valid cause of action for retaliatory discharge. For example, the Illinois Supreme Court ruled that exhaustion of the grievance arbitration procedure was not required.[82] However, the opposite conclusion was reached by the Montana Supreme Court where it dismissed the claim of an employee who failed to submit to the grievance arbitration procedure.[83] The Fourth Circuit, U.S. Court of Appeals, has held that Maryland courts require that a discharged employee, who sues pursuant to a collective bargaining agreement, must exhaust contractual and federal remedies before pursuing a state action in tort.[84]

The doctrine of res judicata was cited by one court in dismissing an employee's state claim.[85] The court found it unnecessary to address the question of whether the retaliatory discharge action was preempted by federal labor law, reasoning that the arbitrator's decision that the employee was fired for absenteeism was res judicata to any other reason for her termination.

---

740 F.2d 1468, 117 LRRM 2073 (CA 9, 1984) (wrongful discharge case of miner fired in retaliation for reporting unsafe mine conditions did not fit public policy exception because policy plaintiff was purportedly protecting stemmed from a federal statute and was not based on state law); Jackson v. Consolidated Rail Co., 717 F.2d 1045, 114 LRRM 2682 (CA 7, 1983) cert. denied, 104 S.Ct. 1000 (1984) (discharge claim significantly interrelated with interpretation of contractual provisions cannot be entertained because it impinges too strongly on federal labor policy elucidated by Railway Labor Act); Lamb v. Brigg Mfg., 700 F.2d 1092, 115 LRRM 4824 (CA 7, 1983) (state cause of action against retaliatory discharges is precluded if claimant is a union employee covered by a collective bargaining agreement).

[80]Desoto v. Yellow Freight Sys., 124 LRRM at 3073.

[81]107 S.Ct. 2425, 125 LRRM 2521 (1987).

[82]Gonzalez v. Prestress Eng'g Corp., 503 N.E.2d 308, 124 LRRM 2252 (Ill. 1986). See also Puchert v. Agsalud, 677 P.2d 449 (Hawaii, 1984). For an exhaustive discussion of recent Illinois cases addressing federal preemption and retaliatory discharge issues, see Green, "Federal Preemption of Suits for Wrongful Discharge under Illinois State Law," 41 Arb. J. 46 (1986).

[83]Brinkman v. Montana, 729 P.2d 1301, 124 LRRM 2328 (Mont., 1986).

[84]Childers v. Chesapeake & Potomac Tel. Co., 881 F.2d 1259, 1265, 131 LRRM 3217 (CA 4, 1989).

[85]Fisher v. Martin Marietta, 815 F.2d 703 (CA 6, 1987), aff'd without a published opinion.

In an action removed under § 301, a federal court determined that it has jurisdiction to address the merits of alleged state law claims during the course of its preemption inquiry and should remand action to a state court if the claim is not preempted. The court, however, may dismiss the claim if the complaint plainly fails to state a cause of action under state law.[86]

Regarding a union's duty of fair representation, there is no definitive answer about what constitutes actionable arbitrariness on the part of the union.[87] A majority of courts agree that the union has to be more than negligent in order to breach the duty of fair representation.[88] Some courts, however, do hold that negligence might in some instances constitute lack of fair representation.[89] However, in *Electrical Workers v. Hechler* the Supreme Court held that any duty of care to a union member that is imposed on a union through contractual arrangement is not sufficiently independent of the collective bargaining agreement to withstand federal preemption.[90]

With respect to Title VII discrimination claims, statistical studies show that a sizeable number of these claims are arbitrated and that the number of cases processed by arbitrators is on the increase.[91] This does not mean, however, that grievants do not exercise the right to de novo review granted to them by *Gardner-Denver*.[92]

Other Supreme Court Decisions Affecting Arbitration

Additional decisions by the United States Supreme Court after the *Trilogy* are summarized as follows:

---

[86]Childers v. Chesapeake & Potomac Tel. Co., 881 F.2d 1259, 1262, 131 LRRM 3217 (CA 4, 1989).

[87]For a good overview of fair representation in its totality, see Kirschner, "Duty of Fair Representation: Implications of Bowen," 1 Lab. Law. 19 (1985); Note, "Adding Injury to the Insult: Bowen and the Duty of the Fair Representation," 67 Marq. L. Rev. 317 (1984).

[88]See Note, "Breaching the Duty of Fair Representation," 17 John Marshall L. Rev. 415 (1986), at 420-424, and the accompanying footnotes.

[89]Dutrisac v. Caterpillar Tractor Co., 749 F.2d 1270, 113 LRRM 3532 (CA 9, 1983) (negligent failure to perform a ministerial act, such as filing a timely application for an arbitration which results in eliminating one of employee's remedies and potentially subjects him to a severe sanction, constitutes actionable breach of fair representation.

[90]107 S.Ct. 2161, 125 LRRM 2353 (1987).

[91]See Hauck, "The Efficacy of Arbitrating Discrimination Complaints," 35 Lab. L.J. 175 (1984).

[92]Alexander v. Gardner-Denver Co., 94 S.Ct. 1011, 7 FEP 81 (1974). Although a sizeable percentage of arbitrator's awards are reviewed by courts, the most pervasive study on the subject reports that courts reverse only 1.2%, and the EEOC only 4.4%, of the arbitral awards, and thus concludes that *Gardner's* significance is more procedural than substantive. See Hoyman & Stallworth, "The Arbitration of Discrimination Grievances in the Aftermath of *Gardner-Denver*," 39 Arb. J. 49 (1984). One study indicates that despite all criticism the conventional arbitral wisdom will render a legally correct award in close to 95% of discrimination cases. See Hauck, 35 Lab. L.J. at 180. Another recent study, which focused primarily on gender discrimination, also indicates that alleged shortcomings of arbitrating discrimination issues might be exaggerated, and finds that the arbitrators are impartial, have prior experience with the subject matter, and are cognizant of the relevant law. The study also suggests that parties in discrimination cases are now afforded increased procedural protection. See Willig, "Arbitration of Discrimination Grievances: Arbitral and Judicial Competence Compared," Proceedings of the 39th Annual Meeting of NAA, 101 (BNA Books, 1987).

Bowen v. U.S. Postal Service: A union that breaches its duty of fair representation by failing to take a meritorious grievance to arbitration will be liable for a portion of the grievant's back-pay damages.[93]

DelCostello v. Teamsters: The most appropriate statute of limitations applicable to actions against a union and an employer for breach of the collective bargaining agreement and breach of the duty of fair representation is the six-month period provided by § 10(b) of the National Labor Relations Act.[94]

McDonald v. City of West Branch: In an action brought under the Civil Rights Act, 42 U.S.C. § 1983, a federal court should not afford res judicata or collateral estoppel effect to an arbitration award made pursuant to a collective bargaining agreement.[95]

Schneider Moving & Storage Co. v. Robbins: Where neither the trust agreements nor the collective bargaining agreements evidence any intent to condition the contractual right of the trustees to seek judicial enforcement of the trust provisions on exhaustion of arbitration procedures contained in the collective bargaining agreements, none will be inferred.[96]

Furniture & Piano Movers Local 82 v. Crowley: The trial court erred by enjoining an internal union election for allegations of misconduct and ordering a new election to be held under the supervision of an arbitrator. The sole remedy available to union members seeking to overturn an election is a suit filed by the Secretary of Labor.[97]

Allis-Chalmers Corp. v. Lueck: Where a claim is asserted under state law but is based on interpretation of the collective bargaining agreement, state law is preempted by federal labor law, and the claim must be dismissed if the employee failed to pursue the contract grievance procedure.[98]

Cornelius v. Nutt: The "harmful error" rule, under Civil Service Reform Act § 7701(c)(2)(A), must be applied by an arbitrator deciding a grievance over discharge in the same manner as it would be by the Merit System Protection Board.[99]

AT&T Technologies v. Communications Workers: Unless the parties choose to submit the issue to an arbitrator, it is for the

[93]103 S.Ct. 588, 112 LRRM 2281 (1983).
[94]103 S.Ct. 2281, 113 LRRM 2737 (1983).
[95]104 S.Ct. 1799, 115 LRRM 3646 (1984).
[96]104 S.Ct. 1844, 115 LRRM 3641 (1984).
[97]104 S.Ct. 2557, 116 LRRM 2633 (1984).
[98]105 S.Ct. 1904, 118 LRRM 3345 (1985).
[99]105 S.Ct. 2882, 119 LRRM 2905 (1985).

courts, not the arbitrator, to determine arbitrability of a grievance.[100]

Chicago Teachers Union Local 1 v. Hudson: The union has an obligation to develop truly neutral methods of resolving disputes over payment of agency shop fees by nonunion members.[101] Following that decision, new Rules for Impartial Determination of Union Fees were adopted by the American Arbitration Association.

Meritor Savings Bank v. Vinson: Under the common law principles of agency, an employer is not automatically liable for the harassing actions of its supervisory employees. An employer may protect itself from liability by instituting a grievance system specifically directed to combat sexual harassment offenses which is organized in a fashion that would encourage the victims of harassment to come forward. However, the court rejected the view that the mere existence of a grievance procedure and a policy against discrimination, coupled with the employee's failure to invoke that procedure, would insulate the employer from liability. The court also held that the mere existence of a grievance procedure does *not* insulate the employer from liability. It is only relevant to the determination of the issue. Evidence of the victim's demeanor and dress may be relevant in determining whether the sexual advances were unwelcome. The dissent, however, argued that a well-tailored grievance procedure should not protect the employer from liability but should rather be a factor relevant to determining the magnitude of damages.[102]

Caterpillar, Inc. v. Williams: A case which is based upon a state claim may not be removed to federal court on the basis of a federal defense, including the defense of preemption; however,

---

[100]106 S.Ct. 1415, 121 LRRM 3329 (1986).

[101]106 S.Ct. 1066, 121 LRRM 2793 (1986).

[102]106 S.Ct. 2399, 40 FEP 1822 (1986). *Vinson* is likely to have a considerable impact on the number of sexual harassment cases arbitrated. Since a well-tailored grievance procedure designed to combat sexual harassment might protect the employer from liability for undiscovered transgressions of its employees, employers may opt to include such a procedure, perhaps one with arbitration as the last step, in the collective bargaining agreement. The victims then will have to arbitrate, if only to preserve the right to have their cases reviewed by the court. Moreover, recent studies addressing the efficacy of arbitration of sexual harassment cases suggest that, had victims had a better understanding of arbitration procedures, they might have chosen to arbitrate. First, arbitration gives a victim an advantage of speedy conflict resolution and often protects the nonemployee visitors who would otherwise not have a Title VII claim. Secondly, the most common remedies sought by the victim in sexual harassment cases are the injunction and reinstatement with back pay. Arbitrators routinely grant the same remedies. Thirdly, in holding the victim's demeanor and dress as factors relevant to the court's decision, the *Vinson* Court reduced the evidentiary advantages the trial procedure might have had over an arbitration proceeding where such information was routinely admitted. For a discussion of arbitration's suitability for resolving gender discrimination issues, see Willig, "Arbitration of Discrimination Grievances: Arbitral and Judicial Competence Compared," Proceedings of the 39th Annual Meeting of NAA, 101 (BNA Books, 1986). For a careful treatment of *Vinson* and an excellent review of past arbitral decisions elucidating relevant considerations for deciding sexual harassment cases, see Monat & Gomez, "Sexual Harassment: The Impact of *Meritor Savings Bank v. Vinson* on Grievances and Arbitration Decisions," 41 Arb. J. 24 (1986).

once an area of state law has been completely preempted, any claim based on that preempted law is considered, from its inception, a federal claim, thus arising under federal law.[103]

Karahalios v. National Federation of Federal Employees Local 1263: In an action brought under Title VII of the Civil Service Reform Act of 1978 by a federal employee within a bargaining unit for which the union was the exclusive bargaining agent, there is no private cause of action against the union for a breach of its statutory duty of fair representation. The exclusive enforcement authority over the duty of fair representation is the Federal Labor Relations Authority.[104]

Legal Status of Federal-Sector Arbitration

The Agencies and Their Role

Federal Service Impasses Panel (FSIP). Regarding review of FSIP decisions, the Federal Labor Relations Authority has differentiated between the provisions of an agreement which have been imposed by a final order of the FSIP and those resulting from interest arbitration awards issued by FSIP mediators/arbitrators. An agency head is authorized to review for legal sufficiency the provisions of a collective agreement imposed by FSIP decisions and orders.[105] The Fourth Circuit, U.S. Court of Appeals, has held, in part agreeing with the Authority, that agreement provisions imposed by the FSIP or by a designee of the Panel may be reviewed by the agency head pursuant to 5 U.S.C. § 714(c).[106] If the agency head disapproves, review of that disapproval may be sought through negotiations or an unfair labor practice.[107]

Interest arbitration awards, which have been issued based on management's voluntary agreement to interest arbitration, are not subject to agency head review, and must be challenged by filing exceptions to the award.[108]

---

[103]107 S.Ct. 2425, 125 LRRM 2521 (1987).

[104]109 S.Ct. 1282, 130 LRRM 2737 (1989).

[105]5 U.S.C. § 7114(c); Interpretation and Guidance, 15 FLRA 564 (1984), aff'd sub nom. AFGE v. FLRA, 778 F.2d 850 (D.C. Cir., 1985). See generally Broida, A Guide to Merit Systems Protection Board Law and Practice, 1979-1987 (Dewey Publications, 1987); Bussey, Federal Civil Service Law and Procedures: A Basic Guide, 2d ed. (BNA Books, 1990).

[106]Department of Defense Dependents Schools v. FLRA, 852 F.2d 779, 128 LRRM 3104 (CA 4, 1988). See also Panama Canal Comm'n v. FLRA, 867 F.2d 905, 130 LRRM 2930 (CA 5, 1989).

[107]5 U.S.C. § 7117 provides a procedure by which an exclusive representative can contest an agency's declaration that particular proposals are nonnegotiable. 5 U.S.C. § 7118 provides for unfair labor practice proceedings.

[108]Department of Defense Dependents Schools v. FLRA, 879 F.2d 1220, 131 LRRM 3042 (CA 9, 1989); Department of Agriculture v. FLRA, 879 F.2d 655, 131 LRRM 3162 (CA 9, 1989); Department of Defense Dependents Schools (Virginia), 27 FLRA 586 (1987), aff'd in part, 852 F.2d 779, 128 LRRM 3104 (CA 4, 1988). See also Air Force Logistics Command, Wright-Patterson A.F.B., 15 FLRA No. 27 (1984), aff'd sub nom. Department of the Air Force v. FLRA, 775 F.2d 727 (CA 6, 1985). 5 U.S.C. § 7122 provides that either party may file exceptions to an arbitration award with the FLRA, which can review the award and modify it on the basis that it is contrary to law, rule, or regulation, or for "other grounds similar to those applied by Federal courts in private sector labor-management relations * * * ."

Role and Scope of Federal-Sector Grievance Procedure and Arbitration

The FLRA has found that since the probationary period is part of the examination, certification, and appointment process, which is excluded from arbitration by statute, grievances involving probationary employees are not grievable or arbitrable.[109]

Also, where nonunion employees elect to pursue a statutory appeal, the union is not obligated to represent them. The obligation of the union is limited to those matters arising out of collective bargaining.[110]

When the union has a choice, under the Act, and elects to file an unfair practice charge rather than submit an issue to arbitration under the grievance procedure, the issuance of a decision by the FLRA may preclude consideration of the merits of a grievance by an arbitrator.[111]

Under the Act a union may not have the right to grieve a job change on the basis of the employee's seniority if that contention is inconsistent with management rights under 5 U.S.C. § 7106.[112]

Scope of Federal-Sector Bargaining and Management-Rights Safeguards

Management Rights—Prohibited Bargaining Items. The provision in 5 U.S.C. § 7106(a) stating that management rights are to be exercised "in accordance with applicable laws" may limit management's right to contract out. The Court of Appeals for the District of Columbia Circuit affirmed a decision by the FLRA requiring the negotiability of a proposal that would mandate that the EEOC comply with OMB Circular A-76, which addresses procedures to be followed by management in making a contracting-out decision.[113] An arbitrator may find that management failed to comply with OMB Circular A-76 and may require that the process be rerun. The decision

---

[109]James A. Haley Veterans Hosp., 82 LA 973 (Wahl, 1984); Department of the Air Force, 82 LA 593 (Wann, 1984).

[110]Treasury Employees v. FLRA, 800 F.2d 1165, 1171 (D.C. Cir., 1986).

[111]Electing to utilize the unfair labor practice route rather than the grievance arbitration procedure may, in some circumstances, result in the aggrieved party being denied a forum to litigate the merits of its dispute. Under the Harry S. Truman Veterans Hosp., 11 FLRA 516 (1983), line of cases, the Authority will dismiss unfair labor practice charges where the dispute results from contractual interpretation, and there has been no clear repudiation of any contractual provisions. If an unfair labor practice charge based on contract interpretation is dismissed by the Authority after the time limit for the filing of a grievance has been passed, the aggrieved party may be left without a remedy. See also Frazier, "Arbitration in the Federal Sector," 41 Arb. J. 70 (1986).

[112]A union may not have the right to grieve a job change based on the employee's seniority because that contention was inconsistent with management rights under 5 U.S.C. § 1706. See Veterans Admin. Medical Center, 83 LA 1219 (Rotenburg, 1984).

[113]EEOC v. FLRA, 744 F.2d 842, 117 LRRM 2625 (D.C. Cir., 1984), cert. granted, 105 S.Ct. 3497 (1985), cert. dismissed, 106 S.Ct. 1678, 122 LRRM 2081 (1986). In the Supreme Court dismissal of certiorari, Justices White and Stevens dissented, with Stevens stating that he would reverse the court of appeals decision.

to contract out is not *per se* subject to review.[114] The arbitrator may not, however, cancel a procurement action.[115]

An award finding arbitrable a grievance seeking to enforce a contract provision denying the agency the right to make a contracting-out decision was set aside because it violated the employer's right to contract out under 5 U.S.C. § 7106(a). Also, a proposal barring contracting out until the grievance procedure was fully exhausted was ruled not negotiable.[116]

Management Rights—Permitted Bargaining Items. An agency's obligation to bargain as to the impact and implementation under 5 U.S.C. § 7106(b)(2) and (3) has been limited to subjects that have more than a minimal impact on unit employees. Regarding the factors it will consider in determining whether a union's request for impact bargaining will be validated, the Authority stated:

> We have reassessed and modified the recent *de minimis* standard. * * * In examining the record, we will place principal emphasis on such general areas of consideration as the nature and extent of the effect or reasonably foreseeable effect of the change on conditions of employment of bargaining unit employees. Equitable considerations will also be taken into account in balancing the various interests involved.
>
> As to the number of employees involved, this factor will not be a controlling consideration. It will be applied primarily to expand rather than limit the number of situations where bargaining will be required. For example, we may find that a change [affecting only a few employees] does not require bargaining. However, a similar change involving hundreds of employees could, in appropriate circumstances, give rise to a bargaining obligation. The parties' bargaining history will be subject to similar limited application. As to the size of the bargaining unit, this factor will no longer be applied.[117]

The negotiations on impact and implementation must also relate to the change that the agency is making with respect to conditions of employment.[118]

Consultation Rights. A union may reduce its right to bargain to only "consultation" by specific waiver language in the collective bargaining agreement.[119]

Non-Government-Wide Rules or Regulations. The FLRA may make a "no compelling need" finding only through the § 7117(b) negotiability appeal, and not through an unfair labor practice proceeding.[120]

---

[114]744 F.2d at 851. See also Department of Health & Human Servs. v. FLRA, 822 F.2d 430, 125 LRRM 2976 (CA 4, 1987); contra Defense Language Inst. v. FLRA, 767 F.2d 1398, 120 LRRM 2013 (CA 9, 1985), cert. dismissed, 106 S.Ct. 2004 (1986).

[115]Blytheville A.F.B. v. AFGE Local 2840, 22 FLRA No. 72 (1986).

[116]See Library of Congress, 23 FLRA No. 15 (1986). See also Department of Treasury, IRS v. FLRA, 862 F.2d 880, 130 LRRM 2024 (D.C. Cir., 1988).

[117]Social Security Admin., 24 FLRA No. 42, pp. 407-408 (1986).

[118]Air Force Logistics Command, Wright-Patterson A.F.B., 22 FLRA No. 53 (1986).

[119]Department of Health & Human Servs., 83 LA 883 (Edes, 1984).

[120]Army Eng'g Center v. FLRA, 762 F.2d 409, 119 LRRM 2854 (CA 4, 1985).

Review of Arbitration Awards

Where the Merit Systems Protection Board has established a substantive rule or standard for reviewing agency actions, that standard is binding on arbitrators. Specifically, in *Cornelius v. Nutt,*[121] the Supreme Court held that arbitrators hearing cases under § 7121(e) of Title 5 must observe the "harmful error rule" required by § 7701(c)(2) as interpreted and defined by the MSPB. The extent to which arbitrators must follow MSPB precedent not involving statutory interpretation, however, was not specifically decided by the Court.

Comptroller General's Role

The Comptroller General has responded to joint requests for interpretation or application of a statute pertaining to labor relations matters.[122] Where the request is not jointly made, the Comptroller General has refused to assert jurisdiction where to do so would be disruptive of the grievance arbitration process.[123]

The Back Pay Act

The FLRA has revised or modified arbitrators' awards involving application of the Back Pay Act where the arbitrator:

(1) Failed to find a causal relationship between the violation and the remedy.[124]
(2) Awarded overtime back pay to an employee without a finding that but for the violation, the employee would have received the overtime.[125]
(3) Awarded payment of additional commuting expenses.[126]
(4) Ordered an employee promoted without first finding that but for the improper failure to promote, the employee would have been promoted.[127]
(5) Awarded back pay for a temporary promotion which predated the effective date of the agreement.[128]
(6) Credited sick leave which is not a part of pay and allowances.[129]

When awarding attorney fees, an arbitrator is required to fully articulate the basis for the award.[130] Regarding the requirements for an award of attorney fees, the Authority has stated:

---

[121]105 S.Ct. 2882, 119 LRRM 2905 (1985).
[122]Kenneth J. Corpman, et al., Comptroller General, B-214845 (Slip Opinion, April 12, 1985).
[123]Valerie Pannuci Reynolds, Comptroller General, B-225918 (Slip Opinion, March 19, 1987).
[124]National Marine Fisheries, 22 FLRA No. 43 (1986).
[125]Naval Air Rework Facility, Norfolk, 21 FLRA No. 55 (1986).
[126]Customs Serv., 23 FLRA No. 51 (1986).
[127]Patent & Trademark Office, 21 FLRA No. 52 (1986).
[128]Social Security Admin., 20 FLRA No. 78 (1985).
[129]Kirkland A.F.B., 19 FLRA No. 30 (1985).
[130]5 U.S.C. § 7701(g).

> As previously recognized by the Authority, a threshold requirement for entitlement to attorney fees under the Back Pay Act is a finding that the grievant has been affected by an unjustified or unwarranted personnel action which has resulted in the withdrawal or reduction of the grievant's pay, allowances, or differentials. *Department of Defense Dependents School and Overseas Education Association,* 3 FLRA 259, 263 (1980). Further, a reading of the Back Pay Act indicates that an award of attorney fees must be in conjunction with an award of back pay to the grievant on correction of the personnel action, that the award of attorney fees must be reasonable and related to the personnel action, and that the award of attorney fees must be in accordance with the standards established under 5 U.S.C. § 7701(g). Section 7701(g) prescribes that for an employee to be eligible for an award of attorney fees, the employee must be the prevailing party. Section 7701(g)(1), which applies to all cases except those of discrimination, requires that an award of attorney fees must be reasonable, and that the fees must have been incurred by the employee.
>
> * * *
>
> The standards established under section 7701(g) further require a fully articulated, reasoned decision setting forth the specific findings supporting the determination on each pertinent statutory requirement, including the basis upon which the reasonableness of the amount was determined * * *.[131]

The arbitrator is not *functus officio* where an award of attorney fees is involved and an award of attorney fees after the award is proper.[132]

Legal Status of Arbitration in State-Sector Employment

The identification of patterns and trends in the area of state-sector employment is, perhaps, becoming less difficult with the passage of time.

With a maturing of labor relations in the public sector, the "traditional prohibition" against strikes by public employees is weakening in some quarters. At least 12 states now provide a right to strike in one variation or another for their employees.[133] In addition, the California

---

[131] Army Support Command, Hawaii, 14 FLRA No. 90, pp. 683-684 (1984).

[132] Philadelphia Naval Shipyard & Metal Trades Council, 32 FLRA No. 63 (1988).

[133] Alaska, California, Hawaii, Idaho, Illinois, Minnesota, Montana, Ohio, Oregon, Pennsylvania, Vermont, and Wisconsin. For listings of pertinent statutory citations as well as discussions on the right to strike in the public sector, see Aaron, "Unfair Labor Practices and the Right to Strike in the Public Sector: Has the National Labor Relations Act Been a Good Model?" 38 Stan. L. Rev. 1097, 1098, and 1109-1119 (1986); Case Notes, "Labor Law: The California Supreme Court Confers a Limited Right to Strike Upon California's Public Employees Through Judicial Fiat," 11 U. Dayton L. Rev. 421, 425-426 and 428 n.58 (California law) (1986); Note, "*County Sanitation District No. 2 v. Los Angeles County Employees Association, Local 660:* A Study in Judicial Legislation," 1986 B.Y.U. L. Rev. 197, 197 n.3 (1985); Bumpass, Jr. & Ashman, "Public Sector Bargaining in a Democracy—An Assessment of the Ohio Public Employee Collective Bargaining Law," 33 Clev. St. L. Rev. 593, 640 n.213 (1984-85). A comprehensive treatment of public-sector collective bargaining, including the right of public employees to strike, is contained in "Developments in the Law—Public Employment," 97 Harv. L. Rev. 1611, 1676-1738 (1984). See also Annotation, "Right of Public Employees to Strike or Engage in Work Stoppage," 37 A.L.R.3d 1147 (1971), and Annotation, "Classes of Public Employees Forbidden to Strike," 22 A.L.R. 4th 1103 (1983). The associated right of public employers to engage in a lockout also has been left untouched by the evolving growth of labor relations in the public sector. See Utility Workers Local 466 v. Labor Relations Comm'n, 389 Mass. 500, 451 N.E.2d 124, 116 LRRM 3150 (1983), where a public employer lockout was held valid although a state law prohibited public employee strikes.

Supreme Court has asserted that public employee strikes are not inconsistent with public policy and are therefore legal unless they are statutorily barred or unless they present a substantial and imminent threat to public health and safety.[134]

Sovereignty Doctrine

The erosion of the sovereignty doctrine as a deterrent to the legalization of collective bargaining and arbitration for public employees continues. The doctrine has been severely criticized by commentators.[135] In addition, in addressing the proposed application of the sovereignty doctrine to a public employment issue, a three-judge panel found that the doctrine had not been breached by the creation of an exclusive collective bargaining representation system under the Minnesota Public Employment Labor Relations Act, since the legislature retained final approval or rejection of any negotiated agreement.[136] In reaching its ruling, the panel rejected the plaintiff's theory that "only * * * some branch of the public employer * * * may constitutionally serve as the employee representative"; otherwise "an impermissible delegation of state sovereignty" would result.[137]

State-Sector Collective Bargaining

Only a few states have not enacted legislation relating to the topic of collective bargaining for their public employees.[138] Of the 43 states

---

[134]County Sanitation Dist. 2 v. Los Angeles County Employees Ass'n, 38 Cal.3d 564, 214 Cal. Rptr. 424, 699 P.2d 835, 119 LRRM 2433, cert. denied, 106 S.Ct. 408, 120 LRRM 3216 (1985). The limited scope of the right to strike as announced in *County Sanitation,*however, was emphasized later in City of Santa Ana v. Police Benevolent Ass'n, 207 Cal. App. 3d 1568, 255 Cal. Rptr. 688 (Cal. Ct. App. 1989) (where work stoppages conducted by police during labor negotiations were held to be illegal *per se*).

[135]The view that the sovereignty doctrine "has almost no continuing influence" and "is no longer a factor" in public-sector bargaining cases, is presented in Westbrook, "The Use of the Nondelegation Doctrine in Public Sector Labor Law: Lessons From Cases That Have Perpetuated an Anachronism," 30 St. Louis U.L.J. 331, 353, 356 (1986). The writer also contends, however, that the separate and different doctrine of nondelegation "can be useful in the analysis of some issues in public sector labor law," although it is often misunderstood, as in the Missouri Trilogy cases of Springfield v. Clouse, 206 S.W.2d 539 (Mo. S.Ct., 1947); State ex rel Missey v. Cabool, 441 S.W.2d 35, 70 LRRM 3394 (Mo. S.Ct., 1969); and Sumpter v. Moberly, 645 S.W.2d 359, 112 LRRM 2787 (Mo. S.Ct., 1982), reh'g denied, 645 S.W.2d 366 (Mo. S.Ct., 1983). *Id.* at 383. A dissatisfaction of the sovereignty doctrine for adversely affecting grievance arbitration as well as other aspects of public employment is expressed in "Developments in the Law—Public Employment," 97 Harv. L. Rev. 1611, 1691-1696, 1718 n.5 and 1719-1724 (1984). In County Sanitation Dist. 2 v. Los Angeles County Employees Ass'n, 699 P.2d at 842, the court in its plurality opinion reviewed and then rejected the sovereignty doctrine, saying that "the use of this archaic concept to justify a per se prohibition against public employee strikes is inconsistent with modern social reality and should be hereafter laid to rest."

[136]Knight v. Minnesota Community College Faculty Ass'n, 571 F. Supp. 1, 111 LRRM 3156 (D. Minn., 1982), rev'd sub nom. Minnesota State Bd. for Community Colleges v. Knight, 104 S.Ct. 1058, 115 LRRM 2785 (1984).

[137]571 F. Supp. at 3.

[138]Alabama, Arizona, Arkansas, Colorado, Louisiana, Mississippi, and West Virginia. See Aaron, "Unfair Labor Practices and the Right to Strike in the Public Sector: Has the National Labor Relations Act Been a Good Model?" 38 Stan. L. Rev. 1097, 1098 (1986). The experience in one of these states, Arizona, where collective bargaining involving public school teachers is held although neither statutorily approved nor prohibited, is documented in Sachen, "Collective Negotiations in Arizona's Public Schools: The Anomaly of Tolerated Illegal Activities," 28 Ariz.

that have passed relevant legislation, North Carolina remains the only state that has statutorily prohibited public employment collective bargaining.[139] A majority of states have passed legislation expressly favoring collective bargaining for either all or designated classes of their employees. Three states, South Carolina, Virginia, and West Virginia, provide the opportunity of a grievance procedure for state, county, and municipal employees as opposed to authorizing collective bargaining.[140]

The split in judicial authority as to whether statutory authorization is needed before public employment collective bargaining is permissible is reported in *AFSCME Local 2238 v. Stratton*.[141] There, adopting the minority position, the court held that public employees in New Mexico did not need an express grant of statutory authority in order to bargain collectively. The court found an implied authorization to bargain collectively as an incidental part of a specific statutory grant for the promulgation of reasonable rules governing labor relations. In Colorado, collective bargaining agreements in the public sector are valid and enforceable even though there is no express statutory authorization.[142]

Grievance Arbitration With and Without Statutory Authorization

Legislative and judicial favor for grievance arbitration progressively increases in the public sector.[143] A majority of the states now provide by legislation for the establishment of grievance and arbitration procedures in public-sector employment.[144] Judicial favor

---

L. Rev. 15 (1986). A general updating on public-sector employment laws is set out in "Special Report: Legislative Roundup," 25 GERR 277 (1986). In "Developments in the Law—Public Employment," 97 Harv. L. Rev. 1611, 1678 (1984), the conclusion is drawn that "[c]ourts have uniformly held *** that public employers are not constitutionally required to bargain collectively with a public employee union."

[139]N.C. Gen. Stat. §§ 95-98 (1985).

[140]See S.C. Code Ann. § 8-17-120 (Law Co-op., 1986)., Va. Code § 2.1-114.5.1, § 15.1-7.1 and § 22.1-308 (1981) and W.Va. Code §§ 29.6A.1 et seq. (1988); see also Aaron, "Unfair Labor Practices and the Right to Strike in the Public Sector: Has the National Labor Relations Act Been a Good Model?" 38 Stan. L. Rev. 1097, 1098 n.11 (1986).

[141]108 N.M. 163, 769 P.2d 76, 131 LRRM 2424 (1989).

[142]Littleton Education Ass'n v. Arapahoe County School Dist. No. 6, 191 Colo. 411, 553 P.2d 793, 93 LRRM 2378 (1976).

[143]For illustrative cases acknowledging public policy in support of grievance arbitration, see Communications Workers Local 4501 v. Ohio State Univ., 24 Ohio St.2d 191, 494 N.E.2d 1082, 1087 (1986); Hunter-Tannersville CSD Bd. of Educ. v. McGinnis, 100 A.D.2d 330, 475 N.Y.S.2d 512, 515 (1984). See also "Arbitration in the Public Sector," 1 Lab. Law. 454 (1985); and "Developments in the Law—Public Employment," 97 Harv. L. Rev. 1611, 1718 (1984).

[144]Aaron, "Unfair Labor Practices and the Right to Strike in the Public Sector: Has the National Labor Relations Act Been a Good Model?" 38 Stan. L. Rev. 1097, 1104-1105 (1986) and "Developments in the Law—Public Employment," 97 Harv. L. Rev. 1611, 1720 (1984). Also see Township of Moon v. Police Officers, 508 Pa. 495, 498 A.2d 1305 (Pa. S.Ct., 1985) (court held that an interest arbitration panel could provide for a grievance arbitration panel in its award in settlement of a collective bargaining dispute).; Dye v. New York City Transit Auth., 57 N.Y.2d 917, 456 N.Y.S.2d 760, 442 N.E.2d 1271 (1982) (court rejected constitutional challenge to a provision of the New York Civil Service Law that permits a waiver of statutory rights for contractual arbitration).

is evident in the cases that have supported arbitration even in the absence of direct statutory authorization.[145]

In one case a court held that grievance arbitration does not involve an improper delegation of legislative authority to nonelected officials in breach of the state constitution:

> An arbitrator is required to perform different functions in the two situations. Binding interest arbitration allows the arbitrator to substitute his judgment for that of public officials on matters the electorate has entrusted to its elected representatives. * * * Grievance arbitration, on the other hand, arises only after the parties have reached complete agreement on terms and conditions of employment. The arbitrator's function is to make factual findings related to a particular situation and to interpret and apply specific contract provisions, reading the agreement as a whole and discerning the intent of the parties without rewriting the agreement. * * * When an arbitrator is required to interpret the provisions of an existing agreement, he acts in a judicial capacity rather than in a legislative one. * * * The authority to interpret an existing contract, therefore, does not constitute legislative authority, and the nondelegation principle is not implicated in grievance arbitration.[146]

An advisory arbitration decision does not preclude subsequent court action on a discharge against a school district.[147]

Interest Arbitration Statutes

Variations prevail among interest arbitration statutes.[148]

---

[145]For cases supporting grievance arbitration in the absence of statutory authorization, see Anne Arundel County v. Fraternal Order, 313 Md. 98, 543 A.2d 841 (Md., 1988); Stratford v. International Fed'n of Professional & Tech. Eng'rs, Local 134, 201 Conn. 577, 519 A.2d 1, 6 (1986) (an arbitration award that resulted from the consent of parties and not from statute upheld); Fire Fighters Local 589 v. Newburgh, 116 A.D.2d 396, 501 N.Y.S.2d 369 (1986) (public policy does not exist disfavoring delegation of issues involving compensation for job-related injury or illness to an impartial third party, in this case a physician). For reference to the allowance of grievance arbitration in the absence of statutory authorization, particularly when collective bargaining is nevertheless approved, see "Developments in the Law—Public Employment," 97 Harv. L. Rev. 1611, 1720-1721 (1984). Although favor in the public sector for grievance arbitration grows, greater scrutiny is seemingly given to the award of an arbitrator in the public sector to ensure that it complies with his authority. For illustrative cases of where a public-sector arbitrator was held to have exceeded his authority, see Gary Teachers Union Local No. 4 v. Gary Community School Corp., 512 N.E.2d 205, 126 LRRM 2870 (Ind. Ct. App., 1987) (by awarding teachers a bonus, arbitrator exceeded his authority as defined by state legislature); Salamanca v. Salamanca Police Unit Local 805, 130 N.Y. Misc.2d 819, 497 N.Y.S.2d 856 (1986) (arbitrator lacked authority to rule on merit and fitness issue exclusively reserved by state constitution and civil service law to Civil Service Commission); Ferris State College v. AFSCME Council 25, Local 1609, 138 Mich. App. 170, 361 N.W.2d 342, 118 LRRM 2409 (1984) (court held that an arbitrator lacked authority to reduce to a suspension penalty of discharge assessed by a public employer against one of its employees); Ford v. Civil Serv. Employees, 94 A.D.2d 262, 464 N.Y.S.2d 481 (1983) (court ordered employee discharged even though arbitrator had found penalty of discharge too severe). For illustrative arbitration decisions in which the arbitrator concluded that because of the scope of an applicable state statute or for some other related reason, he lacked jurisdiction to hear a public employee grievance brought before him, see Springfield Bd. of Educ., 87 LA 16 (Feldman, 1986); City of Houston, 86 LA 1068 (Stephens, 1986); and City of Elyria, Ohio, 84 LA 318 (Laybourne, 1985).

[146]Denver v. Denver Fire Fighters Local 858, 663 P.2d 1032, 1037-1038 (Colo. S.Ct., 1983).

[147]Hoffsetz v. Jefferson County School Dist. No. R-1, 757 P.2d 155 (Colo. Ct. App. 1988) (employee rejection of award); Waterworks Employees Local 1045 v. Board of Waterworks, 44 Colo. App. 178, 615 P.2d 52 (Colo. Ct. App., 1980) (employer rejection of award).

[148]Maine Rev. Stat. Ann. tit. 26 § 1285 (1984) provides for final and binding arbitration for judicial employees on matters other than their salary, pension, and insurance. On these latter topics, the arbitrator can make advisory recommendations only. See also Hawaii Rev. Stat.

Constitutionality of Binding Interest Arbitration. The question of the constitutionality of interest arbitration statutes has not been subject to a uniform answer.[149]

One court concluded that the binding interest arbitration statute set forth adequate guidance for the arbitrator as well as reasonable review procedures and therefore did not constitute an improper delegation of legislative authority.[150] With respect to the delegation and guidance issues, the court stated that accountability "remains viable in the ability of the legislators to terminate or modify any delegation of legislative power that has been made."[151] The statute provided factors for the arbitrator to weigh and for a mandatory selection of the parties' "last best offer," which "significantly circumscribe[d] what might otherwise be deemed a broad delegation of legislative power."[152]

In another case[153] however, a binding interest arbitration clause in a collective bargaining contract was held to constitute an unconstitutional delegation of legislative power under the constitution of the State of Kentucky. The court found that the Transit Authority, a party to the contract, was a governmental entity under the Kentucky constitution and as such could not convey to an arbitrator its statutorily granted powers of discretion in policy matters and decision-making. Issues "covered by the collective bargaining agreement, for the most part, call for the exercise of discretion and judgment, and therefore involve policy and management decisions."[154]

Determining Arbitrability and Compelling Arbitration

The Supreme Court in *AT&T v. Communications Workers*[155] reaffirmed the private-sector principle that substantive arbitrability—whether a collective bargaining agreement creates a

§ 89-11 (1981); Ill. Rev. Stat. ch. 48, § 1601 et seq. (1985); Minn. Stat. Ann. § 179A16(7) (1987); Wash. Rev. Code Ann. § 41.56.030(6) (1985). On December 31, 1986, binding interest arbitration became effective for the New York Metropolitan Transit Authority. Its employees, together with police and firefighters, are the only public employees in New York covered by binding interest arbitration. 25 GERR 42 (1986). For a general discussion of interest arbitration, see Gershenfeld, "Interest Arbitration," Proceedings of the 36th Annual Meeting of NAA, 190-202 (BNA Books, 1984), and "Developments in the Law—Public Employment," 97 Harv. L. Rev. 1611, 1706-1712 (1984).

[149]See City of Rocky River v. State Employment Relations Bd., 43 Ohio St.3d 1, 539 N.E.2d 103, 131 LRRM 2952 (1989) (reversing its earlier ruling of only six months and holding that the state constitution's "home rule" power granted to a municipality was not violated by the binding arbitration procedure provided for in the Ohio's Public Employee Collective Bargaining Act; Klauder v. San Juan County Deputy Sheriffs Guild, 107 Wash. 2d 338, 728 P.2d 1044, 124 LRRM 2179 (1986) (holding that an interest arbitration clause is a nonmandatory subject of bargaining which cannot be renewed without mutual consent of the parties).

[150]Carofano v. Bridgeport, 196 Conn. 623, 495 A.2d 1011 (1985).

[151]495 A.2d at 1016.

[152]Id. at 1017.

[153]Transit Auth. of Lexington v. Transit Union Local 639, 698 S.W.2d 520 (Ky., 1985).

[154]698 S.W.2d at 523.

[155]AT&T Technologies v. Communications Workers, 106 S.Ct. 1415, 121 LRRM 3329 (1986). See also Rhode Island v. AFSCME Local 2883, 463 A.2d 186, 116 LRRM 2819 (R.I., 1983). In School Dist. 42 of the City of Nashua v. Murray, 514 A.2d 1269 (N.H., 1986), it was held that the Public Employee Labor Relations Board had exclusive original jurisdiction to determine arbitrability for purposes of collective bargaining agreement administration.

duty for the parties to arbitrate a particular grievance—is an issue for the courts, unless the parties clearly and unmistakably provide otherwise.[156] Some states have given an administrative board exclusive original jurisdiction to determine arbitrability for purposes of collective bargaining agreement administration.[157]

Court Review of Arbitration Awards

Limited judicial review is available in the public sector when an arbitration award is contrary to public policy. "Incantations of 'public sector' may not be advanced to overturn every arbitration award."[158] The public policy which obliges a court to refrain from enforcing an award must be clear and explicit; absolute.[159]

Although there is limited judicial review of arbitration awards in the public sector, courts will overturn an award contrary to an appropriate public policy.[160] However, the public policy which obliges the court to refrain from enforcement of the award must be clear and explicit. In one case, a court upheld an arbitrator's award reinstating a bus driver discharged for drunk driving, where the discharge was based only on the odor of alcohol on his breath, and not a chemical test.[161] The court found no violation of a clear and explicit public policy. But in another case, a court struck down an arbitrator's award reinstating a discharged employee who shot two bullets through his supervisor's empty car after a shouting match.[162] The court stated that public policy clearly prohibited retaliation with violence.[163]

Errors of law or fact almost never justify vacating an arbitrator's decision.[164] An arbitrator's award will not be overturned for errors of judgment on the law unless "manifest disregard for the law" has occurred.[165]

---

[156]See Jones, "Arbitration From the Viewpoint of the Practicing Attorney: An Analysis of Arbitration Cases Decided by the New York State Court of Appeals From January, 1973, to September, 1985," 14 Fordham Urb. L.J. 523 (1986), by the author of the opinion in the *Liverpool* decision. See also Board of Educ., Rockford School Dist. No. 205 v. Rockford Educ. Ass'n, 125 LRRM 2603 (Ill. App. Ct., 1986).

[157]Coles County Bd. of Educ. Dist. 1 v. Compton, 526 N.E.2d 149, 131 LRRM 2313 (Ill. Sup. Ct., 1988); School Dist. 42 of the City of Nashua v. Murray, 514 A.2d 1269 (N.H., 1986).

[158]Port Jefferson Station Teachers Ass'n v. Brookhaven-Comsewogue Union Free School Dist., 383 N.E.2d 553, 99 LRRM 3438, 3439 (N.Y., 1978).

[159]Transit Union Div. 1300 v. Mass Transit Admin., 504 A.2d 1132, 121 LRRM 2894 (Md., 1986); Enlarged City School Dist. of Troy v. Troy Teachers' Ass'n, 508 N.E.2d 930 (N.Y., 1987). See also Paperworkers v. Misco, Inc., 108 S.Ct. 364, 126 LRRM 3113 (1987), where the Supreme Court further clarified the limits of judicial review of arbitration awards when public policy considerations are involved.

[160]W.R. Grace & Co. v. Rubber Workers Local 759, 103 S.Ct. 2177, 2183, 113 LRRM 2641 (1983).

[161]Transit Union Div. 1300 v. Mass Transit Admin., 504 A.2d 1132, 121 LRRM 2894 (Md., 1986).

[162]U.S. Postal Serv. v. Letter Carriers, 125 LRRM 3190 (W.D. Pa., 1987).

[163]Ibid.

[164]Sylvania Bd. of Educ. v. Sylvania Educ. Ass'n, 121 LRRM 2346 (Ohio Ct. Com. Pls., 1985).

[165]Madison v. Fire Fighters Local 311, 124 LRRM 2131, 2133 (Wis. Ct. App., 1986).

Statutory and Public Policy Limitations on Scope of Bargaining and Arbitration

Express Statutory Removal of Matter From Bargaining. When management rights are statutorily removed from the duty to bargain, procedures regarding the implementation of such subjects remain topics for bargaining.[166]

Some Matters Sometimes Held Nonbargainable.[167] Other matters sometimes held outside the scope of bargaining are:

1. Classification of students according to their abilities.[168]
2. Medical disqualification standards.[169]
3. Teacher evaluations.[170]
4. School calendar.[171]
5. Reclassification of teachers.[172]
6. Decision to abolish positions.[173]

---

[166]For example, see Hawaii Act, § 89-(9)(d): Wisconsin State Employment Labor Relations Act, § 111.91(1)(b).

[167]Hill & Sinicropi, "Public-Sector Concerns/State Restrictions," Management Rights: A Legal and Arbitral Analysis, 140-145 (BNA Books, 1986). Also, the parties may in the collective bargaining agreement prohibit the arbitrator from deciding whether a statute makes a term illegal in the contract, thereby leaving the question for the courts to decide. See Duluth Fed'n of Teachers Local 692 v. School Dist. 709, 361 N.W.2d 834, 122 LRRM 3084 (Minn., 1985).

[168]Rapid City Educ. Ass'n v. Rapid City Area School Dist., 376 N.W.2d 562, 120 LRRM 3424 (S.D., 1985).

[169]SEPTA v. Transport Workers, 525 A.2d 1, 125 LRRM 3051 (Pa. Commw. Ct., 1984).

[170]Wethersfield Bd. of Educ. v. Connecticut State Bd. of Educ., 519 A.2d 41, 125 LRRM 2510 (Conn., 1986).

[171]Board of Educ. of Montgomery County v. Montgomery County Educ. Ass'n, 505 A.2d 905, 123 LRRM 2505 (Md. Ct. Spec. App., 1986), stating that the school calendar and reclassification of teachers are subjects only tenuously related to the mandatory subject of wages, hours, and working conditions and are management's prerogatives.

[172]Township of Old Bridge Bd. of Educ. v. Old Bridge Education Ass'n, 489 A.2d 159, 121 LRRM 2784 (N.J., 1985), holding that the decision to abolish positions is nonnegotiable, but a provision for notice is. See also AFSCME Local 128 v. Ishpeming, 400 N.W.2d 661, 124 LRRM 3182 (Mich. Ct. App., 1987), holding that the impact of the elimination of positions is a mandatory subject of bargaining.

[173]Township of Old Bridge Bd. of Educ. v. Old Bridge Education Ass'n, 489 A.2d 159, 121 LRRM 2784 (N.J., 1985).

Chapter 3

Scope of Labor Arbitration

Interest Arbitration and Contract Clauses

Specific Provision for Interest Arbitration

It is now well settled that interest arbitration clauses[1] are nonmandatory subjects of bargaining. Thus a union's insistence on bargaining to impasse on inclusion of an interest arbitration provision into a contract constitutes an unfair labor practice.[2] Most courts have held that a union cannot rely on an interest arbitration clause in an existing contract to require an employer to agree to a similar clause in a successor contract.[3]

---

[1]For collective bargaining agreements containing specific interest arbitration clauses, see American Metal Prods. v. Sheet Metal Workers Local 104, 794 F.2d 1452, 123 LRRM 2824, 2826 n.1 (CA 9, 1986); Sheet Metal Workers Local 57 Welfare Fund v. Tampa Sheet Metal Co., 786 F.2d 1459, 122 LRRM 2161, 2162 (CA 11, 1986). In both *American Metal Products* and *Tampa Sheet Metal*, the interest arbitration clause provided in part:

> In addition to the settlement of grievances arising out of interpretation or enforcement of this agreement as set forth in the preceding sections of this Article, any controversy or dispute arising out of the failure of the parties to negotiate a renewal of this agreement shall be settled as hereinunder provided:
>
> (a) Should the negotiations for the renewal of this agreement become deadlocked * * *, either party may submit the dispute to the National Joint Adjustment Board.
>
> The dispute shall be submitted to the National Joint Adjustment Board pursuant to the rules by the National Joint Adjustment Board. The unanimous decision of said Board shall be final and binding upon the parties, reduced to writing, signed and mailed to the parties as soon as possible after the decision has been reached. There shall be no cessation of work by strike or lockout unless and until said Board fails to reach a unanimous decision and the parties have received written notification of its failure.

See also Sheet Metal Workers Local 20 v. Baylor Heating & Air Conditioning, 688 F. Supp. 462, 129 LRRM 2108 (S.D. Ind., 1988), aff'd, 877 F.2d 547, 131 LRRM 2838 (CA 7, 1989) (same clause); Sheet Metal Workers Local 104 v. Andrews, 119 LRRM 3516 (N.D. Calif., 1985) (same clause).

[2]Hotel & Restaurant Employees Local 703 v. Williams, 752 F.2d 1476, 118 LRRM 2600 (CA 9, 1985) (arbitrator cannot make interest arbitration clause self-perpetuating by including it in a new contract).

[3]Sheet Metal Workers Local 14 v. Aldrich Air Conditioning, 717 F.2d 456, 114 LRRM 2657 (CA 8, 1983) (holding that an interest arbitration clause is unenforceable insofar as it applies to the inclusion of a similar clause in a new collective bargaining agreement). See also American Metal Prods. v. Sheet Metal Workers Local 104, 794 F.2d 1452, 123 LRRM 2824 (CA 9, 1986);

Once included, however, almost every court recently considering the question has held that interest arbitration provisions are entitled to the same presumptions favoring arbitration as grievance arbitration provisions and are therefore enforceable under § 301 of the NLRA.[4] The rationale for enforcement appears to be the basic role of the courts in § 301 suits. A court's role in a § 301 suit is to ascertain "whether the party seeking arbitration is making a claim which on its face is governed by the contract."[5] Since interest arbitration provisions are most often specifically part of a contract, courts are less hesitant to enforce them.[6]

Arbitrator's Function in Rights Disputes

Unlike the arbitrator's quasi-legislative role in interest disputes, the arbitrator's function in rights disputes is limited to interpretation of the bargained-for agreement. Beginning with its *Enterprise Wheel* decision[7] the Supreme Court limited the arbitrator's role in rights disputes to interpretation and application of the collective bargaining agreement.[8] The Court held that although an arbitrator could look outside the contract for guidance, "he does not sit to dispense his own brand of industrial justice,"[9] and his award is therefore legitimate only insofar as it "draws its essence" from the collective bargaining agreement.[10]

Electrical Workers (IBEW) Local 367 v. Graham County Elec. Coop., 783 F.2d 897, 121 LRRM 2924 (CA 9, 1986); Sheet Metal Workers Local 420 v. Huggins Sheet Metal, 752 F.2d 1473, 118 LRRM 2603 (CA 9, 1985); Sheet Metal Workers Local 263 v. Sheet Metal Contractors Labor Relations Council of Iowa, Cedar Rapids Chapter, 120 LRRM 2191 (N.D. Iowa, 1984). The Board has taken the same position, Advice Memorandum, Sheet Metal Workers Local 162, 109 LRRM 1205 (1981). But see Sheet Metal Workers Local 252 v. Standard Sheet Metal, 699 F.2d 481, 112 LRRM 2878 (CA 9, 1983) (enforcing arbitrator's inclusion of interest arbitration clause in a new contract).

[4]See cases cited in note 3. But see Bally Mfg. Corp. v. Electrical Workers (IBEW) Local 713, 605 F. Supp. 110, 120 LRRM 3166 (N.D. Ill., 1985) (court refusing to enforce interest arbitration provision because contract also contained termination provision, and to enforce interest arbitration provision would deprive termination clause of all meaning, thus perpetuating interest arbitration clause at expense of an equally binding termination clause). For a case dealing with the same issue but arriving at a different result, see Sheet Metal Workers Local 420 v. Huggins Sheet Metal, 752 F.2d 1473, 118 LRRM 2824 (CA 9, 1985).

[5]Steelworkers v. American Mfg. Co., 80 S.Ct. 1343, 46 LRRM 2414, 2415 (1960).

[6]Sheet Metal Workers Local 104 v. Andrews, 119 LRRM 3516 (N.D. Cal., 1985); see also Hotel & Restaurant Employees Local 703 v. Williams, 752 F.2d 1476, 118 LRRM 2600 (CA 9, 1985).

[7]Steelworkers v. Enterprise Wheel & Car Corp., 80 S.Ct. 1358, 46 LRRM 2423 (1960). The *Enterprise Wheel* decision was part of the famous *Steelworkers Trilogy* in which the Court outlined the significance of arbitration in the labor-management context. For a discussion of the *Steelworkers Trilogy*, see Chapter 2 of the Fourth Edition, topic entitled "The Trilogy."

[8]80 S.Ct. at 1361, 46 LRRM at 2425.

[9]Ibid.

[10]Ibid.

In 1981,[11] 1983,[12] and again in 1984,[13] the Court reaffirmed both *Enterprise Wheel* and the "primacy and exclusivity of arbitration within its proper sphere of contract interpretation":[14]

> [E]ven though a particular arbitrator may be competent to interpret and apply statutory law, he may not have the contractual authority to do so. An arbitrator's power is both derived from, and limited by, the collective bargaining agreement. He has no general authority to invoke public laws that conflict with the bargain between the parties. His task is limited to construing the meaning of the collective-bargaining agreement so as to effectuate the collective intent of the parties.[15]

Lower courts have followed the Court's lead and have uniformly restricted the arbitrator's function in rights disputes to the role of contract interpreter.[16] They are routinely called upon to define the

---

[11]Barrentine v. Arkansas-Best Freight Sys., 101 S.Ct. 1437, 24 WH Cases 1284 (1981).

[12]W.R. Grace & Co. v. Rubber Workers Local 759, 103 S.Ct. 2177, 113 LRRM 2641 (1983). In *Grace* the Court issued its oft-cited statement that "a federal court may not overrule an arbitrator's decision simply because the Court believes its own interpretation of the contract would be a better one." 113 LRRM at 2644. For an in-depth discussion of the Supreme Court's opinion in *Grace*, see Christensen, "W.R. Grace and Co., An Epilogue to the Trilogy?" Proceedings of the 37th Annual Meeting of NAA, 21-32 (BNA Books, 1985).

[13]McDonald v. City of West Branch, 104 S.Ct. 1799, 115 LRRM 3646 (1984). In *McDonald*, the Court upheld the res judicata or collateral estoppel effect of an arbitration award rendered in a § 1983 discrimination case. The Court reiterated its stance that the arbitrator's authority "derives solely from the contract." 115 LRRM at 3648.

[14]Quoted language is from Nolan & Abrams, "The Future of Labor Arbitration," 37 Lab. L.J. 437, 438-439 (1986). See also Heinsz, "Judicial Review of Labor Arbitration Awards: The Enterprise Wheel Goes Around & Around," 52 Mo. L. Rev. 243 (1987); Dunsford, "The Role and Function of the Labor Arbitrator," 30 St. Louis U.L.J. 109, 119 (1985) ("In the first great debate about the role of the arbitrator, the prevailing judgment has been to consider the arbitrator an adjudicator and not a mediator or problem solver").

[15]Barrantine v. Arkansas-Best Freight Sys., 101 S.Ct. 1437, 1446-1447, 24 WH Cases 1284 (1981) (citations omitted). See also Alexander v. Gardner-Denver Co., 94 S.Ct. 1011, 7 FEP Cases 81, 87 (1974) ("the arbitrator has authority to resolve questions of contractual rights").

[16]See, e.g., George A. Hormel & Co. v. Food & Commercial Workers Local 9, 879 F.2d 347, 131 LRRM 3018 (CA 8, 1989), reh'g denied, 1989 U.S. App. Lexis 13102 (award vacated because it did not draw its essence from contract); Eberhard Foods v. Handy, 868 F.2d 890, 130 LRRM 2830 (CA 6, 1989) (award should be upheld unless it fails to draw its essence from collective bargaining agreement); Jersey Nurses Economic Sec. Org. v. Roxbury Medical Group, 868 F.2d 88, 130 LRRM 2680 (CA 3, 1989) (award unenforceable because it did not draw its essence from collective bargaining agreement); In re Marine Pollution Serv., 857 F.2d 91, 129 LRRM 2472 (CA 2, 1988) (arbitrator failed to satisfy requirement that award be drawn from essence of collective bargaining agreement); Electrical Workers (IBEW) Local 1842 v. Cincinnati Elec. Corp., 808 F.2d 1201, 1203, 124 LRRM 2473, 2476 (CA 6, 1987) (upholding arbitrator's award interpreting and applying a forfeiture clause because award drew its essence from the contract); Northwest Airlines v. Air Line Pilots, 808 F.2d 76, 124 LRRM 2300 (D.C. Cir. 1987) (award limited to construing collective bargaining agreement upheld); Walsh v. Union Pacific R.R., 803 F.2d 412, 123 LRRM 2789 (CA 8, 1986) ("Matters of contract interpretation are committed to the arbitrator"); Teamsters Local 863 v. Jersey Coast Egg Producers, 773 F.2d 530, 120 LRRM 2505 (CA 3, 1985), cert. denied, 106 S.Ct. 1468, 121 LRRM 3104 (1986) (reversing district court order vacating arbitrator's award because award was "drawn from the four corners of the bargaining agreement"); Ford Motor Co. v. Plant Protection Employees, 770 F.2d 69, 120 LRRM 2008 (CA 6, 1985) (reversing district court's decision to vacate awards because arbitrator restricted himself to interpreting the contract and as such may not be overruled by a court); Morgan Servs. v. Clothing & Textile Workers Local 323, 724 F.2d 1217, 115 LRRM 2368 (CA 6, 1984) (award vacated because arbitrator exceeded authority given him by the contract); Super Tire Eng'g Co. v. Teamsters Local 676, 721 F.2d 121, 114 LRRM 3320 (CA 3, 1983) (reversing district court decision vacating award because award was based on the contract and was not irrational); St. Louis Theatrical Co. v. Stage Employees Local 6, 715 F.2d 405, 114 LRRM 2097 (CA 8, 1983) (upholding vacation of award because arbitrator exceeded authority granted him by parties in collective bargaining agreement); Radio & Television Broadcast Eng'rs Local 1212 v. WPIX, Inc., 716 F. Supp. 777 (S.D.N.Y., 1989), stay denied, 1989 U.S. Dist. Lexis 9193 (enforcing award which did not contravene collective bargaining agreement); Hunt v. Commodity Haulage Corp., 647 F. Supp. 797 (E.D.N.Y., 1986) (award will be upheld where arbitrators have acted within authority granted them by contract between parties);

arbitrator's function in the context of reviewing arbitration awards. The arbitrator's role as contract interpreter is evidenced by the Court's reluctance to vacate or modify an award that "draws its essence" from the contract.[17]

Moreover, a similar conclusion regarding the arbitrator's role is demonstrated by court decisions resolving the question of arbitrability. The Supreme Court has held that an order to arbitrate should not be denied unless it could be said that arbitration of a particular grievance is outside the scope of the collective bargaining agreement.[18] The arbitrator is a creation of the bargained-for agreement and as such is limited by its terms.[19]

Recently, the NLRB has begun to expand the role of arbitrators by deferring cases alleging violations of individuals' basic § 7 rights to

---

Jovijo, Inc. v. Food & Commercial Workers Local 23, 641 F. Supp. 690 (W.D. Pa., 1986) (award upheld because it was "drawn" from agreement); Letter Carriers v. U.S. Postal Serv., 625 F. Supp. 1527, 121 LRRM 2384 (D.D.C., 1986) (award upheld because arbitrator did not exceed his authority); but see High Concrete Structures, Inc. v. Electrical Workers (UE) Local 166, 879 F.2d 1215, 131 LRRM 3152 (CA 3, 1989) (recognizing arbitrator's authority to go beyond express terms of collective bargaining agreement where so agreed by the parties either through an interest or rights arbitration clause in the agreement or through a separate agreement).

The Second Circuit has put a gloss on the *Steelworkers Trilogy* that "an arbitration award will not be vacated when the arbitrator explains his decision in terms that offer even a barely colorable justification for the outcome reached * * *." Pinkerton's NY Racing Sec. Servs. v. Service Employees Local 323, 805 F.2d 470, 473, 123 LRRM 3090, 3092 (CA 2, 1986) and cases cited therein.

[17]Steelworkers v. Enterprise Wheel & Car Corp., 80 S.Ct 1358, 46 LRRM 2423 (1960). See cases cited in note 16. However, the courts have begun to recognize a public policy exception to the arbitrator's authority to interpret the contract. That is, even though the arbitrator's award may "draw its essence" from the contract, it may at the same time be unenforceable because it violates established law or seeks to compel unlawful action. W.R. Grace & Co. v. Rubber Workers Local 759, 103 S.Ct. 2177, 113 LRRM 2641, 2645 (1983). Yet the extent to which an award can be said to violate public policy is in conflict. The Supreme Court in *Grace* first recognized that an arbitrator's award may be unenforceable because it violates public policy. The Court explained that the basis for the public policy exception must be "well defined and dominant" and ascertained "by reference to the laws and legal precedents and not from general considerations of supposed public interests." Numerous courts have read *Grace* to establish an "extremely narrow" exception; Stead Motors v. Automotive Machinists Lodge 1173, 886 F.2d 1200, 132 LRRM 2689 (CA 9, 1989), cert. denied, 58 USLW 3739 (1990); Northwest Airlines v. Air Line Pilots, 808 F.2d 76, 124 LRRM 2300 (D.C. Cir., 1987); Bevles Co. v. Teamsters Local 986, 791 F.2d 1391, 122 LRRM 2666 (CA 9, 1986), cert. denied, 127 LRRM 2048 (1987); E.I. DuPont de Nemours & Co. v. Grasselli Employees Indep. Ass'n of E. Chicago, 790 F.2d 611, 122 LRRM 2217 (CA 7, 1986); Postal Workers v. U.S. Postal Serv., 789 F.2d 1, 122 LRRM 2094 (D.C. Cir., 1986). However, the Fifth Circuit has declined to read the exception narrowly and has vacated arbitrators' awards based on a broader interpretation of what constitutes public policy. Misco, Inc., v. Paperworkers, 768 F.2d 739, 130 LRRM 2119 (CA 5, 1985), cert. granted, 107 S.Ct. 781, vacated and remanded, 108 S.Ct. 364, 126 LRRM 3113 (1987); Meat Cutters v. Great Western Food Co., 712 F.2d 122, 114 LRRM 2001 (CA 5, 1983); see Ray, "Protecting the Parties' Bargain After *Misco*: Court Review of Labor Arbitration Awards," 64 Ind. L.J. 1 (1988).

[18]AT&T Technologies v. Communications Workers, 106 S.Ct. 1415, 1419, 121 LRRM 3329 (1986).

[19]106 S.Ct. at 1418 ("arbitration is a matter of contract"); see also Seafarers v. National Marine Servs., 639 F. Supp. 1283, 1290 (E.D. La., 1986) ("arbitration is a creature of contract with no life independent of its collective bargaining agreement"). The arbitrator's role as contract interpreter is further evidenced by the court's role in § 301 (29 U.S.C. § 185 (1982)) suits to compel arbitration. In actions to compel arbitration, the court's role is to ascertain "whether the party seeking arbitration is making a claim which on its face is governed by the contract." Printing Specialties & Paper Prods. Local 680 v. Nabisco Brands, 649 F. Supp. 253, 256 (N.D. Ill., 1986) (citing Steelworkers v. American Mfg. Co., 80 S.Ct. 1343, 1346, 46 LRRM 2414, 2415 (1960)). Congress has also defined the arbitrator's function as contract interpreter. The NLRA provides in part: "Final adjustment by a method agreed upon by the parties is declared to be the desirable method for settlement of grievance disputes arising over the *application or interpretation of an existing collective-bargaining agreement.* 29 U.S.C. § 173(d) (emphasis added).

the grievance arbitration machinery.[20] Their role has taken on new dimensions as the Board has thrust upon them new authority to apply and interpret legal issues and statutes clearly outside the four corners of the parties' bargained-for agreement.

Yet an arbitrator's adjudicative role remains his foremost priority. For example, historically an arbitrator also acted as mediator: someone who would resolve disputes through settlement and compromise.[21] But today, even though arbitrators are frequently called upon to mediate disputes, their role as mediator is cautioned against.[22] Moreover, arbitrators themselves are now viewing their function as more adjudicative: "Arbitration more and more resembles litigation, arbitrators think of themselves as contract interpreters rather than as 'labor relations physicians***.'"[23]

---

[20]Prior to 1977, the Board showed a reluctance to defer to arbitration grievances alleging a violation of an individual's basic rights under § 7 of the NLRA. General Am. Transp. Corp., 228 NLRB 808, 94 LRRM 1483 (1977). This posture was consistent with § 10(a) of the NLRA which gives the Board jurisdiction to hear unfair labor practice issues. 29 U.S.C. § 160(a). However in United Technologies Corp., 268 NLRB 557, 115 LRRM 1049, 1051 (1984), the Board overruled *General American* and held that it would begin deferring to arbitration cases in which individuals alleged violations of §§ 8(a)(1), 8(a)(3), 8(b)(1)(A), and 8(b)(2) of the NLRA. The Board believed that "[w]here an employer and a union have voluntarily elected to create dispute resolution machinery culminating in final and binding arbitration, it is contrary to the basic principles of the Act for the Board to jump into the fray prior to an honest attempt by the parties to resolve their disputes through that machinery." See also Chevron, U.S.A., 275 NLRB 949, 119 LRRM 1238 (1985) (Board ordering deferral to arbitration of alleged violations of § 8(a)(3)); Spann Bldg. Maintenance Co., 275 NLRB 755, 119 LRRM 1209 (1985) (Board reaffirming *United Technologies* and upholding deferral unless grievance procedure "has been or is likely to be unfair or irregular").

Similarly, in Olin Corp., 268 NLRB 573, 115 LRRM 1056, 1058, 1063 (1984), the Board held that it would defer to an arbitrator's award which ruled on an unfair labor practice charge if "(1) the contractual issue is factually parallel to the unfair labor practice issue, and (2) the arbitrator was presented generally with the facts relevant to resolving the unfair labor practice." Member Zimmerman dissented because he believed that the Board would begin deferring to an arbitrator's award based on a presumption that an unfair labor practice issue has been resolved, without actually knowing if the issue was presented to or considered by the arbitrator. See also Ohio Edison Co., 274 NLRB 128, 118 LRRM 1429 (1985) (NLRB deferred to arbitration panel case in which it was alleged that employer violated § 8(a)(3) of the NLRA). Henkel & Kelly, "Deferral to Arbitration After *Olin* and *United Technologies*: Has the NLRB Gone too Far?" 43 Wash. & Lee L. Rev. 37 (1986); Comment, "The National Labor Relations Board's Policy of Deferring to Arbitration," 13 Fla. St. U.L. Rev. 1141 (1986); Shank, "Deferral to Arbitration: Accommodation of Competing Statutory Policies," 2 Hofstra Lab. L.J. 211 (1985); National Labor Relations Board Office of the General Counsel Memorandum GC 84-5, 115 LRR 334, 344-345 (1984) (interpreting *United Technologies* as allowing deferral to grievance arbitration procedure alleged violations of §§ 8(a)(1), 8(a)(3), 8(a)(5), 8(b)(1)(A), 8(b)(1)(B), 8(b)(2), and 8(b)(3) of the NLRA).

[21]Dunsford, "The Role and Function of the Arbitrator," 30 St. Louis U.L.J. 109, 115 (1985).

[22]Code of Professional Responsibility for Arbitrators of Labor-Management Disputes, pt II § F, ¶2 b, c:

> If one party requests that the arbitrator mediate and the other party objects, the arbitrator should decline the request.
>
> An arbitrator is not precluded from making a suggestion that he or she mediate. To avoid the possibility of improper pressure, the arbitrator should not so suggest unless it can be discerned that both parties are likely to be receptive. In any event, the arbitrator's suggestion should not be pursued unless both parties readily agree."

The Code is found in 3 Lab. Arb. & Dispute Settlements (Nondecisional material) 51.

[23]Nolan & Abrams, "The Future of Labor Arbitration," 37 Lab. L.J. 437, 437 (1985). See also Dunsford, "The Role and Function of the Labor Arbitrator," 30 St. Louis U.L.J. 109, 119 (1985): "In sum, if an arbitrator ventures into mediation, he may learn things and evoke confidences which, should he later be forced to adjudicate, will seriously impair the integrity of the later process."

Rights Arbitration Contract Clauses

Although the courts limit arbitrators to interpretation of the collective bargaining agreement, the arbitrator is a creation of the contract, and the contract defines the scope of his authority.[24] Thus his authority to interpret the agreement depends upon the scope of the arbitration clause. Broad arbitration clauses give an arbitrator expansive authority to decide a multitude of disputes.[25] The Supreme Court has ruled that a broad grievance arbitration provision should be held to encompass all disputed matters not specifically excluded: "[A]rbitration should not be denied unless it may be said with positive assurance that the arbitration clause is not susceptible of an interpretation that covers the asserted dispute. Doubts should be resolved in favor of coverage."[26]

In light of this presumption the courts do not hesitate to support arbitration of an issue unless they are convinced that the clause specifically excludes that issue. For example, the Second Circuit, U.S. Court of Appeals, held that a broad arbitration clause gave an arbitrator the authority to resolve a grievance that required him to interpret a separate employment contract to determine whether the Impartial Chairman had been properly dismissed.[27] The Second Circuit held that even if the separate employment contract was wholly distinct from the collective bargaining agreement, the dispute would be arbitrable under the broad language of the arbitration provision.[28]

---

[24]Safeway Stores v. Food & Commercial Workers Local 400, 621 F. Supp. 1233, 118 LRRM 3419 (D.D.C., 1985) (arbitration is a matter of contract and arbitrator's authority is defined by agreement); see also Seafarers v. National Marine Servs., 639 F. Supp. 1283, 1290 (E.D. La., 1986) ("arbitration is a creature of contract with no life independent of its collective bargaining agreement").

[25]See, e.g., Simkins Indus., 81 LA 592 (Carter, 1983) (broad grievance arbitration clause covers dispute over job rotation even though job rotation not specifically mentioned in contract, because grievance arbitration clause did not limit grievances to only those specific conditions of employment set forth in written agreement); Trans World Airlines, 81 LA 524 (Sys. Bd. of Adjustment; Heinsz, Chm., 1983) (broad arbitration clause covers arbitration over award of attorneys' fees). For an example of a broad arbitration clause, see E.M. Diagnostic Sys. v. Teamsters Local 169, 812 F.2d 91, 124 LRRM 2633, 2634 (CA 3, 1987): "Any dispute arising out of a claimed violation of this Agreement shall be considered a grievance * * *."

[26]AT&T Technologies v. Communications Workers, 106 S.Ct. 1415, 1419, 121 LRRM 3329, 3332 (1986): "In the absence of any express provision excluding a particular grievance from arbitration, * * * only the most forceful evidence of a purpose to exclude the claim from arbitration can prevail." (Citing Steelworkers v. Warrior & Gulf Navigation Corp., 80 S.Ct. 1347, 34 LA 561 (1960)); see also Daniel Constr. Co. v. Electrical Workers (IBEW) Local 257, 856 F.2d 1174, 129 LRRM 2429 (CA 8, 1988), cert. denied, 109 S.Ct. 1140, 130 LRRM 2656 (1989) (where arbitration clause broadly refers to "any dispute over interpretation," only the most forceful evidence of purpose to exclude claim from arbitration can prevail); Pervel Indus. v. TM Wallcovering, 675 F. Supp. 867 (S.D.N.Y., 1987), aff'd, 871 F.2d 7 (CA 2, 1989) (doubts concerning scope of arbitral issues should be resolved in favor of arbitration).

[27]Pitta v. Hotel Ass'n of New York City, 806 F.2d 419, 422, 124 LRRM 2109, 2112 (CA 2, 1986); see also Ceres Terminals, 92 LA 735 (Malin, 1989) (arbitrator has authority to consider master contract provisions in interpreting local's contract); but see FMC Corp., 92 LA 1246 (Stoltenberg, 1989) (interpretation of sales agreement outside scope of arbitrator's authority).

[28]Pitta v. Hotel Ass'n of New York City, 806 F.2d at 423, 124 LRRM at 2112. However, the court directed the parties to appoint another arbitrator because of the impartial chairman's clear personal interest in the outcome of the issue.

In addition, where an exclusionary clause conflicts with a broad arbitration clause, courts will generally rule in favor of coverage.[29]

Even though courts generally resolve a disputed question of coverage in favor of arbitration, where the arbitration provision expressly excludes certain issues, the courts will enforce the exclusion and exclude those issues from arbitration. For example, the Eighth Circuit, U.S. Court of Appeals, addressed the issue of whether the determination of contract duration was covered by an arbitration provision which was limited to "employee grievances." The court held that although such an issue could be covered under a broad arbitration clause, it could not be arbitrated under a narrow clause limited to employee grievances.[30] In another example, a court held that an arbitration clause that specifically excluded jurisdictional disputes from its coverage excluded from the arbitrator's authority the ability to resolve a dispute between two competing union locals over work at a particular job site.[31]

In determining whether a dispute is arbitrable, courts will look not only to the arbitration clause, but to all the terms of the agreement. That is, a broad arbitration clause may be limited by language found elsewhere in the agreement. In one case, a court held that although the arbitration clause was "broadly worded," an exclusionary clause that is "crystal clear and unambiguous" will be given effect to negate the presumption of arbitrability.[32] Similarly, an arbitrator lacks authority to hear a dispute where the contract is silent as to the disputed rights involved and the grievance arbitration clause limits the arbitrator to interpretation of the *written* provisions of the agreement.[33] However, in another case the Third Circuit, U.S. Court of Appeals, held that a broad arbitration clause gave the arbitrator authority to arbitrate a dispute over subcontracting even though the agreement contained an express right of management to subcontract out certain work.[34] The court rejected the employer's position that the subcontracting clause granted the employer an absolute right to contract out bargaining unit work because the subcontracting clause stated that the employer's right to subcontract was "subject to" the restrictions contained in the agreement. The court held that because of the scope of the parties' arbitration clause, it had "no difficulty concluding that the subject matter of the Union's grievance came within the zone of its protected interests under the collective bargaining agreement."[35]

---

[29]H.C. Lawton, Jr. Inc. v. Teamsters Local 384, 755 F.2d 324, 118 LRRM 2825 (CA 3, 1985); Hahnemann Univ. v. Hospital Employees Dist. 1199C, 596 F. Supp. 443 (E.D. Pa., 1984).

[30]Purex Corp. v. Teamsters Local 618, 705 F.2d 274, 277, 112 LRRM 3433, 3436 CA 8, 1983).

[31]Waco Scaffolding Co. v. Carpenters Local 845, 585 F. Supp. 102 (E.D. Pa., 1984).

[32]Woodcrest Nursing Home v. Service Employees Local 144, 788 F.2d 894, 898, 122 LRRM 2201, 2204 (CA 2, 1986).

[33]Sun Life Ins. Co. of Am., 87 LA 598 (Harkless, 1987).

[34]E.M. Diagnostic Sys. v. Teamsters Local 169, 812 F.2d 91, 124 LRRM 2633 (CA 3, 1987).

[35]Id. at 2636. In a dissent, Judge Garth believed that the parties had expressly excluded subcontracting from the arbitration clause. He found that the record demonstrated the necessary "forceful evidence" of intent to exclude subcontracting from arbitration so that regardless of the scope of the arbitration clause, the issue of subcontracting was not arbitrable. See also Dallas

Precontract and Postcontract Grievances

After the Supreme Court's *Nolde* decision, termination of the collective bargaining agreement no longer necessarily extinguishes a party's duty to arbitrate grievances "arising under" the contract. In *Nolde*, the Court ordered the parties to arbitrate a dispute over severance pay even though their agreement had expired,[36] noting that although the dispute arose after the expiration of the agreement, it nonetheless arose under the contract.[37]

Yet the Court's holding in *Nolde* is imprecise. The problem stems from the opinion itself which, though containing a narrow holding,[38] suggests two inconsistent propositions: (1) the obligation to arbitrate survives the expiration of a collective bargaining agreement where the dispute is over a right "arguably created" by the expired agreement;[39] (2) a "presumption of arbitrability" arises when the parties do not clearly express their desire that the duty to arbitrate terminates with the contract.[40]

The disparity between the narrow holding and the conflicting propositions has created general confusion in the lower courts which have ruled inconsistently over the scope of the obligation to arbitrate postcontract grievances.[41] The majority of lower courts have read *Nolde* narrowly, holding that in order for a grievance to be arbitrable after the expiration of the contract, it must involve either rights that "accrued" or "vested" during the term of the agreement or disputes which "arose under" the agreement while it was still in effect.[42]

Power & Light Co., 87 LA 415 (Keller, Chm., 1985) (holding grievance over right not specifically contained in contract arbitrable under grievance arbitration clause even though clause provided that, to be arbitrable, grievance must be covered by a specific provision of agreement, and disputes over matters not referred to in agreement would not be subject to arbitration).

[36]Nolde Bros. v. Bakery Workers Local 358, 97 S.Ct. 1067, 94 LRRM 2753, reh'g denied, 97 S.Ct. 1689 (1977).

[37]94 LRRM at 2756.

[38]94 LRRM at 2757. The Court held that severance pay disputes were arbitrable under the expired agreement.

[39]Id. at 2756.

[40]Id. at 2757.

[41]See, e.g., George Day Constr. Co. v. Carpenters Local 354, 722 F.2d 1471, 115 LRRM 2459 (CA 9, 1984) (court declining to interpret holding in *Nolde* or reconcile conflicting opinions); Ogden, Lees & Gasperini, "The Survival of Contract Terms: The Quagmire Expands," 36 Lab. L.J. 688, 693 (1985). See also notes 42 through 44.

[42]See, e.g., Food & Commercial Workers Local 7 v. Gold Star Sausage Co., 897 F.2d 1022, 133 LRRM 2765 (CA 10, 1990) (postcontract arbitration required only if grievance involves either conduct that occurred partially during contract term or employee rights that accrued or vested during that period); Mine Workers Local 2487 v. Blue Creek Mining Co., 806 F.2d 1552, 1555, 124 LRRM 2294, 2296 (CA 11, 1987) (grievant's rights "accrued" during contract period); Teamsters Local 238 v. C.R.S.T. Inc., 795 F.2d 1400, 122 LRRM 2993 (CA 8, 1986) (right to be discharged for just cause is strictly creature of contract and as such does not survive beyond contract expiration); Graphic Communications Union Local 2 v. Chicago Tribune Co., 794 F.2d 1222, 123 LRRM 2488 (CA 7, 1986) (grievance did not "arise under" expired collective bargaining agreement because it dealt with a future practice to be instituted by employer); Electrical Workers (IBEW) Local 22 v. Nanco Elec., 790 F.2d 59, 122 LRRM 2826 (CA 8, 1986) (dispute over postexpiration contributions to trust fund did not "arise under" contract); Teamsters Local 807 v. Brink's Inc., 744 F.2d 283, 286, 117 LRRM 2306 (CA 2, 1984) (*Nolde* limited to grievances which "arise under the collective bargaining agreement"); Glover Bottled Gas Corp. v. Teamsters Local 282, 711 F.2d 479, 113 LRRM 3211 (CA 2, 1983) (expiration of contract did not preclude arbitration of discharge when activity giving rise to discharge occurred prior to expiration); O'Connor Co. v. Carpenters Local 1408, 702 F.2d 824, 825, 122 LRRM 3316 (CA 9, 1983) (postexpiration dispute over hiring of

However, several courts have interpreted *Nolde* broadly and have held that regardless of whether the rights in dispute "arose under" the contract or "accrued" or "vested" during the term of the contract, unless expressly negated there is a presumption that the parties intended their arbitration obligation to survive beyond the expiration of the agreement.[43] These courts focus and rely on the Supreme

---

nonunion employees not arbitrable because it is not "covered" by expired contract); Pressmen's Union No. 7 v. The Chicago Tribune, 657 F. Supp. 351, 125 LRRM 2137 (N.D. Ill., 1987) (dispute concerning calculation of vacation pay is arbitrable under expired collective bargaining agreement, even though events triggering grievance occurred more than six months after expiration of contract because such rights "accrued under" contract).

A good discussion of the narrow view can be found in Oil Workers Local 4-23 v. American Petrofina Co. of Tex., 586 F. Supp. 643, 648, 649, 117 LRRM 2034 (E.D. Tex., 1984), rev'd on other grounds, 759 F.2d 512, 119 LRRM 2395 (CA 5, 1985), vacated and remanded on other grounds, 106 S.Ct. 2912, 122 LRRM 2655 (1986), in which the court dismissed the broad view as a "misinterpretation" of *Nolde*. The court rejected the union's argument that the "duty to arbitrate survives independent of contract expiration unless (1) there is language clearly to the contrary in the collective bargaining agreement; or, (2) there is conduct of the parties that is so clear that a contrary intent is established." The court noted that "[o]ther decisions have limited Nolde to apply only to accrued rights and benefits; and this Court believes this is the proper view. Otherwise, almost every clause and term of a collective bargaining agreement would stay in effect after agreement was terminated. This certainly would not reflect the intention of the parties; but it certainly would lead to a raft of litigation."

For arbitrators accepting the narrow view, see Basic, Inc., 82 LA 1065 (Dworkin, 1984) (Christmas bonus "vested" under prior contract and therefore payable even though new contract expressly excludes Christmas bonus provision); Shieldalloy Corp., 81 LA 489 (Talmadge, 1983) (right to vacation pay is a right "established by the contract" and is arbitrable even though grievance arises after expiration of agreement); Bekins Moving & Storage Co., 81 LA 1198 (Brisco, 1983) (grievance over birthday holiday pay when birthdays occurred after expiration of contract not arbitrable.

Several courts have focused not on whether the dispute arose under the contract or whether the rights are accrued or vested but on the *Nolde* Court's statement that it would reserve judgment on "the arbitrability of post-termination contractual claims which, unlike the [claim in *Nolde*], are not asserted within a reasonable time after the contract's expiration." Nolde Bros. v. Bakery Workers Local 358, 97 S.Ct. 1067, 94 LRRM 2753, 2757 n. 8 (1977). These courts appear to read *Nolde* as allowing postcontract arbitration as long as the grievance is filed within a reasonable time after the expiration of the contract. In Teamsters Local 703 v. Kennicott Bros., 771 F.2d 300, 120 LRRM 2306 (CA 7, 1985), the Seventh Circuit held that a grievance filed over six months after the expiration of the contract was not filed within a reasonable time and was therefore not subject to arbitration. But see Pressmen's Union No. 7 v. The Chicago Tribune, 125 LRRM 2137 (N.D. Ill., 1987) (holding that *Kennicott* cannot be read to preclude *Nolde's* presumption of arbitrability when the dispute involves a right that accrued under contract but did not ripen until after contract expired). See also Federated Metals Corp. v. Steelworkers, 648 F.2d 856, 107 LRRM 2271 (CA 3, 1981), cert. denied, 102 S.Ct. 567, 108 LRRM 2924 (1981) (grievance filed over nine months after expiration of agreement not unreasonable where grievances arose while union was negotiating for a new agreement after old agreement had expired).

For one court holding that termination of the collective bargaining agreement due to decertification of the union does not deprive the union of the use of the arbitration procedure under the terminated contract, see Automobile Workers v. Telex Computer Prods., 816 F.2d 519, 125 LRRM 2163 (CA 10, 1987). For a discussion of the obligation to arbitrate disputes after a rejection of the collective bargaining agreement in bankruptcy, see Simon & Bishop, "Bankruptcy and Its Impact on Arbitration: A Union View," 39 N.Y.U. Nat'l Conference on Labor (1986).

[43]See, e.g., Culinary Workers Local 226 (Joint Exec. Bd.) v. Royal Center, Inc., 796 F.2d 1159, 123 LRRM 2347 (CA 9, 1986) (holding that arbitration clause survived termination of collective bargaining agreement because broad arbitration clauses presumptively survive termination); Federated Metals Corp. v. Steelworkers, 648 F.2d 856, 107 LRRM 2271 (CA 3, 1981), cert. denied, 102 S.Ct. 567 (1981) (even narrowness of arbitration clause does not foreclose postcontract grievance arbitration); Paperworkers v. Wells Badger Indus., 124 LRRM 2658 (E.D. Wis., 1987) (evidence reveals parties' intent to arbitrate postcontract disputes even though such disputes did not arise under contract); Trustees of Graphic Communications Union Local 229 v. Rapid Copy Inc., 620 F. Supp. 202 (D. Minn., 1985) (holding arbitration clause survives termination of contract because presumption is that parties intended clause to survive); see also Emery Air Freight Corp. v. Teamsters Local 295, 786 F.2d 93, 121 LRRM 3240 (CA 2, 1986) (applying broad reading of *Nolde*).

For an example of an arbitrator accepting the broad view, see MGM Grand Hotels, 86 LA 765 (Rothschild, 1986) (grievances protesting employer's failure to obtain replacements through union's hiring hall are arbitrable even though replacements were hired during strike that

Court's language in *Nolde* that "in the absence of some contrary indication, there are strong reasons to conclude that the parties did not intend their arbitration duties to terminate automatically with the contract."[44] For example, in one case the Ninth Circuit, U.S. Court of Appeals, expressly rejected the narrow view of *Nolde* and held that notwithstanding the fact that the agreement had terminated, courts "must presume that the parties intended the arbitration duty to survive" where no evidence existed to negate the presumption.[45] Therefore, unless proved otherwise, all postexpiration disputes arguably touching on the collective bargaining agreement are subject to arbitration.[46]

Similarly, the Third Circuit, U.S. Court of Appeals, rejected the narrow view of *Nolde* and held that a narrow arbitration clause does not provide sufficient indication of intent to exclude postcontract disputes.[47] The court expressly rejected the distinction between vested and nonvested rights: "We do not believe that the somewhat esoteric determination that the disputed right to a particular benefit has vested or accrued should control the decision whether the duty to arbitrate the dispute survives contract termination."[48]

Until recently, the Board had adopted a broad interpretation of the Court's *Nolde* opinion, holding in one case that the parties' duty to arbitrate survived the termination of the contract when the dispute arose over an obligation created by the contract,[49] and that the employer was obligated to arbitrate the discharge of an employee discharged after the contract term.[50] The Board read *Nolde* to mean:

> Where the parties to a collective-bargaining agreement have agreed to subject certain matters to a grievance and arbitration process, "the parties' obligation under their arbitration clause survive[s] contract termination when the dispute [is] over an obligation arguably created by

---

occurred after contract expired).

For a critical discussion of the broad view of *Nolde*, see Jauvtis, "The Liminal Period: Obligations of Parties Upon Expiration of a Collective Bargaining Agreement," 58 N.Y. St. B.J. 30 (Nov. 1986); Geslewitz, "Case Law Development Since Nolde Brothers: When Must Post-Contract Disputes Be Arbitrated?" 35 Lab. L.J. 225 (1984); Leonard, "Post-Contractual Arbitrability After Nolde Brothers: A Problem of Conceptual Clarity," 28 N.Y.L. Sch. L. Rev. 257 (1983).

[44]Nolde Bros. v. Bakery Workers Local 358, 97 S.Ct. 1067, 94 LRRM 2753, 2756 (1977).

[45]Culinary Workers Local 226 (Joint Exec. Bd.) v. Royal Center, Inc., 796 F.2d 1159, 123 LRRM 2347, 2349 (CA 9, 1986). See also NLRB v. Litton Financial Printing, 893 F.2d 1128 (CA 9, 1990) (reaffirming its interpretation of *Nolde*).

[46]123 LRRM at 2350.

[47]Federated Metals Corp. v. Steelworkers, 648 F.2d 856, 107 LRRM 2271 (CA 3, 1981); see also Seafarers Int'l Union v. National Marine Servs., 820 F.2d 148 (CA 5, 1987), cert. denied, 108 S.Ct. 346 (1987) (rejecting narrow interpretation of *Nolde*).

[48]648 F.2d at 861. Parties who wish to avoid a broad reading of *Nolde* have added to the collective bargaining agreement a provision that only disputes arising "under and during the term of the Agreement" will be arbitrable. See, e.g., Teamsters Local 636 v. J.C. Penney Co., 484 F. Supp. 130, 132 n.1, 103 LRRM 2618 (W.D. Pa., 1980); Gates Canada, Inc. and Rubber Workers Local 733, 82 LA 480 (Brown, 1984) (grievance seeking health benefits for employee who had surgery after contract expired not arbitrable where expired contract had provision that provided for arbitration of grievances solely under "the collective bargaining agreement then in effect"). Such provisions clearly negate any presumption that the parties intended that all postcontract disputes be arbitrable.

[49]American Sink Top & Cabinet Co., 242 NLRB 408, 101 LRRM 1166 (1979).

[50]101 LRRM at 1167.

the expired agreement." That obligation is not terminated merely by the parties' failure to expressly cover this situation. As the Court stated generally in *Nolde*, in the "absence of some contrary indication, there are strong reasons to conclude that the parties did not intend their arbitration duties to terminate automatically with the contract."[51]

Similarly, in another case,[52] the Board found arbitrable the discharge of an employee after the contract had expired when the conduct on which the discharge was based occurred at least in part before expiration of the contract.[53]

However, in a recent decision the Board specifically adopted the narrow view of *Nolde*:

> We acknowledge that *Nolde* contains language with a broader sweep than its narrow holding that a claim to severance pay arguably accruable under the contract is arbitrable even though the plant closed after the contract expired. We conclude, however, in agreement with the circuit courts that have addressed the issue, that a dispute based on post-expiration events "arises under" the contract within the meaning of *Nolde* only if it concerns contract rights capable of accruing or vesting to some degree during the life of the contract and ripening or remaining enforceable after the contract expires.[54]

In this case, the collective bargaining agreements at several of the employer's facilities had expired. Immediately after expiration, the employer sent a letter to the union stating that it would not abide by the grievance arbitration procedure under the expired contract for "grievances filed during the time we are without an agreement."[55] During the interim period between the two contracts the union filed nine grievances. The employer refused to arbitrate each one, stating by letter that it would not "arbitrate grievances based on alleged violations of the contract which occurred during the contractual hiatus."[56]

The Board addressed the issue of whether the employer's repudiation of a grievance arbitration procedure in the expired contract constituted a violation of the employer's duty to bargain under § 8(a)(5) of the NLRA. It found that the employer's refusal amounted to a "whole-

---

[51]Id. at 1166.

[52]Digmar Equip. & Eng'g Co., 261 NLRB 1175, 110 LRRM 1209 (1982).

[53]110 LRRM at 1210. Several commentators and at least one court have criticized the Board's position on ordering arbitration when a discharge might have been based on events which occurred prior to the contract's expiration. County of Ottawa v. Jaklinski, 423 Mich. 1, 377 N.W.2d 668, 120 LRRM 3260 (Mich., 1985); Geslewitz, "Case Law Development Since Nolde Brothers: When Must Post-Contract Disputes Be Arbitrated?" 35 Lab. L.J. 225, 230-232 (1984); Kirkscium, "Post Contract Arbitrability Since *Nolde Brothers*," 54 U. Colo. L. Rev. 103, 107 (1982). These commentators believe that under the Board's reading of *Nolde*, the substantive "just cause" right of a collective bargaining agreement would continue indefinitely. Also, the Board's position may require courts to examine the causes for the disputed discharge, and "the risk that courts would decide the merits of a case in the guise of deciding arbitrability would be enhanced." 120 LRRM at 3268. Finally, indefinite arbitration under the Board's position is likely since almost all discharged employees can arguably allege that their discharge was due at least in part to conduct occurring during the term of the collective agreement.

[54]Indiana & Mich. Elec. Co., Fort Wayne, Ind., 284 NLRB 53, 125 LRRM 1097, 1103 (1987); see also Rose Printing Co. v. Graphic Communications Union Local 241-B, 289 NLRB No. 31, 131 LRRM 1420 (1988) (refusal to arbitrate any grievances after expiration of contract is unlawful based on rationale of *Indiana & Mich. Elec. Co.*).

[55]125 LRRM at 1097.

[56]Ibid.

sale repudiation of its contractual obligation to arbitrate," and that the employer therefore violated §§ 8(a)(5) and 8(a)(1) of the NLRA.[57] The Board held that neither party may unilaterally abandon a procedure by which they have customarily resolved day-to-day worksite disputes.[58] If either party desires to alter the procedures, they must seek to resolve any differences through the arbitration machinery.[59]

Although the Board found that an employer could violate federal law by a blanket repudiation of the obligation to arbitrate postcontract grievances, it nevertheless held that *Nolde* did not require that every postcontract grievance be arbitrated.[60] Specifically rejecting the broad view of *Nolde*, it held that the employer had a duty to arbitrate only those disputes concerning rights that accrued or vested under the prior contract.[61] Because the Board found that the nine grievances filed by the union neither "arose under" the expired contracts, nor involved rights that accrued or vested under the expired contracts, it did not order the employer to arbitrate the grievances.[62]

---

[57]Id. at 1103.

[58]Id. at 1099. The Board reasoned that permitting either party to unilaterally abandon its grievance procedure would not serve the interest of preserving industrial peace.

[59]Ibid. Answering dissenting Chairman Dotson, the Board explained that it was not insisting "upon rigid adherence to an expired and truncated contractual dispute resolution system," but merely insisting "that changes in that dispute resolution system be made only after the parties concerned have agreed to them or otherwise adequately bargained over the matter." Ibid.

[60]Id. at 1103. See quoted language in text at note 40, supra. The Board held that "whether the nine hiatus grievances are arbitrable under *Nolde* turns on whether they 'arise under' the expired agreements." Ibid.

[61]Ibid. Not only did the Board choose to follow the courts that accept the narrow view of *Nolde*, it expressly declined to follow *American Sink* to the extent that it could be read to hold that "the mere invocation of any term of the expired contract triggers the post-expiration duty to arbitrate under *Nolde* * * *." Id. at 1104 n. 9.

[62]The nine grievances in Indiana & Mich. Elec. Co. involved the following events: (1) an employee's suspension for excessive absenteeism; (2) an employee's suspension for improper job performance and sleeping on company time; (3) the employer's failure to assign an employee overtime, and giving the work to a supervisor instead; (4) the employer's failure to provide an employee with proper working conditions and compensation when he was assigned to a job away from his normal work location; (5) the employer's request that an employee report to his new job two days before the date he was told he would be transferred; (6) the employer's failure to pay an employee line mechanic wages for the time he spent working as a leadman; (7) the manner in which the employer assigned routes to an employee and other meter readers; (8) an oral warning given to meter readers for failure to read enough meters in one day; and (9) a supervisor's acquisition of an employee's telephone number and use of it to contact her at home. Id. at 1098 n. 2. After examining the grievances, the Board concluded that rights invoked in each grievance did not "arise under" the expired contracts within the meaning of *Nolde*.

Chapter 4

The Arbitration Tribunal

Tripartite Arbitration Board

The extinction of tripartite arbitration boards predicted by some neutral arbitrators has not occurred. A recent study suggests that such boards continue to be used in grievance arbitration for three reasons: (1) the tradition of tripartite grievance resolution ingrained into the labor-management relationship in industries such as those covered under the Railway Labor Act, (2) distrust of neutral arbitrators, and (3) inertia.[1] It has also been suggested that labor and management support for tripartite arbitration boards could indicate a desire to mediate grievances.[2]

Methods of Selecting Arbitrators

Generally, the parties will be held to their contractual time limits relative to the arbitrator selection process.[3] Where a contract does not contain a specified method of selection or time limits, then the parties' past practice may govern the selection process.[4]

An award will not be enforced if the arbitrator is not chosen in accordance with the method agreed to by the parties. In a case in which an arbitrator's appointment did not conform to the agreement upon which he based his jurisdiction, the defect in the method used to select

[1]Veglahn, "Grievance Arbitration by Arbitration Boards: A Survey of the Parties," 42 Arb. J. 47 (1987).

[2]Ibid.

[3]W.J. Bullock, Inc., 93 LA 33 (Clarke, 1989); Trumbull County Dep't of Human Servs., 90 LA 1267 (Curry, 1988).

[4]Gallagher & Burk, 91 LA 1217 (Richman, 1988); City of Oregon, 90 LA 431 (Stieber, 1988).

the arbitrator left him powerless to implement the agreement.[5] Similarly, where a grievance was not appealed to arbitration in accordance with AAA rules incorporated into the collective bargaining agreement, the arbitrator held that it was procedurally defective and accordingly not arbitrable.[6]

The Tenth Circuit, U.S. Court of Appeals, has held that failure to observe the contractual time limit for processing grievances deprived a special subcommittee of any jurisdiction it might otherwise have had to entertain a grievance.[7] Arbitration opinions generally hold that delays in demanding arbitration or selecting the arbitrator do not bar arbitration where no time limits are contained in the parties' contract.[8]

Labor arbitrators are minimally active in the nonunion sector.[9] A recent survey revealed that fewer than 8 percent of the leading nonunion companies under the umbrella of the National Association of Manufacturers use the services of arbitrators.[10] The methods used for selecting arbitrators at these companies include the following: (1) management chooses "at random" from a list of three names supplied by a "recognized" arbitration association, (2) the grievant chooses from a list provided by the AAA, (3) management and the grievant alternately strike names from a list of five arbitrators supplied by "an appropriate source," and (4) an arbitrator is designated by the AAA when management and the grievant fail to agree.[11] In each case management pays the arbitrator's fee, but at one company employees are required to pay $25 toward the fee when their grievances are denied.[12]

Arbitrators and Their Qualifications

Background, Training, and Supply of Arbitrators

Numerous studies have been conducted into the demographics of the arbitration profession. In general, these studies reveal that the

[5]Avis Rent A Car Sys. v. Garage Employees Local 272, 791 F.2d 22, 122 LRRM 2861, 2864 (CA 2, 1986). For a compilation of citations to the arbitration statutes of the 50 states, see Freedman, Legislation on Dispute Resolution, 313-314 (ABA, 1984). For a general discussion on the role of the arbitrator, see Dunsford, "The Role and Function of the Labor Arbitrator," 30 St. Louis U.L.J. 109 (1985).

[6]Inland Container Corp., 90 LA 532 (Ipavec, 1987).

[7]Barnard v. Commercial Carriers, 863 F.2d 694, 130 LRRM 2073 (CA 10, 1988).

[8]See, e.g., W.J. Bullock, Inc., 93 LA 33 (Clarke, 1989); City of Maumee, 90 LA 946 (Graham, 1988); City of Oregon, 90 LA 431 (Stieber, 1988); Social Sec. Admin., 89 LA 457 (Feigenbaum, 1987).

[9]Bognanno & Smith, "The Demographic and Professional Characteristics of Arbitrators in North America," Proceedings of the 41st Annual Meeting of NAA, 266 (BNA Books, 1989).

[10]McCabe, "Corporate Nonunion Grievance Arbitration Systems: A Procedural Analysis," 40 Lab. L.J. 432 (1989).

[11]Ibid.

[12]Ibid.

typical arbitrator is a white male,[13] near 60 years of age,[14] and practicing part-time.[15] The most frequently requested arbitrators, and thus the busiest, are those with the most experience. These individuals tend to be members of the American Arbitration Association and the National Academy of Arbitrators, and they are in an older age group.[16]

Because a large percentage of labor arbitrators will likely be retiring from practice over the next decade, there is a continuing need to try to develop a future supply to fill the inevitable void that will be created.[17] An American Bar Association panel has found that, while there is interest in the possibility of training attorneys to be arbitrators, there is also skepticism regarding the need for such training: "Arbitration, negotiation, and mediation are what lawyers do every day."[18] Designating oneself an arbitrator is easy enough but obtaining cases is a difficult task, and the ability to obtain cases is the true validation of one's status as an arbitrator.[19] Once new arbitrators have received training in the basic substantive and procedural skills of the profession, labor and management must be willing to provide them with experience in order to guarantee an adequate supply of arbitrators in the future.[20]

Studies and surveys involving the decisionmaking processes of arbitrators reflect a difference in the perception of parties and actual performance. In one survey, the parties indicated they had found that arbitrators' decisions were significantly related to age and experience.[21] Recent studies indicate that in fact age, experience, education, gender, attorney status, and NAA membership have no apparent

---

[13]Bognanno & Smith, "The Demographic and Professional Characteristics of Arbitrators in North America," Proceedings of the 41st Annual Meeting of NAA, 266 (BNA Books, 1989); Berkeley, "The Other Side of the Mirror: Advocates Look at the Future for Female Arbitrators," 40 Lab. L.J. 370 (1989); Petersen & Katz, "Male and Female Arbitrator Perceptions of the Arbitration Process," 39 Lab. L.J. 110 (1988).

[14]Bognanno & Smith, "The Demographic and Professional Characteristics of Arbitrators in North America," Proceedings of the 41st Annual Meeting of NAA, 266 (BNA Books, 1989); Allen & Jennings, "Sounding Out the Nation's Arbitrators: An NAA Survey," 39 Lab. L.J. 423 (1988).

[15]Bognanno & Smith, "The Demographic and Professional Characteristics of Arbitrators in North America," Proceedings of the 41st Annual Meeting of NAA, 266 (BNA Books, 1989).

[16]Kauffman & McKee, "Labor Arbitrator Selection and the Theory of Demand," 42 Arb. J. 35, 38 (1987). See also Bognanno & Smith, "The Demographic and Professional Characteristics of Arbitrators in North America," Proceedings of the 41st Annual Meeting of NAA, 266-289 (BNA Books, 1989); Berkeley, "Arbitrators and Advocates: The Consumers' Report," id. at 290-302, and Fleischli, "Comment," id. at 302-304.

[17]Zimny, Dolson & Barreca, eds., Labor Arbitration: A Practical Guide for Advocates (BNA Books, 1990); Allen & Jennings, "Sounding Out the Nation's Arbitrators: An NAA Survey," 39 Lab. L.J. 423 (1988). See also Berkeley, "The Other Side of the Mirror: Advocates Look at the Future for Female Arbitrators," 40 Lab. L.J. 370, 371 (1989) (advocates responding to 1987 survey expressed overwhelming agreement with the statement that there is a shortage of newer, acceptable arbitrators).

[18]Steen, "The Multi-Door Courthouse Project: Examining the Arbitration Door," Arbitration/Big Case: ABC's of Dispute Resolution, 84 (ABA, 1986).

[19]Lawson & Rinaldo, "Improving Arbitrator Performance: A Modest Proposal," 39 Arb. J. 49 (1984). See also Kauffman & McKee, "Labor Arbitrator Selection and the Theory of Demand," 42 Arb. J. 35 (1987).

[20]Nowlin, "Arbitrator Development: Career Paths, a Model Program, and Challenges," 43 Arb. J. 3, 4 (1988).

[21]Thornton & Zirkel, "The Consistency and Predictability of Grievance Arbitration Awards," 43 Indus. & Lab. Rel. Rev. 294 (1990); Nelson, "The Selection of Arbitrators," 37 Lab. L.J. 703 (1986).

relationship to arbitrators' decisions.[22] Although the parties in one survey said that they did not necessarily select arbitrators who were most likely to decide in their favor,[23] another survey concludes that evaluation of arbitrator performance is affected by whether the arbitrator's award was favorable.[24] A 1987 study suggests that parties seek in an arbitrator characteristics which they themselves possess.[25]

Qualifications Set Forth in Agreement or by Regulation

It has been suggested that requiring arbitrators to undergo an examination similar to a bar examination might serve to remove the "buddy system" currently perceived as being prevalent in the arbitration profession. Such an examination would not only create an objective standard for judging potential arbitrators but would also put them on notice of what is expected of them and enable the profession to police and upgrade the quality of its members.[26] A recent report of the Society of Professionals in Dispute Resolution (SPIDR) Commission on Qualifications adopted the following three central principles: (1) no single entity, but rather a variety of organizations, should establish qualifications for neutrals; (2) the greater degree of choice the parties have over the dispute-resolution process, program or neutral, the less mandatory the qualification requirements should be; and (3) qualifications criteria should be based on performance, rather than paper credentials.[27] The report advocates incorporation of performance-based testing into training and apprenticeship programs.[28] Also, dispute-resolution programs, entities that sponsor neutrals and neutrals themselves "have an ongoing obligation to maintain and improve acquired knowledge and skills through additional training, practice, and study."[29]

One commentator has suggested that the AAA and FMCS establish a review committee to examine applications from individuals whose work brings them into daily contact with labor relations in a nonadvocacy capacity, because they may have a more substantial grounding in the labor relations field than part-time arbitrators. An example of such persons are legal writers for labor services, who abound among several of the legal publishing companies. The AAA/FMCS committee would have the discretion to approve the listing of

---

[22]Thornton & Zirkel, "The Consistency and Predictability of Grievance Arbitration Awards," 43 Indus. & Lab. Rel. Rev. 294 (1990); Deitsch & Dilts, "An Analysis of Arbitrator Characteristics and Their Effects on Decision Making in Discharge Cases," 40 Lab. L.J. 112 (1989); Scott & Shadoan, "The Effect of Gender on Arbitration Decisions," 10 J. Lab. Res. 429 (1989).

[23]Nelson, "The Selection of Arbitrators," 37 Lab. L.J. 703 (1986).

[24]Crane & Miner, "Labor Arbitrators' Performance: Views From Union and Management Perspectives," 9 J. Lab. Res. 42 (1988).

[25]Berkeley, "Arbitrators and Advocates: The Consumers' Report," Proceedings of the 41st Annual Meeting of NAA, 290 (BNA Books, 1989).

[26]Kalet, "Training New Arbitrators," 39 Arb. J. 73 (1984).

[27]"Qualifying Neutrals: The Basic Principles," 44 Arb. J. 48 (1989).

[28]Ibid.

[29]Id. at 49.

these individuals on an arbitration panel or to authorize them to take a certification examination.[30]

Many commentators, advocates, and arbitrators believe that the most effective evaluation procedure is the parties' choice of arbitrators based on the arbitrators' past performance. It has been suggested that inclusion of the following three data items in arbitrator biographies by appointing agencies such as AAA and FMCS will provide additional assistance in selecting arbitrators based on their performance: "(1) Issues award: within ____ days after close of hearing record; (2) Study time: ____ days per hearing day; (3) Waiting period for first available hearing date: ____ weeks."[31]

An ongoing complaint by parties to arbitration is the delay of many arbitrators in rendering their awards. It has been suggested that, if appointing agencies such as the AAA and FMCS do not take a more active internal policing role to remedy this situation, external remedies may be imposed.[32] In the early 1970s the steel industry received a great many complaints about the arbitration process regarding the length of time required for resolution of cases, the high costs, the technicalities, and the lack of satisfaction for the grievant. As a result, the industry initiated expedited arbitration. New arbitrators were included on the steel panels where the types of issues being heard were routine and not precedent setting, which gave employers and union leaders an opportunity to evaluate novice arbitrators and provided a pool for their major decisions. Similarly, the Postal Service has appointed arbitrators to its expedited panels before appointing them to hear the more complex cases, although it generally uses experienced arbitrators even on its expedited panels.[33]

Impartiality

When asked about impartiality in arbitration and absence of misconduct in the profession, Eric J. Schmertz, Dean of Hofstra University School of Law, stated that there "has not been a single instance in which an arbitrator has been accused and proved of having committed misconduct. * * * And one of the reasons is that we serve in a 'fish bowl.' Everything that is done is seen. And we serve on acceptability. We are not appointed by the government, and we don't have lifetime tenure like a judge. * * * And we police our own profession. The parties do too; when someone does a poor job, he or she is not acceptable anymore."[34]

---

[30]Kalet, "Training New Arbitrators," 39 Arb. J. 73 (1984). See Chapter 1 of the Fourth Edition, subtopic entitled "National Academy of Arbitrators."

[31]Berkeley, "The Most Serious Faults in Labor-Management Arbitration Today and What Can Be Done to Remedy Them," 40 Lab. L.J. 728, 731 (1989).

[32]Dilts, "Timeliness of Arbitration Awards: Some Ethical Considerations," 43 Arb. J. 62 (1988).

[33]Kauffman & McKee, "Labor Arbitrator Selection and the Theory of Demand," 42 Arb. J. 35 (1987).

[34]Friedman, "Arbitrators in Oral History Interviews: Looking Back and Ahead," 12 Empl. Rel. L.J. 424, 444-445 (1986).

One survey has suggested that a party's evaluation of arbitrator performance is affected by whether the arbitrator's award was favorable to the party.[35] Parties are cautioned against measuring an arbitrator's neutrality based on the percentage of awards in favor of management and labor. "[T]here is no simple method of determining arbitrator neutrality—that is, no substitute for a case-by-case examination of the arbitrator's knowledge and reasoning. Applying the 50/50 measure will only harm the parties, the arbitrator, and the arbitration process."[36]

A number of methods are used in screening arbitrators to eliminate potential bias. In some jurisdictions, arbitrators are selected on an entirely random basis. In others, a panel of arbitrators is chosen, consisting of one attorney generally perceived to be a "plaintiff's lawyer" and another attorney generally perceived to be a "defendant's lawyer." In the case of a single arbitrator, a formal process is used to select a pool of "neutral" neutrals, from which a random selection may be made.[37] Despite best efforts to ensure impartiality, some longstanding societal prejudices may linger. The results of studies are in conflict as to whether women receive more favorable treatment by arbitrators than men.[38]

The Ninth Circuit, U.S. Court of Appeals, has held that, before a court can vacate an arbitration award because of "evident partiality" on the part of an arbitrator, the party alleging bias must establish facts that create a reasonable impression of partiality.[39] This is a less stringent standard than for federal judges.[40] The court found that an arbitrator's status as a party to the employer's suit to enjoin the arbitration on grounds that it was untimely requested, and the arbitrator's subsequent filing for sanctions against the employer's attorney under Rule 11 of the Federal Rules of Civil Procedure, did not create a reasonable impression of partiality. The district court order vacating the arbitration award was accordingly reversed.[41]

The Sixth Circuit applied a similar analysis to hold that the participation of an employer-side co-chair on the committee deciding a grievance in which his former law partners were involved during their

---

[35]Crane & Miner, "Labor Arbitrators' Performance: Views From Union and Management Perspectives," 9 J. Lab. Res. 43 (1988).

[36]Dilts & Deitsch, "Arbitration Win/Loss Rates as a Measure of Arbitrator Neutrality," 44 Arb. J. 42, 47 (1989).

[37]Steen, "The Multi-Door Courthouse Project: Examining the Arbitration Door," Arbitration/Big Case: ABC's of Dispute Resolution (ABA, 1986).

[38]See, e.g., Scott & Shadoan, "The Effect of Gender on Arbitration Decisions," 10 J. Lab. Res. 429 (1989) (study indicates that the gender of grievants in discipline and discharge cases does not influence the arbitrator's decision); Bemmels, "The Effect of Grievants' Gender on Arbitrators' Decisions," 41 Indus. & Lab. Rel. Rev. 251 (1988) (study of discharge cases in Canada suggests that women received more favorable treatment by arbitrators than did men).

[39]Toyota of Berkeley v. Local 1095, 834 F.2d 751, 127 LRRM 2112, 2116 (CA 9, 1987), cert. denied, 108 S.Ct. 2036, 128 LRRM 2568 (1988).

[40]Id., 127 LRRM at 2115-2116.

[41]Id. at 2116–2117. For additional cases rejecting claims of arbitrator bias, see Teamsters Local 814 v. J&B Sys. Installers & Moving, 878 F.2d 38, 131 LRRM 2799 (CA 2, 1989); NABET v. NBC, 707 F. Supp. 124, 131 LRRM 2995 (S.D.N.Y. 1988); Sanford Home for Adults v. IFHP Local 6, 665 F. Supp. 312, 126 LRRM 3149 (S.D.N.Y., 1987).

partnership, while it would raise an appearance of impropriety requiring a federal judge's recusal from a case, did not create a reasonable impression of partiality in the arbitral setting.[42] In another opinion, however, the Sixth Circuit held that, where the employer and union act jointly to procure an arbitrator who they think will be biased against a grievant, it is simple fairness to set aside the arbitration decision even in the absence of a finding of bias of the arbitrator.[43]

A dispute over a union's alleged dismissal of a permanent impartial arbitrator for an industrywide grievance-arbitration procedure was deemed arbitrable, where a collective bargaining contract clause provided for arbitration of all complaints and disputes involving "any acts, conduct or relations between the parties."[44] The court found that the impartial arbitrator's clear personal interests in the outcome of the dispute, arising from his unilateral termination by the union, disqualified him from hearing the dispute as an arbitrator. It directed the parties to appoint another arbitrator, in accordance with the contract, for purposes of hearing and deciding the issue.[45]

In another case, a neutral arbitrator's failure to disclose a prior business relationship with a principal of one of the parties to an arbitration did not justify a district court's use of its powers under Rule 60(b) of the Federal Rules of Civil Procedure and the United States Arbitration Act to set aside the award.[46] The court stated that the test to be applied is whether, having due regard for the different expectations regarding impartiality that parties bring to arbitration, the party's principal was so intimate—personally, socially, professionally, or financially—as to cast serious doubt on the arbitrator's impartiality.[47] In this case, although the president of one party to the arbitration had been the neutral arbitrator's supervisor for two years and was a key witness in the arbitration, their relationship had ended 14 years before, the arbitrator had no possible financial stake in the outcome of the arbitration, and his relationship with that corporate office during their period together at another company had been distant and impersonal.[48]

The New York Supreme Court, Appellate Division, vacated an arbitration award where a sole arbitrator's contractual relationship with the parent organization of one of the parties was substantial enough to create an inference of bias, where that party was prejudiced by the arbitrator's failure to disclose the relationship.[49] The contractual relationship at issue involved the arbitrator's being one of a panel

---

[42]Apperson v. Fleet Carrier Corp., 879 F.2d 1344, 1360-1361, 131 LRRM 3079 (CA 6, 1989).
[43]Allen v. Allied Plant Maintenance Co., 881 F.2d 291, 132 LRRM 2021, 2027 (CA 6, 1989).
[44]Pitta v. Hotel Ass'n of N.Y.C., 806 F.2d 419, 124 LRRM 2109, 2110 (CA 2, 1986).
[45]Id., 124 LRRM at 2112-2114.
[46]Merit Ins. Co. v. Leatherby Ins. Co., 714 F.2d 673 (CA 7), cert. denied, 104 S.Ct. 529 (1983).
[47]Id. at 680.
[48]Id. at 676-678.
[49]City Sch. Dist. v. Oswego Classroom Teachers, 100 A.D.2d 13, 473 N.Y.S.2d 284 (N.Y. App. Div., 1984).

of eight arbitrators designated to hear and determine disputes between the parent organization and its field representatives.[50]

However, where a party to an arbitration under the Federal Arbitration Act fully disclosed its relationship with the arbitrator prior to the commencement of the hearing, and the arbitration council examined the relationship and determined that the arbitrator should remain on the panel, and where nothing in the record demonstrated that the opposing party was prejudiced, or that there was "evident partiality" on the part of the arbitrator merely because of the existence of some past insubstantial business dealings with the party, the arbitration award was confirmed.[51]

The Second Circuit, U.S. Court of Appeals, in examining whether a father-son relationship between an arbitrator and an officer of one party to the arbitration, expressed its traditional reluctance to inquire into the merits of an arbitrator's award, or to require of an arbitrator the same demanding level of impartiality as that dictated for judges.[52] However, it found that in the absence of evidence relating to the nature of the relationship between the arbitrator and his father (who was an officer in the international union of which the party to the arbitration was a local), it was bound by its strong feeling that sons are more often than not loyal to their fathers, partial to their fathers, and biased on behalf of their fathers. The court therefore, held that the award was grounded in unfairness, and that the relationship rose to the level of "evident partiality" required for vacating the arbitration award.[53]

On the other hand, where an employer failed to object to the selection of members of a contractually established joint arbitration committee at the time they were seated, the employer's objection to the committee's award based on the alleged partiality of the committee members was found to be waived.[54] As a general rule, a grievant must object to an arbitrator's partiality at the arbitration hearing before such an objection will be considered by the federal courts. The exception to this rule is when all facts as to the alleged bias are not known at the time of the hearing.[55]

---

[50]Id., 473 N.Y.S.2d at 287-288.

[51]Milliken & Co. v. Tiffany Loungewear, 99 A.D.2d 993, 473 N.Y.S.2d 443 (N.Y. App. Div., 1984).

[52]Morelite Constr. Corp. v. Carpenters, 748 F.2d 79, 81, 117 LRRM 3009 (CA, 2, 1984).

[53]Id., 117 LRRM at 3012. See standards under which an award may be vacated, 9 U.S.C. §10 (U.S. Arbitration Act). The court defined "evident partiality" to mean "where a reasonable person would have to conclude that an arbitrator was partial to one party to the arbitration." This "reasonable person" standard has been adopted by other courts. See Apperson v. Fleet Carrier Corp., 879 F.2d 1344, 131 LRRM 3079 (CA 6, 1989); Teamsters Local 814 v. J & R Sys. Installers, 878 F.2d 38, 131 LRRM 2799 (CA 2, 1989); NABET v. NBC, 707 F. Supp. 124, 131 LRRM 2995 (S.D.N.Y., 1988). Any arbitrator, nevertheless, should adhere to a policy of disclosing any circumstance likely to create a "presumption of bias" or that the arbitrator believes "might disqualify" him or her as an impartial arbitrator. See Rules 11 and 17, AAA's Voluntary Labor Arbitration Rules; FMCS Regulations, 29 CFR Part 1404; Code of Professional Responsibility 2.B.

[54]Electrical Workers (IBEW) Local 2 v. Gerstner Elec., 614 F. Supp. 874, 121 LRRM 3042, 3044 (D.Mo., 1985).

[55]Apperson v. Fleet Carrier Corp., 879 F.2d 1344, 1358-1359, 131 LRRM 3079, 3090-3091 (CA 6, 1989).

Nevertheless, the courts have the equitable power to intervene in an arbitration proceeding before an award is rendered, where there is "a real possibility that injustice will result," and one court has held that plaintiffs were not required to arbitrate their claims, as required by the bylaws of an organization of which all parties were members, in a charged atmosphere where the appearance of bias permeated the board of arbitrators from which the arbitrators had been selected.[56]

Ability and Expertise

For many lawyers, an arbitrator's expertise is one of the positive aspects of the arbitration system: "Having lawyers or physicians on the panel in products liability or medical malpractice cases may save your client the cost of rebuilding the wheel each time a case is heard."[57]

Not all commentators find that such expertise is among the desirable qualities to be sought in selecting an arbitrator. One commentator has pointed out that an impartial arbitrator may be harder to find than one who is an expert. "[E]ven in intra-industry disputes, is it always desirable to have a decision maker whose mind is filled with preconceived notions about industry reputations and practices?"[58] And another has observed that expertise in the field may serve to handicap the proceedings if the parties look to the arbitrator as an advice giver.[59]

There is, of course, "a tradeoff between impartiality and expertise," according to the Seventh Circuit, U.S. Court of Appeals:

> The expert adjudicator is more likely than a judge or juror not only to be precommitted to a particular substantive position but to know or have heard of the parties (or if the parties are organizations, their key people). * * * [P]eople who arbitrate do so because they prefer a tribunal knowledgeable about the subject matter of their dispute to a generalist court with its austere impartiality but limited knowledge of subject matter.[60]
>
> * * * The professional competence of the arbitrator is attractive to the businessman because a commercial dispute arises out of an environment that usually possesses its own folkways, mores, and technology. Most businessmen interviewed contended that commercial disputes should be considered within the framework of such an environment. No matter how determinedly judge and lawyer work to acquire an understanding of a given business or industry, they cannot hope to approximate the practical wisdom distilled from 30 or 40 years of experience.[61]

---

[56]Rabinowitz v. Olewski, 100 A.D.2d 539, 473 N.Y.S.2d 232, 234 (N.Y. App. Div., 1984).

[57]Meyerowitz, "The Arbitration Alternative," 71 A.B.A.J. 78, 79 (1985).

[58]Bayer & Abrahams, "The Trouble with Arbitration," 11 Litigation 30 (Winter, 1985) (quoting Hart & Sacks, The Legal Process, 342 (1958)).

[59]Cf. Phillips and Piazza, "How to Use Mediation," 10 Litigation 31, 33 (Spring, 1984) (discussing choosing a mediator).

[60]Merit Ins. Co. v. Leatherby Ins. Co., 714 F.2d 673, 679 (CA 7), cert. denied, 104 S.Ct. 529 (1983).

[61]Ibid. (quoting Resolving Business Disputes 51 (AMA, 1965)).

Legal Training

Participants in an Arbitration Workshop sponsored by the National Institute for Dispute Resolution and the American Bar Association, Special Committee on Dispute Resolution, agreed that only attorneys who had fulfilled a minimum legal experience should be allowed to serve as arbitrators.[62]

In a survey yielding 1,040 usable replies from persons on the American Arbitration Association's national list of labor arbitrators, over half of the respondents had degrees in law.[63] In another study involving 74 usable responses to a survey sent to arbitrators, 68.9 percent of the respondents had law degrees.[64]

Arbitrator's Immunity From Civil Liability

In a case in which an arbitrator's award caused an employee to lose a promotion and his place on a recall list, the arbitrator was found to be absolutely immune from suit for damages. The employee acknowledged that the arbitrator had jurisdiction to determine his employment status, despite the employee's contention that the arbitrator intentionally acted in absence of jurisdiction by choosing to adjudicate his rights without giving him notice or the opportunity to be present or represented.[65]

However, in another case the parties to an arbitration proceeding brought an action against the arbitrator as well as the organization sponsoring the arbitration for the arbitrator's failure to render a timely award. The California Court of Appeal reversed a lower court's dismissal of the complaint, and declined to grant quasi-judicial immunity to the arbitrator who breached his contract to render a timely award.[66] As noted by the California Court of Appeal in a subsequent case, this decision was superseded by legislation.[67]

---

[62]Steen, "The Multi-Door Courthouse Project: Examining the Arbitration Door," Arbitration/Big Case: ABC's of Dispute Resolution, 80 (ABA, 1986).

[63]Sprehe & Small, "Members and Nonmembers of the National Academy of Arbitrators: Do They Differ?" 39 Arb. J. 25, 28 (1984).

[64]Nelson, "The Selection of Arbitrators," 37 Lab. L.J. 703, 705 (1986).

[65]Durden v. Lockheed-Georgia Co., 123 LRRM 2262 (N.D. Ga., 1985).

[66]Baar v. Tigerman, 140 Cal. App. 3d 979, 211 Cal. Rptr. 426, 41 ALR 4th 1004 (1983). For articles discussing this case, see Daughtrey, "Quasi-Judicial Immunity Lost by the Arbitrator Who Sat on the Award: Baar v. Tigerman," 22 Am. Bus. L.J. 583 (1985); Note: "Baar v. Tigerman: An Attack on Absolute Immunity for Arbitrators!" 21 Cal. W.L. Rev. 564 (1985); Note: "Arbitrator Potentially Liable for Failure to Render a Decision," 67 Marq. L. Rev. 147 (1983). For an analogous discussion of mediator liability, see Chaykin, "Mediator Liability: A New Role For Fiduciary Duties?" 53 U. Cin. L. Rev. 731 (1984); see also Note: "The Sultans of Swap: Defining the Duties and Liabilities of American Mediators," 99 Harv. L. Rev. 1876 (1986).

[67]See Coopers & Lybrand v. Superior Court, 212 Cal. App. 3d 524, 260 Cal. Rptr. 713, 720 (1989) (the purpose of § 1280.1 was to supersede the holding in *Baar* and to expand arbitral immunity to conform to judicial immunity when the arbitrator is acting under any statute or contract).

Tribunals Under Railway Labor Act

Several recent cases have considered challenges to the power of the National Mediation Board to act at times when there are vacancies on the Board, in light of the board's quorum requirement.[68]

A court held that one member had the power to act for the Board pursuant to a validly issued delegation order. A delegation order provides that an individual member of the Board has the power and authority to carry out any of the work, business, or functions assigned to him by the Board. The court sustained the final certification of the union which was made by the only remaining member of the Board, since the member was acting pursuant to a delegation order.[69]

Essentially the same issue was presented in another case, where the investigation of a representation dispute was conducted by a single Board member, but the official certification of the union as the employee's representative was made by two members, one of whom had been appointed to the Board six days before the union was certified. The court held that the details and procedures used by the NMB to investigate a representational dispute leading to an official certification of an employee representative are largely at the Board's discretion.[70]

In an arbitration opinion under the Railway Labor Act, it was determined that a witness in a proceeding before the System Board of Adjustment could not serve as a partisan Board member in the same case.[71] The ruling turned on the risk of the partisan member's inadvertent introduction of additional "testimony" during an executive session of the Board, as opposed to mere clarification of facts on the hearing record.[72]

National Railroad Adjustment Board

The following circumstances are not sufficient to exempt a worker from the exhaustion-of-remedies requirement under the Railway Labor Act: (1) where the union "grievor" stated that he believed the grievance of the railroad worker had little merit or hope for success; (2) where the worker was not required to use the union "grievor," in whom he had little faith, to ensure that pursuing and exhausting administrative remedies under the Railway Labor Act would not be

[68]Hunter v. National Mediation Bd., 754 F.2d 1496, 119 LRRM 2993 (CA 9, 1985); Jones v. St. Louis-San Francisco Ry., 728 F.2d 257, 115 LRRM 2905 (CA 6, 1984); Railroad Yardmasters v. Harris, 721 F.2d 1332, 114 LRRM 3214 (D.C. Cir., 1983). See also Kanowitz, "Alternative Dispute Resolutions and the Public Interest: The Arbitration Experience," 38 Hastings L.J. 239, 286 (1987).

[69]Railroad Yardmasters v. Harris, 721 F.2d 1332, 114 LRRM 3214 (D.C. Cir., 1983).

[70]Hunter v. National Mediation Bd., 754 F.2d 1496, 118 LRRM 2993 (CA 9, 1985). See also Kanowitz, "Alternative Dispute Resolution and the Public Interest: The Arbitration Experience," 38 Hastings L.J. 239, 286 (1987).

[71]Northwest Airlines, 89 LA 484 (Flagler, 1987).

[72]Id. at 487.

wholly futile; and (3) where the worker claimed that his due process rights under federal and state law were violated by his discharge.[73]

The Eighth Circuit, U.S. Court of Appeals, has held that the district court should exercise its jurisdiction without requiring exhaustion of remedies before the National Railroad Adjustment Board in cases in which the primary question is the interpretation of a Federal Employers' Liability Act release, and questions of interpretation of a railroad industry collective bargaining agreement are only incidental.[74]

Railroad Special Boards of Adjustment

The Sixth Circuit, U.S. Court of Appeals, held that a Public Law Board failed to comply with the requirements of the Railway Labor Act because the Board had acted improperly in rendering an award that was not fully considered by a majority of its members in the manner required by the Act. In that case, two substitute arbitrators were not present on the date of the hearing, did not have the opportunity to hear a tape or read a transcript of the proceedings, did not discuss the award with each other or with the neutral Board member who was present at the hearing, and thus, a majority of the Board did not fully consider appellant's claims because they did not have an opportunity to participate in or consider the oral proceedings.[75]

Airline System Boards of Adjustment

A System Board of Adjustment has jurisdiction to consider whether a rule was reasonable and reasonably applied, not merely to decide whether a safety rule, for example, has been violated.[76] In order to avoid possible inadvertent additional "testimony" during executive sessions and to preserve the Board's integrity both in appearance and in fact, a witness in a proceeding before a System Board of Adjustment may not serve as a partisan Board member in the same case.[77]

An Airline System Board of Adjustment has authority to determine the appropriateness of discipline where the degree of discipline is challenged as being disparate and dissimilar, even though such determination was not specifically encompassed in the request for a ruling on the existence of just cause.[78]

---

[73]Kozina v. Chicago Terminal R.R., 609 F. Supp. 53 (N.D. Ill., 1984). See also Rader v. Transportation Union, 718 F.2d 1012, 114 LRRM 3127 (CA 11, 1983); Kaschak v. Consolidated Rail Corp., 707 F.2d 902, 113 LRRM 2760 (CA 6, 1983).

[74]Tello v. Soo Line R.R., 772 F.2d 458, 460, 120 LRRM 2343, 2345 (CA 8, 1985).

[75]Jones v. St. Louis-San Francisco Ry., 728 F.2d 257, 115 LRRM 2905, 2910 (CA 6, 1984).

[76]Delta Air Lines, 89 LA 408 (Kahn, chair, 1987).

[77]Northwest Airlines, 89 LA 484 (Flagler, chair, 1987).

[78]Trans World Airlines, 93 LA 167 (Eisler, 1989).

Chapter 5

Grievances—Prelude to Arbitration

Attitude of Parties to the Grievance Procedure

The attitude of the parties becomes clear as the grievance moves through the grievance machinery. The terms and provisions of the bargaining agreement may provide for full, partial, or no disclosure. However, unless there are contractual prohibitions, both parties should make a complete disclosure of all the facts, positions taken, and provisions of the agreement relied upon at the earliest possible steps in the grievance procedure.[1] The absence of such disclosure, with its inherent lack of good faith, is not only unfair but unwise. And, even where there is no requirement for written notice to the union of the employer's action, some reasonable method of prompt communication is expected.[2]

Failure to Comply Strictly With Technical Requirements of Grievance Procedure

Strict compliance with the contract provisions of the grievance procedure was considered vital by one arbitrator. In that case a provision stipulated that if the employer failed to respond to a grievance within a specified time period the alleged grievance was to be settled in favor of the union. When the arbitrator found the employer had not complied with the prescribed time limit, he held the employer to the provision.[3]

In another case the arbitrator foreclosed an employer from taking the position that the grievance was untimely because the contractual

---

[1]Consolidation Coal Co., 84 LA 1037 (Duda, 1985); Safeway Stores, 89 LA 627 (Staudohar, 1987) (arbitrator admonishes employer to cease and desist from refusing to provide all available material facts to union); Roadmaster Corp., 89 LA 126 (Doering, 1987) (failure of discharge letter to detail specific incidents of alleged strike misconduct does not by itself warrant vacating discharge).

[2]Sheridan Broadcasting Corp., 83 LA 1263 (Duff, 1984).

[3]Roper Outdoor Prods., Williamsburg Div., 84 LA 261 (Duda, 1985).

grievance procedure mandated that the parties disclose all facts which would be relied upon during the hearing, and the employer failed to serve notice that it intended to oppose the grievance on procedural grounds. The facts relied upon by the employer in making its charge of an untimely filing were available during the processing of the grievance. In failing to make the argument prior to submitting the matter to arbitration, the employer did not strictly comply with the provisions of the contract.[4]

Unions get similar treament. In *Power Wheels*[5] the contract required that any grievance involving the suspension or termination of an employee had to be reduced to writing within five working days. Arbitrator Patricia Thomas Bittel held that verbal notice of the union's intention to file a grievance, given within the five-day period, did not comply with the contractual prerequisites to arbitration.[6]

But even though a contract required discharge grievances to be brought within five working days, Arbitrator Edward W. Wies found that a grievance filed seven days after the discharge was not untimely where the grievant had made the company aware of his grievance and the company was lax in enforcing the time limits in the processing of grievances. The arbitrator held that by accepting the delays, the company had waived its contractual rights on time limits.[7]

Should Grievance Machinery Be Open to All Complaints?

As a rule, grievance statements should not be too general in nature. Failure to cite the relevant contract provisions in the grievance will not prevent an arbitrator from considering such provisions.[8]

In a coal industry case Arbitrator Marvin J. Feldman expressed the view that he was bound by a prior arbitration review board decision and applied the doctrine of res judicata, as the prior decision controlled subsequent grievances based on the same facts and claims by the same parties. In discussing the application of this doctrine to the facts of his case, Arbitrator Feldman stated that "[i]n order to cause the res judicata theory to fail, the following must be shown:

---

[4]Consolidation Coal Co., 91 LA 1011 (Stoltenberg, 1988).

[5]91 LA 1062 (Bittel, 1988).

[6]Id. See also Reliance Elec. Co., 90 LA 641 (Wolff, 1988); Central Business Sys., 90 LA 172 (Fish, 1987).

[7]Sanford Corp., 89 LA 968 (Wies, 1987).

[8]Astro-Valcour, 93 LA 91 (Rocha, 1989) (lack of direct reference to any article or section of collective bargaining contract does not invalidate grievance asserting grievant's belief that discharge was unjust since link between "discharge for proper cause" clause and the grievance is easily discernible); Quaker State Corp., 92 LA 898 (Talarico, 1989) (grievance challenging employer's promulgation of residency requirement as well as discipline imposed under it is arbitrable despite claim that the wording of grievance challenges only the penalty); Augsburg College, 91 LA 1166 (Gallagher, 1988) (grievance asserting past practice of compensating essential-services bargaining unit members for "snow day" is arbitrable even though it contains no reference to specific contract provisions where contract definition of "grievance" can be interpreted to include all disputes about the terms and conditions of employment); Cone Mills Corp., 86 LA 992 (Nolan, 1986).

(1) The previous award was clearly an instance of bad judgment.
(2) The decision was made without benefit of all of the relevant facts.
(3) The decision was based upon obvious and substantial error.
(4) A full hearing was not afforded.[9]

With reference to the exclusion of certain classes of grievances from formal grievance procedures, one arbitrator found that if an employer proceeds with the grievance process without raising a timely objection to the subject matter of the grievance, the employer will have waived its right to raise the issue at the hearing.[10]

The right of former employees to utilize the grievance procedure was raised yet again in another case.[11] In this case a former employee was unable to use the grievance procedure when, after the elimination of his job, he exercised his right to severance pay. It was determined that by exercising this right he forfeited all seniority rights, including his right of access to a grievance procedure.

An arbitrator may not address the reasonableness of the employer's entire substance abuse policy or the employer's duty to bargain prior implementation, where the national union demanded bargaining and the local union negotiated a new contract with knowledge that the policy was to be implemented, but no timely grievance to enforce any bargaining rights was filed, and the grievances before the arbitrator challenged only mandatory testing of one employee and his suspension pending receipt of test results.[12]

Depending on the nature of the issue and the underlying facts, an arbitrator may or may not decide an issue which raises a question under the Labor Management Relations Act.[13]

Where the contract contains a nondiscrimination clause, a Board of Arbitration may consider the issue of racial discrimination in a hearing on a grievance arising from the failure of black employees to qualify for promotion.[14]

Identification and Signature of Individual Grievants; Group Grievances

Waiver of Employee Rights or Signature Requirement

Arbitrators recognize that the grievance process, which is in the agreement between the company and the union, is controlled by the

---

[9]Freeman United Coal Mine Co., 84 LA 1302, 1305 (1985).
[10]Ajayem Lumber Midwest, 88 LA 472 (Shanker, 1987).
[11]Crown Zellerbach Corp., 84 LA 1195 (Nicholas, 1985).
[12]Stone Container Corp., 91 LA 1186 (Ross, 1988).
[13]Compare Supermarket Serv. Corp., 89 LA 538 (DiLauro, 1987) (arbitrator had authority to rule on grievance insofar as claims allege violations of collective bargaining contract but may not rule on whether challenged conduct violates Labor Management Relations Act), with Hartford Provision Co., 89 LA 590 (Sacks, 1987) (arbitrator will decide whether employee is eligible for bargaining unit under Labor Management Relations Act where employer clearly indicated that it wanted arbitrator to make decision and union briefed LMRA eligibility issue).
[14]Arkansas Power & Light Co., 89 LA 1028 (Woolf, 1987).

union. Generally, only the union, and not the employee, has the right to demand that a grievance be taken to arbitration. For this reason, it has been held that a grievance filed by the union may not require the signature of a particular employee.[15]

In addition, the provision in an agreement requiring the employees themselves to file may be unenforceable if the employer had notice of grievances against it and opportunity to be heard.[16]

Waivers, since they result in defeat of the rights of the parties without consideration of the merits of the dispute, are not lightly inferred by arbitrators. Thus two reprimand grievances filed in a dispute concerning discipline and involuntary transfer are arbitrable despite the contention that the union waived them in the process of responding to the employer's request for clarification. The arbitrator concluded that the union never explicitly withdrew the reprimand grievances.[17]

Steps in Grievance Procedure

While some vacillation occurs in the enforcement of contractual time period requirements, in the vast majority of cases these requirements are strictly enforced where the parties have previously and consistently enforced such requirements. Many grievances are refused a hearing due to lack of compliance with such restrictions.[18] Vacillation occurs in cases where no definite time period restriction is contained in the agreement or the contract stipulated a "reasonable" time period within which a grievance may be filed.[19] Certain situations, however, are not subject to contractual time limits. When the subject of a grievance is an ongoing violation, time limit restrictions are lifted.[20] Time limits are also waived if the parties to a grievance allow the grievance to move from step to step in the procedure without making objections of untimeliness.[21]

---

[15]Teamsters Local 744 v. Skokie Valley Beverage Co., 123 LRRM 3175 (N.D. Ill., 1986); Allegheny Ludlum Steel Corp., 86 LA 492 (Mullin, 1986); Niagara Frontier Transp. Auth., 85 LA 229 (Lawson, 1985); District of Columbia Metro. Police Dep't, 82 LA 701 (Feigenbaum, 1984).

[16]Teamsters Local 657 v. Stanley Structures, 735 F.2d 903, 117 LRRM 2119 (CA 5, 1984).

[17]Grossmont Union High School Dist., 91 LA 909 (Weiss, 1988); Astro-Valcour, 93 LA 91 (Rocha, 1989) (no waiver where grievant bypassed the first two steps of grievance procedure and timely filed written grievance at third step where contract provides that grievance arising from suspension or discharge will automatically go to third step).

[18]Cosmic Distrib., 92 LA 205 (Prayzich, 1989); Louie Glass Co., 85 LA 5 (Hart, 1985); Dana Corp., 83 LA 1053 (King, 1984); Mobile Video Servs., 83 LA 1009 (Hockenberry, 1984); Kansas Gas & Elec. Co., 83 LA 916 (Thornell, 1984). Compare Phillips 66 Co., 92 LA 1037 (Neas, 1989) (employer did not sustain burden of proof by preponderance of the evidence that union did not timely file grievance; overwhelming arbitral precedence supports resolving doubts as to compliance with time limits in favor of arbitrability).

[19]Mesker Indus., 85 LA 921 (Mikrut, 1985); Clougherty Packing Co., 85 LA 1053 (Richman, 1985).

[20]Gulf S. Beverages, 87 LA 688 (Caraway, 1986); Pantsmaker, Inc., 83 LA 753 (Roberts, 1984); Board of Educ. Special Dist. 1, 81 LA 41 (Rotenberg, 1983).

[21]Camp Lejeune Marine Corps Base, 90 LA 1126 (Nigro, 1988) (grievance filed five years after alleged wrongful failure to promote is arbitrable where employer processed grievance and did not assert timeliness objection until arbitration); Polygram Distribution, 83 LA 249 (Gibson, 1984); Mid-America Canning Corp., 85 LA 900 (Imundo, 1985).

In addition, earlier steps of the grievance procedure will be considered to have been waived if a company official, other than the one specified in the agreement, accepts and processes the grievance.[22]

Grievance Mediation

In recent years the concept of "grievance mediation" has gained acceptance by the parties, and it has been added as a step to the grievance procedure in some collective bargaining agreements.[23]

The neutral party or "mediator" does not decide the case, nor does he have the power to do so; unlike arbitration, the mediator has no binding power over either of the parties to a grievance. Since he does not have the power to decide the issue, the mediator generally attempts to elicit the facts of the dispute with as little formality as possible. Using creative suggestion, thoughtful questioning, and gentle persuasion, the mediator attempts to guide the two sides toward a mutually acceptable agreement. The major advantage of mediation is the spirit of cooperation that can result from mediatory efforts. Both sides come to the mediation table of their own free will: both sides compromise to develop a solution which is acceptable to both parties. And a solution reached by such method is more likely to work than a binding arbitration decision which, by its very nature, is imposed upon the losing party in a grievance dispute. Winners and losers are not produced by the mediation process; partners, however, often are.

If the grievance cannot be resolved by mediation, the mediator delivers an immediate advisory, nonbinding opinion as to how the issue should be decided under the terms of the agreement. The parties can then use the advisory opinion as the basis for further settlement discussions and/or they can submit the grievance to arbitration.

The three major requirements for effective "grievance mediation" are: "(1) the mediator must be selected from a source outside the company; (2) the mediator must be a party whom both sides can trust; and, (3) each party must approach the mediation with an open mind and a sincere resolve to reach agreement."[24] These requirements presuppose the most important requirement for effective mediation: a competent mediator.

While grievance mediation is still a new and relatively untested method of settling labor disputes, its potential for success is tremendous.[25]

---

[22]Peabody Coal Co., 87 LA 1002 (Volz, 1986).

[23]Goldberg, "The Rise in Grievance Mediation," Proceedings of the NYU 37th Annual Nat'l Conference on Labor, § 13-1 et seq. (Matthew Bender & Co., 1984); Goldberg, "The Mediation of Grievances Under a Collective Bargaining Contract: An Alternative to Arbitration," 77 Nw. U.L. Rev. 270 (1982).

[24]Conti, "Mediation of Work-Place Disputes: A Prescription for Organizational Health," 11 Empl. Rel. L.J. 291, 296 (1985).

[25]See generally Power, "Targeting a New Dimension to Dispute Resolution," 37 Lab. L.J. 524 (1986); Bierman & Youngblood, "Resolving Unjust Discharge Cases: A Mediatory Approach," 30 Arb. J. 48 (1985); Loewenberg, "Structure of Grievance Procedures," 35 Lab. L.J. 44 (1984); Brett & Goldberg, "Grievance Mediation in the Coal Industry: A Field Experiment," 37 Indus. & Lab. Rel. Rev. 49 (1983); Bowers, Seeber & Stallworth, "Grievance Mediation: A Route to Resolution for the Cost-Conscious 1980's," 33 Lab. L.J. 459 (1982).

Grievance Representatives

Right to Union Representation at Early Stage

Union representation of disputes between aggrieved employees and management has received considerable attention from the courts, the NLRB, and arbitrators. While the right to union representation has been invoked to cover many areas of labor-management relations,[26] this Supplement will focus on the right to union representation in the context of discipline and rights protected by the bargaining agreement.

Since the Supreme Court declared in 1975 that individual employees have a right to refuse to submit to investigatory interviews which they reasonably believe may result in discipline without union representation, the NLRB has continued to shape the "contours and limits of the statutory rights" established in *Weingarten*.[27] Reversing its previous holding that *Weingarten* rights extend to nonunion employees, the Board determined that application of *Weingarten* to nonunion settings required employers to recognize and deal with employees on a collective basis violative of the Act's exclusivity principle.[28] Noting that union representatives have certain knowledge, skills, and experience in investigatory interviews, one Board member found that no equivalent quality of representation in a nonunion setting justified an extension of *Weingarten* rights.[29]

The scope of remedies available to employees whose *Weingarten* rights have been violated has also undergone considerable change under current Board policy. Where an employee who had been denied union representation at his investigatory interview was found to have been discharged for cause, the Board declined to order reinstatement with back pay and instead issued a cease and desist order directing the employer to refrain from its unlawful activity.[30] In a case where the employer denied the union representative the right to speak during an investigatory interview, the Board restricted its remedy to the issu-

---

[26]Such claims to union representation and adjudication under a collective bargaining agreement have not been found to create a bar against claims raised pursuant to the Fair Labor Standards Act (Barrentine v. Arkansas-Best Freight Sys., Inc., 101 S.Ct. 1437, 24 WH Cases 1284 (1981)); Civil Rights Act of 1871 (McDonald v. City of West Branch, Mich., 104 S.Ct. 1799, 115 LRRM 3646 (1984)); or statutes regulating trust funds (see Schneider Moving & Storage Co. v. Robbins, 104 S.Ct. 1844, 115 LRRM 3641 (1984), and Central States v. Central Transp., 105 S.Ct. 2833 (1985)). Where administrative agencies have deferred certain cases to arbitration, one circuit has indicated that such deferral does not absolve the agency from explaining its reasons for accepting an arbitrator's award that contravenes agency precedent. Darr v. NLRB, 801 F.2d 1404, 123 LRRM 2548 (D.C. Cir., 1986).

[27]NLRB v. J. Weingarten, 95 S.Ct. 959, 963, 88 LRRM 2689, 2691 (1975).

[28]Sears, Roebuck & Co., 274 NLRB 230, 118 LRRM 1329 (1985), overruling Materials Research Corp., 262 NLRB 1010, 110 LRRM 1401 (1982).

[29]Id., 118 LRRM at 1333. For commentary on the loss of *Weingarten* rights for nonunion employees see Note, "Extending *Weingarten* Rights To Nonunion Employees," 86 Colum. L. Rev. 618 (1986).

[30]Taracorp Indus., 273 NLRB 221, 117 LRRM 1497 (1984), overruling Kraft Foods, 251 NLRB 598, 105 LRRM 1233 (1980).

ance of a cease and desist order although the grievant had been returned to work by an administrative law judge.[31]

Following its holding in *Baton Rouge Water Works*,[32] the NLRB continues to uphold the right of employers to deny union representation where the imposition of discipline has already been determined.[33] However, where a portion of the meeting consists of an investigatory interview, the Board's finding that an employee was denied his *Weingarten* rights has been upheld by a Court of Appeals.[34] Additionally, *Weingarten* rights have been found not to attach to a situation where the employer has a general meeting to discuss company rules[35] or where employees walk out of an investigatory interview after the employer legally denies them the right to union representation.[36]

Also, the employer did not violate the *Weingarten* rights of an employee who was discharged for insubordination where, after being asked to go to the manager's office to fill out an accident report, the employee left the area to get a union representative. Since the incident did not involve an investigatory interview, the *Weingarten* rights did not apply.[37]

Weingarten and its progeny have gained general acceptance among arbitrators who have generally focused their decisions on the presence or absence of the *Weingarten* principles.[38] Where the employee fails to request or waives union representation, arbitrators have generally found employer denial of representation not to be a violation of the contract or *Weingarten*.[39] However, arbitrators have taken note of the extent to which certain employees would be aware of *Weingarten* rights to uphold employer discipline of a union president while mitigating discipline for an employee with limited knowledge of English.[40]

In construing the extent to which *Weingarten* applies to employer investigations, some arbitrators have limited the right to union representation to investigatory interviews only. As a result, arbitral authority exists to prevent union representation during employer searches for physical evidence in automobiles[41] and in meetings

---

[31]Greyhound Lines, 273 NLRB 1443, 118 LRRM 1199 (1985), modifying 273 NLRB 1443 (1985); also see Radisson Muehlebach Hotel, 273 NLRB 1464, 118 LRRM 1601 (1985).

[32]Baton Rouge Water Works, 246 NLRB 995, 103 LRRM 1056 (1979).

[33]See San Antonio Portland Cement Co., 121 LRRM 1234 (1985); Eagle Discount, 275 NLRB 1438, 120 LRRM 1047 (1985).

[34]See NLRB v. S.W. Bell Tel. Co., 730 F.2d 166, 116 LRRM 2211 (CA 5, 1984); Gulf States Mfg. v. NLRB, 704 F.2d 1390, 113 LRRM 2789, reh'g denied, 715 F.2d 1020, 114 LRRM 2727 (CA 5, 1983).

[35]Northwest Eng'g Co., 265 NLRB 190, 111 LRRM 1481 (1982).

[36]Bridgeport Hosp., 265 NLRB 421, 111 LRRM 1585 (1982).

[37]Twin Coast Newspapers, 89 LA 799 (Brisco, 1987).

[38]See Arbitrator Ted T. Tsukiyama's discussion of arbitral application of *Weingarten* in Maui Pineapple Co., 86 LA 907, 911 (1986). See also Arkansas Power & Light Co., 92 LA 144 (Weisbrod, 1989); Tucson Unified School Dist., 92 LA 544 (White, 1989).

[39]Calcasieu Parish Police Jury, 86 LA 350 (Nicholas, 1985); Fry's Food Stores of Ariz., 83 LA 1248 (Weizenbaum, 1984).

[40]Borough of Carlisle Pa., 82 LA 1 (Woy, 1984), and Maui Pineapple Co., 86 LA 907 (Tsukiyama 1986).

[41]Shell Oil Co., 84 LA 562 (Milentz, 1985).

informing employees to submit to drug screening during a physical examination.[42]

In denying an employee union representation during a performance evaluation, one arbitrator held that the union had no right to accompany an employee to a supervisor's performance evaluation before there was a grievance or a grievable event.[43]

Mirroring the NLRB holding in *Baton Rouge*, arbitrators have held that where the purpose of the meeting was to administer discipline and not to conduct an investigatory interview, employer denial of union representation did not violate the principles of *Weingarten*.[44] Arbitrator Jack Clarke reasoned that although he would not decide the propriety of applying federal statutes, the Board's *Baton Rouge* standard led him to deny the union's *Weingarten* arguments in a case where an employee was denied union representation at a meeting where no investigation was conducted but a verbal reprimand was issued.[45]

Grievance Adjustment by Individual Employees

The Supreme Court's decision in *Bowen* held that unions were liable for damages caused by a union's refusal to proceed to arbitration.[46] Since then, various courts have explored the scope of the union's duty of fair representation in § 301 breach of the duty of fair representation actions.

In decisions following *Bowen*, various courts of appeal have continued to give representatives considerable leeway in the processing and presentation of grievances.[47] In upholding a union's decision not to proceed to arbitration in a discharge case, one court of appeals found no violation where the union based its decision on the experience of its labor attorney, the grievant's criminal conviction, the union's analysis of arbitral precedent, and other documentary evidence.[48] However, where a union failed to submit a grievance in a timely manner, the same court found the union's action to be arbitrary despite a finding that good cause for termination existed.[49] Noting that the grievant's resort to a federal district court constituted the harm inflicted by the union's breach of the duty of fair representation, the Ninth Circuit, U.S. Court of Appeals, affirmed the district court's award of $2,000 in damages and refused to characterize the award as attorney's fees.[50]

---

[42]Birmingham-Jefferson County Transit, 84 LA 1272 (Statham, 1985).

[43]Anoka County, Minn., 84 LA 516, 521 (Jacobowski, 1985).

[44]AFG Indus., 87 LA 568 (Clarke, 1986). Also see Fry's Food Stores of Ariz., 83 LA 1248 (Weizenbaum, 1984).

[45]AFG Indus., 87 LA at 572.

[46]Bowen v. U.S. Postal Serv., 103 S.Ct. 588, 112 LRRM 2281 (1983).

[47]Galindo v. Stoody Co., 793 F.2d 1502, 123 LRRM 2705 (CA 9, 1986); Camacho v. Ritz-Carlton Water Tower, 786 F.2d 242, 121 LRRM 2801 (CA 7, 1986); Johnson v. U.S. Postal Serv., 756 F.2d 1461, 118 LRRM 3411 (CA 9, 1985).

[48]Johnson v. U.S. Postal Serv., 118 LRRM at 3414 (CA 9, 1985).

[49]Dutrisac v. Caterpillar Tractor Co., 749 F.2d 1270, 113 LRRM 3532 (CA 9, 1983).

[50]Id., 113 LRRM at 3536-3537.

While *Bowen* extended union liability for violations of its duty of fair representation, the Supreme Court later limited the statute of limitation for § 301 suits to six months.[51] As applied by the courts of appeal, the *DelCostello* statute of limitations has been found to extend to federal employees[52] and employees covered by the Railway Labor Act.[53] Another court found the six-month statute of limitation applicable to actions where the alleged violation of § 301 involved the employer alone.[54] Where an employee brought an action claiming wrongful discharge for exercising his right to workers' compensation in violation of the collective bargaining agreement, the Eighth Circuit held that in bringing the suit eight months after the union informed him it would not go to arbitration the claim was barred under either Missouri statute or *DelCostello's* six-month statute of limitations.[55]

Privileges and Protection of Grievance Representatives

Many collective bargaining agreements recognize the special role of union grievance representatives and provide for certain immunities and privileges.[56] Subject to restraints imposed by courts and arbitrators, these contractual protections serve to insure the union's ability to handle grievances and administer the contract.

Superseniority

Since its *Gulton* decision,[57] the NLRB has continued to invalidate superseniority clauses applied to union officers who do not have "steward-like" grievance handling responsibilities.[58] Viewing superseniority for nongrievance-handling union officers as interference with employee rights to refrain from § 7 activity, the Board has invalidated clauses granting superseniority to union negotiating committees,[59] union executive board members,[60] and those union officials who do not perform steward-like duties.[61]

[51]DelCostello v. Teamsters, 103 S.Ct. 2281, 113 LRRM 2737 (1983).
[52]Pham v. Government Employees (AFGE), 799 F.2d 634, 123 LRRM 2206 (CA 10, 1986).
[53]Triplett v. Railway Clerks Local 308, 801 F.2d 700, 123 LRRM 2975 (CA 4, 1986).
[54]Lacina v. G.K. Trucking, 802 F.2d 1190, 123 LRRM 3179 (CA 9, 1986).
[55]Johnson v. Hussmann Corp., 805 F.2d 795, 123 LRRM 3074 (CA 8, 1986).
[56]Comparable protections may exist for employer grievance representatives. See NLRB v. Electrical Workers (IBEW) Local 46, 793 F.2d 1026, 122 LRRM 2842 (CA 9, 1986) (union fine of member working as supervisor of nonunion contractor violates NLRA as union demonstrated intent to represent employees of nonunion contractor by offering to reduce fine if contractor signs collective bargaining agreement with union). However, the Supreme Court has held that union fines of member-supervisors with no collective bargaining or grievance handling responsibility do not violate the NLRA. NLRB v. Electrical Workers (IBEW) Local 340, 107 S.Ct. 2002, 125 LRRM 2305 (1987), affirming 780 F.2d 1489, 121 LRRM 2563 (CA 9, 1986).
[57]Gulton Electro-Voice Inc., 266 NLRB 406, 112 LRRM 1361 (1983).
[58]Id. at 1364.
[59]Dravo Corp., 276 NLRB 1176, 120 LRRM 1156 (1985).
[60]Cooper Indus., 271 NLRB 810, 117 LRRM 1188 (1984).
[61]International Harvester, 270 NLRB 1342, 116 LRRM 1343 (1984).

Where union officials engage in impromptu meetings with management prior to filing a formal grievance and such meetings become an important part of grievance handling, the Board has found the extension of superseniority lawful.[62] However, unilateral employer action denying insurance and pension benefits to employees on leaves of absence for union business did not violate the NLRA since providing the benefits was not related to shop floor grievance handling.[63] The Board's continued policy of limiting the scope of superseniority benefits to union grievance representatives for layoff and recall purposes established in *Dairylea*[64] has enjoyed wide support among the various circuits when called upon to enforce Board orders.[65]

In considering the effect of a superseniority clause, arbitral authority has both accepted and rejected the *Gulton* standard. In upholding the superseniority of a union vice president, the arbitrator stated that his authority was limited to interpreting the collective agreement rather than applying the current NLRB ruling.[66] Conversely, another arbitrator refused to permit stewards with low overtime status to automatically assume a higher grade position since that would be granting stewards a benefit beyond the layoff/recall rights established by the Board in *Dairylea*.[67]

Where the major purpose of superseniority is to allow efficient union administration of the contract, arbitrators have permitted layoff of union stewards when the work group has been reclassified[68] or when temporary layoff did not impede the union's ability to administer the contract.[69] In a case where superseniority rights conflicted with recall subject to ability to perform the work, the arbitrator held that an employer's assessment of relative ability is irrelevant and outweighed by the superseniority provision where the retained steward can perform the work at an acceptable level.[70]

Plant Access

While union access to an employer's premises for grievance investigation has generally been upheld by arbitrators, access for other

---

[62]Electrical Workers (IUE) Local 663, 276 NLRB 1043, 120 LRRM 1150 (1985).

[63]Mead Packaging, 273 NLRB 1451, 118 LRRM 1184 (1985).

[64]See Dairylea Coop., 219 NLRB 656, 89 LRRM 1737 (1975).

[65]See NLRB v. Niagara Mach. & Tool Works, 746 F.2d 143, 117 LRRM 2689 (CA 2, 1984) (recording secretary and sergeant at arms not eligible for superseniority; Board order enforced); Automobile Workers Local 1384 v. NLRB, 756 F.2d 482, 118 LRRM 2753 (CA 7, 1985) (access to union official and superseniority clause not factors in bumping recording secretary from third to first shift). See also NLRB v. Harvey Hubble Inc., 767 F.2d 1100, 119 LRRM 3460 (CA 4, 1985); NLRB v. Automobile Workers Local 1131, 1161, 777 F.2d 1131, 121 LRRM 2080 (CA 6, 1985). For further examination of the post-*Gulton* cases, see Note, "New Limits on Superseniority: Ignoring the Importance of Efficient Union Operations," 86 Colum. L. Rev. 631 (1986).

[66]Hunter Eng'g Co., 82 LA 483 (Alleyne, 1984). See also Ferro Eng'g, 90 LA 257 (Duda, 1987); U.S. Steel Corp., 89 LA 221 (Dybeck, 1987).

[67]Ex-Cell-O Corp., 85 LA 1190, 1193 (Statham, 1985).

[68]Textron Inc., 83 LA 931 (Flaten, 1984).

[69]Almet/Lawnlite, Inc., 87 LA 624 (Boals, 1985).

[70]U.S. Steel Corp., 85 LA 1113 (Murphy, 1985). Compare Siemens Energy & Automation, 91 LA 599 (Goggin, 1988), where arbitrator found that steward's record did not show any experience in the classification and another steward had been recalled to the department.

nongrievance-related activities has received greater scrutiny. Where a contract required union representatives to make arrangements with the company prior to entering the premises to "discuss matters of contract administration," Arbitrator John F. Caraway ruled that the contract did not allow solicitation of membership by a nonemployee union representative.[71] However, in a case where an employer repeatedly denied the union representative access to investigate violations of the union security clause and on one occasion had the union representative arrested for trespassing, Arbitrator William E. Riker found that the employer interfered with the union's contractual right to visit the premises.[72] Recognizing the union's obligation not to unreasonably interrupt employees during a peak business period, Arbitrator Riker held the employer responsible for creating a confrontational situation where the circumstances called for "a spirit of cooperation and consideration."[73]

Employer rules governing access to the premises must be based on reasonableness. For instance, where a contract permitted union safety officials access to the employer's premises, an arbitrator found the employer's requirement that union officials sign waivers releasing the employer from all liability was unreasonable.[74] However, since the union officials were covered by workers' compensation and since without the waiver union officials would be granted greater rights than employee members, Arbitrator Marvin J. Feldman reasoned that the employer's requirement of waiver of liability for specific visits by union safety officials was reasonable.[75]

Special Immunity

Arbitrators continue to recognize a limited form of immunity from discipline for stewards acting in their official capacity as grievance representatives. Arbitrator M. David Keefe found that company discipline of stewards struck at the "core issue of the union steward's right to represent grieving employees."[76] Although a steward's conduct during grievance handling is generally afforded immunity, Arbitrator Keefe found that discipline could be invoked up to a point. Where a steward insisted on further discussion of a settled grievance, the arbitrator found discharge was too severe a penalty and reduced the employer sanction to a suspension.[77]

Where employer discipline is imposed on union stewards engaged in grievance representation, arbitrators have been reluctant to uphold discipline that interferes with the union's grievance-handling respon-

---

[71]Montgomery Ward & Co., 85 LA 913 (1985).
[72]Piper's Restaurant, 86 LA 809 (1986).
[73]Id. at 810.
[74]Utah Power & Light, 88 LA 310 (1986).
[75]Id. at 314.
[76]Crown Cork & Seal, 88 LA 145, 148 (1986).
[77]Id. at 149, 151.

sibilities. Where an employer fired a steward for alleged theft of legal pads, the arbitrator held that discharge was improper as past practice of the parties permitted stewards to use legal pads for grievances and other union-related activities.[78] Arbitrator Harvey Nathan found the three-day suspension of a union steward for insubordination violated the contract since company representatives unilaterally established the time the steward could file a grievance, and he refused the steward's request to change the meeting time.[79] Imposition of discipline when the steward spoke back to his supervisor, Arbitrator Nathan reasoned, restricted steward access to a supervisor and violated the union's access to the grievance procedure.[80]

While steward conduct in the course of union business is protected, the immunity is not absolute. One arbitrator upheld the suspension of a steward for refusing to remove defamatory postings critical of the company's medical insurance.[81] In upholding the discharge of a union steward for racial harassment of another employee, another arbitrator held that the steward's position created no immunity from plant rules against harassment.[82] Where Arbitrator Roland Strasshoffer found a steward's comments towards a female supervisor to be beyond the level of "shop talk" and intended to "demean and degrade," he held that the supervisor had just cause for termination.[83]

An arbitrator held that an employer had just cause to discharge a shop steward for insubordination when the shop steward refused to take a drug test under a policy which was properly adopted, reasonably announced, and fairly applied.[84] Another arbitrator found that an employer properly issued a reprimand to a union president who failed to indicate the time spent on union business on his time card.[85] Just cause existed to discharge a chief steward for leaving work without permission and threatening the lives of co-workers[86] and for extorting money from employees who were hired through a hiring hall.[87]

Status as a union steward or officer does not create a special duty that permits greater liability for the actions of a steward than for other employees. Where an employer terminated four union stewards for participating in a work stoppage over a change in plant starting time, an arbitrator held that company action in terminating the stewards while issuing reprimands to other employees was based on their union status and could not constitute just cause.[88]

---

[78]Carnation Co., 84 LA 80 (Wright, 1985).
[79]Southern Ind. Gas & Elec. Co., 85 LA 716 (1985).
[80]Id. at 720-721.
[81]Dalfort Corp., 85 LA 70 (White, 1985).
[82]Peninsular Steel Co., 88 LA 391 (Ipavec, 1986).
[83]Hobart Corp., 88 LA 512 (1986).
[84]Crescent Metal Prods., 91 LA 1129 (Coyne, 1989).
[85]Alofs Mfg. Co., 89 LA 5 (Daniel, 1987).
[86]International Paper Co., 89 LA 985 (O'Grady, 1987).
[87]OK Grocery Co., 92 LA 440 (Stoltenberg, 1989).
[88]Schnadig Corp., 85 LA 692 (Seidman, 1985).

Time Limitations

On occasion arbitrators will find a waiver of express and clear time limitations because of extenuating circumstances. Such was the situation when Arbitrator Thomas DiLauro found a grievance timely filed.[89] In this case, the agreement required a grievance to be filed "within seven days after the mailing by registered mail of written notice of such discharge to the Union." The grievance was filed more than six weeks after the mailing of the notice. In finding the grievance timely filed, Arbitrator DiLauro found persuasive these circumstances: the grievant was off duty at the time of the discharge notice using what she believed was an appropriate leave; the grievant was suffering from an anxiety attack and being cared for at the home of a friend; the notice was mailed to the grievant's home, and when the grievant returned to her home she learned of the discharge notice and then immediately filed a grievance protesting her discharge.[90]

Grievance Settlements as Binding Precedents

See Chapter 11 for the precedential value of arbitration awards.

Notice of Intent to Arbitrate

Arbitrator F. Jay Taylor found that a sex discrimination grievance was timely filed two years after the employee (who was pregnant) was denied an opportunity to transfer to light duty. The grievance was filed after the grievant and the union discovered that the company had allowed a male employee to be transferred to light work after a gallbladder operation.[91]

Where the agreement sets a specific time within which the arbitration process must be commenced, failure of a party to request arbitration within the time specified renders the dispute nonarbitrable.[92] Whether or not the time limit has been met[93] or waived[94] is a question for the arbitrator.

---

[89]Sugardale Foods, 87 LA 18 (1986). See Arbitrator Kaufman's decision in Food Employers Council Inc., 87 LA 514 (1986) (grievance asserting typographical error in contract was timely filed although alleged error first appeared 12 years earlier, where contract contained no time limit for filing such grievance, employers had not implemented their interpretation of the disputed provision, and timeliness issue was not raised until arbitration hearing).

[90]Sugardale Foods, 87 LA 18, 21 (1986).

[91]Cities Serv. Co., 87 LA 1209 (1986). For an opposing view, see Rome Cable Corp., 87 LA 519 (Konvitz, 1986). In *Rome* Arbitrator Konvitz analogized time limits in a grievance procedure to a statute of limitations and, in finding the grievance untimely, noted that the grievance arose at the time the wrong was done and that the filing limitation period was not extended by the length of time the grievant remained ignorant of the wrong.

[92]Missouri Minerals Processing, 85 LA 939 (Talent, 1985); Robbins A.F.B., Ga., 84 LA 1173 (Holley, 1985); North Shore Gas Co., 84 LA 1016 (Seidman, 1985).

[93]Old Dominion Wood Preserves, 82 LA 437 (Foster, 1983).

[94]Bard Mfg. Co., 83 LA 749 (Feldman, 1984).

Chapter 6

Determining Arbitrability

For recent developments in this area, see the *AT&T Technologies* case discussed in Chapter 2, at pages 15 and 25–26.

Chapter 7

Arbitration Procedures and Techniques

Source of Procedural Rules

The Code of Professional Responsibility and the Code of Ethics

The Code of Professional Responsibility for Arbitrators of Labor Management Disputes provided the authority and support arbitrators needed to encourage mediation rather than arbitration,[1] and to proceed ex parte when a litigant failed to appear after due notice.[2]

Stating the Issue

Use of Original Grievance

The purpose of filing a grievance is to fully inform the company of the nature of a problem so that the company can make whatever defense is available. If a union fails to notify an employer, either in writing or by discussion, of additional claims that it intends to assert, until after all grievance procedures are finished, such additional claims will not be considered in arbitration.[3]

The filing of the grievance mobilizes the grievance machinery of only the particular bargaining agreement. A grievance filed under a local agreement, with its own grievance procedure, cannot be converted to a grievance under the master agreement.[4]

---

[1]Lloyd W. Aubry Co., 91 LA 679, 680 (Millious, 1988).
[2]Elsass, Inc., 92 LA 905 (Fullmer, 1989); Westlake, Inc., 90 LA 1129 (Armstrong, 1988).
[3]Lakeland Color Press, 82 LA 1151 (Gallagher, 1984).
[4]Ceres Terminals, 92 LA 735 (Malin, 1989).

In the public sector, arbitrators have disallowed the presentation of issues which the employer or the union have failed to raise until the hearing.[5] Generally, issues raised at the hearing must be rooted in prearbitral discussions or grievance steps. Even a claim that prearbitral discussions were flawed because of a misprint in the complaint will not be considered by the arbitrator on the day of the hearing without substantial supportive evidence concerning the error.[6]

Where an issue that was not discussed prior to arbitration is raised at the hearing, it may be permitted if it speaks to the merits of the grievance before the arbitrator, but not if it is simply a collateral complaint.[7]

Issue Pinpointed by Arbitrator

Arbitrators will pinpoint the issues when the parties cannot do so.[8] When one issue in a case with several issues is dormant throughout the prearbitral proceedings, the arbitrator may remand the case to the parties for reprocessing through the grievance procedure after the issue surfaces during the hearing.[9]

Simultaneous Arbitration of Several Grievances

Arbitrator Harold G. Wren, in a case arising in the public sector, departed from the general rule when he denied consolidation of grievances despite two prior arbitration decisions between the same parties which permitted combination.[10] Arbitrator Wren placed the burden on the party moving to consolidate to show that combination would promote efficiency or economy in the arbitral process. In another case, an arbitrator refused to combine a second similar and related grievance because the first grievance had also been the subject of an NLRB unfair labor practice charge which the NLRB deferred to arbitration, and the employer objected to consolidation.[11]

Extent of Permissible Deviation From Prearbitral Discussion of Case

In one case, an agreement required full disclosure of all relevant facts and positions during a prearbitral meeting; the grieving party,

---

[5]National Educ. Ass'n, 86 LA 592 (Wahl, 1985); Florida Power Corp., 86 LA 59 (Bell, 1986); Federal Bureau of Prisons, 82 LA 950 (Kanzer, 1984).

[6]Pennsylvania Dep't of Corrections, 86 LA 978 (Kreitler, 1986).

[7]Mohawk Rubber Co., 86 LA 679 (Groshong, 1986); Hamady Bros. Food Mkt., 82 LA 81 (Silver, 1983).

[8]See Chapter 7 of the Fourth Edition, subtopic entitled "Issue Pinpointed by the Arbitrator," p. 230.

[9]Lyondell Petrochemical Co., 89 LA 95 (Caraway, 1987).

[10]Air Force Logistics Command, 92 LA 60 (1988).

[11]Fedders-U.S.A., 92 LA 418 (Cohen, 1989).

however, opted to bypass the meeting altogether. At arbitration the grievant relied on evidence of past practice, an issue neither proffered nor announced earlier. Over the employer's objection, based on lack of knowledge, Arbitrator Marshall J. Seidman ruled the meeting discretionary, at the whim of the employee, and received the evidence.[12] Where a party fails to address, at the hearing, an issue raised in the original grievance, such issue is deemed waived or abandoned, and the arbitrator will not consider it in the briefing stage.[13]

Arbitrator John J. Flagler refused to permit an employer to raise a defense to a discharge grievance which the employer had never suggested in prearbitral proceedings, since "[t]o do so would be to undermine the integrity of the parties' grievance procedure."[14] Where an employer attempted to add an additional ground for discharge which it had not originally stated, the arbitrator rejected the effort.[15]

Need for Hearing

It is appropriate to dispense with a hearing when only procedural issues, such as the situs of a pending arbitration, are the subject of that arbitration.[16]

Representatives in Arbitration

Parties have the right to be represented by attorneys of their own choosing, despite a challenge based on vague contract language.[17] Moreover, if a conflict exists between two grievants who cannot be represented by a single attorney, each of them, as well as the union, may, with the consent of the parties, have separate representation in the separate arbitration of their cases, even though the bargaining agreement declares the union to be the sole collective bargaining representative.[18]

Privilege to Attend Hearing

Recently, in the public sector, arbitrators have recognized the "totality of the circumstances" in determining if a witness has a need or a right to attend the hearing. Where the entire record sustains proof of the issue, a witness in a sensitive case need not appear if appearing

---

[12]Consolidation Coal Co., 92 LA 813 (1989).
[13]Texas Utils. Elec. Co., 90 LA 625 (Allen, 1988).
[14]Southern Minn. Sugar Coop., 90 LA 243, 247 (1989). This holding is contrary to the general rule described in Chapter 7 of the Fourth Edition, subtopic entitled "Extent of Permissible Deviation from Prearbitral Discussion of Case," p. 234.
[15]Pittsburgh Press Club, 89 LA 826 (Stoltenberg, 1987).
[16]Highgate Pictures, 90 LA 485 (Gentile, 1988).
[17]Rustco Prods., 92 LA 976 (Cronin, 1989). See discussion in Chapter 7 of the Fourth Edition, subtopic entitled "Representatives in Arbitration," p. 241.
[18]General Mills, 92 LA 969 (Dworkin, 1989).

means the witness will suffer a humiliating cross-examination.[19] At the same time, an unnecessary party may be properly denied paid leave from his job to attend a hearing on an issue which speaks to an entire bargaining unit rather than to a specific employee.[20] Other current cases support the concept that nonattendance of a grieving party is not fatal to the hearing if the grievant is adequately and fairly represented by a union official.[21]

Limiting Attendance by Witnesses

Sequestering of witnesses, in appropriate circumstances, can be an effective method of highlighting fabrications and inaccuracies which might not be apparent where witnesses have had an opportunity to hear the evidence presented by other members of the group.[22]

Time, Place, and Notice of Hearing

When one of the parties refuses to cooperate in the selection of a date for the arbitration hearing, after the arbitrator has given the party ample opportunity to participate, it is incumbent upon the arbitrator to proceed without unnecessary delay to avoid the subversion of the arbitral process.[23]

At times the place of the hearing is itself the subject of arbitration when the language of the agreement is susceptible of conflicting interpretations.[24]

Default Awards in Ex Parte Proceedings

Default awards are available, where appropriate, in the public sector. Arbitrators do not hesitate to conduct ex parte hearings in the public sector when a party, which has been afforded ample and continuous notice of the grievance proceedings, fails to appear or to offer any reason for its failure to appear.[25] Such awards continue to be available in the private sector also.[26]

Most arbitrators take great pains to ensure that an absent party has received adequate notice of the scheduled hearing and endeavor to

---

[19]Veterans Admin. Medical Center, 87 LA 405 (Yarowsky, 1986).

[20]Social Security Admin., 87 LA 434 (Hoh, 1986).

[21]Texas Utils. Mining Co., 87 LA 815 (Allen, 1986); American Inks & Coatings Corp., 87 LA 691 (DiLauro, 1986).

[22]Northern States Power, 86 LA 1088 (Boyer, 1986).

[23]Shop 'N Save Warehouse, 86 LA 1098 (Cohen, 1986).

[24]Highgate Pictures, 90 LA 485 (Gentile, 1988) (both New York and Los Angeles were named as sites for the hearing).

[25]Dade County Pub. Health Trust, 86 LA 759 (Chandler, 1986); Oakland Univ., 86 LA 731 (Borland, 1986).

[26]Cross & Trecker, 85 LA 721 (Chalfie, 1985); Eastern Non-Ferrous Foundry, 82 LA 524 (DiLauro, 1984).

secure the attendance of the missing litigant.[27] Awards rendered in these circumstances set forth all the evidence adduced at the hearing in full detail to demonstrate that the arbitrator based the award on the evidence, and not solely on the default of one party.[28]

Court Enforcement of Default Awards

Where an arbitration panel entered a default judgment against an employer who had waited for several hours for the proceeding to commence, but had to leave for other business, and before leaving asked for the hearing to be rescheduled, a federal district court refused to enforce the award.[29] The court found that the panel had violated the due process rights of the employer, and that the bargaining agreement did not contain default procedures or provisions.[30]

Where a union attempts to withdraw a grievance from arbitration on a "non-precedent" and/or "without prejudice" basis, the company may rightfully object to such action and insist that the hearing proceed, with or without the participation of the union.[31]

Withdrawal of Cases From Arbitration

Contrary to the prevailing view, which, in accordance with the common law, permits nonbinding withdrawal prior to issuance of an award,[32] an arbitrator has held that an employee's withdrawal of a grievance after a second-step meeting was res judicata and prevented an examination of the same issue later in the arbitration of a new grievance.[33]

Continuances

The claim of surprise may be the good cause to obtain an offer or grant of a continuance, as was the case where an unforseen issue suddenly emerged.[34]

---

[27]Elsass, Inc., 92 LA 905 (Fullmer, 1989) (devoting substantial space to explaining the steps taken and the rationale for proceeding in this fashion).

[28]Ibid. See also Westlake, Inc., 90 LA 1129 (Armstrong, 1988); Dutko Wall Sys., 89 LA 1215 (Weisinger, 1987).

[29]Chicago Truck Drivers v. Denton Cartage Co., 648 F. Supp. 1009, 124 LRRM 2627 (N.D. Ill., 1986).

[30]Id. at 1011-1012.

[31]Guardian Indus., 86 LA 844 (Joseph, 1986).

[32]See Chapter 7 of the Fourth Edition, subtopic entitled "Withdrawal of Cases From Arbitration," p. 249.

[33]Hawks Nest Mining Co., 92 LA 414 (Volz, 1989).

[34]Consolidation Coal Co., 92 LA 813 (Seidman, 1989); Lyondell Petrochemical Co., 89 LA 95 (Caraway, 1987).

Split Hearings

Arbitrator's Express Retention of Jurisdiction

In one case, the arbitrator directed the parties to negotiate concerning monetary relief in a subcontracting dispute and retained jurisdiction in the event the issue could not be settled.[35]

Transcript of Hearing

Where an employer alone requested a transcript of the proceedings, the employer bore the full cost, even where the arbitrator asked for a courtesy copy and required that the copy be made available to the union if the transcript were to be the official record.[36]

Exhibits

Written statements of facts will not substitute for testimony of "live" witnesses who are under oath and subject to cross-examination, and whose demeanor can be viewed for purposes of credibility determinations.[37]

Oath by Arbitrator and Witnesses

The oath administered by an arbitrator and taken by a witness may influence an arbitrator's resolution of credibility issues.[38]

Settlements at Arbitration Stage

It has been suggested that mediation of grievances at arbitration hearings undermines lower steps of the grievance procedure and could create the appearance of impropriety if mediation fails and the case has to be adjudicated.[39]

---

[35]West Helena-Helena Sportswear Co., 91 LA 1411 (Nicholas, 1988).

[36]United States Dep't of Agric., 93 LA 920, 928-929 (Seidman, 1989); see also Nuturn Corp., 84 LA 1058, 1060 (Seidman, 1985) (employer bore full cost of transcript when union said it would be satisfied with its own tape recording of hearing).

[37]Kent State Univ., 91 LA 895, 899-900 (Curry, 1988).

[38]An arbitrator has credited the testimony of a grievant who testified in person and denied allegations under oath over written, unsworn statements. Kent State Univ., 91 LA 895, 903 (Curry, 1988).

[39]Smith Meter, Inc., 86 LA 1009 (Creo, 1986). Compare Lloyd W. Aubry Co., 91 LA 679 (Millious, 1988), where the arbitrator suggested that the parties make a second attempt to negotiate a settlement, since the Code of Professional Responsibility for Arbitrators recognizes that an arbitrator may undertake mediation, after arbitration has been invoked, if neither party objects, either at the request of a party or at the arbitrator's own suggestion, provided it can be determined that both parties are likely to be responsive.

Briefs

An arbitrator has held that a supplemental statement submitted by an employer after receipt of both parties' briefs may be considered in resolving a dispute over an affirmative action plan. The arbitrator reasoned that the employer's brief and supplemental statement addressed the issue of the appropriate remedy, and that the union was not prejudiced by the supplemental submission.[40]

Reopening the Hearing

A hearing may be reopened for good cause in order for the parties to explore newly discovered evidence. The elements of good cause are grounded in common sense:

1. The request to reopen the hearing must precede the arbitrator's final award.
2. The proffered evidence must not have been available with due diligence at the time of the hearing.
3. The proffered evidence must be pertinent.
4. The proffered evidence must be likely to affect the outcome.
5. Admission of the new evidence must not improperly prejudice the other party.[41]

Remedy Power and Its Use

Scope of Remedy Power

Current cases in the public sector reinforce the general rule that the remedy the arbitrator provides is restricted by limitations contained in the collective bargaining agreement and may be further delimited by statute, regulation, and court decisions.[42] However, the cases also reflect the discretion of the arbitrator to offer as the only remedy the appropriate interpretation of ambiguous contract language.[43] In addition, grievants in the public sector have failed to obtain a favorable remedy, which was otherwise appropriate under provisions of the contract, where they themselves have failed to act promptly and in good faith,[44] or where the employer has shown good

---

[40]District of Columbia Dep't of Fin. & Revenue, 91 LA 1, 3 (Hockenberry, 1988).

[41]See Westvaco, 91 LA 707 (Nolan, 1988) (hearing reopened because request was made before the award was issued; proffered evidence consisted of newspaper article published after the hearing was closed; article could affect decision and raised question concerning grievant's credibility).

[42]Cornelius v. Nutt, 105 S.Ct. 2882, 119 LRRM 2905 (1985); 5 C.F.R. § 550.801 et seq.; Internal Revenue Serv., 89 LA 59 (Gallagher, 1987); Veterans Admin., 88 LA 554 (Byars, 1986).

[43]See City of Cincinnati, 88 LA 1219 (Duda, 1987); Veterans Admin., 88 LA 554 (Byars, 1986); Social Security Admin., 87 LA 1096 (Avins., 1986).

[44]Los Angeles Community College, 87 LA 252 (Kaufman, 1986).

faith in the face of merely arguable contentions.[45] Arbitrators in public-sector cases have, where authorized by the agreement, required payment of hearing costs and attorney's fees, within boundaries of fairness to the prevailing party.[46]

An arbitrator denied a union punitive damages in a case where the employer kept retail stores open on New Year's Day in violation of the contract. The arbitrator noted that no provision for such damages was found in the contract and the violation of the agreement by this employer was the first of its kind.[47]

Should the Given Remedy Be Used?

Parties frequently frame the remedial question via the phrase, "If so, what shall the remedy be?" This broad remedial power should not be wielded to fashion a remedy and award which transcend the underlying grievance, or to permit the arbitrator to fashion his own brand of workplace justice. For instance, an arbitrator ordered a public employer to post a notice "that any verified infraction of the Attorney General's rules and regulations concerning prohibition of misuse of [information] system[s] for personal reason from the date of posting the notice, forward, is a discharge infraction which shall not be remitted for any reason of seniority or outstanding service record."[48] Expansive remedies undermine the collective bargaining process and may restrain arbitrators in future proceedings.

---

[45]Stark County Eng'r, 88 LA 497 (Kates, 1986).

[46]Hines Veterans Admin. Hosp., 85 LA 239 (Wolff, 1985); Chattanooga Gas Co., 83 LA 48 (Mullin, 1984); Department of Army, 82 LA 1133 (Schubert, 1984); U.S. Customs Serv., 81 LA 634 (Kaufman, 1983).

[47]Great A&P Tea Co., 88 LA 430 (Lipson, 1986). See also Silva Harvesting, 88 LA 413 (Pool, 1986); Pride Professional Servs., 88 LA 229 (Gallagher, 1986); Florida Power Corp., 87 LA 957 (Wahl, 1986).

[48]City of Sterling Heights, 89 LA 420, 426 (Keefe, 1987).

Chapter 8

Evidence

Strict Observance of Legal Rules of Evidence Usually Not Required

Arbitrators are permitted to examine the totality of evidence to ensure that it is free of the emotional involvement of the parties and to determine which version of conflicting testimony is more credible.[1]

Under the American Arbitration Association Voluntary Labor Arbitration Rules, Rule 28 provides that the arbitrator is the judge of the relevancy and materiality of the evidence offered and that conformity to legal rules of evidence shall not be necessary.[2] One arbitrator has interpreted Rule 28 to mean that arbitrators are empowered to judge the "relevancy and materiality" of the evidence only, and are not empowered to exclude items as incompetent, so that most evidence, including hearsay, is literally received unless it is of so little probative value that it can be eliminated without impairing proof of the issues. The arbitrator interpreted this rule as not empowering him to exclude hearsay as incompetent, but rather as empowering him to judge the "weight" of the evidence in his final decision. "Relevancy and materiality" include "weight," in that an arbitrator's "duty to resolve factual disputes necessarily implies that he has to 'weigh' the evidence."[3]

The evidence in arbitration is weighed by a "flexible arbitral application of formal rules." The evidence may be oral or written or

---

[1]Hughes Aircraft Co., 86 LA 1112, 1117 (Richman, 1986).

[2]American Arbitration Association Voluntary Labor Arbitration Rule 28 provides:
The parties may offer such evidence as they desire and shall produce such additional evidence as the arbitrator may deem necessary to an understanding and determination of the dispute. An arbitrator authorized by law to subpoena witnesses and documents may do so independently or upon the request of any party. The arbitrator shall be the judge of the relevance and materiality of the evidence offered and conformity to legal rules of evidence shall not be necessary. All evidence shall be taken in the presence of all of the arbitrators and all of the parties except where any of the parties is absent in default or has waived the right to be present.

[3]Lever Bros. Co., 82 LA 164, 167 (Stix, 1983).

both, but there is no instruction that formal rules of evidence need be applied.[4] It should be noted, however, that admissibility is limited to the evidence that existed at the time of the conflict. Changes in the status of the grievant after the conflict has occurred are outside the scope of what may be considered as relevant evidence.[5] However, evidence related to rehabilitation for alcoholism or drug addiction, postdischarge, may be admitted in order that the arbitrator may fashion an appropriate remedy.[6]

Liberal Admission of Evidence

Arbitrators frequently will not exclude certain evidence even where the objection to the material is based on a federal statute or on contract language stating that matters not raised in written grievance may not be raised later.[7]

Despite the policy of arbitrators to liberally admit evidence, arbitrators generally do not admit "contradictory counterproof," finding it collateral under Rule 403 of the Federal Rules of Evidence.[8] Arbitrators will allow great latitude in admitting circumstantial evidence as a logical inference that certain facts exist in circumstances in which direct evidence is lacking.[9] In fact, arbitral decisions have sometimes been reached on the basis of circumstantial evidence even after a suit for criminal charges has been dropped due to a lack of evidence.[10]

What Type of Evidence Should Be Used

In discharge or discipline cases, witness testimony, including the facts which led to the disciplinary action, comprises the most important evidence. Arbitrators have consistently ruled that burden of proof in such cases rests with the employer and that the arbitrator may determine the weight and relevancy of evidence to decide the contro-

---

[4]Republic Airlines, 83 LA 127, 129 (Seidman, 1984).

[5]Pacific Gas & Elec. Co., 88 LA 749 (Koven, 1986) (evidence of an employee's December 1984 arrest for drug possession was held not admissible at arbitration of his November 1984 discharge for refusing to take a drug test); Savannah Transit Auth., 86 LA 1277 (Williams, 1985) (grievant's testimony that she was no longer on medication was not considered in determining propriety of discharge for absenteeism, even though medication caused her chronic absences).

[6]Northwest Airlines, 89 LA 943 (Nicolau, 1984).

[7]Marine Corps Logistics Base, 87 LA 47 (Gentile, 1986). But see Adrian College, 89 LA 857 (Ellmann, 1987). A supervisor's diary was held to be not admissible at a hearing relating to an employee's discharge for poor performance because the employer refused to provide a copy to the grievant or the union prior to the hearing, and the public policy of the State of Michigan prohibits introduction in "judicial or quasi-judicial" proceedings of documents that are privately kept by administrative employees and are excluded from regular personnel files.

[8]Soule Steele Co., 85 LA 336, 342 (Richman, 1985).

[9]Ibid. St. Charles Grain Elevator Co., 84 LA 1129 (Fox, 1985); Wisconsin Dep't of Health & Social Servs., 84 LA 219 (Imes, 1985).

[10]Bethlehem Steel Corp., 81 LA 268 (Sharnoff, 1983). Based on circumstantial evidence, the employer properly dismissed an employee for the theft of a co-employee's pickup truck even though the criminal charges were dropped due to a lack of evidence.

versy.[11] However, the current status of an employee is not material in determining just cause for disciplinary action by an employer stemming from a past conflict.[12]

Where employees have been discharged or severely disciplined on alcohol or drug charges, the employer must produce verifiable evidence. If an employee has been tested, the employer must produce documentation of confirmed test results. If the employer refuses to give an employee a blood test, despite the employee's request for one, the employer may not rely on observations of supervisory personnel for evidence.[13] If a private investigator, especially hired by the employer, or the employee's supervisor observes or suspects alcohol or drug use, the contraband and/or container must be confiscated and produced as evidence.[14] An arbitrator did not require the actual contraband where the investigator produced as corroborating evidence daily reports of the drug activity made and filed with the investigative agency.[15]

"New" Evidence at Arbitration Hearing

In cases where an employer furnished recently acquired evidence at the arbitration hearing, acceptable "new" evidence was distinguished from "surprise" evidence that prejudiced the union. Exhibits that were substantive, relevant, and easily understood were admitted into evidence regardless of their surprise value.[16]

Requiring the Production of Evidence

Use of Subpoenas

The arbitrator may refuse to issue a subpoena requiring an employer to produce a written report completed by a supervisor under the theory that such documents are similar to an attorney's "work product" and are protected, absent contract language to the contrary.[17]

---

[11]Hilton Int'l Co. v. Union de Trabajadores de la Industria Gastronomica de P.R. Local 610, 600 F. Supp. 1446, 119 LRRM 2011 (D.P.R., 1985).
[12]Savannah Transit Auth., 86 LA 1277, 1280 (Williams, 1985).
[13]Durion Co., 85 LA 1127, 1129-1130 (Coyne, 1985).
[14]Air Treads of Atlanta, 83 LA 1323 (Yancey, 1984); U.S. Borax & Chem. Corp., 84 LA 32 (Richman, 1984).
[15]Georgia Pacific, 85 LA 542 (King, 1985). See also Consumer Plastics Corp., 88 LA 208 (Garnholz, 1987).
[16]Wells Aluminum Corp., 86 LA 983 (Wies, 1986); Lever Bros. Co., 82 LA 164 (Stix, 1983).
[17]P.P.G. Indus., 90 LA 479, 481 (Sedwick, 1987).

The union's refusal to comply with an arbitrator's subpoena allowed an arbitrator to draw adverse inferences about the union's case, but it did not justify granting the employer's motion to dismiss.[18]

Evidence Requested by Arbitrator

Arbitrators may request that pertinent evidence be produced. In one case, however, Arbitrator Marshall J. Seidman stated it was beyond his authority to require that a transcription of the hearing be provided to the parties at a shared expense since the collective bargaining agreement between the parties did not specifically require it.[19]

Significance of Failure to Provide Evidence

A party's failure to use witnesses who should be knowledgeable creates an inference against that party. Where an employer failed to have the single accusing witness appear, the arbitrator expressed concern because of the accuser's absence and found insufficient evidence to support the employee's discharge.[20] Also, an arbitrator may note the "well-established" rule that the failure to call a witness who is available to a party gives rise to a presumption that the witness's testimony would be adverse to the position of the party having the ability to call that witness.[21]

In cases where an employee is discharged for substance abuse, sufficient documentation of employee conduct is mandatory to meet the employer's burden of proof, whether it be confirmed medical tests or investigative reports, or actual confiscated contraband. Arbitrators will sustain grievances where the employer fails to provide verifiable evidence. Arbitrator Thomas J. Coyne stated that "to discharge a person for suspected but unconfirmed intoxication is to discharge unjustly."[22] Arbitrator Dorothy Cowser Yancey wrote: "[A]rbitrators do not make decisions based on 'feelings' and 'intuitions.' One man's word is not enough to convince this arbitrator that another man is lying and guilty of committing a rule violation."[23] Another arbitrator sustained a grievance arising out of a warning for alleged neglect of duty and noted the absence of eyewitness testimony and the reliance on circumstantial evidence which was found not to be compelling.[24]

---

[18]Niemand Indus., 88-1 ARB ¶ 8070, 3336-3337 (Sergent, 1987). See generally Hill & Sinicropi, Evidence in Arbitration, 2d ed., 285-290 (BNA Books, 1987); Grenig & Estes, Labor Arbitration Advocacy, 36 (Butterworth, 1989); Bornstein & Gosline, Labor and Employment Arbitration, § 7.01-§ 7.05 (Matthew Bender, 1989).

[19]Nuturn Corp., 84 LA 1058, 1060 (1985). See generally Hill & Sinicropi, Evidence in Arbitration, 2d ed., 95-98 (BNA Books, 1987).

[20]Veterans Admin. Medical Center, 82 LA 25, 27 (Dallas, 1984); St. Charles Grain Elevator Co., 84 LA 1129, 1132 (Fox, 1985).

[21]Southern Cal. Permanente Medical Group, 92 LA 41, 45 (Richman, 1989).

[22]Durion Co., 85 LA 1127, 1129 (1985) (alcohol).

[23]Air Treads of Atlanta, Inc., 83 LA 1323, 1327 (1984) (alcohol). Also see U.S. Borax & Chem. Corp., 84 LA 32, 35 (Richman, 1984) (drugs).

[24]Jaite Packaging Co., 90 LA 1061, 1064 (Fullmer, 1988).

Preservation of Evidence

Unconfirmed suspicion of alcohol or drug use is not grounds for discharge. If an employee is observed and suspected of an alcohol or drug violation, the contraband and/or container must be confiscated and preserved as evidence. Failure by employers to preserve items in question, for inspection and use as corroborative evidence, has led to the reinstatement of the grievant.[25]

Use of Adverse Witnesses

A common limitation on the right to call witnesses from the other side concerns an attempt by management to call the grievant as its first witness in discharge or disciplinary actions.[26]

An arbitrator who permits this practice is, in essence, allowing management to circumvent the long-established rule that the employer must present its case first in matters involving discipline and discharge. The facts surrounding the employer's decision to discipline or discharge are within the employer's knowledge, and, considering the employer's advantage of access to personnel records and of initial disciplinary power, it is only equitable for the employer to present his entire case before the grievant is required to testify. This procedure is not designed to exempt the grievant from testifying, but rather is an attempt to ensure a fair hearing. Should the union attempt to close its case without calling the grievant, the arbitrator does have the authority to require the grievant's testimony unless there are special circumstances that might involve criminal self-incrimination, trade secrets, or classified defense matters involving the grievant. Only in the rare cases in which the arbitrator requires the union to testify first should grievant's testimony precede management's testimony.[27]

Failure of Grievant to Testify

Failure of a grievant to testify, when faced with a forgery charge, allowed an arbitrator to draw the inference that the grievant had no

---

[25]Air Treads of Atlanta, Inc., 83 LA 1323 (Yancey, 1984) (suspected beer cans); U.S. Borax & Chem. Corp., 84 LA 32 (Richman, 1984) (marijuana).

[26]Rohm & Haas, 91 LA 339, 343 (McDermott, 1988) (arbitrator refused to allow the grievant to be called as the employer's first witness in a hearing regarding a discharge for excessive absenteeism since the employer had the burden of presenting its case and would have ample opportunity to cross-examine the grievant); City of San Antonio, 90 LA 159, 162 (Williams, 1987) (arbitrator required the employer to make a *prima facie* case regarding its disciplinary charges before allowing it to call the grievant as a witness and found that the criminal law restrictions against self-incrimination do not apply in labor arbitration); also, see generally Bornstein & Gosline, Labor and Employment Arbitration, § 4.03 [1] [a] [i] [B] (Matthew Bender, 1989); Grenig & Estes, Labor Arbitration Advocacy, 85 (Butterworth, 1989); Hill & Sinicropi, Evidence in Arbitration, 2d ed., 273-278 (BNA Books, 1987); Levin & Grody, Witnesses in Arbitration, 123-125 (BNA Books, 1987); "Procedural Rulings During the Hearing," Proceedings of the 35th Annual Meeting of NAA, 138 (BNA Books, 1983).

[27]See "The Role of the Arbitrator in Ensuring a Fair Hearing," Proceedings of the 35th Annual Meeting of NAA, 30 (BNA Books, 1983).

adequate explanation of his conduct.[28] When a grievant failed to take the stand to refute any of the charges in a drug use related hearing the arbitrator held that the grievant's inaction weighed against him.[29]

The Lie Detector

Results of lie detector tests continue to be criticized because of the subjective dependency of the operator's skill, the subjective dependency on a person's emotional state, and the lack of substantive authority supporting the accuracy of test results.[30]

Arbitrators have consistently reaffirmed that employers cannot take disciplinary action against employees should the employees refuse to submit to a lie detector test.[31] Moreover, a grievant can refuse to take a lie detector test, and this refusal is inadmissible as a presumption of guilt.[32] And, an employee is "perfectly free" to terminate a polygraph test without prejudice to himself, and such termination does not establish his guilt.[33]

A lie detector should not be used to supplant courts and arbitrators as finders of fact.[34] If lie detector evidence is admitted, the grievant's representative should be given an opportunity to cross-examine the accuser, as well as the polygraph operator.[35]

Arbitrators have declined to give any weight to lie detector test results when the employer has relied solely on such tests in discharging an employee.[36] However, Arbitrator Seymour X. Alsher noted

---

[28]Republic Airlines, 83 LA 127, 131 (Seidman, 1984).

[29]Marathon Petroleum Co., 89 LA 716, 720, 723 (Grimes, 1987). See generally Bornstein & Gosline, Labor and Employment Arbitration, § 7.01-§ 7.05 (Matthew Bender, 1989); Estes & Grenig, Labor Arbitration Advocacy, 83-84 (Butterworth, 1989); Hill & Sinicropi, Evidence in Arbitration, 2d ed., 261-268 (BNA Books, 1987).

[30]A.R.A Mfg. Co., 87 LA 182 (Woolf, 1986). The arbitrator gave no weight to a polygraph examination of an employee who allegedly observed the grievant take a compressor because the polygraph examiner failed to submit evidence of required testing experience and had not sworn to the accuracy of the report. Further, the examiner's report did not contain sufficient information for the determination of his qualifications as an expert witness and the arbitrator had no information on the sequence or clarity of the examiner's questions or the raw data the examiner evaluated. Also, see generally Bornstein & Gosline, Labor and Employment Arbitration, § 5.11 [4] (Matthew Bender, 1989); Grenig & Estes, Labor Arbitration Advocacy, 82-83 (Butterworth, 1989); Hill & Sinicropi, Evidence in Arbitration, 2d ed., 199-228 (BNA Books, 1987); "Modern Shamanism and Other Folderol—The Search for Certainty," Proceedings of the 39th Annual Meeting of NAA, 187 (BNA Books, 1987).

[31]Bake Rite Rolls, 90 LA 1133, 1136 (DiLauro, 1988); Texas City Refining, 89 LA 1159, 1164 (Milentz, 1987); Glen Manor Home for the Jewish Aged, 81 LA 1178 (Katz, 1983). But see City of Miami, 92 LA 175, 180 (Abrams, 1989) (arbitrator held that the refusal of an employee, reasonably suspected of assault and robbery, to take the polygraph test was a valid reason for discharge since the test is a legitimate investigative tool). See also Orthodox Jewish Home for the Aged, 91 LA 810, 815, 816 (Sergent, 1988). However, in National Tea Co., 90 LA 773, 775 (Baroni, 1988) the arbitrator found that the employee's refusal to take the polygraph test justified the employer's transfer of the employee to another department since the transfer was based on legitimate business reasons flowing from loss of confidence in the employee because of his refusal.

[32]International Minerals & Chem. Corp., 83 LA 593 (Kulkis, 1984).

[33]Mississippi Power Co., 90 LA 220, 222 (Jewett, 1987).

[34]International Minerals & Chem. Corp., 83 LA 593 (Kulkis, 1984).

[35]Consumer Plastics Corp., 88 LA 208 (Garnholz, 1987). The arbitrator did not give any weight to a lie detector test taken by an undercover agent whose testimony concerning the employee's possession of marijuana on company property provided the sole basis of the employee's discharge and where the union was given no opportunity to question the agent.

[36]Avis Rent A Car Sys., 85 LA 435, 439 (1985).

that "[a]rbitrators are not totally inhospitable to the receipt, consideration and evaluation of evidence obtained by the use of the polygraph."[37]

Arbitrators accept lie detector results only for limited purposes, noting that "such evidence has not attained scientific acceptance as a reliable and accurate means of ascertaining truth or deception."[38] Test results were accepted as corroborative of the truthful demeanor of an already credible undercover agent testifying to firsthand observations where the agent had filed daily reports with the investigative agency.[39] Arbitrators do require evidence of the polygraph test examiner's experience and the accuracy of the test reports themselves.[40] The polygraph examiner and his record of the test should be available for cross-examination at the hearing.[41]

An employer is not required to administer a lie detector test, upon request by the grievant, to assist in proving the grievant's innocence. Lie detector test results are suspect and generally inadmissible in labor arbitration. It is not an error for the employer to refuse such corroborative evidence.[42]

Evidence Obtained by Allegedly Improper Methods

Arbitrators continue to admit evidence obtained through unconsented searches when the employer's tactics are not egregious. In one case, a supervisor's search of an employee's lunch box in the employee's tool locker was permitted, where the tool locker was open to everyone in the shop and the supervisor had earlier observed the employee in a limited-access storeroom with parts not required for the equipment he was repairing. The arbitrator found that the supervisor's search was supported by reasonable cause and was not a dramatic intrusion on the employee's privacy.[43] In another case, marijuana found in the zippered compartment of a wallet which the grievant had lost was admitted into evidence notwithstanding the contention that the finder could have identified the owner of the wallet from the cards and papers in the open portion of the wallet. The arbitrator noted that the motive of the finder in examining the wallet

---

[37] Id. at 439.

[38] Reynolds Metals Co., 85 LA 1046, 1052 (Taylor, 1985).

[39] Georgia Pacific, 85 LA 542 (King, 1985); Consumer Plastics Corp., 88 LA 208 (Garnholz, 1987).

[40] A.R.A. Mfg. Co., 87 LA 182, 186-187 (Woolf, 1986).

[41] Houston Lighting & Power Co., 87 LA 478 (Howell, 1986).

[42] Texas City Refining, 89 LA 1159 (Milentz, 1987); Immigration & Naturalization Serv., 89 LA 1252, 1256 (Baroni, 1987). The results of grievant's polygraph test were given no weight in the hearing on his disciplinary suspension. The test was ordered by the grievant, it was based on limited information provided by the grievant, and it consisted of questions that reflected data that he considered important.

[43] American Welding & Mfg. Co., 89 LA 247, 252 (Dworkin, 1987).

was not prosecution but an attempt to provide positive identification.[44]

Results of blood and urine tests have been admitted into evidence to prove drug usage where the grievants signed an authorization for the tests, even though grievants were told that if they refused to submit blood and urine samples, they would be suspected of being under the influence of a controlled substance and required to prove otherwise.[45]

Confessions

Confessions of employees implicating another employee are viewed with skepticism when used against the implicated employee.[46]

Testimony by Persons From Outside

Opinion Evidence by Expert Witnesses

Arbitrators have permitted "expert" testimony from handwriting experts,[47] a toxicologist,[48] a psychologist/social worker,[49] and polygraph operators.[50]

---

[44]Rust Eng'g Co., 85 LA 407, 410 (Whyte, 1985). In Wayne State Univ., 87 LA 953 (Lipson, 1986), evidence of drugs, which was excluded by the court in criminal proceedings against the grievant, were admitted in his arbitration proceeding, and his discharge was upheld. But cf. Kerr-McGee Chem. Corp., 90 LA 55, 60 (Levin, 1987) (evidence of drug paraphernalia taken from grievant's van in company parking lot excluded from evidence where company did not have reasonable grounds to search the vehicle).

[45]Boone Energy, 85 LA 233, 236 (O'Connell, 1985). See also Roadway Express, 87 LA 224 (Cooper, 1986) (under contract providing for drug and alcohol testing of employees, employer was allowed to demand that an employee undergo a test whenever a responsible supervisor had an honest and reasonable suspicion that the employee might be under the influence of alcohol or drugs).

[46]Rohr Indus., 93 LA 145, 157-158 (Goulet, 1989).

[47]Peninsular Steel Co., 88 LA 391 (Ipavec, 1986); Schlage Lock Co., 88 LA 75, 76-77 (Wyman, 1986).

[48]Trailways, 88 LA 1073, 1076 (Goodman, 1987).

[49]King Soopers, Inc., 86 LA 254, 260 (Sass, 1985).

[50]Ohio State Reformatory, 88 LA 1019, 1027 (Duda, 1987). For a full discussion of the admissibility of testimony regarding polygraph tests, see topic entitled "The Lie Detector," supra.

Chapter 9

Standards for Interpreting Contract Language

Ambiguity

"The sources of contract interpretation include the language of the contract and, to the extent it is ambiguous, bargaining history and past practice."[1] An arbitrator may find contract language ambiguous even though both parties have asserted that it is clear and unambiguous.[2] If the contract language relied upon by a grievant is ambiguous and each party has submitted equally convincing external evidence, the grievant has not sustained his burden of proof.[3]

---

[1]Downington School Dist., 88 LA 59, 61 (Zirkel, 1986). See also Mentor Bd. of Educ., 89 LA 292, 294 (Sharpe, 1987); Sacramento School Dist., 88 LA 113, 116 (Wilcox, 1986); Pittsburgh Brewing Co., 88 LA 95, 96 (Duff, 1986).

[2]Independent School Dist. No. 47, 86 LA 97 (Gallagher, 1985). See United Grocers, 92 LA 566, 569 (Gangle, 1989), citing Nolan, Labor Arbitration Law and Practice, 163 (1979), where Arbitrator Gangle restated a standard for determining when an ambiguity exists:

> The test most often cited is that there is no ambiguity if the contract is so clear on the issue that the intentions of the parties can be determined using no other guide than the contract itself. This test borders on a tautology, however, for it comes perilously close to a statement that language is clear and unambiguous if it is clear on its face. Perhaps a better way of putting it would be to ask if a single, obvious and reasonable meaning appears from a reading of the language in the context of the rest of the contract. If so, that meaning is to be applied.

See also Klein Tools, 90 LA 1150, 1153 (Poindexter, 1988) (contract is not ambiguous if one party negligently uses a term which does not express the meaning intended by that party, or if a party could have received a clarification of the term during negotiations).

However, in Circle Steel Corp., 85 LA 738, 739 (Stix, 1984), the arbitrator stated that "whether a contract is ambiguous is not to be determined simply from the face of the contract (as other authorities hold), but only after taking into consideration the circumstances existing at the time the contract was adopted and the practice of the parties in applying it." The arbitrator found the intent of the parties contrary to the express language of the contract and rendered a decision based on his perception of their intent.

[3]Rockwell Int'l Corp., 82 LA 42, 45 (Feldman, 1984) ("[W]here the evidence is in equipoise and where there is no clear and unambiguous language in the contract to guide the decision making involved and where prior arbitral authority does not contain any common predicate or guidelines for the findings indicated therein, the grievance must fail for lack of proof—there being no probative evidence in the file to sustain the protest as filed."). See also GTE Prods. Corp., 85 LA 754 (Millious, 1985) (lack of contract provision expressly including or excluding layoff time from being a part of continuous service allows the company to make the determination as a managerial right).

"Legislation" Versus "Interpretation"

Arbitrators continue to recognize and apply the U.S. Supreme Court's *Enterprise Wheel*[4] doctrine:

> [A]n arbitrator is confined to interpretation and application of the collective bargaining agreement; he does not sit to dispense his own brand of industrial justice. He may of course look for guidance from many sources, yet his award is legitimate only so long as it draws its essence from the collective bargaining agreement. When the arbitrator's words manifest an infidelity to this obligation, courts have no choice but to refuse enforcement of the award.[5]

If the arbitrator's award does not "draw its essence" from the collective bargaining agreement, it constitutes legislation rather than interpretation and will not be enforced by the courts.[6]

On the other hand, one commentator has suggested that it is not only expected that something of the arbitrator's personality will "creep into his decision," but that it is quite necessary.[7] Advocating the exercise of judgment by arbitrators, Sylvester Garrett points to what he views as the "inescapable truth":

> [T]he ultimate responsibility of an arbitrator in the interpretive process is to rely on his or her background of experience or expertise in the collective bargaining process, with due regard to the relationship of the given parties and their presentations so as to provide as practical and realistic an interpretation as is possible under the given agreement.[8]

Rejecting what he deemed the "myths" of contract interpretation, Arbitrator Garrett quoted Shakespeare in lending advice to future arbitrators in this regard: "And this above all, to thine own self be true and it must follow as the night the day that thou canst not then be false to any man."[9]

While these views might suggest that modern arbitrators should play a more active role, perhaps even to the point of "legislating" just a bit, the arbitral awards indicate that most arbitrators view their authority as limited. Thus, Arbitrator Samuel Chalfie defined the limits of arbitral authority as follows:

---

[4]Steelworkers v. Enterprise Wheel & Car Corp., 80 S.Ct. 1358, 46 LRRM 2423 (1960).

[5]80 S.Ct. at 1361.

[6]The *Enterprise Wheel* doctrine has been recognized as limiting the arbitrator's authority in American Petrofina Co. of Texas, 92 LA 578, 583 (Dunn, 1989); U.S. Dep't of Labor, 92 LA 477, 482 (Grossman, 1989); Cleveland Twist Drill Co., 92 LA 105, 108 (Strasshofer, 1989); Geauga Co., 92 LA 54, 59 (Fullmer, 1988); Checker Motors Co., 91 LA 1198, 1201 (Lipson, 1988); Harvard Indus., 91 LA 849, 855 (Ellmann, 1988); Rolling Acres Care Center, 91 LA 795, 799 (Dworkin, 1988); Arizona Bank, 91 LA 772, 774 (Fine, 1988); Polysar, Inc., 91 LA 482, 484 (Strasshofer, 1988); Synergy Gas Co., 91 LA 77, 91 (Simon, 1987); TPC Liquidation, Inc., 88 LA 696, 699 (Lumbley, 1987); Schuylkill Valley School Dist., 87 LA 1190, 1191 (Zirkel, 1986); Airco Carbon, 86 LA 6, 9 (Dworkin, 1986); Lithonia Lighting Co., 85 LA 627, 629 (Volz, 1985); and May Dep't Stores, 84 LA 53, 55-56 (Morgan, 1985).

[7]Garrett, "The Interpretive Process: Myths and Reality," Proceedings of the 38th Annual Meeting of NAA, 121 (BNA Books, 1986).

[8]Id. at 143.

[9]Id. at 148 (quoting from Hamlet, Act I, Scene iii).

[The arbitrator's] function is not to rewrite that Agreement and certainly it is not to suggest, imply nor to inform the Parties of what changes should be effected, renegotiated or changed even if his sense of justice and fairness so dictate, or even if he believes the Agreement contains inequities. Nor can the Arbitrator allow the economic consequences of an Award [to] influence him in his ultimate decision. The Arbitrator's Award * * * must derive its essence from the Agreement, and * * * tell the Parties what they can or cannot do inside of that Agreement.[10]

Intent of the Parties

Arbitrators seek to interpret collective agreements to reflect the intent of the parties.[11] They determine the intent of the parties from various sources, including the express language of the agreement, statements made at precontract negotiations, bargaining history, and past practice.[12] "Constructions favoring the purpose of the provision are to be favored over constructions which tend to conflict with the purpose of the provision."[13]

The primacy of the rule regarding the effectuation of the parties' intent is evident when compared with other rules of construction.[14] In one case, for example, Arbitrator George Van Pelt acknowledged that "the clear language of the Hours provision of the contract, if taken by itself without relation to any of the facts, would indicate that it was the

---

[10]Lorillard, 87 LA 507, 512 (1986). See Sherwin-Williams Co., 92 LA 464, 470 (Allen, 1989) (arbitrator refused to "fill gaps" and remanded issue to negotiation, where there was no "meeting of minds," no applicable past practice, and no dictionary definition of ambiguous term); Pollock Co., 87 LA 325, 335 (Oberdank, 1986); Associated Grocers, Biard Div., 86 LA 895, 903 (Weizenbaum, 1985); RRS, Inc., 86 LA 664, 666 (Redel, 1985); Goodyear Aerospace Corp., 86 LA 584, 586 (Fullmer, 1985); Brooklyn Acres Mutual Homes, 84 LA 952, 955 (Abrams, 1985).

[11]See, e.g., The News-Sun, 92 LA 713, 715 (Heinsz, 1989); Spokane School Dist. No. 81, 92 LA 333, 335 (Smith, 1989); Bridge Terminal Transp., 92 LA 192, 195 (Gentile, 1988); Brutoco Eng'g Constr., 92 LA 33, 36 (Ross, 1988); Alpha Beta Stores, 91 LA 888, 893 (Richman, 1988); City of Davenport, 91 LA 855, 858 (Hoh, 1988); Lockheed Space Operations Co., 91 LA 457, 462 (Richard, 1988); Container Corp. of Am., 91 LA 329, 332 (Rains, 1988); Montana Power Co., 90 LA 932, 934 (Corbett, 1987); Allied Plant Maintenance Co., 88 LA 963, 965-966 (Bankston, 1987); Silver Lake Bd. of Educ., 88 LA 885, 888 (Madden, 1986); Pabst Brewing Co., 88 LA 656, 660 (Wyman, 1987); Magic Chef, 84 LA 15, 17 (Craver, 1984) (parties did not intend that all employees who handled fiberglass insulation be included in a certain job classification). For cases where arbitrators looked to the intent behind contract provisions in dispute in order to resolve the grievance before them, see Armour Food Co., 85 LA 640 (Thornell, 1985); Jacksonville Shipyard, 82 LA 90 (Galambos, 1983).

[12]See, e.g., Atlanta Wire Works, 93 LA 537, 540 (Williams, 1989); Bard Mfg. Co., 92 LA 616, 619 (Daniel, 1989); Lithonia Lighting, 89 LA 781, 783 (Chandler, 1987); Tiger Maintenance Corp., 89 LA 276, 279 (Hockenberry, 1987); E.M. Smith & Co., 88 LA 1124, 1127 (Dworkin, 1987); Southwestern Elec. Power Co., 87 LA 9, 13 (Williams, 1986) (determining intent of parties from contract language, negotiations, and past practice); Los Angeles Community College Dist., 85 LA 988, 990 (Christopher, 1985) (determining intent of parties from contract language, position memoranda issued by employer, and past practice); Cincinnati Enquirer, 83 LA 567, 570 (Modjeska, 1984) (determining intent of parties from contract language and conduct of parties in processing grievance).

[13]Louisiana-Pac. Corp., 86 LA 301, 304 (Michelstetter, 1986) (purpose determined from evidence of past practice and bargaining history). In Associated Fur Mfg., 85 LA 810, 811 (1985), Arbitrator Jay Kramer stated that "[a] collective bargaining agreement is not a painting in still life. It is a document which tries to portray a living-together relationship of two parties who are interested in 'mutual survival.'" In that context, Arbitrator Kramer commented upon the interpretation urged by the union as follows: "[It would] put a wholly unnatural premium upon excessive technicality and * * * ignore the manifest intent of the [parties]."

[14]Maple Heights Bd. of Educ., 86 LA 338 (1985).

intention of the negotiators * * * that the secretaries would be paid for lunch break * * *."[15] However, despite the clear and unambiguous language, Arbitrator Van Pelt felt it necessary to "look further behind the language to determine the true intent of the parties."[16] In light of the undisputed evidence that there was no agreement with respect to this issue, coupled with the fact that secretaries had never been paid for lunch despite such language in the contract, Arbitrator Van Pelt concluded that "it was the intent of the parties that at no time would the lunch period be included."[17]

Similarly, Arbitrator William Stix fashioned a remedy by seeking to enforce the intent of the parties despite the clear language of the contract.[18] Focusing on the parties' willingness to use common sense, Arbitrator Stix looked to the intent of the language in controversy. Finding that the clear intent was "to reward an employee who actually works three months without absence or tardiness,"[19] he interpreted the contract to mean that, in each three-month period during which perfect attendance was achieved by attendance on 62 successive scheduled working days, a "bonus" day would be earned, despite explicit reference in the contract to "four three-month periods."[20] Arbitrator Stix found such reference to be "merely administrative and not central to the intent of the parties."[21]

Language Which Is Clear and Unambiguous

As stated in the main text, "[i]f the language of an agreement is clear and unequivocal, an arbitrator generally will not give it a meaning other than that expressed."[22] Arbitrators continue to recognize that:

> Past practice, no matter how well established that practice may be, cannot alter the terms of a contract whose clear and unambiguous terms

---

[15] Id. at 340.

[16] Ibid. See Pennsylvania Bureau of Police & Safety, 87 LA 947, 949 (Hogler, 1986) (rejecting union's position that contract was clear and unambiguous and permitted no exception; although mandatory in one respect, qualified in another; therefore, subject to interpretation so as to ascertain meanings of words).

[17] Maple Heights Bd. of Educ., 86 LA 338, 342 (1985).

[18] Circle Steel Corp., 85 LA 738 (1984).

[19] Id. at 740. See also Hueblein Wines, 93 LA 400, 406 (Randall, 1988); Retail Mkts. Co., 92 LA 1234, 1237 (Klein, 1989); Stroh Brewery Co., 92 LA 930, 932 (Berquist, 1989); City of Melbourne, 91 LA 1210, 1211 (Baroni, 1988); Alpha Beta Stores, 91 LA 888, 893 (Richman, 1988); Jefferson Schools, 91 LA 18, 20 (Daniel, 1988); Southern Cal. Edison, 90 LA 5, 7 (Castrey, 1987); Interbake Foods, 89 LA 1118, 1120 (Keefe, 1987); Warner Press, 89 LA 577, 579 (Brunner, 1987); Potlach Corp., 88 LA 1184, 1186 (Corbett, 1987); School Dist. No. 303, 88 LA 1159, 1162 (Goldstein, 1987); Inland Empire Paper Co., 88 LA 1096, 1102 (Levak, 1987); Racine Police Dep't, 88 LA 1038, 1043 (Baron, 1987); Allied Plant Maintenance Co., 88 LA 963, 966 (Bankston, 1987); Primeline Indus., 88 LA 700, 702 (Morgan, 1986).

[20] Circle Steel Corp., 85 LA at 740.

[21] Ibid.

[22] See Chapter 9 of the Fourth Edition, p. 348.

> establish what amounts to negotiated mutual promises by the parties to a contract.[23]
>
> [T]he fact that disputed language is subject to more than one interpretation does not mean that said language is, therefore, unclear.[24]

If the parties' collective agreement clearly and unambiguously describes employee transgressions for which discharge is the negotiated penalty, the arbitrator cannot consider whether those transgressions constitute "just cause" for discharge.[25] Arbitral opinions are legion in which clear and unambiguous contract language is credited by the arbitrator as being dispositive of an issue.[26]

An exception to this rule is in the occurrence of a mutual mistake. "A mutual mistake exists when both parties sign off contract language which does not correspond with their actual agreement. In this limited circumstance, an arbitrator may reform the contract to reflect the true intent of the parties."[27] In order to affect the clear language of the collective bargaining agreement, however, the mistake must be *mutual*. A unilateral mistake by one party does not provide a sufficient basis for contract reformation.[28]

---

[23]Koehring S. Plant, 82 LA 193, 196 (Alsher, 1984) (arbitrator found contract language unclear, justifying consideration of past practice). See Alameda Unified School Dist., 91 LA 60, 62 (Wilcox, 1988); Artichoke Growers Packing Co., 90 LA 120, 122 (Pool, 1987); Lithonia Lighting, 89 LA 781, 783 (Chandler, 1987); Kentucky Center, 89 LA 344, 348 (Volz, 1987); Mentor Bd. of Educ., 89 LA 292, 294 (Sharpe, 1987); Tiger Maintenance Corp., 89 LA 276, 278 (Hockenberry, 1987); Southern Ind. Gas & Elec. Co., 87 LA 1187, 1188 (Kilroy, 1986); Del Monte Corp., 86 LA 134 (Denson, 1985); Bootz Plumbing Fixtures, 84 LA 18 (Seinsheimer, 1984). But see the following cases where the arbitrator considered past practice despite the presence of clear contract language: Woodhaven School Dist., 86 LA 215, 216 (Daniel, 1986); Rice Memorial Hosp., 84 LA 537, 541 (Boyer, 1985).

[24]Sonoma-Marin Publishing Co., 83 LA 512, 516 (Griffin, 1984). See CFS Continental-Los Angeles, 83 LA 458, 461 (Sabo, 1984) ("[T]he clear meaning and language of the Contract is subject to enforcement even though the results are harsh and may be contrary to the general expectations of one of the Parties.").

[25]Cases applying this premise include Consumer Plastics Corp., 88 LA 208 (Garnholz, 1987); Rockwell Int'l Corp., 84 LA 496 (Feldman, 1985); Kimberly-Clark Corp., 82 LA 1090 (Keenan, 1984).

[26]For cases in which clear and unambiguous contract language was determinative, see General Tel. Co. of Sw., 86 LA 293, 295 (Ipavec, 1985); Champion Int'l Corp., 85 LA 877, 880 (Allen, 1985); Oak Grove School Dist., 85 LA 653, 655 (Concepcion, 1985); Florida Power Corp., 85 LA 619, 622 (Flannagan, 1985); Boogaart Supply Co., 84 LA 27, 30 (Fogelberg, 1984); Disneyland Hotel, 83 LA 685, 688 (Weiss, 1984); Nekoosa Corp., 83 LA 676, 679-680 (Flaten, 1984); Red Owl Stores, 83 LA 652, 656 (Reynolds, 1984); Western Mich. Univ., 82 LA 93, 97 (Kahn, 1984). See Motts, Inc., 87 LA 306, 308 (Eyraud, 1986) (citing Clean Coverall Supply Co., 47 LA 272, 277 (Witney, 1966)); Armstrong Rubber Co., 87 LA 147, 149 (Bankston, 1986) (quoting How Arbitration Works, 4th ed., p. 352); City of Taylor, 84 LA 522, 524 (McDonald, 1985) (quoting Arbitrator Witney in Clean Coverall Supply Co., above). In Michigan Dep't of Social Servs., 82 LA 114, 116 (Fieger, 1983), the arbitrator expounded upon the importance of this aspect of the rule, writing, "Not only is it axiomatic that the clear, unambiguous language of the agreement must be honored, but here the contract in exact terms forbids the arbitrator from ignoring 'in any way,' the specific provisions of the contract nor giving, to either party, rights which were not 'obtained in a negotiating process' * * *. Such restriction goes far beyond the simple statement that the arbitrator is bound by the language of the contract." See also Pittsburg & Midway Coal Mining Co., 87 LA 1107, 1108 (Feldman, 1986); Diamond Crystal Salt Co., 87 LA 427, 434 (Keefe, 1986); Pollock Co., 87 LA 325, 332 (Oberdank, 1986); Kroger Co., 86 LA 357, 365 (Milentz, 1986); Owens-Ill. Inc., 86 LA 354, 357 (Darrow, 1985); BASF Wyandotte Corp., 84 LA 1055, 1057 (Caraway, 1985); Arco Pipe Line Co., 84 LA 907, 909 (Nicholas, 1985); Town of Davie, 83 LA 1153, 1157 (Kanzer, 1984); Aeronca Inc., 82 LA 144, 146 (Finan, undated).

[27]Los Angeles County Social Servs. Union, 89-1 ARB ¶ 8189, 3923 (Knowlton, 1988) (error in transfer agreement).

[28]Pillowtex Corp., 92 LA 321, 325 (Goldstein, 1989); Cleo Wrap, 90 LA 768, 769 (Welch, 1988) (arbitrator refused to add paragraph back into contract which was mistakenly deleted by union, where there was no fraud, deceit or unfair labor practice on part of company); Transit Mgmt. of Se. L.A., 88 LA 1055, 1058 (Baroni, 1987).

Interpretation in Light of the Law

Arbitrators often construe collective bargaining agreements in light of statutes and case law.[29] Many times the parties themselves submit grievances in which they explicitly or implicitly require the arbitrator to apply external law.[30] In some cases, however, arbitrators have refused to apply external law in rendering their decision.[31]

Especially in the context of rising numbers of discrimination claims, the arbitrator's role may be viewed as changing. Deborah R. Willig has suggested that while arbitrators may not base their determination entirely upon their views of the applicable legislation without regard to the language of the agreement, where the rights set forth in the agreement are similar to those created by enacted legislation, they must consider the external law.[32] Forced by these circumstances

---

[29]Examples include City of Keokuk, 88 LA 1129, 1132 (Murphy, 1987); Montgomery County Gov't, 86 LA 220 (Hockenberry, 1985) (application of the codes of Montgomery County, the State of Maryland, and Maryland case law in grievance involving police officers); Container Corp. of Am., 84 LA 489 (Nicholas, 1985) (NLRB and circuit court decisions examined to determine who is a "supervisor" under the NLRA); Cooper T. Smith Stevedoring Co., 84 LA 94 (Baroni, 1984) (arbitrator considered NLRB and federal case law in resolving jurisdictional dispute); San Diego Plasterers Trusts, 83 LA 662 (Weckstein, 1984) (arbitrator considered Taft-Hartley Act, § 302, ERISA, and case law in finding that trust instruments should not be amended to require employer or representative of employer trustees to be signatory to collective bargaining agreement with union).

[30]Examples include Pension & Welfare Funds, 87 LA 1237 (Wolff, 1986) (legality of employer pension fund contributions in light of NLRA, § 302(c)(5)(B)); Rock County, Wis., 87 LA 1 (Larney, 1986) (application of FLSA); Lakeville Community Schools, 85 LA 945 (Grinstead, 1985) (consideration of teacher tenure act in interpreting collective bargaining agreement); Litton Sys., 84 LA 688 (Bognanno, 1985) (arbitrator considered whether employer violated § 8(a)(5) and § 8(d) of LMRA); Johnson Controls, 84 LA 659 (Imundo, 1985) (arbitration concerning application of ICC regulations); Local Pension Fund & Nat'l Pension Fund, 84 LA 632 (Holden, 1985) (arbitrator considered ERISA provisions in determining whether it was proper for local union pension fund to impose an administrative fee on reciprocal payments made to National Pension Fund); Bevles Co., 82 LA 203, 207 (Monat, 1983) (arbitrator agreed that "the labor agreement does not exist in a vacuum" in holding that parties intended external law to apply to their collective bargaining agreement); Wyatt Mfg. Co., 82 LA 153 (Goodman, 1983) (arbitrator considered, inter alia, Supreme Court decisions of First Nat'l Maintenance Corp. v. NLRB, 101 S.Ct. 2573, 107 LRRM 2705 (1981), and Fibreboard Paper Prods. Corp. v. NLRB, 85 S.Ct. 398, 57 LRRM 2609 (1964), in considering employer's duty to bargain over partial closure of business).

[31]See, e.g., Reyco Indus., 85 LA 1034 (Newmark, 1985) (refusal to apply law of bailment in lieu of plain language of collective bargaining agreement in determining employer's liability for employee's stolen tools); Koehring S. Plant, 82 LA 193 (Alsher, 1984) (arbitrator refused to observe dicta in Pennsylvania Court of Common Pleas opinion which conflicted with an express provision in collective bargaining agreement). In City of Burlington, 82 LA 21 (Kubie, 1984), the arbitrator declined to consider whether an unemployment-compensation hearing officer's prior determination that grievant was not guilty of misconduct disqualifying him from benefits had a collateral estoppel effect on the instant grievance. The arbitrator held that the hearing officer's determination involved a more difficult standard for the employer to satisfy than the standard of "just cause."

[32]Willig, "Arbitration of Discrimination Grievances: Arbitral and Judicial Competence Compared," Proceedings of 39th Annual Meeting of NAA, 101 (BNA Books, 1987). See, e.g., Fairmont Gen. Hosp., 87 LA 137, 140 (Bolte, 1986). In that case, Arbitrator Bolte was confronted with the question whether the hospital could unilaterally impose a mandatory retirement age in the absence of any such provision. Upon consideration of the Age Discrimination in Employment Act, and the contract itself, he decided that the hospital could not take such a unilateral act. In comparing the mandatory retirement policy reflected in the law (i.e., 70 as age of mandatory retirement) with the antidiscrimination article of the agreement, Arbitrator Bolte concluded that the policy set forth in the agreement was one that was continuing in nature. Focusing on the language of the contract which referred to the "*continuing* policy and practice" of the parties not to discriminate on the basis of age, the arbitrator found that such policy predated not only the passage of the ADEA but also the agreement itself (emphasis added). Thus, he concluded that the parties agreed to a standard different from that set up by the law—one which established no age ceiling. Thus, applying both the applicable law and the traditional standards of contract interpretation, Arbitrator Bolte came to a well-reasoned conclusion.

to consider the relative competence of arbitrators to judges, Arbitrator Willig concluded that arbitrators today "are not afraid to look to applicable statutory and decisional law [and] will apply it if it is relevant."[33] In short, modern arbitrators seem prepared to take on this added responsibility.

Normal and Technical Usage

Arbitrators give words their ordinary and popularly accepted meaning in the absence of anything indicating that they were used in a different sense or that the parties intended some special colloquial meaning.[34] Many arbitrators apply a "reasonable man standard" in interpreting words or phrases in collective agreements.[35] One arbitrator determined that when each of the parties has a different understanding of what is intended by certain contract language, the party whose understanding is in accord with the ordinary meaning of that language is entitled to prevail.[36]

---

[33]Willig, "Arbitration of Discrimination Grievances: Arbitral and Judicial Competence Compared," Proceedings of 39th Annual Meeting of NAA, at 108. But see James A. Haley Veterans Hosp., 82 LA 973, 974, 976 (Wahl, 1984). The traditional constraints still apply. In this case, Arbitrator Wahl felt himself bound by the federal case law on the issue of termination of probationary employees despite the recognition that this decision "regretfully, may deprive [the grievant] of his 'day in court' to have the merits of his termination reviewed. * * * [T]hat is beyond an arbitrator's power to remedy."

[34]Vermont Dep't of Corrections, 93 LA 595, 597 (Toepfer, 1989); Prime Health, 93 LA 334, 337 (Clark, 1989); Newaygo County Road Comm'n, 92 LA 918, 921 (Brown, 1989); Gulf Printing Co., 92 LA 893, 895 (King, 1989) (finding that "three consecutive days" means three days in succession without regard to any modifier such as "work"); Rogers-Wayne Metal Prods. Co., 92 LA 882, 887 (House, 1989); West Penn Power Co., 92 LA 644, 647 (Dworkin, 1989); College Community School Dist., 91 LA 610, 612 (Madden, 1988); Orange Unified School Dist., 91 LA 525, 527 (Collins, 1988); Montana Power Co., 90 LA 932, 933 (Corbett, 1987); Kentucky Center, 89 LA 344, 348 (Volz, 1987); Mentor Bd. of Educ., 89 LA 292, 294 (Sharpe, 1987); Coca-Cola Foods, 88 LA 129, 131 (Naehring, 1986); Anaheim Union High School Dist., 84 LA 101, 104 (Chance, 1984) (finding parties intended a special colloquial meaning for "on site" file). Other cases applying this principle include Mesker Indus., 85 LA 921, 928 (Mikrut, 1985); Wagner Castings Co., 83 LA 507, 511 (Talent, 1984). In L & O Growers Ass'n, 82 LA 814, 815 (Weiss, 1984), the company advanced an argument that lemon trees and orange trees were intended to be treated differently with regard to "wet time," i.e., the time during which a worker is prevented from working by excessive moisture on the trees. The company focused on the fact that lemons rot when they are wet and oranges do not, suggesting that such knowledge was intended to be understood in the contract. Arbitrator Weiss rejected this argument including that "[w]etness on orange trees is not any different than wetness on lemon trees when it comes to the question of whether 'a worker is prevented from working.' Thus, the plain meaning of the language is in accord with its reasonable and common-sense interpretation."

[35]For example, see California State Univ., 86 LA 549, 555 (Koven, 1986) ("In the absence of any agreed-upon definition by the parties themselves, an arbitrator cannot formulate a definition for all times and for every situation. Instead, that term must be defined in terms of what a reasonable person would deem to be 'careful consideration' under a particular set of facts."); Container Corp. of Am., 84 LA 604, 607 (Allen, 1985) (application of the "reasonable man" interpretation of a word in the collective bargaining agreement instead of an interpretation which would stretch or torture the term). Westvaco, 83 LA 904, 907 (Heekin, 1984), involved the assignment of mandatory overtime "with proper notice." The arbitrator determined that the *basic implication* of the common phrase "with proper notice" was that an employee should have enough time to become reasonably prepared for such assignment.

[36]Stuart Hall Co., 86 LA 370, 372 (Madden, 1985). Cf. Gulf Printing Co., 92 LA 893, 895 (King, 1989) (burden falls on party contending for a construction other than that based on ordinary meaning to prove that special circumstances exist warranting particular construction).

Arbitrators often apply their understanding of words or phrases in the contract without asserting any authority.[37] One arbitrator determined that awarding administrative leave with pay when an employee was requested or subpoenaed to appear before a court as a witness *for the People* only covered appearances on behalf of the public interest, and this did not include testimony on behalf of a party in a general civil case.[38] Arbitrator David A. Dilts has stated that, "[u]nless specifically and mutually accepted by the parties as an illness qualifying for sick leave, the definition of illness may not be expanded to include intoxication."[39]

Use of Dictionary Definitions

The use of dictionary definitions in arbitral opinions provides a neutral interpretation of a word or phrase that carries the air of authority.[40] A standard dictionary is appropriate for defining a word or phrase in normal usage, but if a word or phrase has been defined by

---

[37]Examples are contained in Department of Navy, 86 LA 92, 96 (Connors, 1985) (arbitrator applied "most common meaning" of the words "discuss" and "negotiate"); Mid-America Canning Corp., 85 LA 900, 904 (Imundo, 1985) (arbitrator applied his understanding of meaning of "one full calendar year of active employment.").

[38]Michigan Dep't of Social Servs., 82 LA 114 (Fieger, 1983).

[39]Air Force Logistics Command, 85 LA 735, 737 (1985).

[40]Arbitrators have consulted standard dictionaries in Pepsi Cola Bottling Co., 93 LA 520, 524 (Randall, 1989); IRS Ogden Serv. Center, 93 LA 261, 272 (Dilts, 1989); Courier Journal, 93 LA 227, 232 (Tharp, 1989); Sam Blount Co., 93 LA 209, 213 (Holley, 1989); Food Barn Stores, 93 LA 87, 89 (Fogelberg, 1989); Texas Utils. Generating Div., 92 LA 1308, 1313 (McDermott, 1989); City of Wayzata, Minn., 92 LA 664, 666 (Fogelberg, 1989); Grain Processing Corp., 92 LA 265, 269-270 (Hilgert, 1989); Hartman Elec. Mfg., 92 LA 253, 255 (Rybolt, 1989); Dinuba Elementary School Dist., 91 LA 1397, 1399 (Rothstein, 1989); Baltimore Sun, 91 LA 1133, 1138 (Wahl, 1988); Harvard Indus., 91 LA 849, 853 (Ellmann, 1988); Rolling Acres Care Center, 91 LA 795, 800 (Dworkin, 1988); College Community School Dist., 91 LA 610, 612 (Madden, 1988); Champion Int'l Corp., 91 LA 245, 250-251 (Duda, 1988); Steelworkers, 89-1 ARB ¶ 8303 (CCH) (Holley, 1988) (arbitrator consulted The New Webster Encyclopedia Dictionary and Webster's Seventh New Collegiate Dictionary for the meaning of "incidental"). Other decisions where arbitrators used dictionary definitions include; West Va. Wesleyan College, 90 LA 1103, 1105 (Duff, 1988); Cardinal Foods, 90 LA 521, 526 (Dworkin, 1988); Crown Cork & Seal Co., 90 LA 329, 331-332 (Kapsch 1987); City of Elyria, 90 LA 292, 295 (Dworkin, 1987); Naval Medical Clinic, 90 LA 137, 143 (Rothschild, 1987); Associated Milk Producers, 89 LA 1186, 1191 (Wyman, 1987) (arbitrator looked to Webster's New Collegiate Dictionary to define "maintain" and "amendment"); Hillel Day School, 89 LA 905, 908 (Lipson, 1987) (arbitrator looked to Black's Law Dictionary to define "family"); Flowers Baking Co., 89 LA 666, 670 (Rice, 1987) (arbitrator looked to Robert's Dictionary of Industrial Relations to define "full-time job"); Spartan Printing Co., 89 LA 605, 608 (Flaten, 1987) (arbitrator looked to Webster's New Collegiate Dictionary to define "concurrent"); Warner Press, 89 LA 577, 580 (Brunner, 1987) (arbitrator looked to Webster's New Collegiate Dictionary and Black's Law Dictionary to define "possible"); City of Cadillac, 88 LA 924, 926 (Huston, 1987) (arbitrator looked to Webster's Third International Dictionary to define "leave of absence"); Waverly Community School Dist., 88 LA 688, 691 (Berman, 1986) (arbitrator looked to Robert' Dictionary of Industrial Relations to define "salary," "wage," and "fringe benefits"); Pabst Brewing Co., 88 LA 656, 660 (Wyman, 1987); Homestake Mining Co., 88 LA 614, 616 (Sinicropi, 1987) (arbitrator looked to the Random House Dictionary to define "permanent" and "temporary"); Derby Cap Mfg. Co., 87 LA 1042, 1047 (Imundo, 1986) (arbitrator looked to dictionary definition of term "spouse"); Hartz Mountain Indianapolis Branch, 86 LA 1137, 1138 (Seidman, 1986) (arbitrator looked to Black's Law Dictionary for definition of "day"); Kroger Co., 85 LA 1198, 1201 (St. Antoine, 1985) (arbitrator looked to Webster's International Dictionaries and Black's Law Dictionary for meaning of the phrase "and/or"); Albright & Wilson Inc., 85 LA 908 (Shanker, 1985) (arbitrator looked to standard dictionary definition of "inadvertent"); Dubuque Community School Dist., 85 LA 636, 638 (Dilts, 1985) (arbitrator looked to Webster's Dictionary to define word "comparable" as used in requirement that health insurance benefits be comparable to those in stated policy); American Foundry & Mfg. Co., 83 LA 525, 528 (Newmark, 1984) (arbitrator looked to Webster's New Collegiate Dictionary for definition of "immediate").

the parties in their agreement, an arbitrator should not look outside the agreement for a definition. The use of a standard dictionary is inappropriate where the arbitrator is defining "words of art" or technical terms. In those cases, specialized dictionaries are sometimes used.[41]

Agreement to Be Construed as a Whole

"To the greatest extent, the Arbitrator must ascertain and give effect to the parties' mutual intent. That intent is expressed in the contractual language, and the disputed portions must be read in light of the entire agreement."[42]

Giving Effect to All Clauses and Words

Although the clear and unambiguous language of a particular clause in a contract indicated one result, one arbitrator came to a different result in giving effect to all clauses and words in the same contract.[43] Noting that the contract contained a clause indicating that "wages shall be paid for jury duty and/or the answer of a subpoena" as well as a clause providing for time off for union business without pay,[44] Arbitrator Marvin Feldman found that:

> When the negotiators of this agreement indicated and stated that payment shall be made for jury duty and in answer of a subpoena, they understood, presumably, that if the answer of a subpoena was for union business and its furtherance or for personal business, that no payment of wage would be made.[45]

Thus applying the rule of contract interpretation that "each clause is supplementary of the other and not, therefore, in conflict with

---

[41]Ramsey County, 88 LA 1103, 1106 (Miller, 1987) (arbitrator looked to Robert's Dictionary of Industrial Relations and Black's Law Dictionary to define "just cause"). In Dillon Stores Co., 84 LA 84, 88 (Woolf, 1984), the arbitrator consulted Bouvier's Law Dictionary for the definition of "promissory estoppel."

[42]Hemlock Pub. Schools, 83 LA 474, 477 (Dobry, 1984) (applying totality of contract article to find that grievant was not wrongfully denied right to teach physical education classes taught by junior employees in another building). The arbitrator in Wells Badger Indus., 83 LA 517, 520 (Hales, 1984), cited the Third Edition of How Arbitration Works for the proposition that a labor agreement should be construed as a whole in order to arrive at the true intent of the parties. Also see City of Cleveland, 92 LA 1052, 1054 (Sharpe, 1989); Spokane School Dist. No. 81, 92 LA 333, 335 (Smith, 1989); City of Saginaw, 92 LA 137, 141 (Ellmann, 1989); City of Melbourne, 91 LA 1210, 1212 (Baroni, 1988); Northern Ill. Mason Employers Council, 91 LA 1147, 1153 (Goldstein, 1988); Allied Plant Maintenance Co., 88 LA 963, 967 (Bankston, 1987).

[43]Indiana Bell Tel. Co., 88 LA 122, 124 (Feldman, 1986). See Michigan Dep't of Social Servs., 82 LA 114, 116 (Fieger, 1983). Construing a similar provision, Arbitrator Fieger observed the fact that the word "People" was capitalized in the agreement thus giving "some indication of what was meant." However, he looked to the "language of the penultimate paragraph" for the key. In that paragraph, the drafters "conceived that a witness could appear in a role other than as a witness for the 'People,' and specifically state [sic] that when he does, he does not receive administrative leave." Thus, the arbitrator denied the grievance seeking administrative leave to witnesses subpoenaed to testify at an appeal from the denial of unemployment benefits.

[44]Indiana Bell Tel. Co., 88 LA 122, 124 (1986).

[45]Id. at 125.

the other,"[46] Arbitrator Feldman gave effect to both clauses of the contract despite the apparent contradiction in the plain language itself. Another arbitrator stated the rule as follows:

> All words used in an agreement should be given effect. The fact that a word is used indicates that the parties intended it to have some meaning, and it should not be declared surplusage if a reasonable meaning can be given to it consistent with the rest of the agreement.[47]

Avoidance of Harsh, Absurd, or Nonsensical Results

"Contracts are to be given a reasonable construction, so as to avoid harsh, illogical, or absurd results."[48] By comparing arbitral surgery with oral surgery, Arbitrator James Duff illustrated the absurdity of a company's policy regarding "doctor's" excuses for sick days. In that case the company had refused to accept an excuse from a chiropractor on the ground that a "physician's" note was required.[49] Carrying this policy out to its potential limits, Arbitrator Duff described the "genuine predicament" of an employee experiencing the "painful symptoms of a physical condition, such as an aching, abscessed tooth. * * *"[50] Under a strict interpretation of the company's policy of accepting only a "physician's" note, the employee "would be compelled to go through the pro forma gesture of having a physician certify what perhaps only a dentist would truly know about his or her condition."[51] Finding the entire situation absurd, Arbitrator Duff granted the grievance.

---

[46]Ibid.

[47]Armstrong Rubber Co., 87 LA 146, 150 (Bankston, 1986). Other cases where this rule was applied include City of Melbourne, 91 LA 1210, 1212 (Baroni, 1988); Alpha Beta Stores, 91 LA 888, 894 (Riehman, 1988); Plough, Inc., 90 LA 1018, 1020 (Cromwell, 1988); City of N. Las Vegas, 90 LA 563, 566 (Richman, 1988); General Tel. Co. of Sw., 86 LA 293, 295 (Ipavec, 1985) ("It is a rule of contract interpretation that each word and phrase of a contract is to be given meaning on the theory that if the parties to the contract had not intended to give, each word and each phrase, meaning, then they would have deleted such language in order to assist the eventual interpreter."); Pittsburgh Bd. of Pub. Educ., 85 LA 816 (Bolte, 1985); GTE Prods. Corp., 85 LA 754, 757 (Millious, 1985) ("If the parties had intended that continuous service was the same as seniority, then the language of Article 8 separately setting forth continuous service as a condition for payment would be unnecessary and redundant."); Hamady Bros. Food Mkt., 82 LA 81, 84 (Silver, 1983) ("It is presumed as an essential part of any collective bargaining agreement that all terms and conditions stated therein shall be given effect reasonably.").

[48]Schalmont Central School Dist., 87 LA 151, 152 (Babiskin, 1986) (interpreting "days" for purposes of sick leave as "work days" to avoid nonsensical result). Similarly, Arbitrator Dworkin interpreted "work day" to mean "twenty-four hours" to avoid rendering a provision meaningless. West Penn Power Co., 92 LA 644, 648 (Dworkin, 1989). In Portland Water Dist., 87 LA 1227 (Chandler, 1986), the arbitrator interpreted the contract so as to avoid a nonsensical result in favor of a result which was just and reasonable. Similarly, the arbitrator in Charley Bros. Co., 84 LA 655, 658 (Probst, 1985) stated that he was required to establish the appropriate meaning of an agreement consistent with its language which would avoid an obviously absurd result, in finding that an employer properly denied an overtime assignment to an employee who was in the middle of a five-day suspension. In Eagle Iron Works, 85 LA 979, 981 (Thornell, 1985), the arbitrator sustained the grievance because the employer's interpretation of the contract's vacation entitlement provision "would have a harsh result and one not called for by the contract." See also Holiday Inn/Town Square, 90 LA 67, 71 (Cooper, 1987); TPC Liquidation, Inc., 88 LA 696, 698 (Lumbley, 1987).

[49]Consolidation Coal Co., 83 LA 1158, 1159, 1161 (1984).

[50]Id. at 1161.

[51]Ibid.

Arbitrator Patrick A. McDonald applied the doctrine that an arbitrator may reject the extreme positions of both parties where the interpretations urged by the parties were both reasonable but would have led to an absurd result. Thus, he fashioned an interpretation which took into account his understanding of both points of view. Recognizing that the disputed language was inserted into the contract to prevent it from becoming an issue, as well as to prevent the acquisition of benefits by one group not negotiated over by another, Arbitrator McDonald concluded that (1) the general understanding that parity did not exist between the two groups was to be maintained and (2) the interpretation in this case did not dispute that fact but rather established that the present "gap" or disparity could not be widened. Thus, the less logical and more harsh interpretation which would have resulted in the nullification of both was avoided.[52]

To Express One Thing Is to Exclude Another

Arbitrators continue to interpret contract provisions as excluding alternatives where one term is expressly stated.[53]

Specific Versus General Language

Unless a contrary intention appears from the contract construed as a whole, the meaning of a general provision should be restricted by more specific provisions.[54] "In general, Arbitrators hold that when an exception is stated to a general principle, the exception should 'be strictly though, to be sure, properly construed and applied.'"[55] Where two contract clauses bear on the same subject, the more specific should be given precedence.[56]

---

[52]City of Taylor, 84 LA 522, 525 (1985).

[53]See City of Dayton, 88 LA 236, 238 (Heekin, 1986); City of Meriden, 87 LA 163, 165 (Davis, 1986) (statute defines funds from which contribution is to be made; limited to regular pay, longevity pay, and holiday pay. Does not include assessing accumulated sick leave and vacation pay); Iowa Meat Processing Co., 84 LA 933, 935 (Madden, 1985) (prohibition attaching to interdepartmental transfer under § 10 indicates no such prohibitions or conditions for intra-departmental transfer): Allegheny Intermediate Unit, 82 LA 187, 192-193 (McDowell, 1984) (separation of certain benefits to specific section of collective agreement entitled "fringe benefits" was meant to exclude other benefits from provision for "fringe benefits" as used in contract). See also Albright & Wilson Inc., 85 LA 908, 912 (Shanker, 1985); Aeronca Inc., 82 LA 144 (Finan, undated); City of Hollywood, 82 LA 48 (Manson, 1983).

[54]See also Nationwide Indus., 93 LA 286, 288 (Richard, 1989); Chillicothe Tel. Co., 84 LA 1, 3 (Gibson, 1984). See Airco Carbon, 86 LA 6, 9 (Dworkin, 1986) ("A broadly observed principle of contract interpretation, acknowledged in both courts of law and arbitration, holds that specific language prevails over general language.").

[55]See Unitog Co., 85 LA 740, 742 (Heinsz, 1985). In deciding whether the company violated the terms of the collective bargaining agreement when sales promotional employees made deliveries and no payments were made to grievants, Arbitrator Heinsz applied the rule that "when an exception is stated to a general principle, the exception should 'be strictly though, to be sure, properly construed and applied'" (citing Verniton Corp., 77 LA 349, 352 (Shipman, 1981); Fulton-Sylphon Co., 8 LA 983, 984 (Greene, 1947); How Arbitration Works, 4th ed., at 356.

[56]Coca-Cola Foods, 88 LA 129, 131 (Naehring, 1986).

Construction in Light of Context

A contract section in dispute must be read in the context of the other sections in the agreement to establish the intent of the parties.[57]

In one case[58] Arbitrator Maurice Benewitz applied the "golden rule" cited in *A Dictionary of Modern English Usage*[59] as an aid in interpreting a contract provision:

> The golden rule of writing is "that the words or numbers most nearly related should be placed in the sentence as near to one another as possible, so as to make their mutual relation clearly apparent."[60]

Similarly, Arbitrator Benewitz referred to the *Concise Dictionary of Current American Usage*[61] for the proposition that "the pronoun is said to agree in gender * * *, number (*singular or plural*) and person * * * with the antecedent."[62] Based on the foregoing, Arbitrator Benewitz concluded:

> [F]rom the placement of the word and from the number of the referential phrase, * * * the drafters of the language had chosen to limit the length of the specialized news program mentioned under condition (i) but not of the non-news television *which is not mentioned* in condition (i).[63]

Avoidance of a Forfeiture

It is a familiar principle that the law abhors a forfeiture.[64] "If an agreement is susceptible of two constructions, one of which would work a forfeiture and one of which would not, the arbitrator will be inclined to adopt the interpretation that will prevent the forfeiture."[65] But if the contract language mandating a forfeiture is clear and unambiguous, that language must be upheld. As stated by Arbitrator William P. Daniel:

> This arbitrator must respectfully disagree with those arbitrators who would stretch clear language of default to the ultimate limit perceiving some obligation to avoid all forfeitures notwithstanding the parties' clear agreement. It seems appropriate to let the parties determine the

---

[57]Cases which consider context in resolving the meaning of a disputed contract section include Board of Educ. of Prince George's County, 85 LA 999, 1000 (Flannagan, 1985); Zeigler Coal Co., 85 LA 971, 975 (Creo, 1985).

[58]National Broadcasting Co., 86 LA 586, 591-592 (1986).

[59]Fowler, A Dictionary of Modern English Usage, 2d ed., rev'd & ed. by Sir Ernest Gower (Oxford Univer. Press, 1965).

[60]Id. at 21.

[61]Shostak, Concise Dictionary of Current American Usage (Washington Square Press, 1968).

[62]Id., quoted in National Broadcasting Co., 86 LA 586, 592, emphasis added.

[63]86 LA at 592, emphasis added.

[64]In Lithonia Lighting Co., 85 LA 627, 630 (Volz, 1985), the arbitrator stated that "it is a familiar principle that the law abhors a forfeiture of a valuable right, such as the termination of seniority * * *." He applied this principle to set aside the termination of grievant's seniority under ambiguous contract language.

[65]Armstrong Rubber Co., 87 LA 146, 150 (Bankston, 1986). See also Hillel Day School, 89 LA 905, 908 (Lipson, 1987); Allied Plant Maintenance Co., 88 LA 963, 967 (Bankston, 1987).

extent to which defaults will be excused and where the language chosen reflects no such intent but rather an inflexible and absolute application, then the arbitrator has no right to interfere. To resolve doubts and avoid a forfeiture is one thing; to rationalize disregard of a clear contractual mandate is another indeed.[66]

On the issue of "timeliness" of a grievance, it has been held that "[a]mbiguities in [the] contract language must be resolved in a manner most favorable to upholding the timeliness of a grievance."[67]

Arbitrator John F. Caraway applied the rule set out by Arbitrator Lionel Richmond that "[w]hile it is not for an Arbitrator to rewrite the contract, if the contract is ambiguous insofar as time limits are concerned, since the law abhors forfeitures, the ambiguity should be resolved in favor of timeliness."[68] In light of that principle, Arbitrator Caraway interpreted the contract provision requiring the filing of a grievance within five days of the event to mean five working days.[69] Thus, even though the termination occurred on March 11 and the union did not notify the company of the grievance until March 17, it was nevertheless timely filed under his interpretation of the contract.[70]

Precontract Negotiations

Where the contract language to be interpreted is ambiguous, precontract negotiations and bargaining history provide the arbitrator with a tool to determine the parties' intent.[71] For example, Arbitrator Harry Dworkin held that because a union consistently proposed a seniority requirement for entitlement to overtime in different contract negotiations over a period of 25 years, and the company consistently refused to entertain those proposals, this was a valid aid in interpreting and construing the contract language, particularly where the language did not specifically deal with the subject matter, and where there was some ambiguity or lack of clarity.[72]

While arbitrators may be reluctant to read a provision into a contract where a party has attempted but failed to include it, where a

---

[66]Wayne County Intermediate School Dist., 85 LA 673, 675-676 (1985). See Akron City Bd. of Educ., 86 LA 164, 169 (Dworkin, 1986) ("It is broadly held that contractual forfeiture clauses must be enforced, but only if all facts necessary to trigger divestiture are adequately proven.").

[67]Concrete Pipe Prods. Co., 87 LA 601, 604 (Caraway, 1986).

[68]Ibid. (quoting In re Clougherty Packing Co., 13 LAIS 1001 (Richman, 1985)).

[69]87 LA at 604.

[70]Ibid.

[71]Cases in which the arbitrator considered bargaining history in the face of ambiguous contract language include Atlanta Wire Works, 93 LA 537, 541-542 (Williams, 1989); E.M. Smith & Co., 88 LA 1124, 1127 (Dworkin, 1987); Milford Community School Dist., 89-1 ARB ¶ 8060 (CCH) (Baron, 1988); Downingtown School Dist., 88 LA 59 (Zirkel, 1986); Pacific Sw. Airlines, 86 LA 437 (Darrow, 1985); Southern Ind. Gas & Elec. Co., 86 LA 342 (Schedler, 1985); Midwest Printing Co., 85 LA 615 (Ver Ploeg, 1985); W.E. Plechaty Co., 84 LA 571 (Duda, 1985); Ferry-Morse Seed Co., 84 LA 75 (Duda, 1984).

[72]Stone Creek Brick Co., 83 LA 864 (1984). See contra Hussman Corp., 84 LA 137, 141 (Roberts, 1983) (issue of attempting to obtain through arbitration what could not be obtained in negotiations does not apply here because this issue did not arise in negotiations but was merely a proposed election of only exception which was ultimately rejected, therefore grievance sustained).

party has expressly attempted but failed to exclude a particular clause, the arbitrator may well be inclined to view the inclusion of that clause as a clear indication of the success of its proponent. For example, Arbitrator Charles Milentz noted in a case that during negotiations the union president refused to agree to the new-hire classification because it would permit the company to schedule the new-hires for unlimited hours to the detriment of the existing employees.[73] Eventually, however, the union abandoned its refusal and accepted the new-hire provision. The very same reason advanced by the union for rejecting the clause during negotiations was raised once more by the union in the grievance. Recognizing that through the grievance the union was "attempting to obtain through arbitration what it could not through negotiations and a strike," Arbitrator Milentz denied the grievance.[74]

Unlike this express showing of intent, Arbitrator John Murphy considered a case which clearly illustrated the proposition that it is the manifested intent of the parties during negotiations that is to be considered by the arbitrator and not the undisclosed intent.[75] In that instance, the union president testified that throughout the negotiations the union refused to give the employer the right to take an employee off his job to make way for a partially disabled employee. The language ultimately included in the contract reflected the third proposal by the employer and entirely omitted the sentence to which the union objected.[76] While Arbitrator Murphy acknowledged that there was some credible evidence that the senior vice president had been under the impression that the right was not *lost* by its omission, no evidence to this effect was communicated to the union.[77] Remarking that "[the] intent manifested by the parties to each other during negotiations by their communications and their responsive proposals—rather than undisclosed understandings and impressions—is considered by the arbitrators in determining contract language,"[78] Arbitrator Murphy ruled that the contract gave the employer no right to displace senior employees.

However, the complete lack of discussion of a particular subject during negotiations may also be indicative of intent.[79]

---

[73]Kroger Co., 86 LA 357, 364 (1986).

[74]Id. at 365.

[75]Kahn's & Co., 83 LA 1225, 1229-1230 (1984).

[76]Id. at 1230. The omitted language read as follows: "This may require removing an able bodied senior employee to other duties within the department or within the plant that this senior employee is capable of performing." Id. at 1229.

[77]Id. at 1230.

[78]Ibid.

[79]See, e.g., Port Jefferson Pub. Schools, 82 LA 978, 980 (Marx, 1984), wherein it was successfully argued that "[t]he absence of negotiations discussion as to the word "employee," rather than limiting the meaning, goes to make it all-inclusive." See also Brooklyn Acres Mutual Homes, 84 LA 952, 955 (Abrams, 1985) (testimony regarding bargaining history did not include practical situation of what would occur in instant case where no qualified bidders applied; thus, union's testimony does not warrant a conclusion any different from that which could be achieved by a simple examination of clause).

Experience and Training of Negotiators

Arbitrators continue to stress the skill and experience of negotiators when interpreting the bargained-for language in parties' agreements. This approach includes resolving issues of procedural arbitrability in light of the negotiators' skill and experience,[80] as well as resolving the substantive merits of a case based on the presumed ability of skilled and experienced negotiators to articulate their intent.[81]

Focusing upon the lack of discussion over the contract terms urged by the company, Arbitrator Nicholas Duda found it difficult to believe that had such terms been discussed, the experienced union negotiator would not have objected strenuously.[82] Thus, even a silent record may reflect the intent of the parties when viewed in light of the training and experience of the negotiators.

Industry Practice

As stated in the main text, "[r]eference to custom and practice of the industry in which the parties operate may shed light upon the intended meaning of an ambiguous provision."[83]

Prior Settlements as Aid to Interpretation

That such is the case was recognized by Arbitrator Jerry A. Fullmer in a decision, in which he noted that "[i]t is of course, the arbitrator's job to interpret the labor agreement, not write it. This is mentioned only as a factor possibly bearing on subsequent interpretations."[84]

If the parties themselves have previously arrived at a settlement which necessarily includes some form of contract interpretation, their settlement interpretation will be given significant weight by

---

[80]See, e.g., Universal Foods Corp., 82 LA 105, 108 (Belcher, 1984) (holding grievance arbitrable because parties did not provide for end to grievance process if arbitrator not timely selected. "[I]t is obvious that the negotiators were not novices, but were professionals in the most favorable connotation.").

[81]See Woodings-Verona Tool Works, 84 LA 68, 74 (McDermott, 1984) (arbitrator stressed skill of negotiators drafting an agreement and held that they were aware of difference in meaning between "termination" and "layoff" in providing that employees on layoff before a plant closing were not entitled to severance pay). See also Maple Heights Bd. of Educ., 86 LA 338, 340 (Van Pelt, 1985) ("[w]hile it is difficult for this Arbitrator to understand how parties of the caliber dealing with this contract would first, permit a typographical error to become a part of the permanent record, and second, to permit the same error to continue throughout a series of contracts, nevertheless it apparently happened").

[82]W.E. Plechaty Co., 84 LA 571, 576 (1985).

[83]Glasgow School Dist. No. 1-1A, 92 LA 281, 284 (Corbett, 1988); Alpha Beta Stores, 91 LA 888, 894 (Richman, 1988). See Chapter 9 of the Fourth Edition, p. 360.

[84]Goodyear Aerospace Corp., 86 LA 584, 586 (1985).

arbitrators who have been called upon to construe the same contract language.[85]

Interpretation Against Party Selecting the Language

It is a standard rule of contract interpretation that ambiguous language will be construed against the party who proposed or drafted it.[86] "Enforcement of this rule is practical because it promotes careful drafting of language and careful disclosure of what the drafter intends by his language. Enforcement of the rule is also equitable because the party 'at fault' for failure to take such care is the one against whom the ambiguity is construed."[87]

Company Manuals and Handbooks

Unilaterally promulgated company policies which conflict with the terms of the parties' collective bargaining agreement are generally held by arbitrators to be nonbinding.[88]

Relationship of Insurance Policy to Collective Agreement

If the collective bargaining agreement specifically defines the benefits to be offered bargaining unit employees, its mandate is controlling, notwithstanding conflicting provisions in the insurance policy. In a case where the employer's insurance carrier refused to pay benefits because the insured did not meet its definition of "totally disabled," even though she was totally disabled under the terms of the collective bargaining agreement, Arbitrator Nicholas Duda held that the agreement's definition was controlling:

> Travelers was not a party in the negotiations of the Agreement between the parties. A definition in the policy provided by Travelers to the Company may have been inconsistent with or inadequate for the com-

---

[85]Cases in which arbitrators considered prior settlements in rendering their decisions include Allegheny Ludlum Steel Corp., 85 LA 669 (Duff, 1985) (arbitrator looked to reason behind parties' prior settlement on similar issue in holding that grievance before him lacked merit); National Distillers & Chem. Corp., 85 LA 622 (Caraway, 1985) (arbitrator considered employer payment of wages at overtime rates in settlement of past grievances as evidence that union's contract interpretation was proper).

[86]This rule was applied in Mesker Indus., 85 LA 921 (Mikrut, 1985) (calculation of three-month rolling period in absentee control program ambiguous; arbitrator construed language against company which drafted it). See Georgia-Pac. Corp., 87 LA 217, 221 (Cohen, 1986) (citing Brown v. Sharpe Mfg. Co., 11 LA 228, 233 (Healy, 1948), and concluding that since document was drafted solely by company and probationary employees are not expressly excluded therein as in other documents drafted by company, probationary employees are covered by document). Also see Leo's IGA, 92 LA 337, 339 (Corbett, 1989); Silver's, Inc., 89 LA 850, 853 (McDonald, 1987); Potlatch Corp., 88 LA 1184, 1187 (Corbett, 1987).

[87]Independent School Dist. No. 47, 86 LA 97, 103 (Gallagher, 1985).

[88]See, e.g., Simpson Paper Co., 86 LA 503 (Leach, 1985) (arbitrator required company to amend its absentee control policy so as not to conflict with terms of collective agreement).

mitment the Company made to the Union. Any such problem must be resolved by Travelers and the Company. In any event, the Company must live up to its commitment to the Union.[89]

Reason and Equity

In addition to the intentions of the parties, past practice, and even arbitral precedent, Arbitrator Samuel Nicholas noted that he could not "overlook the equity aspects surrounding [the] grievance * * * which serves to guide him in making for a proper and fair interpretation of the language embodied in [the contract]."[90] Thus he considered the great financial burden on employees who had already retired if their petition were denied, particularly since many would find it difficult, if not impossible, to obtain medical coverage due to their advanced age and medical condition. With that in mind, Arbitrator Nicholas found "that the factor of equity buttresse[d] [his] finding that those employees who had already retired would not be affected by the language of the 1984 Agreement."[91]

Arbitrators often apply the "reasonable man standard" to interpret ambiguous contract language.[92] Arbitrators will also use "a rule of reason" to apply contract language in accordance with the parties' intent rather than in a literal fashion which is contrary to their intent.[93] Where a contract allows for discretion on the part of the employer, its exercise may not be arbitrary, capricious, discriminatory, or unreasonable.[94]

Arbitrator Perry A. Zirkel has formulated a novel approach for rendering an equitable remedy in certain arbitral opinions. In apportioning a back-pay award based on the 25 percent equity he found in favor of the grievant, he held:

> In cases where the remedy can be divisible, such as back pay or seniority as compared to reinstatement or reprimand, and where the merits are somewhat split, an all-or-nothing solution does not seem to be equitable or effective. Thus, in this case, the arbitrator concludes that the balance weighs partially—approximately one quarter—in favor of [grievant].[95]

---

[89]Atlantic Richfield Co., 85 LA 916, 920 (1985).

[90]Jim Walter Resources, 87 LA 857, 862 (1986).

[91]Ibid.

[92]See, e.g., Silver Lake Bd. of Educ., 88 LA 885, 888 (Madden, 1986) (arbitrator held that "School Days" were days that included the minimum number of hours required for a school day in the Kansas statute, Kans. Stat. Ann. § 72-1106); Oliver Rubber Co., 82 LA 38 (Daughton, 1984) (arbitrator found that employer reasonably expected an explanation for employee absence, although not expressly called for in contractual call-in provision).

[93]This approach was utilized in Mor Flo Indus., 83 LA 480 (Cocalis, 1984). See also College Community School Dist., 91 LA 610, 612 (Madden, 1988).

[94]For cases applying this principle see Michigan Employment Sec. Comm'n, 84 LA 473 (Fieger, 1985); Hussman Corp., 84 LA 23 (Maniscalco, 1984); Chillicothe Tel. Co., 84 LA 1 (Gibson, 1984).

[95]Chestnut Operating Co., 82 LA 121, 123 (1983).

Most arbitrators hold that if the contract does not provide for an arbitral opinion based on equity, equity cannot be used as a substitute for the express terms of the contract.[96]

> The arbitrator does not sit as a court of equity. He must take his thoughts from the four corners of the agreement and decide the case under the law of the contract rather than under the law of equity. The decision, therefore, lies within the four corners of the agreement and not under some rule that may be better but not within the confines of the agreement.[97]

[96]For cases applying this principle, see St. Paul Pub. Housing Agency, 87 LA 33, 38 (Gallagher, 1986); Los Angeles Unified School Dist., 85 LA 905, 908 (Gentile, 1985); Hemlock Pub. Schools, 83 LA 474, 477 (Dobry, 1984) (holding that arbitrator's "first obligation is to observe the limits of his power as articulated by the labor agreement. The parties created this arbitral forum, and the Arbitrator is duty-bound to honor the restrictions. Under this contract, his authority is narrowly defined: notions of fairness or equity are not relevant considerations.").

[97]Rockwell Int'l Corp., 84 LA 496, 502 (Feldman, 1985). See Lorillard, 87 LA 507, 512 (Chalfie, 1986) ("[arbitrator's] function is not to rewrite that Agreement and certainly it is not to suggest, imply nor to inform the Parties of what changes should be effected, renegotiated or changed even if his sense of justice and fairness should so dictate, or even if he believes the Agreement contains inequities."); Pollock Co., 87 LA 325, 335 (Oberdank, 1986) ("[T]he arbitrator does not sit as a Chancellor in Equity. Rather, his function is to interpret and apply the collective bargaining agreement before him.").

Chapter 10

Use of Substantive Rules of Law

General Considerations

When the parties to a dispute agree to use the private solution of arbitration, they control the appointment and the authority of the arbitrator and by the submission agreement can expressly regulate to what extent, if any, the arbitrator is to consider applicable law.[1]

The courts continue to recognize the vitality of the general rule that awards are not impeachable for errors of law.[2] However, a limited

[1]See Postal Workers v. U.S. Postal Serv., 789 F.2d 1, 122 LRRM 2094 (D.C. Cir., 1986) (court observed arbitrator had authority to rule on legal issues in view of contract clause stating postal service agrees to comply with applicable laws); City of Fort Dodge, 93 LA 759 (Cohen, 1989) (arbitrator noted in construing dispute concerning retirement benefits that parties contractual references to various statutes indicated intention to have statutory provisions apply); Pepsi Cola Bottling Co., 93 LA 520 (Randall, 1989) (arbitrator concluded that a party's use of the term "probable cause" in the context of grounds for drug testing was presumed to apply in its legal sense); ICI Americas, 93 LA 409 (Gibson, 1989) (clause in contract prohibiting discrimination in employment construed by arbitrator to require him to consider the contractual violation in terms of whether there was a violation of Title VII); Star Tribune, 93 LA 14 (Bognanno, 1989) (non-discrimination clause applying to union activity relied on by arbitrator to apply NLRB law in determining whether employee had been discriminated against because of union activity); Alpha Beta Co., 92 LA 1301, 1302 (Wilmoth, 1989) (contract clause stating that neither employer nor union would discriminate against any individual on the basis of, among other things, age "in accordance with the provisions and requirements of state and federal laws" warranted arbitrator to consider court cases on shifting the burden of proof in ruling on grievance alleging discrimination); Florida Power Corp., 87 LA 957 (Wahl, 1986) (arbitrator relied on a contract clause that defined a grievance to include violation of the law "governing employer-employee relationship" as warrant to consider the applicability of the FLSA); but compare Cosmic Distrib., 92 LA 206 (Prayzich, 1989) (arbitrator declined to consider external law regarding wages of returning economic strikers where parties stipulated that the only issue was whether company had violated collective bargaining contract); Cleveland Twist Drill Co., 92 LA 105 (Strasshofer, 1989) (arbitrator ruled that he was not empowered to consider external law, namely the ADEA and NLRA, in ruling on grievance of retirees concerning early retirement and age discrimination claims because the collective bargaining agreement excluded early retirees, thus depriving him of jurisdiction to rule on those issues).

[2]For a comprehensive statement of the rule that awards may not be overturned for a mistake or an error of law, see Judge (formerly professor) Edwards' decision in Postal Workers v. U.S. Postal Serv., 789 F.2d 1, 122 LRRM 2094, 2098-2099 n. 20 (D.C. Cir., 1986). See also Stead Motors of Walnut Creek v. Automotive Machinists Lodge No. 1173, 843 F.2d 357, 127 LRRM 3213 (CA 9, 1988), reh'g en banc, 886 F.2d 1200, 132 LRRM 2689 (CA 9, 1989); Sheet Metal Workers v. Arizona Mechanical & Stainless, 863 F.2d 647, 130 LRRM 2097 (CA 9, 1988); Masters, Mates & Pilots v. Trinidad Corp., 803 F.2d 69, 123 LRRM 2792, 2795 (CA 2, 1986).

For cases under LMRA: Bevles Co. v. Teamsters Local 986, 791 F.2d 1391, 122 LRRM 2666, 2667 n.2 (CA 9, 1986); Ethyl Corp. v. Steelworkers Local 7441, 768 F.2d 180, 183, 119 LRRM 3566, exception to this rule exists where the award is contrary to a "well defined and dominant" public policy which must be "ascertained 'by reference to the laws and legal precedents and not from general considerations of supposed public interest.'" Most courts are construing this exception as a narrow one.[3] Following the Supreme Court's decision in *Misco*, courts have consistently refused to set aside arbitration awards as contrary to public policy.[4] In the area of the "finality"

3568 (CA 7, 1985), cert. denied, 106 S.Ct. 1184, 121 LRRM 2736 (1986) ("a court of equity will not set . . . aside [an arbitrator's award] for error either in law or fact"); Jones Dairy Farm v. Food & Commercial Workers Local P-1236, 755 F.2d 583, 118 LRRM 2841 (CA 7), vacated, 760 F.2d 173, 119 LRRM 2185, cert. denied, 106 S.Ct. 136, 120 LRRM 2632 (1985) (Judge Posner observed that a party submitting legal claims for an arbitrator to rule on cannot later be heard to complain about his erroneous legal ruling); Television & Radio Artists v. Storer Broadcasting Co., 745 F.2d 392, 398, 117 LRRM 2553, 2557 (CA 6, 1984) ("If an arbitration award represents a plausible interpretation of the contract based on essentially factual determinations within the context of the collective bargaining agreement, judicial inquiry should cease and the award should be enforced. This remains so notwithstanding any error in the legal conclusions based essentially upon record supported factual findings, absent a manifest disregard of the law, in situations involving a mixed fact-law determination.").

[3]Paperworkers v. Misco, Inc., 108 S.Ct. 364, 126 LRRM 3113, 3119 (1987); Northwest Airlines v. Airline Pilots, 808 F.2d 76, 124 LRRM 2300 (D.C. Cir., 1987); E.I. DuPont de Nemours & Co. v. Grasselli Employees Indep. Ass'n of E. Chicago, 790 F.2d 611, 614-615, 122 LRRM 2217, 2218-2219 (CA 7), cert. denied, 107 S.Ct. 186, 123 LRRM 2592 (1986) (stating "that judicial review of an arbitration award is extremely limited," but, "[o]f course we should overturn an arbitration award if it violates public policy."); U.S. Postal Serv. v. Letter Carriers, 789 F.2d 18, 20, 122 LRRM 2101, 2103 (D.C. Cir., 1986) ("a court can vacate an arbitration award which compels conduct contrary to a well-defined public policy. * * * [T]he exception is designed to be narrow so as to limit potentially intrusive, judicial review of arbitration awards under the guise of public policy."); Gateway Structures v. Carpenters Local 701, 779 F.2d 485, 489, 121 LRRM 2209, 2212 (CA 9, 1985) (citing with approval George Day Constr. Co. v. Carpenters Local 354, 722 F.2d 1471, 1477, 115 LRRM 2459, 2463 (CA 9, 1984)) ("[W]e are not bound to defer to an award which actually violates the law or any explicit, well defined and dominant public policy."); Orange Belt Dist. Council of Painters Local 48 v. Kashak, 774 F.2d 985, 990, 120 LRRM 3036, 3040 (CA 9, 1985) ("The only exception to this broad deference justifies reversal of an award which actually violates the law of any explicit, well defined and dominant public policy."); Carpenters Local 1160 v. Busy Beaver Bldg. Centers, 616 F. Supp. 812, 814 (W.D. Pa., 1985) ("Inconsistency with public policy is another ground for reversing an arbitrator's decision, but this standard applies only where an award directly conflicts with federal or state law."); Hilton Int'l Co. v. Union de Trabajadores de La Industria Gastronomica de P.R., 600 F. Supp. 1440, 1450, 119 LRRM 2011, 2014 (D.P.R., 1985) ("it is true, * * * that courts may not enforce a collective bargaining agreement or an award which is contrary to public policy. However, in order for public policy to preclude enforcement of an arbitration award, the public policy must be well defined and dominant and must be ascertained by reference to the laws and legal precedents and not from general considerations of supposed public interests."). For recent articles interpreting the public policy exception and its impact on judicial review of arbitrator's decisions, see Parker, "Judicial Review of Labor Arbitration Awards: Misco and Its Impact on the Public Policy Exception," 4 The Lab. Law. 683 (1988) (Arbitrator Joan Parker examines the history of judicial deference to arbitration and notes that, prior to *Misco*, the doctrine of limited judicial review of arbitration awards was undermined by court decisions rejecting awards as inconsistent with overriding public policy; she concludes that *Misco* reaffirms a narrow scope of review.). See also Gould, "Judicial Review of Labor Arbitration Awards—Thirty Years of the Steelworkers Trilogy: The Aftermath of AT&T and Misco," 64 Notre Dame L. Rev. 464 (1989) (Arbitrator William Gould suggests that *Misco* did not go far enough in favoring arbitral finality in order to stem the flow of litigation seeking review of arbitration awards.). See also Edwards, "Judicial Review of Labor Arbitration Awards: The Clash Between the Public Policy Exception and the Duty to Bargain," 64 Chi.[-] Kent L. Rev. 3 (1988).

[4]Daniel Constr. Co. v. Electrical Workers (IBEW), 856 F.2d 1174, 129 LRRM 2429 (CA 8, 1988) (enforcing arbitrator's award of back pay to employees terminated for failing to pass a psychological test which the arbitrator found invalid; employees were not reinstated because they would have been subsequently laid off); Florida Power Corp. v. Electrical Workers (IBEW), 847 F.2d 680, 128 LRRM 2762 (CA 11, 1988) (upholding arbitrator's reinstatement of power company equipment operator for off-duty drug use and possession); S.D. Warren Co., Div. of Scott Paper Co. v. Paperworkers, 846 F.2d 827, 128 LRRM 2432 (CA 1, 1988) (court precluded on public policy grounds from vacating arbitrator's reinstatement of employee for violation of company drug rule; award vacated on other grounds); U.S. Postal Serv. v. Letter Carriers, 839 F.2d 146, 127 LRRM 2593 (CA 3, 1988) (affirming arbitrator's reinstatement of postal worker discharged for off-duty violence toward postmaster, including firing bullets through postmaster's car; arbitrator took

doctrine, however, courts continue to hold that rights under certain statutes may not be precluded. In addition to continuing to recognize rights under the NLRA, FLSA, and Title VII of the Civil Rights Act, courts more recently have refused to enforce awards which have affected rights under 42 U.S.C. § 1983,[5] 42 U.S.C. § 1981,[6] ADEA,[7] and ERISA.[8] Despite the lack of finality, arbitration remains a viable substitute for litigation even with respect to rights under these statutes.[9]

Range of Views as to Application of "Law"

Views of Arbitrators

Most arbitrators continue to agree with Arbitrator Bernard D. Meltzer's first three points in regard to respecting external law.[10] One

into account mitigating factors); Posadas de Puerto Rico Assocs., d/b/a Condada Plaza Hotel & Casino v. Asociacion de Empleados de Casino de P.R., 821 F.2d 60, 125 LRRM 3137 (CA 1, 1987) (award reinstating casino croupier discharged for failing to clap his hands before leaving his table in violation of a company work rule did not contravene public policy behind Puerto Rico gaming regulations); Oil Workers Local 4-228 v. Union Oil Co. of Cal., 818 F.2d 437, 125 LRRM 2630 (CA 5, 1987) (award reinstating discharged employee who used and sold drugs off-premises did not violate public policy); but compare Delta Airlines v. Air Line Pilots, 861 F.2d 665, 130 LRRM 2014 (CA 11, 1989) (court vacated arbitrator's reinstatement of pilot who flew plane while intoxicated).

[5]McDonald v. City of West Branch, 104 S.Ct. 1799, 1804, 115 LRRM 3646 (1984).

[6]Wilmington v. J.I. Case Co., 793 F.2d 909, 40 FEP Cases 1833, 1839-1841 (CA 8, 1986); Rodgers v. General Motors Corp., 739 F.2d 1102, 35 FEP Cases 349, 351 (CA 6, 1984), cert. denied, 105 S.Ct. 1759, 37 FEP 376 (1985); Strozier v. General Motors Corp., 635 F.2d 424, 24 FEP Cases 1370, 1371-1372 (CA 5, 1981).

[7]Cooper v. Asplundh Tree Expert Co., 836 F.2d 1544, 45 FEP Cases 1386 (CA 10, 1988); Johnson v. University of Wisconsin-Milwaukee, 783 F.2d 59, 39 FEP Cases 1822 (CA 7, 1986); Cook v. Pan Am World Airways, 771 F.2d 635, 38 FEP Cases 1344, 1348-1349 (CA 2, 1985), cert. denied, 106 S.Ct. 895, 39 FEP 1548 (1986); Steck v. Smith Barney, Harris Upham & Co., 43 FEP Cases 1736 (D.N.J. 1987) (refusal to order arbitration on termination claim even though court found claim covered by arbitration clause in individual employment agreement).

[8]Burke v. Latrobe Steel, 775 F.2d 88, 6 EBC 2307 (CA 3, 1985).

[9]It is becoming more common for arbitrators to consider and apply statutes and external law in the resolution of grievances. See, e.g., Lakeland Community College, 93 LA 909 (Richard, 1989) (arbitrator considered the ADEA in evaluating college's forced retirement of tenured professor); Bundy Tubing Co., 93 LA 905, 908 (Volz, 1989) (arbitrator ruled that it was proper to look at the provisions of federal law and their impact on the dispute between the parties, namely, whether the employee had to elect COBRA coverage in order to be eligible for the benefits in question); Star Tribune, Co., 93 LA 14 (Bognanno, 1989) (arbitrator applied provisions of NLRA to discharge); Alpha Beta Co., 92 LA 1301 (Wilmoth, 1989) (ADEA and Title VII law on pretext applied by arbitrator); Murphy Oil United States, 92 LA 1148 (Goodman, 1989) (arbitrator applied NLRA and Board decisions in reaching conclusion concerning rights of economic strikers to vacation benefits). See also Core Indus., Mueller Steam Specialties, 89 LA 151 (Goetz, 1987), an employer and union submitted to an arbitrator a dispute, pending for many years, as to whether the union had been properly certified under the NLRA. Despite the holding in Alexander v. Gardner-Denver Co., 94 S.Ct. 1011, 1022-1024, 7 FEP Cases 81 (1974), to the effect that an arbitration award did not bar an employee's statutory right to trial de novo on a discrimination claim under Title VII, an employer and nonrepresented employee submitted the employee's sex and national origin discrimination claims to an arbitrator who found on all issues for the defendant. Heublein Inc., 84 LA 836 (Tait, 1985). In another case, parties to a consent decree in a civil rights suit under 42 U.S.C. § 1983 agreed to submit disputes with respect to application of the decree to arbitration rather than to the court. Sheriff of Lake County, Ill., 82 LA 918 (Eagle, 1984).

[10]Georgia Power Co., 93 LA 846 (Holly Jr., 1989) (employee challenged discharge after a test for drug use, which arose after a search of the grievant's car, proved to be positive; arbitrator comprehensively reviewed Fourth Amendment case law and pertinent arbitrable authorities): County of Monterey, 93 LA 841 (Riker, 1989) (arbitrator applied First Amendment case law in construing issue of whether discipline of employee for communications outside normal channels

arbitrator agreed with Arbitrator Meltzer's fourth point to disregard external law where there is a clear conflict between the collective agreement and the law.[11] In that case, the grievant, who was vice president of his local union, claimed that superseniority accorded him by a provision of the applicable agreement protected him from layoff. The employer argued that the provision was illegal pursuant to the NLRB's *Gulton* decision.[12] Arbitrator Reginald Alleyne, while recognizing that the employer correctly interpreted the law, chose to ignore *Gulton*, stating that:

> Except when agreements provide to the contrary, the grievance-arbitration procedure is best served when arbitrators adhere to areas of conventional contract interpretation, leaving pure questions of contractual legality to those authorized by law to resolve such questions.[13]

Considering a similar issue, Arbitrator C. Gordon Statham reached a different conclusion, reasoning that it would be a violation of the NLRA, as articulated in various NLRB opinions, to construe the agreement to accord seniority preference to union stewards. There-

---

was proper); Pontiac School Dist./Bd. of Educ., 93 LA 745 (Lipson 1989) (arbitrator reinstated school maintenance man discharged for possession of marijuana because there was inadequate proof that substance was marijuana and because school district lacked sufficient basis to search employee's locker; arbitrator made extensive analysis of constitutional provisions concerning probable cause and Fourth Amendment rights); Golden West Broadcasters, 93 LA 691 (Jones, 1989) (arbitrator applied NLRA bargaining law); Consolidation Coal Co., 93 LA 473 (Seidman, 1989) (arbitrator necessarily had to look at law concerning sympathy strikes). Recent scholarly comment may be found in Zirkel, "The Use of External Law in Labor Arbitration: An Analysis of Arbitral Awards," 1985 Detroit C.L. Rev. 31; Scheinholtz & Miscimarra, "The Arbitrator as Judge and Jury: Another Look at Statutory Law in Arbitration," 40 Arb. J. 55 (1985); Meltzer, "Ruminations About Ideology, Law, and Labor Arbitration," Proceedings of the 20th Annual Meeting of NAA, 1, 15, 31 (BNA Books, 1967). Regarding Arbitrator Meltzer's first point, see Minnesota Dep't of Corrections, 88 LA 535 (Gallagher, 1987) (considered Title VII law in construing issue); Capital Dist. Transit Sys., 88 LA 353 (La Manna, 1986); Morton Thiokol Inc., 88 LA 254 (Finan, 1987); Olin Corp., 86 LA 1193 (Penfield, 1986) (in construing propriety of wage set-off, arbitrator considered state statute where contract was silent). Regarding Arbitrator Meltzer's third point, see San Francisco Newspaper Agency, 88 LA 296 (Gentile, 1986); Fermi Laboratory, 88 LA 79 (Wies, 1986) (by litigating statutory issue under NLRA, parties implicitly asked arbitrator to rule on it); Florida Power Corp., 87 LA 957, 960 (Wahl, 1986) (contract provided for arbitrator to pass upon a legal question by defining a grievance to include an alleged violation of law "governing the employee-employer relationship" or "supervisory conduct which unlawfully * * * denies to any employee his job or any benefit arising out of his job." Thus, the arbitrator considered the contention that the grievants performed compensable work under the FLSA.); San Francisco Unified School Dist., 87 LA 750 (Wilcox, 1986) (labor agreement nondiscrimination clause coextensive with Title VII); Veterans Admin. Medical Center, 83 LA 1219, 1224-1225 (Rotenberg, 1984) (contract provided that all matters covered by the agreement were to be governed by applicable federal statutes. Accordingly, the arbitrator was called upon to construe the challenged section of the collective bargaining agreement under 5 U.S.C. § 7106.); Crown Zellerbach Corp., 83 LA 1001 (Howell, 1984); Palo Alto Unified School Dist., 83 LA 156 (Concepcion, 1984); Farmers Union Cent. Exch., 82 LA 799 (Kapsch, 1984) (nondiscrimination referred to EEOC-AAP duties; arbitrator applied Title VII Law in ruling on grievance).

[11]Hunter Eng'g Co., 82 LA 483 (Alleyne, 1984). See also Roadmaster Corp. v. Laborers Local 504, 851 F.2d 886, 889, 128 LRRM 2953, 2955 (CA 7, 1988) ("the arbitrator should restrict his consideration to the contract, even if such decision conflicts with federal statutory law"); U.S. Playing Card Co., 87 LA 937 (Duda, 1986); BASF Wyandotte Corp., 84 LA 1055 (Caraway, 1985); Health Care & Retirement Corp. of Am., 84 LA 919 (Cerone, 1985).

[12]Gulton Electro-Voice Inc., 266 NLRB 406, 112 LRRM 1361 (1983), enforced sub nom. Electrical Workers (IUE) Local 900 v. NLRB, 727 F.2d 1184, 115 LRRM 2760 (D.C. Cir., 1984).

[13]Hunter Eng'g Co., 82 LA at 485. Compare Lucas Western, Inc., 91 LA 1272 at 1272 (1988), where Arbitrator Alleyne held that the employer did not violate the nondiscrimination clause of the state workers compensation act by discharging an employee for absenteeism on his return from industrial injury leave. Contractual provisions requiring the employer to comply with state and federal nondiscrimination laws warranted the arbitrator to consider external laws in that case.

fore, he refused to construe the agreement to afford stewards any more benefits than NLRB guidelines permit.[14]

Some arbitrators still feel that their role is not to assume jurisdiction over areas which are the responsibility of the NLRB and the courts.[15]

Along with other significant issues related to arbitral consideration of external law, Arbitrator David E. Feller addressed those agreements which specifically incorporate external law.[16] He noted that, if the parties incorporate external law into the agreement and make it clear that they want the arbitrator to interpret and apply external law, the arbitrator must do so, even though this will open up the decision to more extensive review in the courts. Arbitrator Feller rejected the view that every collective agreement should be deemed to embody all the law.[17] It is clear, however, that in each case the questions whether external law is expressly incorporated into the relevant provision of an agreement may well determine the result.[18]

---

[14]Ex-Cell-O Corp., 85 LA 1190 (Statham, 1985). This position, attributed to Arbitrator Robert G. Howlett in the Fourth Edition, p. 371, has gained some acceptance. See, e.g., U.S. Steel Corp., 89 LA 221 (Neumaier, 1987) (arbitrator recognized superseniority where there was no conflict with NLRA); City of Toledo, 88 LA 137 (Feldman, 1986) (affirmative action obligation incorporated into contract); Olin Corp., 86 LA 1193 (Penfield, 1986) (arbitrator construed statute on deduction from wages in ruling on grievance); City of Grand Rapids, 86 LA 819 (Frost, 1986) (according to arbitrator, contractual nondiscrimination provision is parallel to Title VII requiring analysis of grievance as if sex discrimination case in court); Saucelito Ranch, 85 LA 282 (Draznin, 1985); Columbus Nursing Home, 82 LA 1004 (Laybourne, 1984) (arbitrator construed garnishment statute in ruling on discharge); Bevles Co., 82 LA 203 (Monat, 1983).

[15]George A. Hormel & Co., 90 LA 1246 (Goodman, 1988) (arbitrator had no authority to interpret FLSA regarding pay for wash-up time), FMC N. Ordinance Div., 90 LA 934 (Bognanno, 1988) (arbitrator had no authority to decide unfair labor practice claim); Holly Farms, 90 LA 509 (McDermott, 1987) (arbitrator was without authority to decide claim under state handicap law); Antrim City Sheriff's Dep't, 89 LA 928 (Frost, 1987); S.D. Warren Co., 89 LA 688 (Gwiazda, 1985) (arbitrator declined to consider questions of public policy and state law in considering discharge of employees found in possession of or selling drugs on company property); Flowers Baking Co., 89 LA 666 (Rice, 1987) (arbitrator had no authority to decide claim to severance pay under ERISA); Indiana Bell Tel. Co., 88 LA 401, 404 (Feldman, 1986) ("[T]his arbitrator has no jurisdiction over any NLRB defenses, that activity being the proper subject for another forum."); Florida Power Corp., 87 LA 957, 960 (Wahl, 1986) ("This Arbitrator stands with those of his colleagues, who would avoid a judicial role, such as interpreting a statute, whenever possible; that function belongs to a court. The arbitrator's normal role and the area in which he can be most helpful is to interpret and apply the Agreement which the parties have entered into."); City of Bethany, Okla., 87 LA 309, 312 (Levy, 1986) ("It is not for the arbitrator to assume, and he will not assume, jurisdiction over the Fair Labor Standards Act, as that is a federal statute, or regulation and is subject to the jurisdiction of an administrative law judge. The arbitrator will not decide whether or not the FLSA was applicable to this situation, and particularly to the work week and the exclusion of captains and assistant chiefs as to overtime."). But compare Bake Rite Rolls, 90 LA 1133 (DiLauro, 1988) (arbitrator reinstated employee discharged for refusal to take polygraph test in violation of state law); Fleming Foods of Cal., Inc., 90 LA 1071 (Askin, 1988) (payment of severance pay to union officers on leave of absence not precluded by LMRA); Mike-Sell's Potato Chip Co., 90 LA 801 (Cohen, 1988) (arbitrator had jurisdiction to consider whether two subsidiaries were a "single employer"). See also Owens-Illinois, 83 LA 1265 (Cantor, 1984); Elwell-Parker Elec. Co., 82 LA 327 (Dworkin, 1984).

[16]Feller, "Relationship of the Agreement to External Law," Labor Arbitration Development, A Handbook, 33 (BNA Books, 1983).

[17]Id. at 37.

[18]Food Barn Stores, 93 LA 87 (Fogelberg, 1989) (reliance on FLSA concerning meaning of uniform); Star Tribune, 93 LA 14 (Bognanno, 1989); City of Springfield, 92 LA 1298 (Yarowski, 1989). Compare McCreary Tire & Rubber Co., 85 LA 137, 140 (Fischer, 1985) ("ERISA requirements as such do not govern the issue insofar as the contractual status is involved"), and Los Angeles Community College Dist., 87 LA 252 (Kaufman, 1986) (where agreement did not incorporate external law, external law was not applied), with Florida Power Corp., 87 LA 957, 960 (Wahl, 1986) (where agreement authorized arbitrator to pass upon a legal question, external law was applied). See generally Zirkel, "The Use of External Law in Labor Arbitration: An Analysis of Arbitral Awards," 1985 Detroit C.L. Rev. 31 (author examined 100 cases decided between 1972

U.S. Supreme Court Statements Regarding Arbitral Consideration of External Law

In *Gardner-Denver*,[19] in the context of Title VII, and in *Barrentine*,[20] in the context of the FLSA, the Supreme Court considered whether an arbitration decision arising out of a collective agreement should preclude a subsequent suit in federal court based on statutory rights arising out of the same underlying facts. In both instances, the Court ruled that a subsequent suit was not precluded by the prior arbitration award.[21] Although not strictly addressing an arbitrable consideration of external law, the Court's ruling in *Lingle v. Norge Division of Magic Chef, Inc.*,[22] represents a view consistent with *Gardner-Denver* and its progeny in holding that a state court retaliatory discharge action was not preempted by § 301 of the NLRA because the employee's state law tort claims were independent of the labor contract. While arbitration agreements in private employment contracts are increasingly being used for discharges, the *Gardner-Denver* notion that the existence of an arbitration provision will not preclude the exercise of a statutory right continues to have vitality.[23]

In *McDonald v. City of West Branch*,[24] the Court followed its *Gardner-Denver* and *Barrentine* rulings and held that an arbitration award that a discharge was for "just cause" could not preclude a subsequent suit brought under 42 U.S.C. § 1983 challenging the discharge. The Court expressly based its ruling on the same considerations relied on in the earlier cases: (1) the arbitrator's expertise "pertains primarily to the law of the shop, not the law of the land,"[25] and hence he may not have the expertise to resolve the issues that might arise in § 1983 actions; (2) because the arbitrator's authority derives solely from the contract, he may lack authority to invoke public laws in conflict with a labor agreement; (3) arbitration may be an inadequate substitute for judicial proceedings because a union may not vigorously represent a grievant; and (4) arbitral fact-finding is not as complete as or equivalent to judicial fact-finding.[26]

---

and 1982 in light of mode of analysis and citation of legal authority, noting that external law was more evident in context out of which dispute arose than in content).

[19]Alexander v. Gardner-Denver Co., 94 S.Ct. 1011, 7 FEP Cases 81 (1974). For additional material re *Gardner-Denver*, see Hoyman & Stallworth, "The Arbitration of Discrimination Grievances in the Aftermath of Gardner-Denver," 39 Arb. J. 49 (1984).

[20]Barrentine v. Arkansas-Best Freight Sys., 101 S.Ct. 1437, 24 WH Cases 1284 (1981).

[21]For further discussion of these two cases, see The Fourth Edition, topic entitled "U.S. Supreme Court Statements Regarding Arbitral Consideration of External Law," pp. 374-375 and notes 27-29.

[22]108 S.Ct. 1877, 128 LRRM 2521 (1988).

[23]For example, see Anderson v. Dean Witter Reynolds, 449 N.W.2d 468, 51 FEP 1075 (Minn. Ct. App., 1989) (court ruled that arbitration provision of individual employment agreement did not warrant stay of litigation under Minnesota Human Rights Act or preclude independent action alleging violation of the civil rights laws).

[24]104 S.Ct. 1799 (1984).

[25]Id. at 1803.

[26]Judge Posner, of the Seventh Circuit, has indicated that the result in *McDonald* "suggests that the Supreme Court doubts the competence of arbitrators * * *." Hudson v. Chicago Teachers Union Local 1, 743 F.2d 1187, 1196, 117 LRRM 2314 (CA 7, 1984). For a view contrary to that of the *McDonald* court, see DeSimone v. Board of Educ., S. Huntington Union Free School, 612 F. Supp.

Capability of Arbitrators to Deal With External Law

Changes and uncertainty in NLRB deferral law, as well as an increase in cases that trigger deferral, have led some commentators and courts[27] to question the capability of arbitration as an institution, and, by implication, the capability of arbitrators to properly apply NLRA law.

For example, Professor Charles J. Morris[28] has suggested that deferral places an "awesome responsibility" on arbitrators that dictates changes in the way such cases are handled. Among other things, he has recommended that arbitrators who are uncomfortable with NLRA issues should decline to handle such cases, and that a standard of review appropriate to the statutory nature of a deferred case should be adopted.[29] Professor Morris has said that the *Enterprise Wheel*[30] standard (which draws its essence from the contract) "may no longer suffice, at least not in such simplistic form."[31] As an alternative, he recommends that, where the arbitrator applies the NLRA, the standard of review should be something akin to whether the award is "repugnant to the purpose and policies of the Act."[32]

Some Ramifications or Consequences of Arbitrator's Choice Respecting External Law

In one case, the Seventh Circuit, U.S. Court of Appeals, reversed a district court ruling which set aside an arbitration award.[33] In reviewing an award which held that an employer was prohibited from contracting out janitorial work formerly performed by bargaining unit members, the lower court set aside the award because the arbitrator had based his opinion on an NLRB decision which had been repudiated. The lower court found that the arbitrator had misinterpreted external law. In reversing the lower court, the Seventh Circuit found that the question before the arbitrator was not a "pure" question of law

---

1568, 1573 (E.D. N.Y., 1985) ("While we are bound by the Court's holding and therefore recognize that the availability of arbitration does not bar a § 1983 action, we respectfully disagree with the Court. We believe that where government employees have bargained for the creation of an arbitration procedure, there is nothing unjust in requiring such employees to pursue arbitration rather than a § 1983 action. Arbitrators will have far greater expertise in employment disputes and state civil service law than federal judges or jurors."). See also Dean Witter Reynolds Inc. v. Byrd, 105 S.Ct. 1238 (1985). In the context of the Federal Arbitration Act, the Court ruled that a federal court should compel arbitration of pendent state claims subject to arbitration. In part, it reasoned, citing *McDonald*, that, because an award may not have preclusive effect, there should be less reluctance to order arbitration.

[27]See, e.g., Taylor v. NLRB, 786 F.2d 1516, 122 LRRM 2084, 2088-2089 (CA 11, 1986); Ray, "Individual Rights and NLRB Deferral to the Arbitration Process: A Proposal," 28 B.C. L. Rev. 1 (1986); Moses, "Deferral to Arbitration in Individual Rights Cases: A Re-examination of Spielberg," 51 Tenn. L. Rev. 187 (1984).

[28]Morris, "NLRB Deferral to the Arbitration Process: The Arbitrator's Awesome Responsibility," 7 Indus. Rel. L.J. 290 (1985).

[29]Morris, at 309-310.

[30]Steelworkers v. Enterprise Wheel & Car Corp., 80 S.Ct. 1358, 46 LRRM 2432 (1960).

[31]Morris, at 310.

[32]Id. at 311-312.

[33]Jones Dairy Farm v. Food & Commercial Workers Local P-1236, 760 F.2d 173, 119 LRRM 2185 (CA 7), cert. denied, 106 S.Ct. 136, 120 LRRM 2632 (1985).

but rather one involving interpretation of the parties collective agreement, past practice, and the like. The Court ruled that the arbitrator did not commit "so gross an error that it would warrant setting aside his award."[34]

In a similar vein, the First Circuit, U.S. Court of Appeals, upheld an arbitration award which had examined the propriety of an employee's discharge in light of both the agreement and the Puerto Rico Workmen's Accident Compensation Act (the PRCA). The arbitrator ruled that the discharge violated the collective bargaining agreement as well as the PRCA. The award was upheld even though the remedy provided was not consistent with the PRCA because the award drew its essence from the agreement.[35]

Statutory Law

Some Specific Statutes

Where there is a dispute between a specific statute and the bargaining agreement, arbitrators continue to consider the effect of the statute on the issue in question.[36]

Title VII of the Civil Rights Act

An increasing number of arbitrators have relied on Title VII doctrine to decide their cases,[37] especially where the agreement explicitly stated that the parties would comply with the antidiscrimination law.[38]

If a nondiscrimination clause existed in the agreement, arbitrators have construed this to require their consideration of Title VII.[39] If the agreement contained no mention of antidiscrimination,

[34]119 LRRM at 2187.

[35]In Hotel DaVinci, 797 F.2d 33, 123 LRRM 3060 (CA 1, 1986). For similar results, see Postal Workers v. U.S. Postal Serv., 789 F.2d 1, 122 LRRM 2094 (D.C. Cir., 1986), and U.S. Postal Serv. v. Letter Carriers, 789 F.2d 18, 122 LRRM 2101 (D.C. Cir., 1986).

[36]Regarding arbitral consideration of veterans statute, see Capital Dist. Transit Sys., 88 LA 353 (La Manna, 1986). Arbitrators have considered the FLSA in the following cases: City of Joliet, 88 LA 303 (Hill, 1986); Florida Power Corp., 87 LA 957 (Wahl, 1986); Rock County, Wis., 87 LA 1 (Larney, 1986); but have declined to rule on the FLSA in City of Bethany, Okla., 87 LA 309, 312 (Levy, 1986).

[37]Since publication of the Fourth Edition of this book, additional cases have been decided where arbitrators relied on Title VII doctrine. In addition to the cases cited in notes 38 and 39, see Lakeland Community College, 93 LA 909 (Richard, 1989); ICI Americas, 93 LA 409 (Gibson, 1989); Alpha Beta Co., 92 LA 1301 (Wilmoth, 1989); Department of Correctional Servs., 92 LA 1059 (Babiskin, 1989); Schlage Lock Co., 88 LA 75 (Wyman, 1986); Centerville Clinics Inc., 85 LA 1059 (Talarico, 1985); Heublein Inc., 84 LA 836 (Tait, 1985); Bethlehem Steel Corp., 84 LA 225 (Sharnoff, 1985); Crown Zellerbach Corp., 83 LA 1001 (Howell, 1984); National Weather Serv., 83 LA 689 (Gaunt, 1984).

[38]See, e.g., Palo Alto Unified School Dist., 83 LA 156 (Concepcion, 1984); Texas Lime Co., 83 LA 116 (Ness, 1984); Farmers Union Cent. Exch., 82 LA 799 (Kapsch, 1984).

[39]Arbitrators have construed nondiscrimination clauses as requiring them to consider Title VII Law. See, e.g., Minnesota Dep't of Corrections, 88 LA 535 (Gallagher, 1987); San Francisco Unified School Dist., 87 LA 750 (Wilcox, 1986); City of Grand Rapids, 86 LA 819 (Frost, 1986).

arbitrators have continued to recognize that the concepts of just cause and unlawful discrimination are now merged.[40]

Court Decisions

Where the U.S. Supreme Court has rendered a decision on a point in question, arbitrators continue to give very serious consideration to the ruling.[41] In a very unique ruling, the Fifth Circuit, U.S. Court of Appeals, ordered the remand to the arbitrator of his decision to reinstate a drug user, to allow him to consider the public policy question.[42] After the Fifth Circuit's decision, but before the remand hearing with the arbitrator, the Supreme Court reversed the same court's decision in *Paperworkers v. Misco*.[43] The arbitrator on remand determined that the Supreme Court's decision on the issue was controlling and that "the instructions of the Fifth Circuit have been severely and substantially limited" by the Court's subsequent *Misco* decision.[44]

Relying on the Court's *Buffalo Forge* decision,[45] one arbitrator held that a sympathy strike did not violate a no-strike clause.[46] The arbitrator did not address the fact that the Supreme Court, unlike the arbitrator, was constrained by the Norris-LaGuardia Act. Another arbitrator considered himself bound by the law of the federal circuit in interpreting the word "may" in a discharge clause.[47] The arbitrator concluded that a provision stating the employer "may" discharge an employee where contractual preconditions are met did not also require the employer, pursuant to the law of that circuit, to meet an implicit "just cause" standard. As part of what may be seen as a growing trend, at least two arbitrators, relying on state court decisions, found employee handbooks to be part of a labor contract.[48]

In many instances, however, arbitrators disagree with the decisions handed down and refuse to follow them.[49] Although an arbi-

---

[40]Centerville Clinics, Inc., 85 LA 1059, 1062 (Talarico, 1985).

[41]E-Systems, Inc., 86 LA 441 (Traynor, 1986) (grievances ruled not arbitrable since retiree-grievants were not employees within the meaning of the NLRA) (citing Allied Chem. & Alkali Workers v. Pittsburgh Plate Glass Mfg. Co., 92 S.Ct. 383, 78 LRRM 2974 (1971)); Municipality of Anchorage, 82 LA 256 (Hauck, 1983); Wyatt Mfg. Co., 82 LA 153 (Goodman, 1983).

[42]Oil Workers v. Union Oil Co., 818 F.2d 437, 125 LRRM 2630 (CA 5, 1987).

[43]108 S.Ct. 365, 126 LRRM 3113 (1987).

[44]Union Oil Co., 92 LA 777, 790 (Nicholas, 1989).

[45]Buffalo Forge v. Steelworkers, 96 S.Ct. 3141, 92 LRRM 3032 (1976).

[46]V.J. Gautieri Inc., 82 LA 371 (Denson, 1984).

[47]Kimberly-Clark Corp., 82 LA 1090 (Keenan, 1984).

[48]Ohio Power Co., 94 LA 463 (Strasshofer, 1990) and Georgia Pacific Corp., 87 LA 217 (Cohen, 1986).

[49]City of Sterling Heights, 89 LA 723 (Keefe, 1987) (finding policeman had raped victim, in spite of contrary jury verdict in criminal trial); Stark County Eng'r, 88 LA 497 (Kates, 1986); Reynolds Metals, 85 LA 1046 (Taylor, 1985) (arbitrator not bound by criminal conviction); Allegheny Intermediate Unit, 82 LA 187 (McDowell, 1984) (rejecting dicta of court).

trator may not feel constrained to follow court decisions, he may, without question, seek guidance from these decisions.[50]

Arbitrators, when called upon to decide issues relating to a single employer, alter ego and successory, universally rely upon court and NLRB decisions.[51] This is also true in cases involving sexual harassment.[52] Arbitrators in public-sector arbitrations, whether municipal, state, or federal, tend to rely heavily upon court cases for authority, or at least for guidance.[53] Where a union claimed that a company violated the duty of good faith and fair dealing, alleged by the union to be part of every contract, the arbitrator found after analysis of case law that the principle had not been adopted by West Virginia, but also found that if it had, the company had not violated it.[54]

Administrative Rulings

Official interpretations by executive departments of the government continue to be given significant weight where relevant.[55] Obviously, in cases Collyerized by the NLRB, in order to properly rule

[50]Teledyne Monarch Rubber, 89 LA 565 (Shanker, 1987) (excellent discussion of the relocating and transfer of work issue, and its relation to NLRB and court decisions stemming from Milwaukee Springs II, 765 F.2d 175, 119 LRRM 2801 (D.C. Cir. 1985); Hughes Aircraft, 89 LA 205 (Richman, 1987) (substantial use of court decisions to determine principle of "equitable tolling" in an otherwise untimely grievance); Misco, Inc., 89 LA 137 (Fox, 1983) (relying in part on failure of prosecutor to prosecute employee for possession of marijuana and award of compensation by unemployment bureau to sustain grievance protesting discharge) (decision underlying the 1987 Supreme Court case, Paperworkers v. Misco, 108 S.Ct. 365, 126 LRRM 3113 (1987)); Hopeman Bros., 88 LA 373 (Rothschild, 1986); Capital Dist. Transit Sys., 88 LA 353 (La Manna, 1986); Sea-Land Freight Serv., 87 LA 633 (D'Spain, 1986); Hillhaven Corp., 87 LA 360 (Corbett, 1986) (successor obligations re past practices); Georgia Pacific Corp., 87 LA 217 (Cohen, 1986) (handbook as implied contract); Burnside-Graham Ready Mix, 86 LA 972 (Wren, 1986) (successor problem in merger situation); Federal Wholesale Co., 86 LA 945 (Cohen, 1985); Firestone Tire & Rubber Co., 83 LA 12 (Lipson, 1984) (employee v. independent contractor); Eastern Non-Ferrous Foundry, 82 LA 524 (DiLauro, 1984); Old Dominion Wood Preserves Inc., 82 LA 437 (Foster, 1984); Ethyl Imco, 82 LA 290 (Yarowsky, 1983); Bevles Co., 82 LA 203 (Monat, 1983); Southern Cal. Rapid Transit, 82 LA 126 (Draznin, 1983); U.S. Gov't Printing Office, 82 LA 57 (Feldesman, 1983).

[51]Tandem Properties, 92 LA 325 (Koven, 1989); Mike-Sell's Potato Chip Co., 90 LA 801 (Cohen, 1988); Hillhaven Corp., 87 LA 360 (Corbett, 1986); Burnside-Graham Ready Mix, 86 LA 972 (Wren, 1986).

[52]Kraft, Inc., Sealtest Foods, 89 LA 27 (Goldstein, 1987); IBP, 89 LA 41 (Eisler, 1987).

[53]City of Dearborn, 89 LA 766 (Ellmann, 1987) (duty to negotiate and waiver of right); North County Transit Dist., 89 LA 768, 771 (Collins, 1987) (right to order drug test); Williams AFB, 89 LA 671 (Smith, 1987) (award of attorney fees to union); Chicago Police Dep't, 89 LA 631 (Goldstein, 1987) (legal defense in civil lawsuit); Michigan DOT, 89 LA 551 (Borland, 1987) (grant of continuance; excellent discussion of relative considerations); Social Sec. Admin., 89 LA 457 (Feigenbaum, 1987) (laches defense); City of Decatur, 89 LA 447 (Petersen, 1987) (no beard rule); Clover Park School Dist., 89 LA 76 (Boedecker, 1987) (right to cross-examine complainant in sexual harassment); Ramsey County, 89 LA 10 (Gallagher, 1987) (cost of defense for civil action in sexual harassment case).

[54]Wierton Steel Corp., 89 LA 201 (Sherman, 1987); but see Geauga Co., 92 LA 54 (Fullmer, 1988).

[55]Kaiser Permanente, 89 LA 841, 845 (Alleyne, 1987) (NLRB award of interest on back-pay claims found to be persuasive for similar remedy in private sector); Hartford Provision Co., 89 LA 590 (Sacks, 1987) (no violation of union security by refusal of company to put son and nephew of owner into union, based on NLRB criteria); U.S. Steel, 89 LA 221 (Neumeier, 1987) ("super seniority" of local union president); Witco Chem., 89 LA 349 (Rothstein, 1987) (duty to notify union of unit changes, and remedy); Core Indus., 89 LA 151 (Goetz, 1987) (by settlement agreement of parties, arbitrator decided NLRB refusal-to-bargain charges based upon objections to election); Florida Power Corp., 87 LA 957 (Wahl, 1986) (use of DOL Interpretative Bulletin in resolving "mealtime pay" dispute).

on the alleged unfair labor practices, arbitrators are compelled to address and decide these issues within the guidelines developed by over 50 years of decisional authority of the Board.[56] Administrative rulings may be relied upon but are not necessarily controlling.[57]

In a discharge case involving AIDS, the guidelines of the Centers for Disease Control (CDC) were given no weight where they were at odds with a state statute defining a communicable disease. The arbitrator found the employer's written policy concerning AIDS was in accord with the state statute and reasonable, although contrary to the CDC policy guidelines.[58]

Arbitrators continue to give very little weight to the conclusions and actions of state unemployment compensation commissions.[59] Where an employer disregarded the seniority provisions of a contract to accommodate the Ohio Industrial Commission's desire to return an injured worker to useful employment, an arbitrator found the contract provisions controlling.[60] However, when a discharged employee attempted to excuse his poor attendance by claiming the employer unlawfully failed to accommodate his religious convictions, the arbitrator refused to consider the defense, since the state and federal agencies charged with enforcement of that discrimination claim had found in favor of the employer on that issue, albeit by refusing to issue a complaint.[61]

Agency Principles

Generally, a principal may be held responsible for the act of his agent if it is within the scope of the agent's given authority, even if the act is not authorized by the principal in question.[62] However, if there is no existing basis for the act, the employer will not be bound by the act of a supervisor or management employee.[63]

---

[56]Twin Coast Newspapers, 89 LA 799 (Brisco, 1987); Joe Wheeler Elec. Coop., 89 LA 51, (Yancy, 1987).

[57]Geauga Co., 92 LA 54 (Fullmer, 1988) (NLRB's refusal to issue complaint where employer failed to reinstate certain strikers is not res judicata as to grievance by union on same issue); Boardman Co., 91 LA 489 (Harr, 1988) (finding of successor liability in spite of NLRB's refusal to issue complaint against the successor); Sam Brown Co., 89 LA 645 (Newmark, 1987) (employer violated agreement by not requiring sole employee to join union, finding contrary NLRB cases to be inapposite); City of Crystal, 89 LA 531 (Bard, 1987) (EEOC guidelines in police pregnancy-maternity leave); Barnard Eng'g, 86 LA 523 (Brisco, 1985) (NLRB decisions used for guidance in determining alter-ego work diversion); but see United Elec. Supply Co., 82 LA 921 (Madden, 1984) (considered EEOC Guidelines as a general standard in discharge for sexual harassment).

[58]Nursing Home, 88 LA 681 (Sedwick, 1987).

[59]Boise Cascade Corp., 90 LA 791 (Nicholas, 1988); Rust Eng'g Co., 85 LA 407 (Whyte, 1985); City of Burlington, 82 LA 21 (Kubie, 1984); but see Misco, Inc., 89 LA 137 (Fox, 1983).

[60]Container Corp. of Am., 83 LA 708 (Graham, 1987).

[61]JPI Transp. Prod., 93 LA 716 (Kindig, 1989).

[62]Stockton Unified School Dist., 89 LA 754 (Gallagher, 1987) (supervisor work assignment binding, even if assignment had been "specifically forbidden"); but see Hanna Mining Co., 82 LA 1219 (Garrett, 1984), where employer was not bound by erroneous statement of supervisor where employer was acting in fiduciary capacity.

[63]General Motors Corp., 92 LA 624 (Kahn, 1988) (settlement of a local grievance by a shift supervisor and local union cannot contravene master national agreement which is clearly contrary); Jefferson Schools, 91 LA 18 (Daniel, 1988) (where collective bargaining agreement provided for modification only by school board and union, board not bound by agreement signed only by assistant superintendent and union); Agrico Chem., 86 LA 799 (Eyraud, 1985) (agent had no authority to bind employer to lifetime contract).

Collective agreements cannot be changed by a union field representative unless such authority is clearly vested in him by the union membership.[64] An arbitrator will hold the principal bound by the act of its agent if the agent is cloaked with "apparent" authority to act.[65]

The same agency principles apply to employees. Where an employee was discharged after he told an undercover agent the name of a fellow employee from whom the agent could purchase drugs, the arbitrator found that hearsay could not establish an agency relationship between the employee and the seller.[66]

Contract Principles

Arbitrators continue to recognize the fundamental principles of contract law, such as the obligation to perform contractual commitments in spite of hardships.[67] The principle that there is no binding contract without a meeting of the minds has also been applied by arbitrators.[68]

Generally, the intent of a written agreement is that it will not go into effect unless signed by the parties.[69] Other documents may be incorporated into a labor agreement by reference. In one case, where a handbook and a contract frequently contained identical language, the arbitrator found the handbook to be incorporated by reference into the contract.[70] The common law principle that parties to a contract should administer its provisions in good faith cannot be utilized to overcome specific contract language.[71]

Where a city unexpectedly lost revenue for providing contract police service to other communities, impossibility of performance was not a defense to a claim for back pay for laid-off policemen until they found other suitable employment.[72]

---

[64]Rubber Workers Local 670 v. Rubber Workers, 882 F.2d 613, 125 LRRM 2969 (CA 6, 1987); but for the opposite side of that coin, see Mohawk Rubber Co., 93 LA 777 (Aronin, 1989), holding grievance committee's settlement binding on union membership that voted to override settlement and go to arbitration, where contract permits settlement by committee and contains no provision to allow settlement to be overturned.

[65]Todd-Pacific Shipyards, 86 LA 171 (Draznin, 1985) (where company attorney handled first and second steps of grievance and agreed there would be no suspension, later suspension by vice president held invalid; union must be able to rely on word given in grievance meeting).

[66]Southern Cal. Permanente Medical Group, 92 LA 41 (Richman, 1989).

[67]Airco Carbon, 86 LA 6, 9 (Dworkin, 1986) ("No arbitrator is empowered to relieve a party of a bad bargain or to improve an existing contract."); Cascade Corp., 82 LA 313 (Bressler, 1984).

[68]Plumbers & Pipe Fitters Pension Plan, 87 LA 1177 (Everitt, 1986); Sea-Land Freight Serv., 87 LA 633 (D'Spain, 1986); Pollock Co., 87 LA 325 (Oberdank, 1986); Bunny Bread, 85 LA 1118 (Krislov, 1985).

[69]Family Food Park, 86 LA 1184 (Petersen, 1986).

[70]Hayssen Mfg., 82 LA 500 (Flaten, 1984); but see General Tel. of Cal., 89 LA 867 (Collins, 1987) ("Supervisor's Guide to Successful Labor Relations" issued by company to supervisors not binding on company absent contractual provision to that effect).

[71]Geauga Co., 92 LA 54 (Fullmer, 1988) (company was accused of manipulating overtime and recall—but within the terms of the agreement—so as to terminate the seniority of employees on layoff more than 24 months).

[72]City of Evansdale, Iowa, 92 LA 688, 691 (Miller, 1989).

Remedies for Mistake

Arbitrators have recognized the remedy of reformation in order to correct a mutual mistake.[73] However, where the mistake is not mutual, relief will not be granted.[74]

An arbitrator will not set aside terms of an agreement simply because, at the time of the signing of the agreement, one of the parties failed to realize the full ramifications of the provision signed.[75]

Where an employer makes an error in the nature of a "mistake of law" or "mistake of judgment" with full knowledge of all the facts, any monies paid out may not be recovered.[76] Where a company's final offer contains a modification of the fund contribution formula, and it is accepted by the union, the subsequent failure of the union to present that clause to the membership for ratification, or the inadvertent inclusion of the old clause in the new agreement, is held for naught: the offer and acceptance controls.[77]

Unjust Enrichment

The principle of unjust enrichment could not be applied where there was an absence of any fraud, duress, mistake, or other inequitable condition, even though the employer was enriched by the employee's handiwork.[78]

Waiver and Estoppel

Arbitrators often apply the underlying concept of waiver and estoppel without being too concerned with the fine legal distinctions.[79]

---

[73]Gates Rubber Co., 93 LA 637 (Cohen, 1989) (even though substantial paragraph left out of printed contract, arbitrator found clerical error and gave effect to initialed draft of the negotiators); St. Louis Post-Dispatch, 92 LA 23 (Heinsz, 1988) (burden of proof on party claiming mistake to prove it by clear and convincing evidence); Cleveland Pneumatic, 91 LA 428 (Oberdank, 1988) (apparent clerical error in COL Index figure in contract); in correcting a 12-year-old typographical error, arbitrator held, "[T]he arbitrator's function in reforming an agreement is not to effect a change in the parties' agreement but to give effect to the parties' original intention." Food Employers Council, 87 LA 514, 517 (Kaufman, 1986).

[74]Pillowtex Corp., 92 LA 321 (Goldstein, 1989); Klein Tools, 90 LA 1150 (Poindexter, 1988); Cleo Wrap, 90 LA 768 (Welch, 1988); typographical error did not reflect the intention of the parties; hence no meeting of the minds. Maple Heights Bd. of Educ., 86 LA 338 (Van Pelt, 1985); Summit County Brewers & Distribs. Ass'n, 84 LA 840 (Kates, 1985).

[75]Summit County Brewers & Distribs. Ass'n, 84 LA at 840.

[76]"[M]oney paid under a mistake of fact or a mutual mistake may be recovered * * * money paid under a mistake of law or of judgment may not be recovered." Olin Corp., 86 LA 1193, 1197 (Penfield, 1986).

[77]Bay Meadows Racing Ass'n, 90 LA 770 (Christopher, 1988).

[78]Amherst Coal, 84 LA 1181 (Wren, 1985).

[79]For an excellent discussion of the differences among waiver, estoppel, laches, and past practice, see City of Great Falls, 88 LA 396 (McCurdy, 1986). See also Michigan Bell Tel., 90 LA 1186 (Howlett, 1988); Fleming Foods of Mo., 89 LA 1292 (Yarowsky, 1987); Lennox Indus., 89 LA 1065 (Gibson, 1987); City of Dearborn, 89 LA 766 (Ellmann, 1987); U.S. Steel, 89 LA 300 (Dybeck, 1987); Reyco Indus., 81 LA 1133 (Rohlik, 1983).

There can be no waiver of a contract right without knowledge that the right is being abridged.[80]

While arbitrators generally hold that acquiescence by one party to violations of an express rule by the other party precludes action in regard to past transactions, they do not consider that acquiescence precludes application of the rule to future conduct.[81]

The failure to act upon a right given by a contract may be considered by the arbitrator along with other evidence to help establish the intent of the parties in agreeing to certain language.[82]

One arbitrator has held "that failure to enforce a right under a contract does not usually constitute a waiver unless the other party is prejudiced, damaged, or injured by the fact it was misled. In other words, there must be serious reliance before there can be an estoppel."[83] Most arbitrators do not require such a strong showing, but do require fairly strict minimum standards, such as clear evidence.[84]

Where a company has given assurances or made representations which employees have relied on, arbitrators have held that the company is estopped from denying the claim.[85] Where a company reinstated a discharged worker after one day off, based upon an assumed settlement with the union that the union did not sign, the union is not estopped from proceeding with the grievance for the day's pay, since no fully executed settlement existed.[86]

Public employers, under proper circumstances, and where equity would require, may be bound by the doctrine of equitable estoppel.[87] However, the arbitrator differentiated between the public agency discharging its duties under law and the agency acting as an employer engaged in the collective bargaining process.

Principles of Damages

Arbitrators are considered to have the authority to award monetary damages for contract violations even though the contract does not

---

[80]City of Miami, 89 LA 87 (Abrams, 1987).

[81]Federal Wholesale, 86 LA 945 (Cohen, 1985); Del Monte Corp., 86 LA 134 (Denson, 1985) (requiring union notice to company if union intends to enforce a right which it had failed for some time to enforce); Houston Publisher's Ass'n, 83 LA 767 (Milentz, 1984); Peabody Coal Co., 82 LA 1251 (Roberts, 1984); Port Drum Co., 82 LA 942 (Holman, 1984); City of Gainesville, Fla., 82 LA 825 (Hall, 1984); L&O Growers Assocs., 82 LA 814 (Weiss, 1984); Service Care Inc., 82 LA 590 (Talarico, 1984).

[82]Tecumseh Bd. of Educ., 82 LA 609, 613 (Daniel, 1984).

[83]SNE Corp., 82 LA 731, 734 (Flaten, 1984) (requiring serious reliance for estoppel).

[84]Farrell Lines, 86 LA 36 (Hockenberry, 1986) (clear and unmistakable); for distinction between waiver and "zipper clause" see Walgreen Co., 85 LA 1195 (Wies, 1985); Department of Health & Human Servs., 83 LA 883 (Edes, 1984); Firestone Tire & Rubber Co., 83 LA 12 (Lipson, 1984).

[85]Jim Walter Resources, 87 LA 857 (Nicholas, 1986) (representation to retirees at exit interview that they had insurance for life); Michigan Dep't of Social Servs., 87 LA 398 (Frost, 1986); Armco, Inc., 86 LA 928 (Seidman, 1985) (medical treatment undertaken in reliance on personnel department official's assurance of plan coverage; theory of promissory estoppel prevents company from denying coverage that was otherwise properly denied); but see Keebler Co., 86 LA 963 (Nolan, 1986), denying estoppel where no substantial *and* detrimental reliance shown.

[86]Buckeye Steel Casting, 92 LA 630 (Fullmer, 1989).

[87]City of Reno, 87 LA 707 (Richman, 1986).

specifically provide such remedy, since the parties have empowered the arbitrator to resolve their dispute.[88]

Compensatory Damages

Arbitrators continue to adhere to the principle that arbitrators have an inherent power under a contract to award monetary damages to place the parties in the position they would have been had there been no violation.[89] Ordinarily, the amount of damages should be limited to the amount necessary to make the injured party whole, unless the contract states otherwise.[90]

Generally, arbitrators require a showing of injury to justify damages, and will deny monetary relief where the injury is too speculative.[91] In some instances, where the amount is difficult to determine and there is no method available to determine the amount, the arbitrator, after consideration of all pertinent facts and circumstances, should use his own judgment.[92]

Damages Payable to Company or Union

Under the Civil Service Reform Act of 1978, the union, on a grievant's behalf, was allowed to file a claim for reasonable attorney's fees.[93]

Where a violation was the first of its kind committed by an employer, the contract contained no provision for damages, and the employees who worked did so voluntarily and were paid at the required holiday rate, the union was not entitled to punitive or compensatory damages from an employer who stayed open on a holiday.[94] Conversely, where a procedural defect caused by an employer resulted in the need for arbitration, the employer was assessed for the costs of the proceeding.[95] In another case, an employer was required to pay damages to a union where it violated the subcontracting provision of the parties collective bargaining agreement.[96]

---

[88]Cadillac Gage Co., 87 LA 853 (Van Pelt, 1986); Farrell Lines, 86 LA 36 (Hockenberry, 1986). See also FMC Corp., 92 LA 1247 (Stoltenberg, 1989) (arbitrator declined to fashion a remedy which would have required interpretation of an agreement other than the collective bargaining agreement).

[89]Cadillac Gage Co., 87 LA 853 (Van Pelt, 1986).

[90]Kelsey-Hayes Co., 85 LA 774 (Thomson, 1985).

[91]Holiday Inn of E. Peoria, 93 LA 181 (Draznin, 1989); Alpha Beta Co., 90 LA 1081 (Ross, 1988); Monterey Coal Co., 89 LA 989 (Fullmer, 1987); United States Playing Card Co., 87 LA 937 (Duda, 1986); Shell Oil Co., 87 LA 473 (Nicholas, 1986); Kroger Co., 85 LA 1198 (St. Antoine, 1985); Columbia Pictures Indus., 80 LA 1030 (Christopher, 1983).

[92]Lorimar-Telepictures Prods., 90 LA 1115; (Christopher, 1988).

[93]See Arbitrator Wolff in Hines Veterans Admin. Hosp., 85 LA 239 (1985).

[94]See Arbitrator Lipson in Great Atl. & Pac. Tea Co., 88 LA 430 (1986).

[95]Union Oil Co. of Cal., 91 LA 1206 (Klein, 1988).

[96]Brutoco Eng'g Constr., 92 LA 33 (Ross, 1988).

Punitive Damages

States disagree regarding the power of arbitrators to award punitive damages. Some courts have held that public policy prohibits arbitrators from awarding punitive damages.

Federal courts have been far less reluctant to permit punitive damage awards.[97] There is a clear federal policy to encourage arbitration. Therefore, federal courts place a heavy burden on those who attempt to assert an arbitrator has exceeded his authority.[98] In addition, if the contractual arbitration provision permits the award of punitive damages, and is enforced by the federal court pursuant to such labor policy, such a provision will be enforced despite contrary state law or policy.[99]

Attorney Fees

While it is not customary to award attorney fees against the offending party, where an employer acts in bad faith an arbitrator may choose this remedy to make a grievant whole.[100] Furthermore, with regard to federal agency disputes, the Civil Service Reform Act of 1978 does make provision for awarding such fees to the prevailing party.[101]

Mitigating Damages—Deduction of Outside Compensation

When awarding back pay to an employee, particularly in discharge or discipline cases, many arbitrators allow the employer's liability to be reduced by the amount of unemployment compensation or compensation from other employment paid to the employee during the relevant period,[102] providing such income was not a normal part of the grievant's income prior to discharge.[103]

Many arbitrators believe that an employee who has been wronged by an employer has an affirmative duty to mitigate, as far as he reasonably can, the amount of the loss.[104]

---

[97]See, e.g., Machinists v. Northwest Airlines, 858 F.2d 427, 129 LRRM 2588 (CA 8, 1988); Bonar v. Dean Witter Reynolds, 835 F.2d 1378 (CA 11, 1988); Electrical Workers (UE) Local 1139 v. Litton, 704 F.2d 393, 113 LRRM 2015 (CA 8, 1983), on rehearing 728 F.2d 970, 115 LRRM 2633 (CA 8, 1984).

[98]Pullman Power Prods. Corp. v. Local 403, 856 F.2d 1211, 129 LRRM 2500 (CA 9, 1988).

[99]Belko v. AVX Corp., 251 Cal. Rptr. 557 (Cal. Ct. App., 1988); Shaw v. Kuhnel & Assocs., 102 N.M. 607, 609, 698 P.2d 880, 882 (1985); Willoughby Roofing & Supply v. Kajima Int'l, 598 F. Supp. 353, 360 (N.D. Ala., 1984), aff'd, 776 F.2d 269 (CA 11, 1985).

[100]Synergy Gas Co., 91 LA 77 (Simmons, 1987), aff'd, 853 F.2d 59, 129 LRRM 2041 (CA 2, 1988); but see Arizona Bank, 91 LA 772 (Fine, 1988).

[101]Howard P. Foley Co. v. Electrical Workers (IBEW) Local 639, 789 F.2d 1421, 122 LRRM 2471 (CA 9, 1986); Veterans Admin., 88 LA 554 (Byars, 1986); Federal Correctional Inst., 90 LA 943 (White, 1987); Hines Veterans Admin. Hosp., 85 LA 239 (Wolff, 1985).

[102]I.W. Recreational Servs., 93 LA 302 (Richard, 1989); Flying Tigers Line, 91 LA 647 (Concepcion, 1988); Teamsters Local 58, 85 LA 745 (Boedecker, 1985); Yoh Sec., Inc., 85 LA 196 (Goldsmith, 1985). But see O'Keefe's Aluminum Prods., 92 LA 217 (Koven, 1987), in which arbitrator accepted grievant's excuse for failing to mitigate loss.

[103]Alumax Aluminum Corp., 92 LA 29 (Allen, 1988).

[104]Gase Baking Co., 86 LA 206 (Block, 1985).

Other Avoidable Damages; Delayed Arbitration

Where a delay in the arbitration process was caused by the failure of a company to respond, the arbitrator denied the union's request that the company bear the expense of the second arbitration hearing, since the agreement stated that the expense of arbitration was to be borne equally by both parties.[105]

Parol Evidence

The parol-evidence rule continues to be advanced and generally applied in arbitration cases.[106]

---

[105]Regional Transp. Dist., 87 LA 630 (Feldman, 1986). But see Michigan Dep't of Transp., 89 LA 551 (Borland, 1987); Denver Public Schools, 88 LA 507 (Watkins, 1986).

[106]Technocast, Inc., 91 LA 164 (Miller, 1988); Weil-McLain, 86 LA 784 (Cox, 1986); City of Depere, 86 LA 733 (Greco, 1986); Eureka Sec. Printing Co., 85 LA 1040 (DiLauro, 1985); Ferry-Morse Seed Co., 84 LA 75 (Duda, 1984).

Chapter 11

Precedent Value of Awards

It should be noted that probably less than 5 percent of all arbitration awards are ultimately published by the several firms providing this service. In addition, as recently as 1984, The Bureau of National Affairs, Inc. advised that only one case was being published for every 12 cases submitted for publication.[1] There is a belief that the issuance of NAA Opinion 11 in May 1983, which required NAA members to seek permission to publish *after* the award had been issued,[2] may have caused a reduction in the number of cases submitted for publication by NAA members, thereby resulting in the publication of the decisions of less experienced arbitrators. In 1985, the National Academy of Arbitrators amended the Code of Professional Responsibility to permit arbitrators to ask the parties for permission to publish either at the hearing or at the time the award is issued. A brief review of the 1988-89 Volumes (Nos. 89-92) of the LA Reports indicates that approximately 50 percent of the published awards are by NAA members.

An arbitrator should give deference to an earlier arbitration award in a dispute between the same parties where the circumstances are substantially the same, no substantial change has occurred either in the facts or the contract language, and the parties have renegotiated their contract and made no relevant change.[3]

Precedent Value of Legal Decisions

The legal concept of stare decisis, applied by judges in deciding similar cases, has not been transferred to the arbitration context intact.[4]

---

[1]Peterson & Rezler, "Employer and Union Attitudes Toward the Publication of Arbitration Awards," 40 Arb. J. No. 2, 40 (1985).

[2]Id. at 44.

[3]Cannelton Indus., 90 LA 705 (Stoltenberg, 1988); Florida Power Corp., 87 LA 957 (Wahl, 1986).

[4]Logan Co., 90 LA 949 (High, 1988); City of Oak Creek, 90 LA 710 (Baron, 1988); Michigan Dep't of Mental Health, 83 LA 237 (Borland, 1984).

Authoritative Prior Awards

Even though the Arbitration Review Board under the National Bituminous Coal Wage Agreement has been abolished, its full-opinion decisions continue to have precedential effect on cases to which they apply.[5] The decisions of a former chairperson of such board are entitled to no greater weight than those of other coal arbitrators.[6] An arbitration award dealing generally with the issue of job duties falling within a job classification does not preclude an arbitrator from deciding specific allegations in a subsequent grievance relating thereto.[7]

Temporary Arbitrators

The obligation to follow a prior arbitration award, which had found that a particular attendance control program was enforceable and that an illness could be treated as an occurrence, was explained by Arbitrator Jonathan Dworkin as follows:

> Regarding the issue of whether an absence should be excused if proven by medical documentation to have been unavoidable, the Arbitrator's scope is limited by the Aiges decision. The Agreement contemplates that arbitral awards on a subject are final and binding, at least during a contractual term. This means an award which interprets contractual rights and obligations is conclusive on all subsequent grievances which call for interpretations of the same rights and obligations. The Aiges decision governs this dispute insofar as it holds the Attendance Control Program enforceable.[8]

Under the theory of res judicata a final decision in a case is not to be changed by litigation in another case involving the same parties and the same issues. As applied to arbitration the doctrine means "that one may not receive an adverse award and then file grievance after grievance over the same matter in the hope of ultimately finding an arbitrator who will rule in one's favor."[9] An arbitration decision

---

[5]Cannelton Indus., 90 LA 705 (Stoltenberg, 1988) (res judicata applied where company failed to show that previous award was "clearly an instance of bad judgment; was made without the benefit of some important and relevant facts; was based on a substantial error of law or fact or conflicts with a Board decision. * * * A subsequent arbitrator is not to substitute his judgment for that of the prior arbitrator simply because he might have ruled differently in deciding the dispute." 90 LA 708-709.); Arch on the Green, 89 LA 892 (Seidman, 1987); North River Energy Co., 88 LA 447 (Witney, 1987).

[6]Freeman United Coal Mining Co., 87 LA 665 (Clarke, 1986).

[7]Arch of West Va., 90 LA 1220, 1222 (Volz, 1988) (res judicata is not applied where the factual and contractual issues are "quite different"); Engelhard Indus., 82 LA 680 (Nicholas, 1984); Arch of Ill., Inc., 82 LA 625 (Hewitt, 1984).

[8]Howard Paper Mills, 87 LA 863, 866 (1986).

[9]International Ass'n of Fire Fighters, 86 LA 1201, 1203 (Alleyne, 1986). Also see Ideal Elec. Co., 92 LA 1192 (Duda, 1989) (res judicata required that prior decision be followed as subject case involved same labor agreement, same parties and same fact situation; however, principle would not apply if arbitrator had been shown work involved was different from work in previous case, or if there were clear and convincing proof that previous arbitrator was "clearly wrong and incorrect in his interpretation and application of the Agreement."); Todd Pac. Shipyards, 91 LA 30 (Alleyne, 1988) (where arbitrator, in deciding he could not reexamine facts found by previous arbitrator in earlier case involving same parties, same collective bargaining agreement, and same underlying issues arising out of same fact pattern, noted that in a court proceeding a similar issue would present a question of collateral estoppel); Logan Co., 90 LA 949 (High, 1988) (where arbitrator applied doctrine of collateral estoppel since case involved same parties and same issues as previously decided case and noted "the reason for the doctrine of collateral estoppel is to put to rest the issues which are decided and have already been litigated."); Consolidation Coal Co., 82 LA 889 (Abrams, 1984).

involving a different plant of the employer and a different local union may be given great weight where the contract language is identical and where the union's primary negotiator at both plants was the same person.[10] This is particularly true where the contract language was not changed after the award and it had been followed in contract administration.[11] For a second arbitrator to change a prior decision, which the parties have not seen fit to change, would encourage repetitive arbitrations of the same issues, unless there has been a substantial change in the facts of the case or in the pertinent language of the contract.[12]

Persuasive Prior Awards

The approach taken by the Elkouris on the subject of voluntary quit versus discharge was followed by Arbitrator Leonard Irsay.[13] A review of arbitral decisions shows that arbitrators take into account an employee's past work record in applying just cause to penalties, being inclined to reduce penalties in part upon consideration of a long and good past record, and not interfering with the disciplinary decision where the past record is poor.[14]

As to making findings as to the credibility of witnesses, Arbitrator E. Lad Sabo wrote:

> Basically there are four (4) fundamental standards which can be relied upon to judge the competency of Witnesses. These standards are *perception, memory, communication,* and *interest.* It is this last factor which is of paramount importance in any Arbitration Proceeding. Testimony colored by interest or bias can often take the form of deliberate falsification or at least will simply consist of putting one's "best foot forward," which is to say, coloring testimony in a way favorable to the result that the Witness' interest compels him to seek.

---

[10]Cone Mills Corp., 86 LA 992 (Nolan, 1986).

[11]Freeman United Coal Mine Co., 84 LA 1302 (Feldman, 1985). Also see Port Drum Co., 82 LA 942 (Holman, 1984).

[12]Westvaco, 92 LA 1289 (Nolan, 1989); Florida Power Corp., 87 LA 957 (Wahl, 1986). In the following cases prior decisions were not followed: Where facts were not asserted, Fairmont Gen. Hosp., 91 LA 930 (Hunter, 1988) (prior discharge for off-duty shoplifting not claimed to be harmful to employer and newer case claimed violation of subsequently promulgated rules) or where facts changed, Northern Suburban Mass. Transit Dist., 90 LA 809 (Meyers, 1988) (improvement in medical condition in 6-year period since initial decision that employee was disabled). In Weyerhauser Co., 92 LA 361 (1989), Arbitrator Anne Holman Woolf determined not to follow a prior decision where there had been no renegotiation of the agreement between the time of the award and the date of the incidents giving rise to the grievance. In her opinion she also pointed out the need to write fully reasoned opinions if prior awards are to be persuasive on subsequent arbitrators, noting that the lack of discussion in the prior decision regarding the interpretation of the language of the labor agreement prevented her from "evaluating the reasonableness, soundness and validity of that decision" and resulted in her declining to follow the prior award. Similarly, in Federal Wholesale Co., 92 LA 271 (Richard, 1989), a prior decision barring subcontracting was not followed where the previous arbitrator recognized but did not factually find "a special business need" which was found by the second arbitrator in the subsequent case and allowed the company to remain in business.

[13]Fordham Univ., 85 LA 293 (1985) (citing pp. 615-616 of the Third Edition, How Arbitration Works (1973), corresponding pp. 655-656 in the Fourth Edition (1985)).

[14]General Tel. Co. of Ind., 85 LA 251 (Winton, 1985).

> It is also to be noted that in evaluating conflicting Testimony the Arbitrator must further acknowledge the existence of a "code" which inhibits or discourages Union Members from testifying against one another. Thus, there is an inherent bias or interest in the testimony of any Union Member when it involves conflict with another Union Member. The *same* comments may be applicable to certain levels of Employer Representatives.[15]

As to citing a long line of previous decisions in writing an arbitration opinion, Arbitrator Peter Seitz pointed out that the citing of prior published awards can be abused. He stressed the fact that in recent years the overwhelming number of published decisions are written by relatively inexperienced arbitrators. He opined that the vast body of arbitration decisions by the most experienced arbitrators have never been published and concluded that "[i]f there is a 'body of arbitral law' it may be likened to an iceberg, of which only the tip is perceptible; * * *."[16]

As to making reference to workers' compensation awards, Arbitrator David T. Borland gave to such an award "significant weight," stating that it should be treated "much like a prior arbitration award, * * * not in any manner to reflect the obligatory *stare decisis* principle, but more from the advisory arbitral principle, recognizing prior determinations of the same issues, principles, and participants in both proceedings."[17]

---

[15]Lucky Stores, 83 LA 760, 765 (1984). Arbitrator Sabo added at p. 765: "The purpose of the Arbitration Procedure is to *seek* the *truth* of the matter and to adjudicate the rights and privileges of the parties as spelled out in the Labor Agreement and on the *Total Record*, as presented by the Parties."

[16]"The Citation of Authority and Precedent in Arbitration (Its Use and Abuse)," 38 Arb. J. No. 4, 60 (1983).

[17]Highland Park Pub. Schools, 90 LA 986, 998-999 (1988).

Chapter 12

Custom and Past Practice

Custom and Practice as Part of the Contract

Arbitrators continue to hold custom and past practice enforceable through arbitration, even though not expressed in the collective bargaining agreement.[1] Although there remain no universally accepted standards for determining which unwritten practices rise to the level of binding ones,[2] a large number of arbitrators continue to refer to the standards articulated by Arbitrator Jules J. Justin in *Celanese Corporation of America.*[3] If it is not proven that the practice is unequivocal, clearly enunciated and acted upon, and readily ascertainable over a reasonable period of time as a fixed practice accepted by both parties, a binding past practice will usually not be found.[4] Of course, an

---

[1]E.g., Dixie Mach. Welding & Metal Works, 88 LA 734 (Baroni, 1987). Parties may expressly incorporate past practices as a part of their collective bargaining agreement by reference, and thus plainly render them enforceable through arbitration. Alabama By-Prods. Corp., 83 LA 1270 (Clarke, 1984).

[2]In Klickitat County, 86 LA 283 (1985), Arbitrator Martin Smith held that, since definitions of past practice vary, arbitrators are free to formulate their own criteria for establishment of binding practices.

[3]24 LA 168, 172 (1954). These criteria, or similar ones, have been articulated and accepted by Arbitrator McDermott in Texas Util. Generating Div., 92 LA 1308, 1312 (1989); Cyrol in Wyman-Gordon Co., 91 LA 225, 230 (1988); Bittel in City of Marion, 91 LA 175, 179 (1988); and by Hockenberry in Farrell Lines, 86 LA 36, 39 (1986); Ruben in Packaging Corp. of Am., 85 LA 700, 705 (1985); Pratte in Belleville Shoe Mfg. Co., 84 LA 337, 341 (1985); Hilgert in Fashion Shoe Prods., 84 LA 325, 329-330 (1985); Kaplan in Washington Metro. Airport Police Branch, 84 LA 203, 208 (1985); Fitzsimmons in Emerson Elec. Co., 83 LA 895, 897 (1984); White in Ethyl Corp., 82 LA 603, 604 (1984); and Groshong in Charleston Naval Shipyard, 82 LA 476 (1984).

[4]See Illinois Power Co., 93 LA 611, 614 (Westbrook, 1989) (no binding practice where not mutually accepted or consistently applied unit-wide); Country Lane Foods, 88 LA 599, 602 (Strasshofer, 1986) (no proof of mutuality); Waverly Community School, 86 LA 161, 163 (Daniel, 1986) (no proof of mutual acceptance); Revco Indus., 85 LA 1034, 1039 (Newmark, 1985) (proof of one or two instances insufficient to establish practice); Montgomery Ward & Co., 85 LA 913, 915 (Caraway, 1985) (no proof of employer knowledge of and acquiescence in alleged practice); International Paper Co., 85 LA 790, 791-92 (Sloane, 1985) (proof of 10 exceptions to strong tradition does not establish practice); Midwest Printing Co., 85 LA 615, 619 (Ver Ploeg, 1985) (no binding practice where prior occurrences may have been in error); Johnson Controls, 85 LA 594, 600 (Garnholz, 1985) (no proof of mutuality); General Tel. of Cal., 85 LA 476, 481 (Collins, 1985) (no proof of mutual acceptance); Equal Employment Opportunity Comm'n, 84 LA 1231, 1237 (Mikrut, 1985) (proof of three incidents insufficient to establish practice).

arbitrator must first find that a practice exists before its binding effect may be considered.[5]

Just as the standards for determining whether a practice is binding are not universally accepted, the analyses used in determining what types of practices are binding vary among arbitrators. Whether categorized as "working conditions," "major terms of employment," or "benefits" of special value to employees, certain past practices are held to be binding because to hold otherwise would defeat the reasonable expectations of the employees.[6] On the other hand, an employer may not be bound to continue providing a purely gratuitous benefit, even if employees might have come to rely on it.[7] Even a significant economic benefit may not be binding if it is shown the benefit has not been provided consistently.[8]

Arbitrators are reluctant to find that a management right is extinguished by lack of its exercise. Thus, the failure to enforce a requirement that workers hold a valid driver's license[9] and the failure to enforce a rule against personal toll telephone calls[10] were held not to be binding past practices. In some cases, however, because of the employees' expectation of nonenforcement, the employer is required to give adequate notice before beginning to enforce an existing policy.[11]

---

[5]See Trumbull County Dep't of Human Servs., 90 LA 1267, 1272 (Curry, 1988) (method of operation or procedural custom does not constitute practice); Bay Area Rapid Transit Dist., 87-1 ARB ¶ 8084, p. 3341 (Concepcion, 1986) (prior absence of a newly established drug testing policy does not establish a past practice); S.D. Warren Co., 89 LA 688, 699 (Gwiazda, 1985) (where not acted upon, the terms of a posted notice do not constitute a practice, S.D. Warren Co. Div. v. Paperworkers Local 1069, 632 F. Supp. 463, 122 LRRM 2186 (D. Me. 1986), rev'd on other grounds, 815 F.2d 178, 125 LRRM 2086, (CA 1), vacated, 108 S.Ct. 497, 126 LRRM 3360 (1987), rev'd on other grounds, 845 F.2d 3, 128 LRRM 2175 (CA 1, 1988)). In a companion case, the First Circuit upheld the arbitrator's decision on other grounds. 846 F.2d 827, 128 LRRM 2432 (CA 1), cert. denied, 109 S.Ct. 555, 129 LRRM 3072 (1988).

[6]See Reliance Elec. Co., 90 LA 641, 645 (Wolff, 1988) (company nurse constituted benefit and working condition); City of Miami, 89 LA 86, 89 (Abrams, 1987) (work schedule is job benefit); Ferndale School Dist., 88 LA 468, 471 (Stoltenberg, 1987); Airco Carbon, 86 LA 6, 11 (Dworkin, 1986) (management could not unilaterally amend erroneous incentive pay standard in use for 30 years); Clinchfield Coal Co., 85 LA 382, 385 (Rybolt, 1985) (employees have right to rely on practice they believe in effect); Hoover Co., 85 LA 41, 42 (Shanker, 1985) ("past practice * * * set the context and understanding within which the employees operated"); Rola, 84 LA 998, 1000 (Baroni, 1985) (unfair to change practice without contract negotiations); Johnson Controls, 84 LA 553, 559-561 (Dworkin, 1985) (employer bound by practice of providing pay for missed overtime rather than make-up opportunity); City of Detroit, 84 LA 301, 305-307 (Roumell, 1985) (employer bound by practice of posting promotional opportunities); Saginaw Mining Co., 82 LA 735, 738 (Feldman, 1984) (employer bound by practice of providing employees monthly printout of excused absences). But see Honeywell Inc., 92 LA 181, 184 (Lennard, 1989) (smoking privilege held to be detriment and not benefit, and therefore did not constitute binding practice); Dayton Newspapers, 91 LA 201, 211 (Kindig, 1988) (smoking found to be personal right, not a contractual right); City of Anaheim, 91 LA 579, 583 (Bickner, 1988) (administrative procedures that convey incidental advantages are not binding).

[7]In Minnesota Dep't of Labor & Indus., 83 LA 621, 625 (1984), Arbitrator Gallagher stated, "An agreement to be bound is not implied * * * when the practice is not controversial or when * * * it benefits both parties." See also Scott Paper Co., 82 LA 755, 757 (Caraway, 1984); Ohio Precision Casting, 82 LA 117, 120 (Murphy, 1983). But see Dental Command, 83 LA 529 (Allen, 1984) (practice of allowing smoking in lab is binding).

[8]Charleston Naval Shipyard, 82 LA 476 (Groshong, 1984).

[9]City of Sharon, 86 LA 932 (Probst, 1985).

[10]General Tel. Co., 80 LA 138 (Maxwell, 1985).

[11]Ibid.

Management's fundamental right to make work assignments is often upheld in the face of an allegedly contrary practice.[12] Unilateral changes implemented to promote safety and to enhance a company's image have also been approved if they are reasonable and related to a legitimate objective.[13] Moreover, arbitrators frequently base their awards on a demonstrated past practice that supports management's exercise of a right.[14]

Regulation, Modification, or Termination of Practice as Implied Term of Contract

A practice which has been held to be binding is generally enforceable for the duration of the collective bargaining agreement in effect when the issue arises.[15] Thereafter, an employer may effectively repudiate a past practice by giving timely and proper notice of its intent to do so before or during collective bargaining negotiations.[16] Where the factual basis for the practice ceases, the practice may be modified or extinguished during the agreement.[17] An otherwise binding past practice does not survive after bargaining that results in a major modification of the practice.[18] A successor employer may not be bound by the practices of its predecessor.[19]

Contract Clauses Regarding Custom

Arbitrators continue to give effect to contract clauses that purport to nullify prior practices.[20] Such so-called "zipper clauses" commonly

---

[12]Armour Foods, 85 LA 1013 (Madden, 1985); E.G. & G. Florida, 85 LA 585 (Richard, 1985); Dow Corning Corp., 83 LA 1049 (Seidman, 1984); Butler County Mushroom Farm, 82 LA 170 (Jones, 1984). But see City of Miami, 89 LA 86, 89 (Abrams, 1987) (work schedule is benefit).

[13]Acorn Bldg. Components Inc., 92 LA 68, 73 (Roumell, 1988) (restrictions on smoking related to safety considerations upheld despite past practice); Creative Prods., 89 LA 777, 780 (McDonald, 1987) (employer allowed to limit radio use to ear-plug type to improve traffic safety and to protect company image because of visitors on premises).

[14]Arvin Indus., 88 LA 1188 (Volz, 1987); City of Depere, 86 LA 733 (Greco, 1986); E & J Gallo Winery, 86 LA 153 (Wyman, 1985); Armour Foods, 85 LA 1013 (Madden, 1985); Alabama By-Prods. Corp., 85 LA 1107 (Kilroy, 1985); Cigna Healthplans of Ga., 84 LA 422 (Rothschild, 1985); Arco Oil & Gas Co., 84 LA 235 (Baroni, 1985); FMC-Ordinance Div., 84 LA 163 (Wyman, 1985); St. Louis County Water Co., 83 LA 1162 (Holman, 1984); St. Regis Corp., 82 LA 1244 (Coyne, 1984); Jenison Pub. Schools, 82 LA 1100 (Roumell, 1984); Kroger Co., 82 LA 340 (Murphy, 1984).

[15]Arch of Ill., 84 LA 185, 189-190 (Feldman, 1985) (a practice may not be repudiated during the term of the agreement in which it is used). See also Jafco Inc., 82 LA 283, 286 (Armstrong, 1984) (employer may not stand silent on practice during contract negotiations and later unilaterally change practice regarding premium pay).

[16]General Foods Mfg. Corp., 82 LA 889, 891-893 (Williams, 1984).

[17]See Copley Press, 91 LA 1324, 1331 (Goldstein, 1988); E.G. & G. Fla., 85 LA 585, 594 (Richard, 1985); General Tire & Rubber Co., 83 LA 811, 813 (Feldman, 1984); Miners Clinic, 83 LA 445, 448 (Probst, 1984); Butler County Mushroom Farms, 82 LA 170, 171 (Jones, 1984).

[18]Thrifty Corp., 85 LA 780, 782-783 (Gentile, 1985).

[19]Family Food Park, 86 LA 1184, 1188 (Petersen, 1986). But see Williams-Russell & Johnson, 91 LA 1214, 1217 (Byars, 1989) (employer practice of paying contributions to employee IRA accounts for leave hours as well as work hours upheld despite contract language requiring contributions only for each hour worked where practice had been applied by predecessor, adopted and applied consistently by employer, survived challenge during contract negotiations, and was unchallenged in subsequent talks).

[20]E.g., Augsburg College, 91 LA 1166, 1173 (Gallagher, 1988); Wyandot Inc., 82 LA 1263, 1265 (Strasshofer, 1984); Hesco Indus., 81 LA 649 (Chapman, 1983).

take the form either of an acknowledgement that the written contract constitutes the parties' entire agreement and a waiver of the right to bargain about other conditions,[21] or a specific affirmation that management rights are not limited by prior practices.[22] When a union or an employer[23] agrees to a "zipper," it waives its right to rely on practices established during prior contract terms.[24] Although exceptions have been found and the waiver held ineffective where the practice is continued after the execution of the "zipper," other cases hold that in the face of such a specific "waiver," the continuation of a benefit practice in the first year of a three-year agreement does not "revive" the benefit.[25] Whatever their effect on purely practice-created rights or benefits, as a matter of logic "zipper clauses" should not affect the use of practice as an aid to interpreting ambiguous language.[26]

Other parties have attempted to limit the effect of a prior course of conduct by inserting language in the grievance and arbitration provisions of contracts that restricts the arbitrator's use of past practice to the interpretation of ambiguous language.[27]

Among contract clauses preserving past practice, there are those that require future adherence to precedent established in previously arbitrated or settled grievances. In one such case, Arbitrator A. Langley Coffey gave res judicata effect to a settlement in a prior case reached 20 years earlier.[28]

Question of Arbitrability

The split of authority continues over the arbitrability of a dispute concerning a practice-based entitlement where the language of the arbitration clause restricts the use of the grievance and arbitration machinery to issues arising under "the agreement." Under language excluding from the grievance procedure "[c]omplaints with reference to matters not included in the agreement" and defining a "grievance"

---

[21]NLRB v. Southern Materials Co., 447 F.2d 15, 77 LRRM 2814 (CA 4, 1971).

[22]Hayssen Mfg. Co., 82 LA 500 (Flaten, 1984); Hesco Indus., 81 LA 649 (Chapman, 1983).

[23]E.g., Container Corp. of Am., 91 LA 329, 333 (Rains, 1988) (employer held to have waived practice).

[24]NLRB v. Southern Materials Co., 447 F.2d 15, 77 LRRM 2814 (CA 4, 1971).

[25]School City of Hobart, 86 LA 557, 563 (Alexander, 1985) ("[C]lear meaning (of the zipper clause) is not overcome by the relatively short period of the benefits and the lack of evidence that the benefits were mutually intended and understood to continue indefinitely.").

[26]In Houston Publishers Ass'n, 83 LA 767 (Milentz, 1984), management claimed that there was a binding practice of ignoring the status quo practice-preservation clause, but the arbitrator gave effect to the clause, holding that its clear language overcame the claimed practice to the contrary. See also Reardon & Leahy, "Does Past Practice Protect Unions and Their Workers?," 37 Lab. L.J. No. 9, 646, 650, at n. 21 (1986).

[27]Textron, Burkart Randall Div. v. Machinists Lodge 1076, 648 F.2d 462, 107 LRRM 2836 (CA 7, 1981).

[28]Ethyl Corp., Houston Plant, 83 LA 124, 126 (1984). The contract clause at issue in that case read as follows: "A settled grievance which involves the interpretation of a particular provision of the bargaining agreement will be followed in disposing of a subsequently filed grievance requiring interpretation of the same contractual provision and involving substantially similar facts and circumstances." One court held that a prior contrary award must be given res judicata effect because of the "final and binding" clause. Trailways Lines v. Trailways, Inc., Joint Council, 121 LRRM 3025, 3029 (E.D. Mo., 1985).

as "covered by a specific provision of the agreement," one arbitrator found arbitrable a dispute over the discontinuance of free State Fair tickets.[29] As in other such cases, the rationale—derived from the Supreme Court's decision in *Warrior & Gulf*[30]—is that once a practice has attained binding contractual status, it is to be considered "equally a part of the agreement although not expressed in it."[31] Another basis for a finding of arbitrability is language defining a grievance as a "question concerning wages, hours or working conditions," without limiting the subject matter to "the agreement."[32]

In other cases where the written contract was entirely silent on the issue of the benefit claimed by the union, arbitrators have sustained management objection to arbitrability on the ground that their authority is limited by typical contract language to disputes arising under "the agreement."[33]

Role of Custom and Practice in Interpretation of Ambiguous Language

Whatever questions may exist about inferring implied terms exclusively from the existence of a past practice, there continues to be no question that past practice is properly used as an aid to interpreting ambiguous contract language.[34] In addition to practices in the nature of specifically defined and consistent prior conduct, arbitrators have discerned in the parties' prior inconsistent conduct an intent to apply generally a "rule of reason" in interpreting an ambiguous provision, and have supplied "reason" where the parties could not find it for themselves.[35]

---

[29]Dallas Power & Light Co., 87 LA 415 (White, 1985).

[30]United Steelworkers v. Warrior & Gulf Navigation Co., 80 S.Ct. 1347, 46 LRRM 2416 (1960), one of the decisions comprising the well-known *Steelworkers Trilogy*.

[31]Dallas Power & Light Co., 87 LA 415, 418 (White, 1985). See also Simkins Indus., 81 LA 592 (Carter, 1983). Cf. Adkins v. Times-World Corp., 771 F.2d 829, 120 LRRM 2216, 2218 (CA 4, 1985).

[32]E.g., Johnson Controls, 84 LA 553, 559-561 (Dworkin, 1985).

[33]Reyco Indus., 85 LA 1034, 1040 (Newmark, 1985).

[34]E.g., Massey Buick v. Machinists Lodge 63, 119 LRRM 2146 (W.D. Pa., 1984). For recent examples, see Checker Motors Co., 91 LA 1198, 1201 (Lipson, 1988) (determination of application of insurance clause governing coverage); San Bernardino School Dist., 90 LA 214, 216 (Collins, 1987) (defining term "malicious act"); Transamerica Delaval, 84 LA 190 (Brisco, 1985) (management right to require overtime work); City of Burlington, Iowa, 83 LA 973, 976 (Traynor, 1984) (management right to determine method of scheduling vacations); Allied Maintenance Corp., 82 LA 620 (Williams, 1984) (entitlement to overtime work); Metropolitan Medical Center, 82 LA 538 (Miller, 1984) (history of management regulation of certain conduct without union objection; specifically, the contract required payment of a uniform allowance if the employer proscribed uniforms, but in practice the employer had prohibited some forms of inappropriate dress without paying a uniform allowance. The prohibition of inappropriate dress was not interpreted to trigger the obligation to make a uniform allowance payment); Koehring S. Plant, 82 LA 193, 196 (Alsher, 1984). Compare Basin Elec. Power Coop., 91 LA 675, 679 (MacLean, 1988) (past practice only used to interpret ambiguous language in existence at time of the occurrences of the practice).

[35]Circle Steel Corp., 85 LA 738 (Stix, 1984) (contract clause allowing bonus days off as a reward for good attendance is ambiguous as applied to periods which include layoffs; intent to apply "rule of reason" was discerned from parties' past conduct in awarding bonus days in variety of different circumstances). See also Transamerica Delaval, 84 LA 190 (Brisco, 1985); City of Burlington, Iowa, 83 LA 973, 976 (Traynor, 1984); Allied Maintenance Corp., 82 LA 620 (Williams, 1984); Metropolitan Medical Center, 82 LA 538 (Miller, 1984) (where contract required payment of a uniform allowance if employer proscribed uniforms, but in practice employer had prohibited some forms of inappropriate dress without paying a uniform allowance. The prohibition of inappropriate dress was not interpreted to trigger obligation to make a uniform allowance payment); Koehring S. Plant, 82 LA 193, 196 (Alsher, 1984).

As with practices that by themselves create contractual rights, practices to be used as interpretational aids must be understood by or known to both parties,[36] and "should be unequivocal, well recognized and acted upon, consistent, frequent, of reasonable duration, and mutually accepted."[37] The failure of one party to object to the other's action generally satisfies the condition of mutuality, since "[t]he criterion of concurrence does not require an act of affirmation; acquiescence to the practice is deemed sufficient * * *."[38] Just as the failure to use a right expressly contained in the written agreement does not waive the right, a hiatus in the use of a right acquired by practice does not, by itself, eliminate the effect of the practice.[39]

Of course, often a difficult threshold issue is whether the contract's provisions are ambiguous, permitting an arbitrator to look to extrinsic guidance such as past practice.[40] Arbitrator Alvin L. Goldman stated as the test of ambiguity whether the "contractual language is subject to more than one single, reasonable, apparent understanding."[41] Ambiguity is not found on the face of the language itself, but on its application to the facts at hand.[42] Indeed, proof of a consistent prior practice may itself persuade the arbitrator of the ambiguity of a contract provision which is seemingly clear on its face. For example, where the contract provided paid-up life insurance benefits to retirees with "20 years service" and the practice had been to grant the benefit based on service *in the industry* whether with one or several employers, Arbitrator Irwin Dean found that the seemingly clear service requirement was ambiguous.

> Where the parties to an agreement have, through a consistent course of dealing over an extended period of time, ascribed a particular meaning to a term which might in general usage connote some other fact of meaning, the particular meaning developed by the parties should, it seems, be preferred over the meaning ascribed by general usage * * *.[43]

Custom and Practice Versus Clear Contract Language

Many recent arbitration cases and court decisions affirm the principle that parties to an arbitration proceeding are bound by unam-

---

[36]Detroit Lakes Educ. Ass'n, 83 LA 66 (Gallagher, 1984).

[37]Super Valu Stores, 87 LA 453, 457 (Goldman, 1986) (citing Elkouri & Elkouri at p. 362 of the Fourth Edition (1985)) (case in which arbitrator found insufficient incidence of seniority-based assignment of work to casual employees, and that alleged practice was equivocal because on those occasions when such assignments had been made it could have been for other reasons). For a discussion of the standards of effectiveness to which practices generally are held, see Dobbelaere, Leahy & Reardon, "The Effect of Past Practice on the Arbitration of Labor Disputes," 40 Arb. J. No. 4, 27 (1985).

[38]Dillon Stores Co., 84 LA 84, 87 (Woolf, 1984).

[39]Transamerica Delaval, 84 LA 190 (Brisco, 1985).

[40]See Chapter 9 of the Fourth Edition, topic entitled "Ambiguity." Where arbitrators have declared an ambiguity improperly, courts have not hesitated to find that the award does not "draw its essence" from the contract and have vacated such awards on that basis. E.g., Morgan Servs. v. Clothing & Textile Workers Local 323, 724 F.2d 1217, 115 LRRM 2368, 2372 (CA 6, 1984).

[41]Super Valu Stores, 87 LA 453, 456 (1986).

[42]Circle Steel Corp., 85 LA 738 (Stix, 1984).

[43]Associated Textile Sys., 86 LA 761, 765 (1985).

biguous language despite a contrary past practice,[44] even where the practice may have been followed for many years.[45]

Amendment of Contract

While the weight of authority and the better rule are to the effect that unambiguous contract language will prevail over a contrary practice, occasionally arbitrators are persuaded that the parties' conduct is attended with sufficiently reliable indicia of an intent to amend the written provisions of the agreement.[46] Reviewing courts also are sometimes persuaded to enforce an award that gives effect to a practice that is contrary to unambiguous language. "[A]n arbitrator's award that appears contrary to the express terms of the agreement may nevertheless be valid if it is premised upon reliable evidence of the parties' intent."[47]

Gap-Filling

Rights or benefits that are defined generally or that do not specify the consequences of a violation are given specific application by reference to past practice.[48] For example, where a contract gave a union steward the right to a "reasonable time to attend to necessary union business," the practice of permitting the steward to conduct a card check on company time was sustained.[49] Where a contract granted paid leave for emergencies, the practice of not having treated snow days as emergencies controlled.[50] Typical of the "gap-filling" uses of

---

[44]Hoteles Condado Beach v. Local 901, 763 F.2d 34, 119 LRRM 2664 (CA 1, 1985); Heublein Wines, 93 LA 400, 406 (Randall, 1988); Texas Util. Generating Div., 92 LA 1308, 1313 (McDermott, 1989); Warner Cable of Akron, 91 LA 48, 52 (Bittel, 1988); Hayward School Dist., 89 LA 14, 16 (Concepcion, 1987); Toledo Area Regional Transit Auth., 87 LA 193 (Duda, 1986); May Dep't Stores, 84 LA 53 (Morgan, 1985); Dole Can Plant, 83 LA 253 (Tsukiyama, 1984); City of Gainesville, Fla., 82 LA 825 (Hall, 1984); Consolidation Coal Co., 82 LA 819 (Feldman, 1984); Associated Wholesale Grocers, 81 LA 1126 (O'Reilly, 1983) (employee bumping rights); Veterans Admin., 81 LA 946 (Dunn, 1983) (promotion practices).

[45]E.g., City of Meriden, 87 LA 163 (Davis, 1986) (despite a 15-year practice, acquiesced in by union, of deductions from pay, company was bound by clear language to the contrary); BASF Wyandotte Corp., 84 LA 1055 (Caraway, 1985) (where a 15-year practice of paying committee members for their full shift on day of negotiations, unambiguous contract language to the contrary, was given effect: "where a conflict exists between the clear and unambiguous language of the contract and a long-standing past practice, the Arbitrator is required to follow the language of the contract * * *. While the Arbitrator recognizes that it is difficult to accept the overturn of a fifteen (15) year past practice, the Arbitrator is required to do so in light of the clear and certain language * * *.").

[46]E.g, Michigan Dep't of State Police, 92 LA 403, 407-408 (Borland, 1989). See generally Hill & Sinicropi, "Resolving Conflicts With Contract Language," Management Rights: A Legal and Arbitral Analysis, 49-53 (BNA Books, 1986).

[47]Electrical Workers (IBEW) Local 199 v. United Tel. Co., 738 F.2d 1564, 117 LRRM 2094, 2097 (CA 11, 1984). Contra Machinists Dist. Lodge 72 v. Teter Tool & Die Co., 630 F. Supp. 732, 121 LRRM 3270, 3273 (N.D. Ind., 1986) (award drawing its essence not from language of contract but from bargaining history not enforced).

[48]E.g., Kent State Univ., 91 LA 895, 904 (Curry, 1988); Central Brass Mfg. Co., 91 LA 386, 391 (Dworkin, 1988); Wyman-Gordon Co., 91 LA 224, 229-230 (Cyrol, 1988); City of Sweet Home, 89 LA 255, 257 (Runkel, 1987).

[49]S.F.C. Bldg. Corp., 88 LA 706 (Canestraight, 1987).

[50]School Dist. of City of Beloit, 82 LA 177 (Greco, 1984).

past practice are those cases in which an arbitrator must choose between alternative possible remedies, such as whether to award back pay or make-up work to correct a violation of an employee's entitlement to overtime work.[51]

[51]Johnson Controls, 84 LA 553, 559-561 (Dworkin, 1985).

Chapter 13

Management Rights

Inroads Made by Legislation

The Duty to Bargain: Right of Unilateral Action

The duty to bargain on subjects falling within the terms "rates of pay, wages, hours of employment, or other conditions of employment," is a legally enforceable duty imposed on the employer by the original National Labor Relations Act.[1]

Other mandatory subjects of bargaining which have evolved as a result of litigation are employee safety,[2] termination of union privileges,[3] employer's payments to union trust fund,[4] use of recreation fund,[5] disbursement of state funds allocated to increase wages and benefits,[6] costs of arbitration hearing transcripts,[7] allocation of severance and vacation pay following closure of plant,[8] layoff decisions,[9] Christmas

---

[1]For articles containing discussion of duty to bargain and unilateral action see Crough, "The Viability of Distinguishing Between Mandatory and Permissive Subjects of Bargaining in a Cooperative Setting: In Search of Industrial Peace," 41 Vand. L. Rev. 557 (1988); Brittain & Heshizer, "Management Decision Bargaining: The Interplay of Law and Politics," 38 Lab. L.J. 220 (1987); Ellmore, "Subcontracting: Mandatory or Permissive Subject of Bargaining?," 36 Lab. L.J. 773 (1985); George, "To Bargain or Not to Bargain: A New Chapter in Work Relocation Decisions," 69 Minn. L. Rev. 667 (1985); Note, "Section 8(d) of the NLRA and the Duty to Decision-Bargain Over Work Relocation: Some Observations on Management Rights After Milwaukee Spring II," 36 Syracuse L. Rev. 1055 (1985); Susser, "NLRB Restricts Mandatory Bargaining Over Managerial Changes," 35 Lab. L.J. 415 (1984).

[2]Asarco, Inc. v. NLRB, 805 F.2d 194, 123 LRRM 2985 (CA 6, 1986); Oil, Chem. & Atomic Workers v. NLRB, 711 F.2d 348, 113 LRRM 3163 (D.C. Cir., 1983).

[3]NLRB v. BASF Wyandotte Corp., 798 F.2d 849, 123 LRRM 2320, 2322 (CA 5, 1986) (unilateral termination of use of office, phone, and copy machine formerly extended to union president).

[4]American Commercial Lines, 291 NLRB No. 143, 131 LRRM 1561 (1988); Southwestern Steel & Supply v. NLRB, 806 F.2d 1111, 123 LRRM 3290 (D.C. Cir., 1986).

[5]Getty Ref. & Marketing Co., 279 NLRB 924, 122 LRRM 1150, 1151 (1986).

[6]Sheltering Pines Convalescent Hosp., 255 NLRB 1195, 107 LRRM 1145 (1981).

[7]Communications Workers, 280 NLRB 78, 124 LRRM 1009 (1986).

[8]Armour & Co., 280 NLRB 824, 123 LRRM 1266 (1986).

[9]Stamping Specialty Co., 294 NLRB No. 56, 131 LRRM 1740 (1989); Lapeer Foundry & Mach., 289 NLRB No. 126, 129 LRRM 1001 (1988).

bonuses,[10] profit-sharing benefits,[11] insurance programs,[12] drug and alcohol testing of current employees,[13] change in paid lunch policy,[14] the number of members on a union grievance committee,[15] banned use of all personal radios,[16] elimination of shift work,[17] implementation of a light duty program,[18] use of a mandatory, rotating leave-without-pay roster to reduce staffing,[19] replacement of economic strikers by permanent subcontract,[20] and change of driver dispatch procedure.[21]

There remains no duty to bargain over a managerial decision that would otherwise be a mandatory bargaining subject if there are "compelling economic considerations" underlying the decision,[22] or if the decision is not "a material, substantial, and significant one affecting the terms and conditions of employment of bargaining unit employees."[23]

Following the Supreme Court's *First National Maintenance*[24] decision, the NLRB held in *Otis Elevator* that "decisions which affect the scope, direction, or nature of the business" are excluded from § 8(d) of the Act.[25] As for the particular subject of subcontracting, the Board stated that if the employer's decision to subcontract (or to reorganize, consolidate, or relocate) turned on a reduction of labor costs, it would be a subject of mandatory bargaining,[26] but if it turned on "a fundamental change in the scope and direction of the enterprise," it would not be.[27]

---

[10]Freedom WLNE-TV, 278 NLRB 1293, 122 LRRM 1214 (1986).

[11]Ibid.

[12]R.E.C. Corp., 296 NLRB No. 163, 132 LRRM 1286 (1989); Advertiser's Mfg. Co., 294 NLRB No. 51, 132 LRRM 1024 (1989).

[13]Star Tribune, 295 NLRB No. 63, 131 LRRM 1404 (1989); Johnson-Bateman Co., 295 NLRB No. 26, 131 LRRM 1393 (1989) (preemployment drug and alcohol testing is not a mandatory subject of bargaining). See also RCA Corp., 296 NLRB No. 154, 132 LRRM 1348 (1989); United Cable Television Corp. of Conn., 296 NLRB No. 21, 132 LRRM 1058 (1989).

[14]Van Dorn Machinery Co., 286 NLRB 1233, 128 LRRM 1265 (1987).

[15]Southwestern Portland Cement Co., 289 NLRB No. 161, 131 LRRM 1063 (1987).

[16]Murphy Oil U.S.A., 286 NLRB 1039, 127 LRRM 1111 (1987). But cf. J.R. Simplot Co., 238 NLRB 374, 99 LRRM 1684 (1978).

[17]Fast Food Merchandisers, 291 NLRB No. 121, 131 LRRM 1436 (1988). See also Metropolitan Teletronics Corp., 279 NLRB 957, 122 LRRM 1107, enf'd, 819 F.2d 1130, 127 LRRM 2048 (CA 2, 1987).

[18]Jones Dairy Farm, 295 NLRB No. 20, 131 LRRM 1497 (1989); see also Southern Cal. Edison Co., 284 NLRB 1205, 126 LRRM 1324 (1987).

[19]Rocky Mountain Hosp., 289 NLRB No. 139, 130 LRRM 1493 (1988).

[20]Land Air Delivery v. NLRB, 862 F.2d 354, 130 LRRM 2118 (D.C. Cir., 1988), cert. denied, 110 S.Ct. 2063, 132 LRRM 2623 (1988).

[21]Teamsters Local 171 v. NLRB, 863 F.2d 946, 130 LRRM 2033 (D.C. Cir., 1988), cert. denied sub nom. A.G. Boone Co. v. NLRB, 109 S.Ct. 2063, 131 LRRM 2400 (1989).

[22]Mike O'Connor Chevrolet-Buick-GMC Co., 209 NLRB 701, 85 LRRM 1419 (1974), enf. denied on other grounds, 512 F.2d 684, 88 LRRM 3121 (CA 8, 1975). See also Bundy Corp., 292 NLRB No. 69, 131 LRRM 1645 (1989); Van Dorn Machinery Co., 286 NLRB 1233, 128 LRRM 1265 (1987).

[23]United Technologies Corp., 278 NLRB 306, 308, 121 LRRM 1156 (1986) (unilateral implementation of health care bill-correction plan).

[24]First Nat'l Maintenance Corp. v. NLRB, 101 S.Ct. 2573, 107 LRRM 2705 (1981).

[25]Otis Elevator Co., 269 NLRB 891, 115 LRRM 1281, 1283, corrected, 269 NLRB 891, 116 LRRM 1075 (1984).

[26]See, e.g., Milwaukee Spring II, 268 NLRB 601, 115 LRRM 1065 (1984), aff'd, 765 F.2d 175, 119 LRRM 2801 (D.C. Cir., 1985).

[27]Otis Elevator, 269 NLRB 891, 115 LRRM 1281, 1283, corrected, 269 NLRB 891, 116 LRRM 1075 (1984); see, e.g., Inland Steel Container Co., 275 NLRB 823, 119 LRRM 1293 (1985); Garwood-Detroit Truck Equip., 274 NLRB 113, 118 LRRM 1417 (1985); Brittain & Heshizer, "Management Decision Bargaining: The Interplay of Law and Politics," 38 Lab. L.J. 220 (1987);

Other Legislation

Congress continues to limit management rights by enacting legislation designed to protect employees. Recent examples are the Worker Adjustment Retraining Notification Act, requiring that employees be given 60 days advance notice of covered plant closings and mass layoffs;[28] the Drug Free Workplace Act, requiring covered employers to establish drug awareness programs;[29] and the Employee Polygraph Protection Act, which limits employers' use of polygraph examinations on applicants and employees.[30]

Inroads Through Arbitration

Management spokesmen continue to use "protective" clauses in regard to arbitration of disputes. One such spokesman has suggested that the Arbitrator "(a) shall have no power to change, detract from, substitute his judgment for, or add to the provisions of this agreement."[31]

Control of Operation Methods

Arbitrators continue to agree that management has the right to make changes in operations methods even if the changes result in the discontinuance of the union so long as the act itself is not wrongful.[32] Employers may exercise their discretion to eliminate individual jobs as well as entire job classifications.[33]

Wage Adjustments Following Changes in Operation Methods

Where a change in the manner of operations is negligible, the employer is not required to negotiate a piece rate change with the union even though the contract requires the employer to temporarily

---

Note, "NLRB Narrows Duty to Bargain Over Management Decisions: Otis Elevator II and Its Progeny," 21 Wake Forest L. Rev. 725 (1986).

[28] 29 U.S.C. §§ 2101 et seq. (1989) (effective February 4, 1989).

[29] 41 U.S.C. § 701 (1988).

[30] 29 U.S.C. § 2001 (1988).

[31] Metal Container Corp., 83 LA 564, 566 (Naehring, 1984).

[32] Union Carbide, 84 LA 788 (Seinsheimer, 1985). Cf. Witco Chem. Corp., 89 LA 349 (Rothstein, 1987) (employer violated contract by failing to notify union of decision to contract truck driving duties and eliminate job classification).

[33] Duquesne Light Co., 90 LA 758 (Duff, 1988) (senior field service representative classification properly eliminated where contract recognized employer's right to relieve employees from duty for lack of work); Downtown St. Paul Partners, 90 LA 67 (Cooper, 1987) (management right clause permitted employer to close hotel restaurants and bar and lay off employees); Flowers Baking Co. of W. Va., 89 LA 113 (Flannagan, 1987) (checker-loader classification properly eliminated where contract gave employer right to "cease any job").

set the wage scale and to notify the union in the event of any new or experimental operation.[34]

Hourly Rated Employees

Recent cases support the principles stated in the Fourth Edition.[35]

Incentive Employees

In reviewing the rates of incentive employees, arbitrators sometimes apply the maintenance of prior earnings standard. This standard cannot be applied, however, where the contract expressly recognizes that the employer, at its discretion, may find it necessary or desirable from time to time to establish new incentive rates or adjust existing incentive rates because of certain conditions.[36]

If a change in the workload is negligible, the employer is not required to negotiate a change in incentive rates.[37]

Production Standards, Time Studies, and Job Evaluation

If the bargaining agreement gives management exclusive right to manage the plant and direct the employees, the employer has the right to order an employee to increase the speed of a machine that could yield an output approximately at the ceiling for incentive earnings.[38] Arbitrators continue to agree that management has the right to enforce reasonable production standards through discipline.[39]

It is common practice to determine production standards through time studies, and where the contract specifically states that any bona fide change in the methods, machines, tools, fixtures, materials, design, quality, specifications, or other conditions that affect work

---

[34]Jack T. Baillie Co., 84 LA 285 (Concepcion, 1985) (change in manner of loading haul trucks by eliminating manual handling and allowing all handling to be done by forklift, where handling by loaders merely requires insertion of sticks and making higher stacks, cartons are no longer burned, and rhythm of loading is extended).

[35]Southern Cal. Edison Co., 90 LA 5 (Castrey, 1987) (senior lineman/splicer assuming responsibility of crew foreman entitled to wage upgrade where contract provides that senior journeyman on crew is upgraded when foreman is absent); Amana Refrigeration, 89 LA 751 (Bowers, 1987) ("assemblers" assigned to operate two new machines simultaneously entitled to wages at "machine-operator" rate); Kentucky Center for the Performing Arts, 89 LA 344 (Volz, 1987) (employer properly paid basic hourly rate and not higher performance/rehearsal rate for "run through" rehearsals where contract does not define "rehearsal" and industry practice is to pay higher rate only for dress rehearsal). See Chapter 13 of the Fourth Edition, pp. 485-486.

[36]Timken Co., 85 LA 377 (Morgan, 1985). See also USX Corp., 90 LA 1279 (Garrett, 1988) (employer properly paid incentive employee at standard hourly rate for time spent taking audiology test at employer's direction).

[37]Jack T. Baillie Co., 84 LA 285 (Concepcion, 1985).

[38]Weston Paper & Mfg., 85 LA 454 (Cyrol, 1985).

[39]Laidlaw Waste Sys., 90 LA 570 (Clifford, 1987) (employer properly discharged 9-year employee for failure to meet production requirements). But see Featherlite Trailers of Iowa, 90 LA 761 (Schwartz, 1987) (manufacturing company improperly discharged assembly-line employee where company failed to define work standards.)

content requires a new time study, the employer has no right to unilaterally revise its 30-year-old method of calculating incentive pay.[40]

Job and Classification Control

Establishing, Eliminating, and Combining Jobs and Classifications

Arbitrators continue to apply well-established principles in cases addressing the establishment, elimination, and combination of jobs and classifications.

Management may establish jobs or classifications unless restricted by the collective bargaining agreement.[41] Where the agreement contains rigid job classifications, management may not be permitted to unilaterally establish new classifications.[42] However, arbitrators often reject the view that job classifications in an agreement automatically preclude elimination or modification of jobs or classifications.[43]

The decisions continue to uphold management's right to eliminate jobs (and allocate any remaining jobs) when justified by improved technology or production efficiencies.[44] Similarly, cases have sustained management's right to eliminate classifications under the same circumstances.[45]

The trend toward allowing employers to combine jobs or job classifications in determining methods of operation remains evident in recent awards.[46]

---

[40]Airco Carbon, 86 LA 6 (Dworkin, 1986).

[41]Day & Zimmerman, 91 LA 1003 (Belcher, 1988) (employer did not violate contract by requiring employees in newly created maintenance mechanic/operator classification to perform duties of explosive operator); Pan Am World Servs., 84 LA 1161, 1166 (Bowers, 1985) (reclassification of position violated contract); Arco Oil & Gas Co., 84 LA 235, 238-240 (Baroni, 1985) (employer had right to change classification where contract language was broad).

[42]Menasha Corp., 84 LA 989, 992 (Duff, 1985) (where there is no substantial change in job content, unilateral reclassification is not permitted).

[43]See Container Corp. of Am., 91 LA 329 (Rains, 1988) (wage provision requiring parties' consent to change "hourly rates and job classifications" schedules did not restrict management's right to eliminate job classifications); Hennepin Paper Co., 83 LA 214 (Gallagher, 1984) (mere specification of wage rates places no restriction on employer to reorganize work); Engelhard Indus., 82 LA 680 (Nicholas, 1984).

[44]See Courier Journal, 93 LA 227 (Tharp, 1989) (employer properly placed new video display terminals in advertising department and transferred work to that department); Bethlehem Steel Corp., 86 LA 880 (Henle, 1986); Union Carbide, 84 LA 788, 791 (Seinsheimer, 1985); Formosa Plastic Corp., 83 LA 792 (Taylor, 1984); United States Steel Corp., 82 LA 534 (Jones, 1984); Roadmaster Corp., 82 LA 225 (Granack, 1983) (employer had right to redesignate job as nonunit position where job bore little resemblance to old position).

[45]See Container Corp. of Am., 91 LA 329 (Rains, 1988) (employer properly eliminated bargaining unit positions during paper mill modernization in order to improve efficiency of operations); Mead Corp., 84 LA 875, 879-881 (Sergent, 1985).

[46]See United States Steel Corp., 85 LA 1026 (Petersen, 1985) (employer did not violate contract by combining jobs which were both position-rated jobs in same seniority unit); Cigna Healthplans of Cal., 84 LA 422, 427 (Rothschild, 1985); Hennepin Paper Co., 83 LA 214 (Gallagher, 1984).

Interjob and Interclassification Transfer of Duties

Absent limitations in the agreement, management retains the right, under recent decisions, to transfer work from one classification to another.[47]

Relying on management rights provisions, arbitrators have recognized the right of an employer to transfer work from one seniority unit to another where there is no prohibition in the agreement and where the transfer is effected for the sake of increased productivity.[48]

Assignment of Duties and Tasks

Recent decisions affirm management's right to assign duties and tasks,[49] although the presence or absence of job descriptions in an agreement may determine the extent of this right.[50] In the absence of detailed job descriptions, employers have been permitted to assign employees a broad range of tasks related to their regular duties.[51] On the other hand, detailed job descriptions, especially if negotiated, may preclude substantial changes in job content.[52] Minor changes in duties may be permissible, even if the agreement contains detailed job descriptions.[53]

---

[47]See Iowa-Illinois Gas & Elec. Co., 91 LA 1181 (Volz, 1988) (employer properly transferred work from bargaining unit electricians to salaried electronic technicians where electricians' job description did not specifically cover disputed work); Century Plaza Hotel, 83 LA 1314 (Kaufman, 1984); Stokely-Van Camp, 83 LA 838 (Nicholas, 1984); Columbus Jack Corp., 83 LA 797 (Duda, 1984).

[48]See Allied Prods., 90 LA 651 (Baroni, 1988) (employer properly told maintenance-department repairman to use forklift instead of assigning duties to equipment operator where broad management-rights clause gave employer exclusive right to determine assignments); Stokely-Van Camp, 83 LA 838 (Nicholas, 1984); Bethlehem Steel Corp., 82 LA 758 (Henle, 1984) (employees in original seniority unit need not be offered opportunity to follow work to new location unless work transferred constitutes "essence" of job in question).

[49]See Frito-Lay, 93 LA 48, 54 (Creo, 1989) (employer properly introduced hand-held computers to be used by driver-salesmen where contract reserved to management the right to "improve sales methods, operations or conditions"); Ralston Purina Co., 85 LA 1 (Cohen, 1985) (no contract violation where employees are assigned to do two jobs simultaneously); Otis Elevator Co., 84 LA 1260, 1264 (Heinsz, 1985) (employer upheld in not assigning employee to do overtime work); Associated Elec. Coop., 84 LA 1020, 1025 (Penfield, 1985); Litton Sys., 84 LA 273, 276-277 (Marcus, 1985) (no contract violation where assignments to employees outside department do not result in loss of work opportunities to department personnel); Lake Erie Screw Corp., 84 LA 175 (Dworkin, 1985); Stokely-Van Camp, 83 LA 838 (Nicholas, 1984).

[50]See Youngstown Hosp. Ass'n, 88 LA 251 (DiLeone, 1986).

[51]See Friction Div. Prods., 92 LA 225 (Dorsey, 1988) (janitor-custodians who removed bags from dust collectors were not temporarily performing a higher rated job since removal of bags was a minor function); Associated Elec. Coop., 84 LA 1020 (Penfield, 1985); Lake Erie Screw Corp., 84 LA 175 (Dworkin, 1985); Magic Chef, 84 LA 15 (Craver, 1984) (employer had right to assign new duties without reclassifying position).

[52]Allied Plant Maintenance Co., 88 LA 963 (Bankston, 1987) (employer improperly directed maintenance mechanics to clean machinery since the contract clearly allocated the task of cleaning the plant to janitors); Cadillac Gage Co., 87 LA 853 (Pelt, 1986) (employer violated contract and was ordered to pay wages for one-half hour of unit work to union when manufacturing manager sorted bolts); United States Steel Corp., 82 LA 910 (Shore, 1984).

[53]Nashville Gas Co., 88 LA 580 (Kilroy, 1986) (employer did not violate contract when it required service dispatchers to put new customer information on electric "tracker" system since their primary duties had not changed or increased); Bethlehem Steel Corp., 85 LA 1079 (Henle, 1985).

Employers have been permitted to assign unskilled work to skilled workers.[54] Similarly, arbitrators continue to allow employers to assign new duties or reallocate old duties to accommodate technological change or to increase productive efficiency where no contractual restrictions on management's right to assign work are violated.[55]

Arbitrators remain divided on the issue of the assignment of work outside an employee's classification.[56] One case held that the assignment of work outside the employee's work classification is proper if temporary.[57]

Recent decisions also affirm management's right to assign work which overlaps one or two jobs or classifications to one or the other of such job classification.[58] The same principle has been applied to allow an employer to assign work to both jobs or classifications which the work overlaps.[59] Temporary or emergency assignments across job or classification lines have generally been upheld.[60]

Although management often has wide authority to assign duties and tasks, employees retain the right to challenge wage rates applied to new jobs.[61] Temporary assignments also continue to merit higher pay rates in appropriate circumstances.[62]

Hiring of Employees

Employers enjoy considerable latitude in hiring. An employer's right to insist upon and receive accurate information on employment applications and other preemployment documents remains un-

---

[54]See Hubinger Co., 83 LA 1211 (Jacobowski, 1984); St. Regis Corp., 82 LA 1244 (Coyne, 1984).

[55]Courier Journal, 93 LA 227 (Tharp, 1989); Bethlehem Steel Corp., 85 LA 681 (Lilly, 1985); Stokely-Van Camp, 83 LA 838 (Nicholas, 1984).

[56]Compare Stokely-Van Camp., 83 LA 838 (Nicholas, 1984) (employer's right to assign work outside classification upheld), with Amax Coal Co., 82 LA 846 (Witney, 1984) (employer precluded from assigning work outside classification). Also see Youngstown Hosp. Ass'n, 88 LA 251 (DiLeone, 1986) (after layoff, remaining work was assigned to a non-bargaining-unit employee).

[57]See Amax Coal Co., 83 LA 1029 (Kilroy, 1984).

[58]See Morton Thiokol, Inc., 88 LA 254 (Finan, 1987) (no violation where engineers were assigned to paint equipment as incidental to housekeeping functions); Youngstown Hosp. Ass'n, 88 LA 251 (DiLeone, 1986); but see Amax Coal Co., 82 LA 846 (Witney, 1984) (classification provisions were violated where grievant was assigned out of classification while employee of another classification performed primary duty expressed in job title of grievant's classification).

[59]See Morton Thiokol, Inc., 88 LA 254 (Finan, 1987) (employer did not violate the contract or past practice by requiring engineers and firemen to paint pieces of equipment that were assigned to them for cleaning even though "painting" was within job description of another skilled classification); Safeway Stores, 83 LA 472 (Ray, 1984).

[60]See Warner Press, 89 LA 577, 580 (Brunner, 1987) (contract which required that temporarily transferred employees be returned to regular jobs "as soon as possible" meant "as soon as practicable" and therefore employer had right to keep employee on transfer assignment for the remainder of the shift); Standard Register Co., 83 LA 1068 (Abrams, 1984); Dow Corning Corp., 83 LA 1049 (Seidman, 1984); Amax Coal Co., 83 LA 1029 (Kilroy, 1984); Tecumseh Prods. Co., 82 LA 738 (Cabe, 1984).

[61]See Joyce Int'l, 93 LA 122 (Bognanno, 1989) (employer properly paid Group I wage to Group II employees who were bumped into lowest classification due to layoff); Amana Refrigeration, 89 LA 751 (Bowers, 1987) (labor-grade 3 "assemblers" assigned to operate machines were entitled to wages for such work at labor-grade 4 "machine operator" rate where work was more akin to work performed by machine operators); Brass Prods. Co., 85 LA 465 (Lipson, 1985).

[62]See Florida Power Corp., 85 LA 619 (Flannagan, 1985); Engelhard Indus., 82 LA 680 (Nicholas, 1984).

changed, and employees failing to respect this right have found arbitrators mostly unsympathetic.[63]

This wide latitude enjoyed by employers also extends to an employer's obligation to hire for the purpose of filling a vacancy. Without some compelling justification, arbitrators have refused to require employers to fill vacancies.[64]

As in the past, specific contract provisions can limit management's ability to hire. For example, an employer may be required to recall qualified laid-off employees before hiring new employees.[65] Similarly, seniority provisions may be violated if a position is filled with a new employee rather than a current employee with the most seniority,[66] unless management can show that current employees lack the ability to perform in such a position.[67]

Exclusive hiring hall provisions still generate arbitration awards. In two recent cases the employer was found to be in violation of such provisions for hiring from the outside even where the referrals from the local union hall refused to cross picket lines to travel to the employer's work site.[68]

Determination of Size of Crews

Of the few reported decisions in this area, the cases are split over whether management may determine crew size.[69] The right to determine crew size has given way on occasion to health considerations and solicitude for the burden placed on remaining employees when crew size is reduced.[70]

---

[63]See Salt River Project, 91 LA 1193 (Ross, 1988) (grievant failed to list drug-dealing conviction on "felony questionnaire" with original application for employment); Mor-Flo Indus., 89 LA 762 (King, 1987) (employee was properly discharged for intentionally withholding information concerning lower-back injuries during preemployment interview); Laclede Gas Co., 86 LA 480 (Mikrut, 1986); Morton Thiokol, Inc., 85 LA 834 (Williams, 1985); Owens-Illinois, 83 LA 1265 (Cantor, 1984).

[64]See Bethlehem Steel Corp., 90 LA 577 (Oldham, 1987) (permitted temporary vacancies to remain unfilled); Lear Siegler, Inc., 83 LA 1083 (Duda, 1984); National Steel Corp., 82 LA 870 (Sherman, 1984).

[65]See Diamond Power Specialty Co., 83 LA 1277 (Kindig, 1984) (dictum). Cf. Singer Co., 86 LA 917 (Wahl, 1986) (employer violated contract by failing to promote grievants while they were on layoff).

[66]See Oberlin College, 93 LA 289 (Fullmer, 1989) (employer violated contract by improperly awarding library position to applicant from outside bargaining unit instead of to library assistant, where previous arbitrator had ruled that vacancy must be given to internal applicant provided one was qualified); Chillicothe Tel. Co., 84 LA 1 (Gibson, 1984); Potomac Elec. Power Co., 82 LA 352 (Everitt, 1984).

[67]See Illinois Cereal Mills, 88 LA 350 (Petersen, 1986); Emery Mining Corp., 85 LA 1211 (Feldman, 1985); National-Standard Co., 85 LA 190 (Duda, 1985); Monsanto Co., 85 LA 73 (Madden, 1985); Brooklyn Acres Mut. Homes, Inc., 84 LA 952 (Abrams, 1985); Lockheed-Georgia Co., 84 LA 701 (Daly, 1985); Dakota Elec. Ass'n, 84 LA 114 (Boyer, 1985); St. Paul Dispatch & Pioneer Press, 82 LA 1273 (Ver Ploeg, 1984); Rohm & Haas Texas, 82 LA 271 (Taylor, 1984).

[68]See Freesen, Inc., 88 LA 41 (Schwartz, 1986); Mautz & Oren, Inc., 87 LA 379 (Franke, 1986).

[69]Bethlehem Steel Corp., 92 LA 553 (Witt, 1988) (employer improperly reduced crew size); Dinagraphics, 92 LA 453 (Heekin, 1989) (employer did not violate contract by unilaterally assigning a crew of three employees, rather than a crew of four, to operate press). Compare Kroger Co., 86 LA 357, 368 (Milentz, 1986), with Hubinger Co., 83 LA 1211 (Jacobowski, 1984).

[70]See Keebler Co., 86 LA 963 (Nolan, 1986). Cf. Western Fuel Oil Co., 89 LA 772 (Kaufman, 1987) (employer's reduction in staffing did not violate the contract or jeopardize employees' health and safety).

Technological and Process Changes

Additional rulings have been made that absent a specific restriction in the agreement, management may reduce crew size for reasons of substantial changes in technology or process. Specifically, where technological changes result in a substantial decrease in the workload or a significant change in operations, crew size reduction may be justified.[71]

Changes in Type of Operations, Methods, and Procedures

Management's right to eliminate positions and reassign remaining duties when methods of operation have changed has also been upheld.[72]

Production Needs and Reduced Operations

Unless there is evidence of bad faith by management or a specific contract restriction,[73] arbitrators uphold reductions in crew size if there is evidence that production needs have been substantially curtailed.[74]

Work Load and Idle Time

An alleged reduction in crew size may be nothing more than an attempt to reclassify an existing job. One arbitrator found a contract violation where an employer ostensibly eliminated evening and Saturday telephone operator jobs by reclassifying the incumbents as console attendants and reducing their wages. The employer relied on a reduction in the workload caused by implementation of a new telephone system, but the arbitrator concluded that although the level of work was less

---

[71]See Union Carbide, 84 LA 788, 791 (Seinsheimer, 1985) (introduction of digital electronic weighing system reduced workload of stores clerks to "practically a de minimis level"); Grinnell College, 83 LA 39, 43 (Nathan, 1984) (elimination of day-shift weekday telephone operator due to introduction of new telephone system was justified). Arbitrator Nathan reached a different conclusion in the same case regarding night-shift and Saturday operators who had been reclassified due to introduction of the new system, and had their wages lowered. The arbitrator concluded with respect to those persons that although the intensity of their workload had decreased, their duties were essentially the same and the lighter workload did not justify unilaterally reclassifying them or reducing their wages.

[72]See Container Corp. of Am., 91 LA 329 (Rains, 1988) (employer properly eliminated three bargaining unit positions during modernization where action was necessary to improve efficiency of operations); Mead Corp., 84 LA 875, 879-880 (Sergent, 1985); Engelhard Indus., 82 LA 680, 683 (Nicholas, 1984).

[73]See Formosa Plastics Corp., 83 LA 792, 796 (Taylor, 1984); United States Steel Corp., 82 LA 534, 537 (Jones, 1984); but see Georgetown Steel Corp., 84 LA 549, 552 (Schroeder, 1985) (arbitrator sustained reduction of crew on weekdays when use of foremen to do bargaining unit work was de minimis, but found violation of clause prohibiting supervisors from doing unit work, when crew reduction on weekends resulted from foremen being assigned more than *de minimis* amount of unit work).

[74]Brunswick Pulp & Paper Co., 91 LA 307 (Taylor, 1988) (nondisciplinary terminations upheld where employer showed terminations were caused by attrition, seasonal reduction in relief requirements, and new equipment).

intense due to the new system, the essential duties of the job remained unchanged. Thus, the position was not, in fact, eliminated.[75]

Elimination of a position even where the duties of the job are reassigned may be justified so long as it does not impose an undue burden on employees in another job classification.[76] However, reassignment of duties may put at issue the proper pay for the employees to whom the duties are assigned. One arbitrator held that where a lead operator's job was eliminated and some of the duties were assigned to other bargaining unit members, the employees who were assigned to those duties should be paid the lead operator's rate when performing such duties.[77]

Use of Supervisors or "General Help"

The question of the propriety of reassigning crew work to supervisors or "general help" continues to turn primarily on the frequency of the work being assigned outside the crew. Where the amount of work being done by others is infrequent or minimal, elimination of jobs and reassignment may be justified.[78]

Safety or Health Hazard

One arbitrator upheld an airport authority's right to lay off firefighters where the management rights clause preserved the right to take steps to reduce costs and the evidence did not establish that an increased hazard would result to the public or to other firefighters.[79]

Vacancies

It continues to be the general rule that in the absence of specific restriction in the agreement, management has the exclusive right to

---

[75]Grinnell College, 83 LA 39, 43 (Nathan, 1984). The arbitrator also found the employer was justified in eliminating the day-shift operator's job and assigning day-shift telephone work to a nonunit employee since the nature of the work itself on day shift had changed.

[76]See Textron Aerostructures, 91 LA 665 (Nicholas, 1988) (employer properly eliminated bargaining unit inspector and permitted visual inspection by salaried personnel where inspection by bargaining unit duplicated inspection required by vendor); Morton Thiokol, Inc., 86 LA 1102, 1106 (Ipavec, 1986).

[77]Engelhard Indus., 82 LA 680, 683 (Nicholas, 1984). See also Amana Refrigeration, 89 LA 751 (Bowers, 1987) ("assemblers" assigned to operate machines were entitled to wages for such work at "machine operator" rate).

[78]See Kelsey Memorial Hosp., 88 LA 406 (Pincus, 1986) (employer did not violate contract by reducing employee's hours and later laying him off despite union's belief that this action resulted from supervisors' performance of bargaining unit work); Georgetown Steel Corp., 84 LA 549, 551-552 (Schroeder, 1985) (elimination of weigh-clerk position on weekdays, when foremen's performance of their duties was *de minimis* was justified, but foreman performance of weigh-clerk tasks on weekends was not *de minimis* and elimination of that job on weekends violated the contract); Formosa Plastics Corp., 83 LA 792, 797 (Taylor, 1984) (elimination of field-time clerk job was held justified where foreman workload did not significantly increase by assuming remaining field-time clerk duties); United States Steel Corp., 82 LA 534, 537 (Jones, 1984) (elimination of spare parts attendant and reassignment of duties to craftsmen held justified).

[79]See Airport Auth., 86 LA 237, 243 (Christopher, 1985). For a different result based on a contractual procedural requirement, see Keebler Co., 86 LA 963, 967 (Nolan, 1986) (contract that required maintenance of status quo pending resolution of grievances was held to require employer to maintain crew of boiler operators pending outcome of arbitration over union claims of safety hazard).

determine whether a vacancy should be filled.[80] But where duties associated with the vacancy are reassigned and continue to be performed by employees in other jobs, arbitrators will examine whether the employer has intentionally avoided contractually required procedures for filling jobs.[81]

A contract clause requiring the posting of a vacancy where there was an increase in the normal complement of a classification was interpreted to apply only where management determined a vacancy in fact existed. Infrequent transfer of employees to assist in the department did not prove that one did.[82]

Arbitrators have been reluctant to find that management's discretion regarding filling vacancies is restricted by an asserted past practice, such as a custom of posting vacancies. Thus, one arbitrator held that management's prerogative to decide whether or when to fill a vacancy falls within the general management right to direct the work force and may not be infringed upon by past practice.[83]

Scheduling Work

Restrictions on management's right to schedule may be express or implied in contract language.[84] Aside from contractual restrictions,

---

[80]See Bethlehem Steel Corp., 90 LA 577 (Oldham, 1987) (change in working conditions was sufficient to allow temporary vacancies in toolroom attendant position to remain unfilled); Morton Thiokol, Inc., 86 LA 1102, 1106 (Ipavec, 1986); Rock Island Ref. Corp., 86 LA 173, 176 (Morgan, 1985); Quaker Oats Co., 84 LA 390, 392 (Edelman, 1985); Consolidation Coal Co., 84 LA 36, 39 (Rybolt, 1984) (employer not required to fill vacancies where conditions fluctuated and vacancies deemed not permanent); NN Metal Stamping, 83 LA 801, 804 (Abrams, 1984); Miners Clinic, 83 LA 445, 448 (Probst, 1984); Paxall, Inc., 82 LA 708, 712 (Gallagher, 1984).

[81]See Homestake Mining Co., 88 LA 614 (Sinicropi, 1987) (employer violated contract by assigning employee to load-dispatcher duties on relief basis without posting position as permanent vacancy and paying him applicable rate); North River Energy Co., 85 LA 449, 452 (Witney, 1985) (company manipulated job duties and failed to post jobs "for sole purpose of avoiding" duty to post); Jim Walter Resources, 85 LA 290, 293 (Feldman, 1985) (fact that employee has been on "temporary assignment" for 1.5 years indicates there is a permanent vacancy which must be filled). For similar reasoning, see dictum in Quaker Oats Co., 84 LA 390, 392 (Edelman, 1985) (even though company has right to determine to leave position vacant, there may be violation if job duties are reassigned to others, resulting in undue burden or other indications that there remains need for vacated position).

[82]In NN Metal Stamping, 83 LA 801, 804 (Abrams, 1984), the contract requiring posting of a vacancy if "the normal complement" of a classification was increased. The arbitrator found that, while there had been some employees temporarily transferred into the shipping department to assist with some of the duties of the shipping clerks, it was not done on an everyday basis so as to indicate there had been an increase in the "normal complement" of the shipping-clerk classification. See also Lear Siegler, Inc., 83 LA 1083, 1085 (Duda, 1984).

[83]See National Elec. Benefit Fund, 87 LA 914, 920-921 (Lubic, 1986).

[84]See Fort Dodge Laboratories, 87 LA 1290, 1293 (Smith, 1986) (reference in contract to "regularly scheduled" workweek meant employer could not set schedule with different starting times on different days of the week); Indiana Shop 'N Save, 87 LA 548, 552 (Hannan, 1986) (contract requiring part-time employees to be scheduled maximum number of hours for which they are available means senior part-time employees must be scheduled up to 32-hour maximum before junior part-timers receive any hours over the contractual minimum of 17); Kroger Co., 86 LA 357, 361 (Milentz, 1986) (employer's scheduling practice violated contract clause saying two employees would not be scheduled where one could be scheduled to do the work); H. Meyer Dairy Co., 84 LA 131, 134 (Ghiz, 1985) (employer violated contract by not providing required notice prior to schedule change); Schnadig Corp., 83 LA 1194, 1197 (Goldman, 1984) (contract prohibited unilateral changes in starting or quitting time); Red Owl Stores, 83 LA 653, 656 (Reynolds, 1984) (contract required at least one employee be on duty at all times); but see Broekhuizen Produce Co., 82 LA 221, 224 (Roumell, 1984) ("maintenance of standards" clause which makes reference to hours of work nevertheless does not establish a guarantee of hours).

management should consider, before altering schedules, its statutory duty under the National Labor Relations Act, or in the case of public-sector employers, any applicable state public-sector bargaining laws to bargain with the union prior to changing wages, hours, or other terms and conditions of employment. One arbitrator considered this legal duty in issuing an award for the union over a schedule change.[85] Of course, a union's right to bargain over such changes can be waived in the contract by specific language in a management rights clause or other provision giving management the right to make unilateral schedule changes, although such a waiver must be in clear and unmistakable language.[86]

Contractual references to a "normal" or "regular" workweek continue to be interpreted in arbitration. The weight of arbitral authority is that unless there is a specific intent to the contrary, such language does not guarantee a specific schedule or restrict management's right to schedule work.[87] However, one arbitrator found a restriction in a contractual reference to a "regularly scheduled" workweek. The contract said that the workweek would be "five consecutive or regularly scheduled days of eight hours each," which the arbitrator concluded prohibited management from establishing a schedule where employees had varying starting times during the week, since such a schedule was not "regular" as required by the contract.[88]

Where an employer shut down its plant for Thanksgiving week but retained junior electricians for maintenance and inspection work, the seniority provisions of the contract were violated since the shutdown constituted a layoff and not a mere scheduling decision as asserted by the employer.[89]

Some arbitrators have recognized management's right to exercise its scheduling prerogative even when the purpose in doing so was specifically to avoid overtime payments.[90]

---

[85]See JM Mfg. Co., 84 LA 679, 683 (Sisk, 1985).

[86]See Ador Corp., 150 NLRB 1658, 1669, 58 LRRM 1280 (1965). See also United States Dep't of Health & Human Servs., 83 LA 883, 887 (Edes, 1984); Morris, The Developing Labor Law, 2d ed., 640-641 (BNA Books, 1983) and 5th Supplement, 332-334 (BNA Books, 1989).

[87]In Coca-Cola Foods, 88 LA 129, 132 (Naehring, 1986), the arbitrator held that provision in the contract for a "normal work day" of 9.5 hours and a "normal work week" of 47.5 hours did not bar the employer from scheduling more or fewer hours. The arbitrator found that use of the word "normal" not only did not guarantee a fixed number of hours, it implied to the contrary that under some circumstances an abnormal number of hours might be scheduled. For a similar interpretation of the word "normal" see FMC Corp., 85 LA 18, 21 (Karlins, 1985). Similarly, in Family Food Park, 86 LA 1184, 1187-1188 (Petersen, 1986), the arbitrator held that reference in the contract to a "basic work week" of 40 hours did not guarantee a 40-hour week or require that scheduling be governed by seniority.

[88]Fort Dodge Laboratories, 87 LA 1290, 1293 (Smith, 1986). See also Bethlehem Steel Corp., 92 LA 430 (Sharnoff, 1989) (employer violated contract by unilaterally changing work schedule from "normal" 8-hour day, 5-day week to 12-hour day, 3-day week).

[89]Olin Corp., 83 LA 346, 352 (Wolff, 1984). The arbitrator suggested that the employer may have been within its rights to reduce the workweek from five days to four as a means of addressing the shortage of work, but that when it chose to close the entire plant for one week it effected a layoff as that term is commonly understood.

[90]See Western Airlines, 85 LA 311, 314 (Brisco, 1985); Service Care, 84 LA 736, 738 (Duff, 1985). See also Fedders-U.S.A., 92 LA 418 (Cohen, 1989) (employer had right under contract to change starting time from 7:00 a.m. to 6:00 a.m. and stop paying overtime to employees who were called prior to 7:00 a.m.); ITT Fed. Elec. Corp., 83 LA 1201, 1205 (Gentile, 1984) (recognizing that specific contract requirements may prohibit use of scheduling to avoid overtime payment).

Emergency Changes in Work Schedule

Emergency changes in schedule due to acts beyond the company's control and, where applicable, refusal to pay reporting pay have been recognized as a management right.[91] But where delay in notifying employees of an emergency change is unreasonable, employers often are held liable for reporting pay.[92] One arbitrator held that an employer was not obligated to provide prior notice of an emergency change in schedule since the contract did not explicitly require the employer to do so.[93] Employers may also be liable for reporting pay if the emergency condition was something the employer could reasonably have foreseen or controlled.[94]

Emergencies, Acts of God, and Conditions Beyond the Control of Management

As is noted in the Fourth Edition, management rights may be expanded in the event of emergencies.[95]

Overtime

Right to Require Overtime

A contract provision requiring advance notice for voluntary overtime does not limit management's right to require mandatory overtime or require management to give advance notice.[96] Similarly, where a "normal" workday is 9.5 hours and a "normal" workweek is

---

[91]See Sawbrook Steel Castings Co., 85 LA 763, 768 (Witney, 1985); Coerver Indus., 82 LA 1042, 1045 (Carter, 1984). See also Osceola Farms, 93 LA 128 (Abrams, 1989) (employee properly refused to pay double-time premium for days on which heavy rain forced cancellation of harvesting where employees who reported before cancellation received reporting pay).

[92]See Georgia Pac. Corp., 86 LA 1244, 1246 (Chandler, 1986) (contract which required reasonable attempt to notify employees if employer had advance awareness of emergency was held violated where employer failed in its attempts to restore power at 7:00 and 10:00, and did not contact employees scheduled to report at 11:00); Compco Corp., 85 LA 725, 729-730 (Martin, 1985) (although company was justified in emergency shutdown due to weather, failure to make any reasonable attempt to notify employees reporting to work required payment of reporting pay); Missouri Valley, Inc., 82 LA 1018, 1020 (Yaney, 1984) (reporting pay must be paid when radio station that employer relied on to broadcast notice failed to do so. Burden was on employer to provide notice, and contract said employees "may," not "must," call radio station for information if there is uncertainty).

[93]Solar Plastics, 91 LA 361 (Reynolds, 1988) (employees were properly paid for four hours of work when they reported for a regular shift but were locked out because the manager forgot to open the plant); Sawbrook Steel Castings Co., 85 LA 763, 768 (Witney, 1985). The arbitrator held that the change was due to circumstances beyond the employer's control, and that unsuccessful attempts to notify employees, although not required, were made.

[94]See, e.g., Sawbrook Steel Castings Co., 85 LA 763, 768 (Witney, 1985) (if emergency circumstances were such that employer could reasonably have avoided or controlled them, reporting pay might have been required).

[95]Consumers Market, 92 LA 221 (Yarowsky, 1989) (defining "emergency" as any circumstance that would prevent on-time delivery of food products to stores, arbitrator held food distributor within its rights when, because of unscheduled absenteeism, it required overtime work to stock a new store). See Chapter 13 of the Fourth Edition, pp 529-531.

[96]Chromalloy Am. Corp., 83 LA 89, 85 (Taylor, 1984).

47.5 hours, management is not precluded from scheduling work in excess of those hours.[97]

Equalization of Overtime

Where the agreement contains a modified equalization provision and it is apparent that overtime has been awarded unequally, the employer has an obligation not to further skew overtime figures before taking steps to equalize the distribution of overtime.[98]

While management must attempt to meet the underlying objections of the equalization provision, the appropriate test of management's diligence rests on the circumstances of each case, and three unanswered late-night telephone calls were held to be sufficient justification to permit overtime assignment to another employee.[99] Arbitrators disagree about management's right to provide make-up overtime in lieu of pay, where the employer has breached its overtime obligation.[100]

Remedy for Violation of Right to Overtime

Management attempts to change a policy or practice of paying for lost overtime opportunities to one of "make up" overtime is generally viewed as a past practice which can be modified only by bargaining or other appropriate modification procedures.[101]

Some arbitrators issue "cease and desist" orders as the remedy for overtime assignment violations on the theory that a monetary award would be too speculative.[102]

Even though there was no provision in the contract for making a monetary award, one arbitrator awarded compensation to an employee for a good faith error on management's part in awarding overtime, on the basis that a provision allowing for misapplication of overtime to be grieved entitled the grievant to compensation for the lost overtime.[103] However, a misdialed weekend telephone number did not result in an overtime pay remedy, since the error was inadvertent, but the grievant was deemed entitled to the next available overtime call-in.[104]

---

[97]Coca-Cola Foods, 88 LA 129, 131-132 (Naehring, 1986).

[98]Del Monte Corp., 86 LA 134 (Denson, 1985). See also Lockheed Space Operations Co., 91 LA 457 (Richard, 1988) (employer contractually required to equalize overtime may not deny overtime requests of newly certified operators in favor of more experienced operators).

[99]Albright & Wilson, Inc., 85 LA 908, 912 (Shanker, 1985).

[100]Compare Georgia-Pacific Corp., 93 LA 4 (Thornell, 1989) (where contract was silent as to remedy, grievant was entitled to lost pay rather than make-up work) with Lithonia Lighting Div., Nat'l Serv. Indus., 89 LA 781 (Chandler, 1987) (where contract is silent, make-up work is permissible remedy if not inconsistent with past practice and if provided within reasonable time).

[101]See Johnson Controls, 84 LA 553, 559-561 (Dworkin, 1985); see also General Foods Mfg., 83 LA 889, 892 (Williams, 1984), for a similar result, even though management announced during bargaining that it would no longer be bound by the practice.

[102]See United States Playing Card Co., 87 LA 937, 943 (Duda, 1986).

[103]Arco Chem. Corp., 82 LA 146, 148-149 (Nicholas, 1984). See also General Foods Mfg. Corp., 83 LA 889 (Williams, 1984).

[104]Liquid Carbonic Corp., 84 LA 704 (Richman, 1985).

Right to Subcontract

Standards for Evaluating Propriety of Subcontracting

Arbitrators continue to consider the particular circumstances of each case in determining the standards under which management has the right to subcontract. Where the labor agreement is silent about subcontracting, one important factor considered by arbitrators is the effect of subcontracting on the bargaining unit or unit employees. Where subcontracting has little or no effect on the unit or its members, it is likely to be upheld by an arbitrator.[105] Where subcontracting is used either to replace current employees or in lieu of recalling employees on layoff, it is less likely to be upheld.[106] The employer's justification for subcontracting work also is an important factor. Arbitrators are more likely to uphold the contracting out of work where it is justified by sound business reasons.[107]

Notice of Intent to Subcontract; Duty to Bargain

Even though the collective bargaining agreement requires notice of intent to subcontract, the contractual notice requirement is not violated if the employer lacks the necessary equipment and qualified employees and if subcontracting of work is not expected to become routine.[108]

The current Board approach for determining whether an employer's decision is a mandatory subject of bargaining is reflected in *Otis Elevator Co.*, where the Board held that a duty to bargain arises when the decision turns on labor costs, rather than on a change in the direction or nature of the enterprise.[109] The Board followed the

---

[105]See Ideal Elec. Co., 93 LA 101 (Strasshofer, 1989) (employer properly subcontracted company mail delivery where no truck drivers had recall rights, duties required only half hour per day, no employees on layoff, and no layoff resulted); Certainteed Corp., 88 LA 995 (Nicholas, 1987) (that employees were fully employed and unavailable is one factor favoring propriety of subcontracting); M.A. Hanna Co., 88 LA 185 (Petersen, 1986) (subcontract proper where unit welders were unfamiliar with contractor's special processing methods and procedures); Ohio Valley Fed. Credit Union, 82 LA 805 (Duda, 1984) (subcontract of new membership recruitment work justified where credit union needed rapid increase in membership to meet expansion needs).

[106]See MSB Mfg. Co., 92 LA 841 (Bankston, 1989) (employer violated labor agreement by subcontracting delivery where four of thirteen unit positions were lost and average earnings of remaining unit members decreased); American Standard, Trane Co. Div., 89 LA 1112 (McIntosh, 1987) (contracting janitorial services improper where 186 unit employees were laid off); North Star Steel Co., 87 LA 40 (Miller, 1986) (subcontract improper where six unit employees were laid off and available).

[107]See Federal Wholesale Co., 92 LA 271 (Richard, 1989) (severely financially distressed employer justified in subcontracting work to obtain substantial operational savings); Champion Int'l Corp., 91 LA 245 (Duda, 1988) (subcontracting proper in face of general contractual prohibition excepting "where necessary to help finish a job" where bargaining unit could supply 200-300 man hours and subcontractor used over 900 man hours to finish job); M.A. Hanna Co., 88 LA 185 (Petersen, 1986) (subcontracting proper where unit welders were unfamiliar with special processing methods and procedures); Ohio Valley Fed. Credit Union, 82 LA 805 (Duda, 1984) (subcontracting proper to fill special need for member recruitment).

[108]M.A. Hannah Co., 88 LA 185 (Petersen, 1986).

[109]269 NLRB 891, 115 LRRM 1281 (1984).

Supreme Court's approach in *First National Maintenance Corp.*[110] and noted that the same analysis applied to subcontracting decisions. The Fifth Circuit, U.S. Court of Appeals, affirmed the Board's *Otis Elevator*[111] approach in *Steelworkers Local 2179 v. NLRB*.[112]

Under the Board's interpretation of *Fibreboard*,[113] the decision to subcontract in *Fibreboard* was a mandatory subject of bargaining because it turned upon a reduction in labor costs, rather than upon a fundamental change in operations.[114]

One arbitrator has ruled that a union has the right to bargain over the *impact* of subcontracting on the bargaining unit, even where it is clear that the employer has the right unilaterally to contract out the work in question.[115]

Arbitral Remedies Where Subcontracting Violated the Agreement

Arbitrators continue to award a wide variety of remedies where an employer has been found improperly to have subcontracted work. Recent remedies have included: (1) an order prohibiting further subcontracting so long as bargaining unit members are available to do the work, combined with a monetary award to unit members to make restitution for lost earnings;[116] (2) an order that the employer cease and desist from subcontracting, but without monetary damages because the subcontracting was done in good faith;[117] and (3) an award of damages to the union where it was impossible to identify the individual workers who were displaced by the improper subcontracting.[118]

Assigning Work Out of Bargaining Unit

In *Teledyne Monarch Rubber*,[119] the arbitrator rejected an economic justification for a partial plant removal, even though the agreement was silent on the issue of removals. The arbitrator ruled that the employer could not transfer its assembly operations to a nonunion facility during the term of the collective bargaining agreement without the consent of the union, where the transfer would eliminate 15 to

---

[110]101 S.Ct. 2573, 107 LRRM 2705 (1981).
[111]Otis Elevator Co., 269 NLRB 891, 115 LRRM 1281, 1283 n.5.
[112]822 F.2d 559, 125 LRRM 3313 (CA 5, 1987). For recent Board decisions following the same approach, see Garwood-Detroit Truck Equip., 274 NLRB 113, 118 LRRM 1417 (1985) (decision to subcontract mounting and service work not a mandatory subject of bargaining because decision was significant change in business operations); Fraser Shipyards, 272 NLRB 496, 117 LRRM 1328 (1984); UOP, Inc., 272 NLRB 999, 117 LRRM 1429 (1984).
[113]Fibreboard Paper Prods. Corp. v. NLRB, 85 S.Ct. 398, 57 LRRM 2609 (1964).
[114]Otis Elevator Co., 269 NLRB 891, 115 LRRM 1281 (1984).
[115]Witco Chem. Corp., 89 LA 349 (Rothstein, 1987).
[116]MSB Mfg. Co., 92 LA 841 (Bankston, 1989).
[117]American Standard, Trane Co. Div., 89 LA 1112 (McIntosh, 1987).
[118]Brutoco Eng'g Constr., 92 LA 33 (Ross, 1988).
[119]89 LA 565 (Shanker, 1987).

30 percent of the bargaining unit jobs. The employer argued that the bargaining unit would lose even more jobs because of loss of business if the removal were disallowed; however, this argument was rejected on the ground that it should properly be considered by the union in bargaining over the transfer proposal.

Plant Rules

Absent a contractual restriction, management has the right unilaterally to establish reasonable work rules, including rules governing attendance.[120] Attendance policies that disregard all excuses, including personal or sick days to which employees are contractually entitled, or that treat all categories of absence as carrying equal weight have been struck down as unreasonable.[121]

In an increasing number of cases arbitrators have considered rules restricting smoking in the workplace. Smoking policies are generally upheld where the specific rules are considered reasonable and are not in violation of a contract provision.[122]

While management must bargain, upon demand, with regard to rules affecting conditions of employment, a union may lose its right to bargain over the substance of an absentee and tardiness program if it has previously refused to bargain over work guidelines.[123]

Posting of Rules

Where management fails to post/publicize a notice that the penalty for infringement of a rule has been increased, the discharge of an employee may be set aside.[124]

Layoff of Employees

If a contract contains no clause making exceptions for special skills, seniority supersedes ability for purposes of a permanent layoff.[125] However, where an agreement is silent as to the application

---

[120]General Foods Corp., 91 LA 1251 (Goldstein, 1988) (unilateral adoption of attendance policy upheld); Dial Corp., 90 LA 729 (Hilgert, 1988) (no duty to bargain over disciplinary rules). For a general discussion of management's right to implement rules, see Hill & Sinicropi, "Plant Rules," Management Rights: A Legal and Arbitral Analysis, 65-81 (BNA Books, 1986).

[121]St. Joseph Mercy Hosp., 87 LA 529 (Daniel, 1986).

[122]Wyandot, Inc., 92 LA 457 (Imundo, 1989); Central Tel. Co. of Nev., 92 LA 390 (Leventhal, 1989); Honeywell, 92 LA 181 (Lennard, 1989); Acorn Bldg. Components, 92 LA 68 (Roumell, 1988); J.R. Simplot Co., 91 LA 375 (McCurdy, 1988); Worthington Foods, 89 LA 1069 (McIntosh, 1987); Lennox Indus., 89 LA 1065 (Gibson, 1987).

[123]Litton Sys., 84 LA 688 (Bognanno, 1985).

[124]Menasha Corp., 90 LA 427 (Clark, 1987); see also Texstar Corp., 84 LA 900 (Thornell, 1985); Great Plains Bag Corp., 83 LA 1281 (Laybourne, 1984); Distribution Center of Columbus, 83 LA 163 (Seidman, 1984); Bekins Moving & Storage Co., 82 LA 642 (Daughton, 1984).

[125]George A. Hormel & Co., 85 LA 1069 (Miller, 1985); but see Standard Havens, Inc., 92 LA 926 (Madden, 1989) (retention of junior employees proper where agreement allows consideration of seniority, ability, qualifications, and physical fitness); Thombert, Inc., 912 LA 1275 (Yarowsky, 1988) (retention of junior probationary employees because of prior experience proper).

of seniority to layoff, and there is no showing of past practice of taking seniority into effect, the intent of the parties is that it would not be a consideration.[126]

Since arbitrators define the term "layoff" to include any suspension from employment arising out of a reduction in the work force, a plant shutdown that occurred during Thanksgiving week due to a decline in orders constituted a layoff,[127] as did a company's nonscheduling of 10 employees for one week.[128] Similarly, implementation of a "short time" distribution practice was found to require compliance with contractual seniority and layoff provisions.[129]

Laid-off employees who are entitled under the contract to be reinstated to "permanent" positions are entitled to a position understood at the outset to be other than "temporary."[130] Nevertheless, such a contractual provision does not guarantee a reinstated employee lifetime employment.[131]

Bumping

In a contract that contains a provision giving senior employees the right to bump junior employees in a layoff situation, but specifies that ability and experience, along with seniority, will be determining factors in making layoff decisions, the employer may properly disallow senior employees without training to bump junior apprentices who have completed a 27-30 month apprenticeship.[132] However, where the contract requires only that a senior employee be "qualified" for the position sought in order to bump a junior employee, it is improper to deny the senior employee's bumping rights on the basis of a safety policy promulgated unilaterally by the employer.[133] Moreover, where a contract requires the employer to consider ability and

---

[126]Lamar & Wallace, Inc., 83 LA 625 (Bowers, 1984).
[127]Olin Corp., 83 LA 346 (Wolff, 1984).
[128]Bethlehem Steel Corp., 83 LA 745 (Sharnoff, 1984).
[129]Lufkin Indus., 90 LA 301 (Nicholas, 1988).
[130]Firestone Tire & Rubber Co., 90 LA 1154 (Cohen, 1988).
[131]Ibid.
[132]Murphy Oil U.S.A., 86 LA 54 (Allen, 1985); see also Dentsply Int'l, 85 LA 24, 28-29 (Murphy, 1985); Chromalloy-Sturm Mach. Co., 84 LA 1001, 1006 (Imundo, 1985); Brooklyn Acres Mut. Homes, Inc., 84 LA 952, 955-956 (Abrams, 1985); Container Corp., 84 LA 604, 608 (Allen, 1985); Cascade Corp., 82 LA 313, 326 (Bressler, 1984); but see Joy Mfg., 82 LA 1205, 1208 (Schedler, 1984) (since words "experienced" or "qualified" did not appear in layoff or recall provisions, employer could lay off experienced employee and replace him with a senior employee without experience). See also Teepak, Inc., 83 LA 205, 211 (Fish, 1984) (employer may place a limit on number of employees who may bump into a particular classification within a certain time period so as to avoid having too many untrained employees in any one classification).

For cases regarding a senior employee's entitlement to a reasonable trial period to demonstrate his present ability, see United States Steel Corp., 82 LA 655, 657 (Knapp, 1984); Culligan USA, 82 LA 213, 215 (Tamoush, 1984); but see Macomb County Road Comm'n, 82 LA 721, 724 (Roumell, 1984) (senior employee whose qualifications are questionable is not entitled to trial period in layoff situation, but is entitled to reasonable break-in period). See also General Battery Corp., 82 LA 751, 754 (Schedler, 1984).

For a case supporting management's right to require testing to determine a senior employee's qualifications for a position to which he wishes to bump, see International Salt Co., 91 LA 710 (Shieber, 1988).

[133]Lockheed Space Operations Co., 91 LA 457 (Richard, 1988).

seniority in its transfer decisions, the company's right to transfer employees is not considered absolute.[134]

An employer was justified in laying off a senior driver for one day for lack of work and refusing to allow him to bump a junior employee, because the weight of the contractual reduction-in-force language favored a waiting period before bumping rights could be asserted.[135]

Promotion and/or Transfer of Employees

A city employer acted within its rights when it transferred a police inspector to the night shift, despite contract provisions regarding shift preference, since management had the right to determine the number of officers within a rank needed on any shift and the inspector was the only officer of his rank.[136]

An employer was entitled to promote a junior employee, despite contract language requiring promotion by seniority, where considerations of past practice and efficient operations afforded management the right to consider special abilities in filling a vacancy, and the junior employee previously had held the position in question for four years.[137]

An employer improperly refused to allow senior employees to "bid down" to jobs in lower classifications where there was no union concurrence in employer policy of disallowing such a move, and the contract provided that employees had the right to transfer to vacant positions.[138]

Demotion of Employees

Management may not describe a demotion as a transfer in order to avoid compliance with the agreement's rules regarding layoff.[139] However, an arbitrator upheld a nondisciplinary demotion where the contract permitted demotion for inadequacy or deterioration in performance.[140]

An employer demoted an employee improperly, even though the employee had requested the job change, where the employee assumed his job grade and salary would remain the same and the employer failed to advise him to the contrary.[141]

---

[134]City of Omaha, 83 LA 411 (Cohen, 1984).
[135]United Parcel Servs., 90 LA 670 (Statham, 1988).
[136]City of Marion, 91 LA 175 (Bittel, 1988).
[137]Bell Helicopter Textron, 93 LA 233 (Morris, 1989).
[138]Diversitech Gen., 90 LA 562 (DiLeone, 1988); but see Lakewood Bd. of Educ., 90 LA 375 (Graham, 1987) (employer properly awarded promotion to junior employee over senior employee whose selection would have been a demotion).
[139]Marvel Poultry Co., 83 LA 1199, 1200 (Bernhardt, 1984).
[140]Foodland Supermarket, 87 LA 92 (Ling, 1986) (cashier with more than 20 overages/shortages had been repeatedly warned over a five-year period).
[141]Rogers-Wayne Metal Prods. Co., 92 LA 882 (House, 1989).

Merit Increases

Where a contract provided for "minimum salaries" and contained no restrictions on management's right to pay higher rates, management properly awarded merit increases.[142]

Bonuses

A Christmas bonus which had vested under an expired contract was awarded by an arbitrator even though the new contract stated the bonus was no longer in effect.[143] An employer's decision to change a 55-year practice of giving a basket of food at Christmas and to give a gift certificate instead was upheld.[144] However, where a contract stated that "privileges" enjoyed by employees at the time of signing would be continued unless circumstances made doing so "impossible," the employer could not discontinue its long practice of giving a Christmas ham.[145]

Compulsory Retirement

The 1986 amendments to the Age Discrimination in Employment Act remove the 70-year age limitation applicable to employees who are protected under the Act.[146] With limited exceptions, for example, for persons in "a bona fide executive or a high policymaking position," compulsory retirement of employees 65 or older is prohibited.[147]

Disqualifying Employees for Physical or Mental Reasons

Where an employee's physical condition renders him unable or unfit to perform his job, management's right to terminate the

---

[142]CIT Mental Health Servs., 89 LA 442 (Graham, 1987).

[143]Basic, Inc., 82 LA 1065 (Dworkin, 1984). See also Village Meats, 91 LA 1023 (Shanker, 1988) (employees entitled to pro rata safety bonus despite being laid off prior to end of eligibility year).

[144]Emery Indus., 89 LA 603 (Duff, 1987) (long practice not sufficient to make gift basket obligatory).

[145]Alloy Products Corp., 90 LA 390 (Redel, 1988).

[146]29 U.S.C. § 631(a).

[147]29 U.S.C. § 631(c). See Fairmont Gen. Hosp., 87 LA 137 (Bolte, 1986) (employer could not enforce mandatory retirement at age 70 where labor contract did not provide for mandatory retirement age; Age Discrimination in Employment Act held inapplicable because employee was 70 years of age and not protected by the Act as it existed at that time); see also Putnam Hosp. Center, 87 LA 985, 989 (Altieri, 1986) (employer improperly discharged employee on her 70th birthday in violation of antidiscrimination provision of labor contract).

employee has been upheld in many instances.[148] Mental unfitness (psychiatric problems or mental illness) of employees also gives the right of termination to management,[149] especially where an employee's physical or mental condition renders his continued employment unduly hazardous to himself or others.[150]

Conversely, many arbitrators have ordered management to return an employee to work where evidence indicates the employee is able to do the job safely and satisfactorily,[151] especially if the employee has had the condition for a long time and has performed satisfactorily and safely to date.[152]

Significance of Workers' Compensation Disabilities and Costs

An arbitrator ruled that a contractual provision for termination of an employee on sick leave does not apply to an occupational disease covered by workers' compensation.[153]

---

[148]See Mercy Convalescent Center, 90 LA 405 (O'Grady, 1988) (nursing home properly discharged employee suffering from conjunctivitis); Florida Power Corp., 87 LA 1213, 1220-1221 (Singer, 1986); Phillip Morris, U.S.A., 87 LA 975, 977 (Flannagan, 1986); Papercraft Corp., 85 LA 962, 966 (Hales, 1985); Missouri Minerals Processing, 85 LA 939, 945 (Talent, 1985); National-Standard Co., 85 LA 401, 403 (Butler, 1985); Bethlehem Mines Corp., 84 LA 484, 488 (Hewitt, 1985); Porritts & Spencer, Inc., 83 LA 1165, 1168 (Byars, 1984); United States Steel Corp., 82 LA 913, 916 (Tripp, 1984); see also Agrico Chem. Co., 86 LA 799, 805 (Eyraud, 1985) (employer properly removed employee from light duty and placed him on involuntary medical leave); Mead Corp., 86 LA 201, 206 (Ipavec, 1985) (employee who accidentally inhaled chlorine gas and missed two years of work was properly denied vacancy in pulp mill job where employee still suffered symptoms and job required working with chlorine); Transportation Management of Tenn., 82 LA 671, 676 (Nicholas, 1984) (employer properly disqualified employee from position as commercial bus driver following heart attack).

[149]See East Ohio Gas Co., 91 LA 366 (Dworkin, 1988) (acute anxiety depression); Danly Mach. Corp., 87 LA 883, 886 (Cox, 1986) (multiple phobias); Savannah Transit Auth., 86 LA 1277, 1279-1280 (Williams, 1985) (medication and emotional problems following death of spouse); Amoco Oil Co., 86 LA 929, 932 (Holman, 1985) (fear of fire and explosion); but see Tenneco Oil Co., 83 LA 1099, 1104 (King, 1984) (company failed to prove that discharge was for just cause where employee's psychiatrist recommended one month absence from work).

[150]See Union Oil Co., 87 LA 612, 615 (Nicholas, 1986) (employee would be endangering his health by climbing to heights above six feet after cerebral hemorrhage and surgery); Peabody Coal Co., 84 LA 511, 515 (Duda, 1985) (large abdominal hernia potential hazard to employee if reemployed); Spang & Co., 84 LA 342, 346 (Joseph, 1985) (return to heavy lifting duties would create high risk to employee with back problems). See also National Rolling Mills, 84 LA 1144, 1150 (DiLauro, 1985); Owens-Ill., 83 LA 1265, 1269 (Cantor, 1984); Mobile Video Serv., 83 LA 1009, 1012 (Hockenberry, 1984).

[151]Farm Fresh Catfish Co., 91 LA 721 (Nicholas, 1988) (dismissal for safety reasons improper where based on single fainting incident on production floor); Metropolitan Sports Facilities Comm., 90 LA 868 (Bognanno, 1988) (improper to discharge maintenance worker who had performed job on limited basis for five years); Morgan Adhesives Co., 87 LA 1039, 1041-1042 (Abrams, 1986) (reinstatement without back pay where alcoholic employee had good work record and was pursuing medical and psychological treatment); Sperry Corp., 86 LA 520, 523 (Byars, 1986) (contract did not allow employer discretion to deny leave of absence based on employee's ability to work); Gase Baking Co., 86 LA 206, 211 (Block, 1985) (employer improperly denied employee's request to bump into position because of pulmonary problem where that problem had caused employee to miss only one day of work in period of several years); Youngstown Hosp. Ass'n, 82 LA 31, 35 (Miller, 1983) (discharge disproportionate discipline for absenteeism; alcoholism as mitigating circumstances). See also Alton Packaging Corp., 83 LA 1318, 1322-1323 (Talent, 1984); SCM Corp., 83 LA 1186, 1188 (Speroff, 1984); Manufacturing Co., 82 LA 614, 619 (Ray, 1984).

[152]See True Temper Corp., 87 LA 1284 (Nicholas, 1986) (one-arm employee had maintained excellent 10-year work record with company).

[153]Lithonia Lighting Co., 85 LA 627, 631 (Volz, 1985). See also T. Marzetti Co., 91 LA 154 (Sharpe, 1988) (attendance discharge proper despite claim that penalty points for absences due to industrial accidents violate public policy); Mead Paper Co., 91 LA 52 (Curry, 1988) (proper to

Right to Require Physical Examination

Employers have the right to require employees to take audiogram tests required under federal hearing regulations on their off days, when a 14-hour period away from workplace noise is needed to determine whether the employees are suffering hearing loss as a result of their employment.[154]

An employer was entitled unilaterally to adopt a requirement for a comprehensive physical examination for guards/firefighters; however, the specific program adopted was required to be reasonable if its application could lead to disciplinary action.[155] By contrast, where a construction industry employer had an exclusive hiring agreement with a union, an arbitrator held that the employer could not require all individuals referred by the union to submit to a physical examination.[156] Nor could an employer, in the absence of contractual language or past practice, unilaterally impose a requirement that all employees submit to a blood test as a part of a "wellness" program.[157]

Drug and Alcohol Testing

With increasing national concern about the effects of drug and alcohol abuse on the workplace, employers have increasingly resorted to methods to detect and control the problem. Among the measures being taken is implementation of programs to test employees for use of drugs or alcohol. As a result, arbitrators are being required to resolve challenges to implementation of such programs and discipline cases resulting from them.

The National Labor Relations Board has held that drug and alcohol testing of incumbent employees is a mandatory subject of bargaining and that, absent a "clear and unmistakable waiver" of the union's bargaining rights, an employer must bargain with the union

---

discharge employee with 59 work-related accidents as "unsuited for industrial work"); Shamrock Indus., 84 LA 1203, 1206 (Reynolds, 1985); Peabody Coal Co., 83 LA 1138, 1145 (Roberts, 1984); but see Hillsboro Glass Co., 88 LA 107, 113 (Traynor, 1986) (upholding management's decision to deny job bid to employee who had been awarded 12.5% permanent partial disability); Roadway Express, 87 LA 465, 472 (Chapman, 1986) (company permitted to present evidence of excessive workers' compensation claims); E. & J. Gallo Winery, 86 LA 153, 161 (Wyman, 1985) (upholding employer's termination of employee who accepted vocational rehabilitation and monetary settlement for industrial injury); Papercraft Corp., 85 LA 962, 966 (Hales, 1985) (discharge proper where employees receiving workers' compensation benefits are unable to perform job duties).

[154]ITT Continental Baking Co., 84 LA 41 (Traynor, 1984); see also Jefferson Lines, 84 LA 707 (Gallagher, 1985); Caterpillar Tractor Co., 83 LA 226 (Smith, 1984).

[155]FMC, N. Ordinance Div., 90 LA 834 (Bognanno, 1988); see also Pacific Towboat & Salvage Co., 89 LA 287 (Perone, 1987) (employer entitled to require employee returning from absence to submit to physical by mutually agreeable physician).

[156]TCI Gen. Contractor, 93 LA 281 (Christenson, 1989).

[157]Southern Champion Tray Co., 92 LA 677 (Williams, 1988). See generally Hill & Sinicropi, "Medical Screening," Management Rights: A Legal and Arbitral Analysis, 165-190 (BNA Books, 1986).

prior to implementing a testing policy.[158] Arbitrators have reached differing conclusions concerning whether contract language or other circumstances support a management right unilaterally to establish testing policies. In some circumstances, arbitrators have upheld unilateral implementation of testing policies because of contract language preserving the right of management to enforce reasonable rules or safety requirements.[159] On the other hand, some arbitrators have refused to recognize a right to adopt such policies unilaterally even where the contract reserves management's right to adopt reasonable work rules.[160]

Even where management has the right to adopt a drug or alcohol testing policy, the specific provisions of the policy are sometimes struck down as unreasonable.[161] In some cases, discipline has been overturned where it was determined that there was not a reasonable basis to require testing. Thus, requiring testing on return from layoff was found improper where the contract called for requiring a physical if there was reasonable cause to question fitness for work.[162] Similarly, an anonymous telephone call was held an insufficient basis to require testing, since the arbitrator believed a drug test to be "too intrusive an invasion of privacy to be conducted on the basis of an anonymous call."[163]

Selection and Control of Supervisors

An arbitrator determined that the discharge grievance of an employee who had been demoted back into the bargaining unit from a supervisory position was arbitrable, as the employee was not a "new" employee and was not subject to the contractual probationary period.[164]

---

[158]Johnson-Bateman Co. 295 NLRB No. 26, 131 LRRM 1393 (1989). A dispute arising from the unilateral modification of an existing physical examination requirement covering incumbent railway employees is a "minor dispute" under the Railway Labor Act, subject to compulsory and binding adjustment-board arbitration. Consolidated Rail Corp. v. Railway Labor Executives' Ass'n, 109 S.Ct. 2477, 131 LRRM 2601 (1989).

[159]See Dow Chem. Co. U.S.A., 91 LA 1385 (Baroni, 1989); Texas Utils. Elec. Co., 90 LA 625 (Allen, 1988); B.F. Shaw Co., 90 LA 497 (Talarico, 1988); Ashland Oil, 89 LA 795 (Flannagan, 1987); Albuquerque Publishing Co., 89 LA 333 (Fogelberg, 1987); Fleming Foods of Mo., 89 LA 1292 (Yarowsky, 1987).

[160]See Phillips Indus., 90 LA 222 (DiLeone, 1988); Laidlaw Transit, 89 LA 1001 (Allen, 1987) (alcohol and drug policy not within the scope of a contractual provision authorizing employer to issue reasonable work rules).

[161]Stone Container Corp., 91 LA 1186 (Ross, 1988) (policy of testing all employees involved in industrial accidents and calling for automatic suspension pending receipt of test results deemed unreasonable); Sharples Coal Corp., 91 LA 1065 (Stoltenberg, 1988) (policy calling for observed urination in some circumstances deemed unreasonable); Vulcan Materials Co., 90 LA 1161 (Caraway, 1988) (policy imposing random testing held to violate contract provision prohibiting discipline without just cause); Maple Meadow Mining, 90 LA 873 (Phelan, 1988) (rule permitting discipline for off-duty misconduct having no impact on the job is overly broad); Young Insulation Group of Memphis, 90 LA 341 (Boals, 1987) (rule mandating discharge solely on basis of test results showing more than 10 ng/ml of metabolite of marijuana in urine sample deemed unreasonable). See also Denenberg & Denenberg, "Employee Drug Testing and the Arbitrator: What Are the Issues?" 42 Arb. J. No. 2, at 19 (1987).

[162]ITT Barton Instruments Co., 89 LA 1196 (Draznin, 1987).

[163]Southern Cal. Gas Co., 89 LA 393 (Alleyne, 1987).

[164]County of Westmoreland, Pa., 92 LA 790 (Duff, 1989).

Chapter 14

Seniority

Source of Seniority "Rights"

It is well recognized that seniority rights are created and exist only to the extent provided by the collective bargaining agreement. Accordingly, these rights may be modified or abrogated by subsequent negotiations between the parties. As the Ninth Circuit, U.S. Court of Appeals, declared: "Employee seniority rights are not 'vested' property rights which lie beyond the reach of subsequent union-employer negotiations conducted in the course of their evolving bargaining relationship."[1]

In renegotiating the seniority provisions of a collective bargaining agreement, however, the union's bargaining discretion is limited by its status as the exclusive bargaining representative for all its members[2] and by its duty of fair representation to each.[3] In addition, the freedom of bargaining representatives and employers may also be restrained by the courts' use of the doctrine of estoppel.[4] The Ninth Circuit, U.S. Court of Appeals, used this doctrine in one case to prevent a union and a company from using the terms of a modified collective bargaining agreement to deprive an employee of her claim to her original "date of hire" seniority.[5]

---

[1]Hass v. Darigold Dairy Prods. Co., 751 F.2d 1096, 1099, 118 LRRM 2530, 2532 (CA 9, 1985).
[2]Ibid.
[3]Ibid.
[4]Ibid. See also Terones v. Pacific States Steel Corp., 526 F.Supp. 1350, 1356 (N.D. Cal., 1981); Bob's Big Boy Family Restaurants v. NLRB, 625 F.2d 850, 853-854, 104 LRRM 3169 (CA 9, 1980).
[5]Hass v. Darigold Dairy Prods. Co., 751 F.2d 1096, 118 LRRM 2530, 2533 (CA 9, 1985), where, prior to transferring from full-time to part-time status for health reasons, employee sought and obtained assurances from the union that her original hire date seniority would not be forfeited as a result of the transfer. However, when she returned to full-time status, the employee learned she had lost her original seniority date. The union refused to process the employee's grievance, maintaining that under the collective bargaining agreement, she was not entitled to retain the original seniority date because a letter of understanding executed by the company and the union, which established separate seniority lists for full-time and part-time employees, modified the contract.

While seniority rights may be modified during the course of negotiations between the parties, they may also be subject to unilateral modification, when warranted, by a change in conditions or circumstances.[6] Thus, the Seventh Circuit, U.S. Court of Appeals, upheld the finding of an arbitrator that a company did not violate its collective bargaining agreement by unilaterally changing its seniority system after 30 years from a dual chapel seniority system, which maintained different lists for day and night operations, to a companywide seniority system.[7] The Court noted the arbitrator's reasoning that:

> [E]ven though the dual chapel seniority system was an established past practice, such practices can be changed either by a clause to the contrary in a collective bargaining agreement or unilaterally by either party when the conditions upon which the practice was based are substantially changed or eliminated.[8]

Contractual Seniority Rights, the Civil Rights Act, and Arbitration

Section 703(h) of the Civil Rights Act of 1964 permits the routine application of a seniority system absent proof of an intention to discriminate.[9] However, this immunity applies only to "bona fide" seniority systems, and the inquiry into whether a challenged seniority system is bona fide revolves around the presence of discriminatory motive or purpose.[10] To qualify as bona fide, the system must be established and administered without discriminatory intent. The ultimate finding is based upon a consideration of the totality of the circumstances surrounding the adoption and maintenance of the seniority systems.[11]

For example, the Fourth Circuit, U.S. Court of Appeals, found in one case that a system which afforded preference to current employees over outside applicants constituted a bona fide or valid seniority system within the meaning of Section 703(h) in spite of the disparity

---

[6]See Printing Pressmen's Local 7 v. Chicago Newspaper Publishers Ass'n, 772 F.2d 384, 120 LRRM 2511 (CA 7, 1985). See also Rohm & Haas Tex., 93 LA 137 (Allen, 1989) (notwithstanding provision in collective bargaining agreement that most junior employees be selected for involuntary temporary assignments, employer properly assigned unwilling senior bargaining unit employee to worker's committee, where employer's proposal requiring employees to attend meetings that are reasonably related to the performance of duties was added to subsequent agreement); Kroger Co., 92 LA 346 (Pratte, 1989) (past practice of using companywide seniority eliminated in contract negotiations); but see Exxon Shipping Co., 89 LA 731 (Katz, 1987) (employer violated agreement when it unilaterally changed basis for seniority).

[7]120 LRRM at 2512.

[8]Ibid.

[9]See Teamsters v. United States, 97 S.Ct. 1843, 14 FEP Cases 1514, 1526 (1977). Challenges to seniority systems on the basis of discrimination are not limited to the classes of employees protected by Title VII. For example, in Alpha Beta Co., 92 LA 1301 (Wilmoth, 1989), a 50-year-old employee challenged the denial of his job bid alleging that he was discriminated against based on his age. Citing Price Waterhouse v. Hopkins, 109 S.Ct. 1775, 49 FEP Cases 954 (1989), the arbitrator denied the grievance, holding that the employer's decision would have been the same without any consideration of age.

[10]Gantlin v. West Va. Pulp & Paper Co., 734 F.2d 980, 34 FEP Cases 1316, 1324 (CA 4, 1984).

[11]34 FEP Cases at 1325. See also Harvey v. United Transp. Union, 878 F.2d 1235, 51 FEP Cases 394, 406 (CA 10, 1989).

between the number of blacks in the geographic area and the number employed.[12] The court declared that "the County's preference system measures in a race-neutral way, and moreover, what it measures—the state of being a county employee or not—is neither a factor subject to manipulation for prejudicial ends, nor does it lend itself to use for the purpose of racial discrimination."[13]

It is generally recognized that seniority practices having a disparate impact are not actionable where the negotiated seniority system is bona fide and not the result of an intention to discriminate.[14] For example, a court found that the seniority system set forth in a collective bargaining agreement was bona fide despite its discriminatory impact on black employees.[15] The court noted that a discriminatory effect alone is not enough to show that a seniority system is not bona fide.[16]

Similarly, in a case where it was found that a seniority point system was neutral, legitimate, and applied equally to all races,[17] a court declared that in the absence of any evidence to establish that the seniority system had its genesis in racial discrimination, and that it was negotiated or maintained for that or any other illegal purpose, the fact that the system may ultimately be found to perpetuate past discrimination does not make it unlawful.[18]

Another case provides a prime example of a valid bona fide seniority system which perpetuated pre-Act discrimination.[19] There the court found that, although the seniority system had and continued to have the inevitable effect of perpetuating disparities and disadvantages associated with race, the plaintiffs had no basis for relief,[20] since neither the union nor the company had been motivated by racial considerations in establishing the seniority system.[21]

---

[12]Allen v. Prince George's County, 737 F.2d 1299, 38 FEP Cases 1220 (CA 4, 1984).

[13]38 FEP Cases at 1222.

[14]Gantlin v. West Va. Pulp & Paper Co., 734 F.2d 980, 34 FEP Cases 1316, 1323 (CA 4, 1984). See also Lorance v. AT&T Technologies, 109 S.Ct. 2261, 49 FEP Cases 1656, 1659-1661 (1989).

[15]Calloway v. Westinghouse Elec. Corp., 642 F. Supp. 633, 41 FEP Cases 1715 (M.D. Ga., 1986). Plaintiffs testified that while they had seniority and submitted bids, they did not receive the promotions or upgrades sought. While the court declared that their testimony was evidence of discriminatory impact, it was only circumstantial evidence of discriminatory intent. 41 FEP Cases at 1738.

[16]41 FEP Cases at 1738.

[17]Black Law Enforcement Officers v. City of Akron, 40 FEP Cases 322 (N.D. Ohio, 1986).

[18]Id. at 334. Candidates who obtained a 70% on the combined scoring of a job knowledge test, test battery, and performance appraisal were eligible to receive points for seniority. Seniority was then calculated at a rate of one point for each of the officer's first four years of service and 0.6 points for each year of the next 10 years, with a maximum of 10 points. The court found that the plaintiffs failed to show that the City of Akron intentionally employed the seniority system for the purpose of discriminating against the plaintiffs because of their race. Id. at 335.

[19]Goodman v. Lukens Steel Co., 580 F. Supp. 1114, 39 FEP Cases 617 (E.D. Pa., 1984), modified on other grounds, 777 F.2d 113 (CA 3, 1986), aff'd, 107 S.Ct. 2617, 44 FEP Cases 1 (1987). See also Salinas v. Roadway Express, 735 F.2d 1574, 35 FEP Cases 533 (CA 5, 1984), where the court held that a dual seniority system for road and city drivers does not violate Title VII although it may perpetuate pre-Act discrimination.

[20]Goodman v. Lukens Steel Co., 580 F. Supp. 1114, 39 FEP Cases 617, 628-629 (E.D. Pa., 1984).

[21]Id. at 628. The court found that the unit seniority system established at Lukens was adopted because it represented the standard practice throughout the steel industry, and was assumed to be best suited to operating efficiency. Furthermore, the court noted that even if the seniority system at Lukens had been established for the express purpose of perpetuating racial disparities, a shift to plant-wide or some other seniority systems would have been unlikely to provide any net benefit to black employees, then or in the future. Ibid.

However, where disparities and discriminatory practices result from intentional discrimination, no seniority system is immune from liability and remedial action. For example, where a court found that several unions had unlawfully created and maintained a discriminatory seniority system, it ruled that the system was not bona fide and that the unions involved were liable to the plaintiffs under Title VII.[22]

Similarly, another court declared that where the operation of a hiring hall referral system is the mechanism for intentional discrimination, there is no bona fide seniority system.[23] Likewise, the fact that a union limited its membership to whites until 1960 is a factor which a court must consider in determining whether a seniority system intentionally discriminates against minorities.[24]

A finding of unlawful employment practices gives rise to the issue of the type of relief to be awarded and to whom the relief is available. Section 706(g) provides that if a court finds that the respondent "has intentionally engaged in or is intentionally engaging in an unlawful employment practice * * *, the court may enjoin the respondent from engaging in such unlawful employment practices and order such affirmative action as may be appropriate * * * or any other equitable relief as the court deems appropriate * * *." The boundaries of judicial discretion are aptly illustrated in *Sheet Metal Workers Local 28 v. EEOC*.[25] In 1964, the New York State Commission for Human Rights determined that the union had excluded blacks from membership and apprenticeship programs in violation of state law. After more than 20 years of protracted litigation, including various affirmative action plans and contempt citations for the union's failure to comply, the case reached the Supreme Court. The union argued that the membership goals and other court orders which required granting membership preferences to nonwhites were expressly prohibited by § 706(g). The Supreme Court rejected the union's argument holding that § 706(g) does not prohibit a court from ordering, in appropriate circumstances, affirmative race-conscious relief as a remedy for past discrimination. The Court declared:

> Specifically, we hold that such relief may be appropriate where an employer or a labor union has engaged in persistent or egregious dis-

---

[22]Terrell v. United States Pipe & Foundry Co., 39 FEP Cases 571, 578 (N.D. Ala., 1985). Addressing the avowedly racist policies of the Machinists and Boilermakers unions, the court observed that the Machinists original constitution expressly restricted membership to "white, free born male citizens of some civilized county * * *." It also noted that the Boilermakers were also historically an all-white labor union. Id. at 577.

[23]Commonwealth of Pa. v. Operating Eng'rs Local 542, 770 F.2d 1068, 38 FEP Cases 673 (CA 3, 1985). Citing Teamsters v. United States, 97 S.Ct. at 1864, the court affirmed that a bona fide seniority system is one that has been maintained free from any illegal purpose. 38 FEP Cases at 676.

[24]Harvey v. United Transp. Union, 878 F.2d 1235, 51 FEP Cases 394 (CA 10, 1989). See also Wards Cove Packing Co. v. Atonio, 109 S.Ct. 2115, 49 FEP Cases 1519 (1989) (nonwhite plaintiffs alleged, inter alia, that employer's hiring hall agreement with predominantly nonwhite union resulted in overrepresentation of nonwhites in less desirable, lower paying jobs; Court remanded case to determine if specific elements of employer's hiring process, including hiring hall arrangement, had significantly disparate impact on nonwhites).

[25]Sheet Metal Workers Local 28 v. EEOC, 106 S.Ct. 3019, 41 FEP Cases 107, 117 (1986).

crimination or where necessary to dissipate the lingering effects of pervasive discrimination.[26]

Considering the union's long history of "foot dragging resistance" to court orders, the Supreme Court noted that simply enjoining them from once again engaging in discriminatory practices would clearly have been futile. Hence, the district court had properly determined that affirmative race-conscious measures were necessary to put an end to petitioner's discriminatory ways.[27]

Another example of the Supreme Court's response to "foot dragging resistance" to affirmative race-conscious relief is illustrated in *United States v. Paradise*.[28] In that case, the Court upheld a district court's order requiring a one-for-one promotion system to eradicate pervasive, long-standing discrimination against black state troopers which had not been remedied by a 1972 court order, a 1979 consent decree, or a 1981 consent decree.

In *Franks v. Bowman Transportation Co.*, the Supreme Court held that the § 703(h) exemption of "bona fide" seniority systems was not intended to "restrict relief otherwise appropriate once an illegal discriminatory practice occurring after the effective date of the Act is proved."[29] In most cases, a court need only order an employer or union to cease engaging in discriminatory practices, and award make-whole relief to the individuals victimized by those practices. However, in some instances it may be necessary to require the employer or union to take affirmative steps to end discrimination to effectively enforce Title VII.[30]

The availability of race-conscious remedies under Title VII to preclude unlawful discriminatory employment practices is not questioned.[31] However, the application of race-conscious remedies in the wake of bona fide seniority systems has been scrutinized in the aftermath of the decisions rendered in the *Stotts* case.[32]

In *Stotts* the Supreme Court held that a consent decree entered in settlement of Title VII litigation could not be modified in order to override the application of a bona fide seniority system.[33] Although courts and arbitrators have been called upon to construe *Stotts* as prohibiting all affirmative race-conscious relief, they have refused to do so. The courts' determination of whether *Stotts* precludes the application of race-conscious remedies hinges on three factors: (1) the

---

[26]41 FEP Cases at 116.
[27]Id. at 129.
[28]107 S.Ct. 1053, 43 FEP Cases 1 (1987).
[29]96A S.Ct. 1251, 1263, 12 FEP Cases 549, 555 (1976).
[30]Sheet Metal Workers Local 28 v. EEOC, 106 S.Ct. 3019, 41 FEP Cases 107, 118 (1986).
[31]See Firefighters Local 93 v. City of Cleveland, 106 S.Ct. 3063, 41 FEP Cases 139, 148 (1986), where the Court noted that whatever limits § 706(h) places on the power of the federal courts to compel employers and unions to take certain actions that the unions or employers oppose or would otherwise not take, § 706(g) by itself does not restrict the ability of employers or unions to enter into voluntary agreements providing for race-conscious remedial action.
[32]See Commonwealth of Pa. v. Operating Eng'rs Local 542, 38 FEP Cases 673, 675 (CA 3, 1985).
[33]Firefighters Local 1784 v. Stotts, 104 S.Ct. 2576, 34 FEP Cases 1702 (1984). See also White v. Colgan Elec. Co., 781 F.2d 1214, 39 FEP Cases 1599 (CA 6, 1986).

existence of a bona fide seniority system; (2) the existence of a consent decree and the specific provisions contained therein; and (3) whether there has been an adjudication of intentional discrimination. Where cases may be distinguished from *Stotts* on the basis of these factors, courts have read *Stotts* narrowly to prohibit the judiciary from modifying decrees, entered without a finding of discrimination, in such a manner as to override bona fide seniority systems.[34]

However, a seniority system which is created or maintained with discriminatory intent is by definition not bona fide. Thus, *Stotts* is not applicable in cases seeking remedies for past intentional discrimination. For example, where the Third Circuit, U.S. Court of Appeals, found a pattern and practice of intentional discrimination in the operation of the union's hiring hall referral system, the court found *Stotts* inapplicable on two grounds.[35] First, *Stotts* involved the modification of a consent decree where there had been no judicial finding of intentional discrimination. Conversely, the *Pennsylvania* case involved an injunction decree entered after a long trial designed to remedy a judicial finding of intentional classwide discrimination.

Second, *Stotts* involved a bona fide seniority system and addressed the concerns of balancing the rights of innocent nonminorities against minorities suffering from the effects of past discrimination. Whereas, in the *Pennsylvania* case, the seniority system was not bona fide in that it was found to be the vehicle of intentional discrimination.[36] Thus, while the court-ordered relief in *Stotts* had the effect of overriding the legitimate expectations of other employees created by a bona fide seniority system, the Third Circuit declared in its per curiam opinion that:

> Here, where the referral system itself was the mechanism for intentional discrimination, there is no bona fide seniority system, and therefore, there are no legitimate expectations based on the referral system. Where a seniority system has been maintained with discriminatory intent, those individuals who gain seniority within that system are direct intentional beneficiaries of the illegal discrimination; their "expectations" are therefore illegitimate and do not warrant protection.[37]

---

[34]Commonwealth of Pa. v. Operating Eng'rs Local 542, 770 F.2d 1068, 38 FEP Cases 673, 675 (CA 3, 1985). See Firefighters Local 93 v. City of Cleveland, 106 S.Ct. 3063, 41 FEP Cases 139 (1986); Turner v. Orr, 759 F.2d 817, 37 FEP Cases 1186 (CA 11, 1985); EEOC v. Sheet Metal Workers Local 638, 753 F.2d 1172, 36 FEP Cases 1466 (CA 2, 1985), aff'd, 106 S.Ct. 3019 (1986); Vanguards of Cleveland v. City of Cleveland, 753 F.2d 479, 36 FEP Cases 1431 (CA 6, 1985); Diaz v. American Tel. & Tel. Co., 752 F.2d 1356, 36 FEP Cases 1742 (CA 9, 1985); Kromnick v. School Dist. of Phila., 739 F.2d 894, 911, 35 FEP Cases 538 (CA 3, 1984), cert. denied, 105 S.Ct. 782, 36 FEP Cases 976 (1985); Grann v. City of Madison, 738 F.2d 786, 795, n.5, 35 FEP Cases 296 (CA 7), cert. denied, 105 S.Ct. 296, 35 FEP Cases 1800 (1984); NAACP v. Detroit Police Officers Ass'n, 591 F. Supp. 1194, 35 FEP Cases 630 (E.D. Mich., 1984).

[35]Commonwealth of Pa. v. Operating Eng'rs Local 542, 38 FEP Cases 673, 676 (CA 3, 1985).

[36]Ibid. See Arthur v. Nyquist, 712 F.2d 816, 32 FEP Cases 822 (CA 2, 1983), where the Second Circuit affirmed a district court order that overrode the seniority system involving teachers in the Buffalo system, on the basis of prior findings of intentional discrimination by the school system, cert. denied sub nom. Buffalo Teachers Fed'n v. Arthur, 104 S.Ct. 3555, 34 FEP Cases 1887 (1984).

[37]Commonwealth of Pa. v. Operating Eng'rs Local 542, 38 FEP Cases 673, 676 (CA 3, 1985).

Consequently, where there is an adjudication of intentional discrimination, no seniority system is immune from Title VII liability. However, where the parties have entered into a consent decree and there has been no adjudication of intentional discrimination, bona fide seniority systems will be immune and legitimate expectations arising therefrom will be protected.

Nonetheless, the inherent tension between the imposition of race-conscious remedies and the legitimate expectations arising from bona fide seniority systems continues to be a matter for the courts to address. In one instance, white firefighters brought suit alleging reverse discrimination in promotions as a result of a consent decree entered into by the employer and black firefighters in a prior lawsuit.[38] Citing *Stotts,* the Supreme Court held that a voluntary settlement in the form of a consent decree cannot settle the claims of other employees who were not parties to the agreement.[39] In a second case, however, where a court held a "fairness hearing" with notice to class members prior to approving a consent decree, the decree was upheld in the face of a challenge by a union which had not participated in the settlement negotiations.[40] It has also been held that race-conscious relief in the form of classwide seniority will not be awarded for mere membership in the disadvantaged class where there has been no showing by class members that they were actual victims of discrimination.[41]

Likewise, the resolution of conflicts between collective bargaining agreements and conciliation agreements has followed a similar path. In the *W.R. Grace* case, the Supreme Court held that absent a judicial determination, a conciliation agreement concerning seniority provisions entered into between the EEOC and an employer, without union participation or consent, could not take precedence over the terms of the collective bargaining agreement.[42] The Fifth Circuit, U.S. Court of Appeals, has followed this approach, refusing to order specific performance of a conciliation agreement, entered into by the EEOC and the employer without the union's participation, which provided for the retroactive application of seniority rights to several employees or prospective employees who were not promoted or hired allegedly because of race.[43] The Fifth Circuit refused to enforce the conciliation agreement because it infringed on the terms of the collective bargaining agreement and because the union had not had an opportunity to participate in an adjudication that a Title VII violation had occurred. Similarly, the Seventh Circuit Court of Appeals permitted white plaintiffs to intervene in a discrimination suit filed by racial

---

[38]Martin v. Wilks, 109 S.Ct. 2180, 49 FEP Cases 1641 (1989).
[39]49 FEP Cases at 1646.
[40]Eirhart v. Libbey-Owens-Ford Co., 692 F.Supp. 871, 47 FEP Cases 1070 (N.D. Ill., 1988).
[41]Perez v. FBI, 714 F.Supp. 1414, 49 FEP Cases 1349 (W.D. Tex., 1989).
[42]W.R. Grace & Co. v. Rubber Workers Local 759, 103 S.Ct. 2177, 113 LRRM 2641 (1983).
[43]EEOC v. Safeway Stores, 714 F.2d 567, 32 FEP Cases 1465 (CA 5, 1983), cert. denied, 104 S.Ct. 2384, 34 FEP Cases 1400 (1984).

minorities.[44] Citing *W.R. Grace,* the Court held that equitable decrees are not to be made without consideration of the interests of third parties who may be affected.[45] A different result was reached in an arbitration proceeding, where the union participated in the lawsuit.[46]

A challenge to a discriminatory seniority system must be timely filed. Accordingly, when a seniority system is facially nondiscriminatory in form and application, it is the date of the adoption of the seniority system which triggers the limitations period under § 706(e).[47] Thus, where female employees alleged that a 1979 contractual change from plantwide to classification-based seniority was a result of an intent to discriminate against women, the adoption of the system triggered the limitations period for a Title VII charge. Therefore, the female employees' charges—filed in 1982 at the time of their seniority-based demotions—were untimely.

Seniority Units

Seniority rights are often based upon different units. For example, the agreement may provide for plant, unit, and classification seniority, with plant seniority determining vacation or benefits, unit seniority determining promotional opportunities and job security in a particular seniority unit, and classification seniority determining promotional opportunities plantwide.[48]

The accrual of seniority may vary for different classifications of employees.[49]

Seniority Standing and Determining Length of Service

Seniority Standing

In computing seniority standing, the contract may be explicit as to the order of seniority. For example, one contract stated that seniority begins to accumulate on the date and the hour on which the employee begins to work.[50]

---

[44]United States v. City of Chicago, 870 F.2d 1256, 50 FEP Cases 682 (CA 7, 1989).

[45]Id. at 1262. For further discussions of race-conscious relief and the rights of third parties, see Kramer, "Consent Decrees and the Rights of Third Parties," 87 Mich. L. Rev. 321 (1988), and Comment, "Collateral Attacks on Employment Discrimination Consent Decrees," 53 U. Chi. L. Rev. 147 (1986).

[46]In City of Toledo, 88 LA 137 (1986), Arbitrator Feldman found that the terms of a settlement stipulation, entered in a race discrimination suit in which the union was a party and which provided for specific promotion ratios, overrode the provisions of a collective bargaining agreement which was allegedly violated when a black employee was promoted in accordance with the settlement of the lawsuit.

[47]Lorance v. AT&T Technologies, 109 S.Ct. 2261, 49 FEP Cases 1656 (1989).

[48]Firestone Synthetic Rubber & Latex Co., 85 LA 489 (Marcus, 1985).

[49]Hazelwood Farm Bakeries, 92 LA 1026 (Yarowsky, 1989) (arbitrator determined that employer's two-track seniority system for regular and temporary employees was bona fide).

[50]Mode O'Day Co., 85 LA 297 (Thornell, 1985).

Where the seniority date of employees is the same, the company and the union may be required to cooperate to adopt a nondiscriminatory method of determining the relative priority between the employees.[51]

Seniority Lists

The contract often requires the company to maintain and to post seniority lists in each department for each employee.[52] It may also provide for challenging the list, but arbitrators continue to be disinclined to cut off an employee's right to challenge an erroneous seniority list.[53]

Service Outside the Seniority Unit

Seniority obtained in the bargaining unit may be retained upon transfer to an exempt position,[54] or reinstated after a layoff.[55] Similarly, seniority may be retained by separate agreement.[56]

Arbitrators generally hold that employees cannot be credited with seniority for any service performed prior to entry into the bargaining unit.[57] However, an employee may be credited with seniority for service performed outside the bargaining unit if failure to do so would create a prima facie case of discrimination.[58]

Extension of Seniority Rights to Different Plant or Successor Employer

Closing or Relocation of Plant

If a collective bargaining agreement does not provide for companywide seniority or integration of seniority lists, and a plant-

---

[51]Schnucks Super Saver, 84 LA 282 (Heinsz, 1985). See also St. Louis Park School Dist., 90 LA 543 (Miller, 1988) (arbitrator approved use of basic qualifications as tiebreaker for two employees with same seniority date).

[52]Firestone Synthetic Rubber & Latex Co., 85 LA 489 (Marcus, 1985).

[53]Kelsey-Hayes Co., 85 LA 774, 778-778 (Thomson, 1985) (employee's grievance claiming he was laid off out of line due to employer's use of incorrect seniority date was held to be timely filed when brought more than 40 months after layoff occurred under a contract requiring all grievances be taken up "promptly." Arbitrator found employee's medical condition prevented him from detecting error until new seniority list was posted at time grievance was actually filed).

[54]See Union Carbide Corp., 91 LA 181 (King, 1988) (employee promoted to supervisory position initially retained seniority, but lost it upon transfer to another plant).

[55]Bethlehem Steel Corp., 92 LA 1283 (Valtin, 1989) (employee's seniority was reinstated after employee agreed to repay severance pay).

[56]Simpson Timber Co., 90 LA 1273 (LaRocco, 1988) (employer entered into oral agreement to allow employee to go on layoff status and continue to accumulate seniority in return for employee's promise never to attempt to return to work with employer); Concessions Int'l, 90 LA 1252 (Boedecker, 1988) (employees who transferred from existing enterprise at airport to minority business that "negotiated access" to airport complex kept full seniority rights they had with original employer, since original employer's contract bound minority business).

[57]Allegheny County Comm'rs, 83 LA 464 (Mayer, 1984) (management improperly credited employees with time they worked in nonunit jobs at employer's landfill operation before work was assigned to outside contractor and employees were transferred to unit jobs in road department).

[58]FRP Co., 90 LA 1106 (Statham, 1988) (arbitrator upheld award of seniority earned outside bargaining unit to black employee where white employee had previously received same treatment and to do otherwise would have constituted prima facie case of race discrimination).

closing agreement specifically states that such employees will be covered by all of the contract's "new hire" provisions, an employer may properly treat employees from the closed plant as "new hires" when they are transferred to another plant.[59]

Merger or Sale of Company

In its *Fall River Dyeing & Finishing Corp. v. NLRB* decision,[60] the Supreme Court continued to uphold the NLRB's successorship doctrine by refusing to limit the *Burns* holding.[61] The Court upheld an NLRB order requiring the successor employer to bargain with the union that had represented its predecessor's employees. The Court explained that continuity of the bargaining relationship is of particular importance to the employees when a business is sold and the plans of the new employer are unclear: "[D]uring this unsettling transition, the union needs the presumptions of a majority status to which it is entitled to safeguard its members' rights and to develop a relationship with the successor." Without that presumption, "an employer could use a successor enterprise as a way of getting rid of a labor contract and of exploiting the employees' hesitant attitude towards the union to eliminate its continuing presence." The Court endorsed the agency's finding of "substantial continuity," even though there was a seven-month hiatus between the demise of the predecessor employer and the start-up of the new firm and stated that although the employer was not bound by the predecessor's contract with the union, it "has an obligation to bargain with that union so long as the new employer is in fact a successor of the old employer and the majority of its employees were employed by its predecessor."[62]

Successorship or issues related to successorship continue to confront the arbitrators. Recent cases deal with (1) whether the successor company has any obligation under the predecessor's collective bargaining agreement;[63] and (2) whether the predecessor has an obliga-

[59]Safeway Stores, 87 LA 606 (Gentile, 1986).

[60]107A S.Ct. 2225, 125 LRRM 2441 (1987). For further information on merger and successorship, see Selzer, "Rights and Liabilities of Successor Corporation: Patent Licenses, Leases, and Collective Bargaining Agreements," 22 Creighton L. Rev. 815 (1989); Chatfield-Taylor, "Successorship and the Obligation to Bargain: Clarifying the Steps Toward a High Subjective Analysis," 27 Washburn L.J. 685 (1988); Mace, "The Supreme Court's Labor Law Successorship Doctrine After *Fall River Dyeing*," 39 Lab. L.J. 102 (1988); Fasman & Fischer, "Labor Relations Consequences of Mergers and Acquisitions," 13 Empl. Rel. L.J. 4 (Summer, 1987); Silverstein, "The Fate of Workers in Successor Firms: Does Law Tame the Market?" 8 Indus. Rel. L.J. 153 (1986); "Sweeping Up the Divestiture's Debris: Application of the Successor Employer Doctrine to Ma Bell and Her Relatives," 37 Fed. Com. L.J. 455 (1985); Bernstein & Cooper, "Labor Law Consequences of the Sale of a Unionized Business," 36 Lab. L.J. 327 (1985); "Successorship Doctrine: A Hybrid Approach Threatens to Extend the Doctrine When the Union Strikes Out," 28 St. Louis U.L.J. 263 (1984); Miller & Lindsay, "Mergers & Acquisitions: Labor Relations Considerations," 9 Empl. Rel. L.J. 427 (Wint., 1983-1984).

[61]NLRB v. Burns Int'l Sec. Servs., 92 S.Ct. 1571, 80 LRRM 2225 (1972).

[62]Fall River Dyeing & Finishing Corp., 107A S. Ct. 2225, 125 LRRM 2441, 2446-2447 (1987).

[63]For cases holding that the successor did *not* have obligations under the predecessor's agreement, see Arbitrator Fullmer in Arch of Ill., 89 LA 654 (1987) (holding that successor was not liable for paying pro rata vacation pay to employee injured on job. Successor was not bound by predecessor's contract, past practice, or custom); Peterson in Family Food Park, 86 LA 1184 (1986) (predecessor's past practice of assigning hours of work on the basis of seniority was not carried

tion to require its successor to assume the predecessor's collective bargaining agreement as a condition of the transfer of the business.[64]

Loss of Seniority

Arbitrators continue to uphold contractual provisions that provide for the loss of seniority in the event of layoff for a certain period of time,[65] or in the event of any lengthy absence from work resulting from illness or injury.[66]

In certain situations, however, they may rule otherwise. Thus, a laid-off employee, who successfully bid to a new department from which he was subsequently laid off, was held to have maintained seniority in his original department, even though he ignored a recall notice to the new department.[67] Similarly, an employee who, while serving in the National Guard, was granted an extended leave of absence by his employer to work for a different employer in a job related to his National Guard duties, was permitted to accumulate seniority during the leave period.[68]

In yet another case, an arbitrator ruled that a provision terminating seniority when an employee severs services from a company did

---

over when successor purchased the business and hired its predecessor's former employees); Talarico in Servicare, Inc., 82 LA 590, 592-593 (1985) (holding that the successor was not liable to pay an employee for accrued sick leave, even though the successor hired all the former employees of the predecessor and agreed to "take over" the contract between the union and the predecessor. Talarico's decision is based on the fact that the successor specifically denied responsibility for accrued benefits prior to agreeing to adhere to the terms and conditions of its predecessor's contract). For cases holding that the successor had obligations under the predecessor's agreement see Arbitrator Stoltenberg in Peabody Coal Co., 92 LA 1086 (1989) (ordering successor to continue predecessor's past practice of payment of matching death benefit for non-mine-related deaths); Stoltenberg in Arch of W. Va. 90 LA 891 (1988) (ordering successor to continue predecessor's practice of paying employees on weekly basis, rather than biweekly; successor was bound by terms of a national agreement, local agreement, and past practice); Wren in Burnside-Graham Ready Mix, 86 LA 972 (1986) (ordering a joint venture established by the merger of two companies to dovetail the two companies' seniority lists, using length-of-service method, since the joint venture as an entity succeeded to the contract rights and obligations of two companies).

[64]See Arbitrator Jacobowski in Marley-Wylain Co., 88 LA 978 (1987) (employer violated collective bargaining agreement, which was made binding on successors and assigns, where it failed to require buyer's assumption of agreement); Goodman in Wyatt Mfg. Co., 82 LA 153, 162-163 (1983) (holding that the predecessor was not obligated to require its successor to assume the predecessor's contract, because the contract did not contain an expressed provision requiring the predecessor to secure from the successor a commitment to be bound by the contract, and there was no bargaining history to indicate an intent to at least imply such an obligation).

[65]See Arbitrator Stephens in Fleming Foods of Tex., 84 LA 376, 377-378 (1985); Fogelberg in Boogaart Supply Co., 84 LA 27, 30 (1984).

[66]See Arbitrator Byars in Porritts & Spencer, Inc., 83 LA 1165, 1168 (1984); Cromwell in Trojan Luggage Co, 81 LA 366, 368 (1983). In Lithonia Lighting Co., 85 LA 627, 631 (Volz, 1985), the arbitrator held that absence due to a work-related injury did not constitute "sick leave." Therefore, the employee was entitled to keep seniority under the agreement, which terminated seniority after three years of sick leave.

[67]Pacific Sw. Airlines, 88 LA 639 (Williams, 1986).

[68]Great Lakes Carbon, 88 LA 644 (Singer, 1987) (employee could not reclaim former job by bumping since, by accepting private employment, he had violated contractual provision prohibiting gainful employment during a leave).

not deprive the employee, who had received full retirement benefits, of his continued seniority with the company.[69]

On the other hand, if a leave of absence has been improperly obtained, it is considered a resignation, and the employee must return to work as a new hire without seniority.[70]

Seniority Provisions

When a company is promoting an employee to a supervisory position rather than a "rank and file" position, the employer may give greater perference to "fitness and ability" than to seniority.[71]

An arbitrator also allowed a senior employee, in order to avoid layoff, to bump into a position awarded to a more qualified junior employee, even though the position was an upward bump, where the grievant had "present ability to perform work."[72]

An employer unreasonably applied a relative ability standard by improperly selecting a less senior bidder on the ground that he was "more qualified" than the grievant, where the contract mandated a sufficient ability standard and the grievant had the requisite skills to qualify for the position.[73]

Despite claims that the grievant had never performed work without supervision, the project was overbudget because the first technician could not perform the work, and the employer needed an experienced technician who could diagnose and solve problems, an arbitrator held that an employer improperly bypassed the grievant for a less senior, more experienced technician where the contract required an assignment to be offered to the "next senior technician with ability" and there was no evidence that the technician did not have the ability to perform the work.[74]

Modified Seniority Clauses

Under a "sufficient ability" clause, an arbitrator upheld the seniority rights of laid-off employees to apply for and receive promotion to vacant positions, where the posted notice of job openings specified it was not a recall notice, the jobs carried a higher rate of pay,

---

[69]World Airways, 83 LA 401, 405 (Concepcion, 1984) (pilot, who had reached mandatory age of retirement, 60, and who had retired while on medical leave of absence was entitled to use seniority to downgrade to second officer position, having been certified as fit to return to duty, under contract stating that when leaves are granted on account of sickness or injury, crewmember shall retain and continue to accrue seniority until able to return to duty).

[70]Rose Printing Co., 88 LA 27 (Williams, 1986).

[71]Sebastiani Vineyards, 85 LA 371, 375 (Rothstein, 1985).

[72]Metalloy Corp., 91 LA 221 (Daniel, 1988).

[73]Warner Cable of Akron, 91 LA 48 (Bittel, 1988); Southern Minn. Sugar Co., 90 LA 243 (Flagler, 1987).

[74]Executive Jet Aviation, 91 LA 601 (Kindig, 1988).

the employees met seniority and qualifications requirements, and had greater seniority than the co-workers who were selected.[75]

Determination of Fitness and Ability

Arbitrators have upheld management's action when it did not involve an abuse of discretion.[76] Under a contract containing a modified seniority provision, an arbitrator upheld an employer who regarded two candidates as equal in ability and emphasized seniority in choosing a candidate over the union's objection.[77]

Review of Management's Determination: Evidence and Burden of Proof

In "relative ability" cases, some arbitrators continue to provide management's decisions with a presumption of validity, imposing a burden upon the union to show that management's judgment was arbitrary and capricious.[78] However, in one recent case, the arbitrator required the union to first prove the senior employee's equal qualifications, whereupon the burden of proof shifted to the employer to demonstrate that the selected employee was substantially better in ability and performance.[79]

Where there is a "sufficient ability" clause, arbitrators generally place the burden of proof on the employer to show that a bypassed senior employee is not competent for a job. However, where there was a long-established past practice that allowed the employer to select group leaders on the basis of ability to lead, guide, and instruct, rather than seniority, an arbitrator placed the burden of proof on the union.[80]

Factors Considered in Determining Fitness and Ability

In exercising its right to determine whether an employee is qualified for a particular job, the company may adopt any reasonable method for determining whether an employee has the ability to per-

---

[75]Singer Co., 86 LA 917 (Wahl, 1986).

[76]Gibson in Chillicothe Tel. Co., 84 LA 1 (1984); Hunter in Penn Traffic Co., 84 LA 463, 466 (1985); also see Arbitrator Probst in New Enter. Stone & Lime Co., 85 LA 885, 888 (1985).

[77]General Tel. Co., 87 LA 943 (Daniel, 1986).

[78]FECO Engineered Sys., 90 LA 1282, 1285 (Miller, 1988). See also Zenith Elecs. Corp., 90 LA 1020 (Hilgert, 1988) (union sufficiently demonstrated from preponderance of testimony and evidence that grievant had equal ability and fitness to perform job awarded to junior employee); Carnation Pet Foods, 89 LA 1288 (Berger, 1987) (union bears burden of proof to show management's judgment was arbitrary, capricious, discriminatory, or in bad faith).

[79]Wapato School Dist., 91 LA 1156 (Gaunt, 1988).

[80]E-Systems, 84 LA 194 (Steele, 1985). See also Oil-Dri Prod. Co., 89 LA 1035, 1036 (Rice, 1987) (union has burden to prove beyond preponderance of evidence that employer violated "sufficient ability" clause).

form the particular job.[81] This includes an employee's need for supervision as a relative factor in determining a lack of qualifications,[82] as well as technical knowledge, leadership ability, and initiative to show superior qualifications. In fact, it has been held to be management's duty to consider factors other than technical knowledge to ensure that the selection process is completely reliable.[83]

Use of Tests

An employer was upheld in giving written job knowledge tests to assess the sufficiency of qualifications of applicants.[84] However, test results may not be the sole determining factor of ability, as was pointed out by Arbitrator Marlin M. Volz:

> While arbitrators * * * generally permit the discreet use of testing, they strongly disfavor utilizing tests as the sole means of determining ability to perform work, much preferring that test results be considered as only one factor in making the determination. * * * It is apparent that this ability can be demonstrated through past experience, training, and education as well as achieving a passing performance on a test.[85]

A test previously used as one of several factors in determining fitness and ability may not become the sole or primary criterion where the qualifying level of the test was changed and the senior bidder was not advised of the change or that the test would be the sole criterion.[86]

Furthermore, an employer may not base its decision on a test that did not sufficiently relate to the specific job to prove ability or inability of the grievant to perform the necessary work.[87]

Experience

Experience continues to be a factor in determining fitness and ability where the particular experience considered is related to the job in question.[88] In fact, the selection of a junior employee for an assembly department leadman position was upheld even though the employer failed to consider a senior employee who had equal assembler ability and leadman experience and was capable of learning the job quickly, where, because of prior experience, the selectee could perform the job without a break-in period and the employer had the right under past practice to consider special ability.[89]

---

[81]International Salt Co., 91 LA 710 (Shieber, 1988).

[82]Leach Mfg. Co., 82 LA 235 (Harrison, 1984).

[83]Siemens Energy & Automation, 91 LA 598 (Goggin, 1988); Carnation Pet Foods, 89 LA 1288 (Berger, 1987). See also State of Minn., 91 LA 68 (Bognanno, 1988).

[84]Dakota Elec. Ass'n, 84 LA 114, 119-120 (Boyer, 1985).

[85]Peabody Coal Co., 87 LA 758, 762 (1985). See also Watkins, Inc., 93 LA 660 (Hoh, 1989); FECO Engineered Sys., 90 LA 1282 (Miller, 1988).

[86]Zenith Elecs. Corp., 90 LA 1020 (Hilgert, 1988).

[87]FECO Engineered Sys., 90 LA 1282 (Miller, 1988).

[88]State of Minn., 91 LA 68 (Bognanno, 1988) (junior candidate's statewide experience was superior to grievant's, who only worked with local governmental unit).

[89]Bell Helicopter Textron, 93 LA 233 (Morris, 1989).

Lack of experience was not a factor, however, where the contract required the assignment to be offered to the "next senior technician with ability," and there was no evidence that the senior technician did not have the ability to perform the work.[90] Nor was experience a factor in the application of a "relative ability" clause when the employer properly promoted a junior employee based on "superior" performance in an interview.[91]

Trial or Break-in Period on the Job Versus Training

There continues to be support for the view that an employee should be granted a trial period to demonstrate his ability on the job if his test results do not conclusively determine his ability.[92]

However, an arbitrator denied a grievant entitlement to a trial period under a clause which awards the job to "the senior employee in the plant who bid on the job and who within a reasonable period of time could be expected to prove, to the company's satisfaction, that he or she is qualified to do the job," stating that the definition of "a reasonable period of time" is within the company's discretion, even though the grievant was only given a trial period of less than one hour.[93]

Opinion of Supervision

Supervisory opinion regarding the ability of employees continues to be given weight in arbitral decisions. Thus a senior employee's bid for a posted job was properly rejected where overwhelming evidence was established that due to the employee's lack of interest, effort, or ability, he had "been generally deemed to be the least competent of the employees holding any given classification to which he had been assigned."[94]

Similarly, a senior employee was properly bypassed for promotion where several supervisors had documented that his qualifications did not meet the minimum requirements of the job.[95]

However, where a supervisor viewed the grievant as having a negative attitude, being a poor performer, and being untrustworthy, but the employee had never been counseled or warned about substandard conduct and the supervisor's allegations were unsupported generalities, the arbitrator held that the employer had improperly denied the senior employee's job bid.[96]

---

[90]Executive Jet Aviation, 91 LA 601 (Kindig, 1988).

[91]Kroger Co., 89 LA 1307 (Byars, 1987).

[92]Peabody Coal Co., 83 LA 1080 (Seidman, 1984) (employee who passed six parts of seven-part written test and who had overall passing average was held entitled to take performance test under employer's procedure for filling available positions by giving performance test to employee who passes every part of seven-part written test).

[93]Oil-Dri Prod. Co., 89 LA 1035, 1036 (Rice, 1987).

[94]Okeelanta Corp., 88 LA 420 (Richard, 1986).

[95]Cross & Trecler Co., 85 LA 721 (Chalfie, 1985) (employee's deficiencies included inability to adequately read blueprints and each of minimum math skills).

[96]Helm, Inc., 92 LA 1295 (Feldman, 1989).

Educational Background

An employer was upheld in awarding a position to a junior employee with a college education rather than to a senior employee whose experience was not closely related to the position in question.[97] However, an arbitrator held that an employer could not select a newly hired employee with a four-year college degree over a senior employee with nine years of job-related experience.[98]

Attendance Records

Attendance may be the controlling factor for determining fitness and ability where responsibility and reliability are critical to the job.[99] In fact, an employer has a right to command reasonable standards of attendance and punctuality on the part of its employees[100] and may consider attendance in determining applicants' promotional qualifications, even where it is not a contractually-approved standard.[101] Therefore, an employer may legitimately award a supervisory position to candidates who have the specific abilities and qualifications required on the job rather than to senior candidates who have either demonstrated communication problems or attendance and performance problems.[102]

However, one arbitrator has held that an employer improperly disqualified two employees for promotion under a "relative ability" clause by considering their use of annual leave not scheduled in advance, even though the employer had considered sick leave in promotion decisions under such a clause.[103]

Disciplinary Record

In determining fitness and ability, an employer may properly consider the prior negative experience of a senior employee who has a record of discipline for causing property damage, abuse of equipment, and poor performance when he previously held the job.[104]

However, an employer may not automatically disqualify a candidate on the basis of a disciplinary action without considering the nature of the action and its relation to the work to be performed.[105]

---

[97]Atlantic Richfield Co., 83 LA 960 (Allen, 1984).
[98]County of Stearns, 90 LA 1181 (Kapsch, 1988).
[99]Walgreen Co., 93 LA 482 (Baroni, 1989).
[100]Seaway Foodtown, 89 LA 158 (Chalfie, 1987).
[101]Ohio Univ., 92 LA 1167 (Dworkin, 1989).
[102]Sebastiani Vineyards, 85 LA 371 (Rothstein, 1985) (employer required candidates to have basic math skills, possess leadership ability, operate all bottling line machines, and pass 90-day probationary period).
[103]Letter Carriers Health Plan, 92 LA 295 (Hockenberry, 1989).
[104]Crown Zellerbach Corp., 84 LA 277 (Allen, 1985).
[105]Roseville Community Hosp., 92 LA 421 (Concepcion, 1989).

Employee's Physical and Psychological Fitness

Normally an employee cannot justifiably claim physical fitness for a position which contributes to or would cause a recurrence of the employee's ill health. However, an arbitrator held that an employer improperly denied the request of a physically impaired employee who had missed only one day of work and whose ability to perform the work had been confirmed by a neutral physician's report.[106]

However, where an employee had a physical defect that could cause injury to himself and others, an employer properly denied a position to the employee.[107]

Where an employee was placed on medical leave after he admitted having a psychological condition that prevented his performing assigned duties, the employer justifiably refused to reinstate him until he obtained a full medical release stating that he could return to work with or without restrictions.[108]

Sex as a Factor

A junior female employee may be awarded a cleanup job over a senior male bidder where sex is a bona fide occupational qualification (BFOQ) and the senior male bidder does not have the qualifications required by conventionally accepted standards.[109]

Personal Characteristics of Employee

An employer's failure to award a posted job to the only bidder because he was "hyper," or did not work safely, was a contract violation. The arbitrator questioned the meaning and validity of the term "hyper" and ruled that since the employer had failed to show the grievant was not capable or qualified, the grievant must be afforded an opportunity to prove otherwise.[110]

---

[106]Gase Baking Co., 86 LA 206 (Block, 1985) (employee with emphysema wanted to bump into a janitorial position which would have exposed him to more heat, humidity, and flour dust). See also ACF Indus., 90 LA 125 (High, 1987) (employer may require laid-off employees to undergo physical examination before return to active payroll, where contract was silent, but employer had past practice of administering preemployment physicals and extraordinary circumstances existed as result of recall of large number of employees who had been laid off for up to three years).

[107]United States Steel Corp., 82 LA 913 (Dybeck, 1984) (employee's eye injury resulted in little or no depth perception and job required great accuracy of judgment of speed and direction of molten metal).

[108]Danley Mach. Co., 87 LA 883 (Cox, 1986).

[109]Airco Carbon, 86 LA 25 (Stoltenberg, 1985). See also Reynolds Elec. & Eng'g Co., 91 LA 1289 (Morris, 1988) (employer was not required under nondiscrimination clause of contract to train female employee so that she could bump into position that had always been filled by men, where she did not have required "ability to perform available work"); Southern Cal. Gas Co., 91 LA 100 (Collins, 1988) (employer did not violate nondiscrimination clause when it denied female promotion because she did not meet revised minimum qualifications, where requirements were reasonable and there was no evidence that new requirements had adverse impact on women).

[110]Carling National Breweries, 83 LA 385 (Lewis, 1984). See also Helm, Inc., 92 LA 1295 (Feldman, 1989) (employer improperly denied senior employee's job bid because of alleged negative attitude, poor performance, and untrustworthiness, where allegations were unsupported generalities and employee was never counseled or warned about substandard conduct).

However, an employer was not deemed guilty of discriminating against an employee because of race or national origin when it denied her promotional opportunities for several positions, where she did not have the skills and ability to do the work required by the job.[111]

Age as a Factor

The Age Discrimination in Employment Act of 1967, as amended in 1987, removes the age-70 upper limit on coverage under the Act.[112]

Drug Abuse as a Factor

Arbitrators have held that mandatory drug testing of applicants for a promotion or transfer is unreasonable since it is not testing for fitness for present duty but for off-duty drug use and is an invasion of privacy.[113]

Thus, an employer improperly required laid-off employees to submit to drug screening as a condition for recall and refused to reinstate three who tested positive for marijuana, as layoff status does not, by itself, create reasonable cause to test and the asserted practice of drug testing recalled employees was not applied uniformly.[114]

Interview Results

Interview results, while not always determinative, may have a bearing on fitness and ability if they are fair and related to the job to be performed. Therefore, an employer may, under a "relative ability" clause, properly select a junior employee with a few months' experience over a senior employee with several years of experience, on the basis of "superior" performance during an interview.[115] Additionally, an employer's promotion of a junior employee was upheld, even though the labor agreement listed job performance as a criterion of relative ability, where two interviewers rated the grievant less qualified than the junior employee in eight out of ten comparisons.[116]

An interview, however, cannot be subjective or the questions too far removed from the nature of the duties required.[117]

---

[111]Heublein, Inc., 84 LA 836 (Tait, 1985). See also Hyatt Regency Oakland, 92 LA 1016 (Silver, 1989) (arbitrator held employer did not violate contract when it failed to select black senior engineer for promotion, where supervisor constantly criticized his work and there was no objective evidence that supervisor's attitude toward engineer was racially motivated).

[112]29 U.S.C. §§ 623, 631.

[113]Boston Edison Co., 92 LA 374 (Nicolau, 1988).

[114]ITT Barton Instruments Co., 89 LA 1196 (Draznin, 1987).

[115]Kroger Co., 89 LA 1307 (Byars, 1987).

[116]Redlands Unified School Dist., 91 LA 657 (Bickner, 1988).

[117]County of Stearns, 90 LA 1181 (Kapsch, 1988).

Chapter 15

Discharge and Discipline

Scope of Management Right

Probationary Employees

Although most probationary periods are for a period of 30 to 90 days of work with an employer, the time worked by an employee may not count if the work occurs outside the bargaining unit. In one case, for instance, an employee who worked for more than 10 years as a clerical worker outside the bargaining unit was laid off and then recalled to a job within the unit represented by the union. Despite a relationship with the company spanning almost 16 years, the grievant was determined to be a probationary employee.[1]

It has been held that the purpose of a probationary period in a collective bargaining agreement is to provide a time during which an employer can determine whether an employee is suited for a particular task. Thus where a clause in a collective bargaining agreement provided for a 45-day probationary period, the employer could not use this provision to create a temporary labor pool. Rather, the probationary period had to be used as a bona fide trial period to determine employees' ability to perform.[2]

A company's designation of a new employee as either "permanent" or "temporary" does not necessarily determine whether the employee is probationary. In one case an employee was hired as a "permanent employee" to replace another who was involved in a drug-treatment program. Notwithstanding the designation "permanent

[1]Bethlehem Steel Corp., 91 LA 293 (McDermott, 1988).

[2]Superwood Corp., 91 LA 322 (Gallagher, 1988). When a just-cause clause exists in a collective bargaining agreement, the failure to state explicitly that a lower standard of proof is needed to discharge probationary employees entitles these workers to the same rights as full employees. Pacific Power & Light, 89 LA 283 (Sinicropi, 1987).

employee," the arbitrator considered the new employee probationary.[3]

In another case the company attempted to classify a newly hired employee as "temporary." When the company later discharged the "temporary" employee and relied upon the provision in the agreement pertaining to the discharge of "probationary" employees, the arbitrator refused to allow the termination to stand. The arbitrator found that, because the collective bargaining agreement precluded classification of the employee as "temporary," and because the company nonetheless attempted to apply such status, there was never any intent to provide proper probationary training.[4]

Discharge Versus Resignation

In a case dealing with drug testing, an arbitrator deemed that an employee's resignation to avoid such testing was voluntary, but ordered reinstatement because the drug tests were not administered consistent with company rules.[5]

In any event, an employee must clearly intend and desire to sever the employment relationship in order to effect a voluntary resignation. Where a resignation is coerced,[6] or where an employee refuses to comply with management's request to engage in conduct not required under the contract,[7] such terminations are viewed as discharges rather than voluntary resignations. In *Continental White Cap*, the arbitrator reiterated that there are three ways an employee can resign voluntarily: (1) by written statement, (2) by oral statement, or (3) by

---

[3]Somerset Printing, 91 LA 1233 (Levy, 1988).

[4]Superwood Corp., 91 LA 322 (Gallagher, 1988). Two other cases underscore the importance of the language in the bargaining agreement in determining the rights of the company and its new hirees: In Security Contractor Servs., 90 LA 228 (Riker, 1987), the collective bargaining provisions established probationary status for new employees and restricted their access to the grievance procedures. These provisions were rendered ineffective where the same agreement also provided that "any" employee has the right to file a grievance. In Metro Pittsburgh Pub. Broadcasting, 89 LA 934 (Talarico, 1987), the company was permitted to provide a probationary employee with two weeks notice of discharge when there was only one week of the probationary period remaining. This had the effect of allowing the employee to work past his probationary period where he would otherwise have become a permanent, regular employee. The arbitrator noted the absence of any contractual agreement prohibiting the practice by the employer.

[5]Texas Utils. Generating Co., 82 LA 6 (Edes, 1983). To similar effect, Whiteway Mfg. Co., 86 LA 144 (Cloke, 1986); Fordham Univ., 85 LA 293, 295 (Irsay, 1985) ("[A] voluntary quit is a right exclusively reserved to an employee based on his or her actions. The critical factors to be considered in any effort to distinguish between voluntary quit and discharge are the circumstances surrounding the disputed action and intent on the part of the employee involved."). See also Federal Mogul Corp., 86 LA 225 (Blinn, 1986) (mitigating factors considered despite a contract provision deeming certain action to constitute a voluntary quit). Compare Bruce Hardwood Floors, 92 LA 259 (King, 1989) (employee determined to have voluntarily quit when he left job site, even though he was persuaded by his supervisor, in the parking lot, to return and work remainder of shift, since supervisor lacked authority to rehire the employee).

[6]MacMillan Bloedel Containers, 92 LA 592 (Nicholas, 1989) (where employees were given choice of resignation or summary discharge, resignations were viewed as constructive discharge).

[7]Continental White Cap, 90 LA 1119 (Staudohar, 1988) (refusal to sign company warning against continued absenteeism not tantamount to resignation where signature not required under agreement or company rules).

course of action (or inaction) that indicates an intention to sever the employment relationship.[8]

Conduct Away From Plant

Where conduct away from the plant involves the possession or use of drugs, arbitrators routinely rely upon the effect of the conduct on the employer's business.[9]

It continues to be the rule that off-duty/off-premises altercations, verbal abuse, or threatening behavior towards other employees or a supervisor provides sufficient nexus to the workplace to justify discharge.[10]

Off-Duty Misconduct on Company Premises

Management's right to discipline off-duty employees for misconduct on company premises is not always upheld. One arbitrator refused to sustain the discharge of an employee where the altercation took place at a company picnic on the company farm and was related to company-furnished intoxicants and poor supervision by the company.[11] Similarly, an employer could not discharge an employee for drug possession where the employee was not on company property as an employee or on the way to work, the incident occurred outside of working hours, and his presence on company property was unrelated to his employment.[12] On the other hand, another arbitrator upheld the discharge of an employee for violation of a company rule which

---

[8]Id. at 1121.

[9]Lockheed Aeronautical Sys., 92 LA 669 (Jewett, 1989) (off-duty/off-premises sale of marijuana must have nexus to conduct on job to constitute just cause for discharge; employee reinstated); Bard Mfg., 91 LA 193 (Cornelius, 1988) (absent showing of adverse impact on company workplace and failure of company to investigate, felony conviction not per se basis for discharge); Pennwalt Corp., 89 LA 565 (Kanner, 1987) (discharge of employee based upon off-duty/off-premises use of cocaine which caused three days absence from work not justified where employee had acknowledged drug problem and sought treatment one year prior and otherwise had good work record); Warner-Lambert Co., 89 LA 265 (Sloane, 1987) (employer lacked just cause to discharge employee arrested for possessing handgun and cocaine where no adverse impact demonstrated on business); Pacific Bell, 87 LA 313 (Schubert, 1986) (right to discharge for off-duty misconduct is not automatic and conviction for off-duty possession of cocaine does not demonstrate an employee used drugs on job so as to furnish basis for discharge for just cause). For cases upholding dismissal of employee see USAir, 91 LA 6 (Ables, 1988) (off-duty/off-premises purchase of narcotics by airline flight attendant, followed by arrest while in uniform, provided grounds for discharge where nexus to company operations was provided by criminal prosecutor, who informed company of arrest and expressed his concern, because "I fly USAir."); American Brass Co., 89 LA 1193 (Ahern, 1987) (employee's off-duty/off-premises arrest for possession of cocaine supported inference of intent to bring illegal drugs onto company property, that he had done so previously, and was, therefore, in violation of published company policy against bringing drugs to work); Wayne State Univ., 87 LA 953 (Lipson, 1986) (discharge for off-duty drug use proper where employee's job required considerable contact with community and his off-duty drug use clearly had impact on workplace).

[10]Keebler Co., 92 LA 871 (Roumell, 1989) (however, arbitrator modified discharge based upon seniority and good work record).

[11]AFG Indus., 87 LA 1160 (Clarke, 1986); Kalamazoo Rd. Comm'n, 88 LA 1049 (Lewis, 1987) (discipline of employees who each drank two beers during unpaid lunch was improper, even though company rule prohibited drinking on company time, because unpaid lunch period was not considered to be company time).

[12]Texas Utils. Generating Co., 82 LA 6 (Edes, 1983).

forbade "bringing, possession or use of intoxicants or controlled or illegal drugs on company property," even though the employee, who was charged with possession of drugs with the intent to sell, was arrested across the street from the plant by the police shortly before his shift was to begin.[13]

In yet another case, the arbitrator held that the employer could not discharge an employee who was arrested on premises for possession of marijuana when there was no company rule prohibiting possession and no evidence that the employee had actually used the marijuana while on company premises.[14]

Midconduct Prior to Employment

An employer was permitted to discharge an employee who was arrested and convicted for criminal conduct that occurred prior to employment. The arbitrator found that discharge was appropriate because the conduct involved dishonesty and the company would not have hired the employee had it known of the conduct.[15]

Employer Action Pending Court Hearing on Conduct of Employee

An employer was found to have just cause for suspending an employee charged with distributing drugs, and to convert the suspension to discharge following the employee's conviction, where the employer had made a good faith investigation, and thus had reason to believe the employee would be found guilty, and had also instituted a drug-testing program, exercising its managerial right to check employees and to lessen adverse publicity on business.[16]

However, where an employer's investigation revealed evidence of drug use and dealing on company premises during work hours, discharge prior to the employee's arrest and conviction was upheld since the conduct violated company rules and the company reserved the sole right to discharge for such violations.[17]

Although a company may restrict its discipline to suspension upon the arrest of an employee, the employer may be allowed to discharge the employee upon conviction, even where the conviction is

---

[13]American Brass Co., 89 LA 1193, 1194 (Ahern, 1987).

[14]Greyhound Exhibitgroup, 89 LA 925 (McIntosh, 1987).

[15]Alpha Beta Co., 91 LA 1225 (Wilmoth, 1988). See topic entitled "Employer Action Pending Court Hearing on Conduct of Employee," infra.

[16]Lanter Co., 87 LA 1300 (Thornell, 1986). Cf. Alpha Beta Co., 91 LA 1225 (Wilmoth, 1988) (summary discharge after arrest for grand theft was not supported in absence of company investigation; proper discipline pending outcome of criminal charges would be suspension. However, discharge was allowed to stand for other reasons).

[17]S.D. Warren Co., 89 LA 689 (Gwiazda, 1985), rev'd for other reasons, 845 F.2d 3, 128 LRRM 2175 (CA 1), cert. denied, 109 S.Ct. 555, 129 LRRM 3077 (1988). See topics entitled "Burden and Quantum of Proof" and subtopic entitled "Proof in Group Discipline Cases," infra.

later removed upon successful completion of court-supervised probation.[18]

Types of Penalties

In drug cases the right of the employer is limited in regard to withholding work from employees[19] and subjecting employees to drug testing[20] or searches.[21]

In another case, an arbitrator stated that a disciplinary layoff must be for a specific time and the employee and union are entitled to know the exact length of the layoff.[22]

In certain instances, management has been allowed to use penalties other than warnings, suspensions, and discharge. In one situation, it was determined that a company was justified in transferring employees who had refused to take polygraph tests concerning inventory shrinkage, despite the union's contention that this action was improper discipline under the collective bargaining agreement.[23]

Burden and Quantum of Proof

Despite the trend of requiring proof beyond a reasonable doubt in discharge cases involving the use of drugs or other conduct which would constitute criminal activity, a number of arbitrators apply a lesser standard when the criminal drug usage manifests itself as a violation of company rules.[24] Indeed, one arbitrator succinctly stated that "drug cases are all over the lot"[25] regarding the standard of proof necessary to warrant discharge. Arbitrator Suzanne Gwiazda expressed the issue well:

---

[18]USAir, 91 LA 6 (Ables, 1988). See topic entitled "Conduct Away From Plant," supra.

[19]Oliver Rubber Co., 92 LA 38 (Daughton, 1984).

[20]Tribute Co., 93 LA 201 (Crane, 1989) (an on-the-job accident alone was not sufficient to justify imposition of a drug test requiring just cause); Boston Edison Co., 92 LA 375 (Nicolau, 1988) (company not allowed to use drug testing where it failed to prove any need for test, test did not determine employee's fitness to perform, and company had other means of obtaining its objective); Young Insulation Group, 90 LA 341 (Boals, 1987) (drug testing without probable cause improper where no relationship to job performance is proved). However, a number of arbitrators have begun to allow random, mandatory drug testing, especially where jobs involve safety or health concerns. Texas City Ref., 89 LA 1159 (Milentz, 1987); Marathon Petroleum Co., 89 LA 716 (Grimes, 1987); Ashland Oil, 89 LA 795 (Flannagan, 1987); see also Albuquerque Publishing Co., 89 LA 333 (Fogelberg, 1987) (mandatory, random drug test upheld under collective bargaining agreement which allowed company to establish reasonable work rules to assure orderly operations).

[21]Vista Chem. Co., 92 LA 329 (Duff, 1989) (clause allowing employer to search employees' clothing for drugs should be limited to situations where employer has "reasonable suspicion" and where search is confined to "extent necessary to insure the safe and productive conduct" of business).

[22]Cascade Corp., 82 LA 313, 326 (Bressler, 1984).

[23]National Tea Co., 90 LA 773 (Baroni, 1988). See also Southwest Petro-Chem, 92 LA 492 (Berger, 1988) (employer allowed to impose discipline of demotion instead of discharge when the employee's conduct would have warranted the company terminating him).

[24]Rohr Indus., 93 LA 145, 156 (Goulet, 1989); Carter-Wallace, Inc., 89 LA 587 (Katz, 1987).

[25]Rohr Indus., 93 LA 145, 156 (Goulet, 1989).

> The real question is not whether a formulated phrase used in criminal law should be "borrowed" * * * it is whether arbitrators should require different standards of proof in different kinds of cases.[26]

Gwiazda expressed the general trend in such cases, that the more consequential the case the more proof should be required.[27]

Generally three factors are considered in determining the standard of proof necessary, though none alone seems to be determinative. Arbitrators consider whether the employee's conduct constituted criminal behavior, whether it involved moral turpitude, and whether the sanction imposed was discharge or some lesser discipline. Depending upon their perception of the nature of the employee's drug violation, arbitrators have imposed each of the three evidentiary standards—preponderance of the evidence,[28] clear and convincing,[29] and beyond a reasonable doubt.[30]

Proof in Group Discipline Cases

In the case of an illegal strike, arbitrators will generally require the employer to base discipline upon proof of each individual employee's involvement and degree of participation in the group activity. However, the fact that an employer is not able to identify each employee participating in the strike will not prevent the employer from taking reasonable disciplinary action against those employees whom it proves actually did participate.[31]

Likewise, where a single company investigation of several employees resulted in their simultaneous discharge, grievances by different individuals involving different circumstances could not be lumped together and treated as one.[32]

Review of Penalties Imposed by Management

Where a police officer was suspended from work after a court found him guilty of felony, suspended his sentence, and placed him on

---

[26]S.D. Warren Co., 89 LA 689, 702-703 (1985), rev'd for other reasons, 845 F.2d 3, 128 LRRM 2175 (CA 1), cert. denied, 109 S.Ct. 555, 129 LRRM 3077 (1988).

[27]Ibid.

[28]Carter-Wallace, Inc., 89 LA 587 (Katz, 1987) (preponderance of evidence was used when drug possession at work was characterized as violation of company rules, not criminal conduct, and did not involve moral turpitude). But see Rohr Indus., 93 LA 145 (Goulet, 1989) (clear and convincing standard used when drug possession was characterized as violation of company rules and did not involve moral turpitude).

[29]Rohr Indus., 93 LA 145 (Goulet, 1989) (clear and convincing standard); MacMillan Bloedel Containers, 92 LA 592 (Nicholas, 1989) (clear and convincing standard); Southern Cal. Permanente Medical Group, 92 LA 41 (Richman, 1989) (clear and convincing standard).

[30]S.D. Warren Co., 89 LA 689 (Gwiazda, 1985) (beyond a reasonable doubt standard) (reversed on appeal for other reasons). See also Greyhound Food Mgmt., 89 LA 1138, 1141 (Grinstead, 1987) ("Attempting to steal orange juice valued at 58 cents involves moral turpitude and requires standard of proof beyond a reasonable doubt.").

[31]See Super Valu Stores, 86 LA 622 (Smith, 1986); Detroit Edison Co., 82 LA 226 (Jones, 1983). But see Mann Packing Co., 83 LA 552 (Concepcion, 1984).

[32]S.D. Warren Co., 89 LA 689 (Gwiazda, 1985) (however, arbitrator applied same standard of proof for each grievant) (reversed on appeal for other reasons).

probation, the arbitrator held that he lacked jurisdiction to decide the merits of the work suspension since the statute provided for arbitration only when an employee who has been indicted for felony is found not guilty, and there had been no final disposition of the felony in the subject case.[33]

Authority of Arbitrator to Modify Penalties

In one case, an arbitrator found that he was precluded from reviewing the harshness of a penalty because the parties stipulated that the sole issue before the arbitrator was whether the grievant had been disciplined for just cause for participating in picketing while on vacation.[34] Based on the evidence and circumstances surrounding the parties' stipulation, Arbitrator Dallas L. Jones determined that his authority had been limited by the parties to that issue.

In another case, an arbitrator determined that he lacked authority to review or modify the discharge of an employee who was terminated under a "last-chance" agreement that had been entered into voluntarily by the parties. The arbitrator held that if such agreements were ignored or freely overturned by arbitrators, the parties would be discouraged from providing such opportunities to employees with disciplinary problems.[35]

Arbitrator William L. McKee concluded that he had no authority to overturn the discharge of a 30-year employee who had taken from the company goods worth less than five dollars. The arbitrator, nevertheless, "implored" the company to reinstate the grievant because of his long service record and valued contribution. He also pointed out: "In their consideration of this request, the company's managers would do well to refocus the light on themselves to see if they ever have left the plant with a company pencil, paper clip, or legal pad in their pockets or briefcases."[36]

Factors in Evaluating Penalties

Nature of the Offense: Summary Discharge Versus Corrective Discipline

Offenses committed by employees are generally split into two categories, extremely serious and less serious. Those which are extremely serious (i.e., stealing, striking foreman) usually justify summary discharge without any attempt at corrective discipline. The less serious offenses (i.e., tardiness, absence without permission) are

---

[33]City of Houston, 86 LA 1068 (Stephens, 1986).
[34]Detroit Edison Co., 82 LA 226 (1983).
[35]Inland Container Corp., 91 LA 544 (Howell, 1988).
[36]Bridgford Frozen-Rite Foods, 91 LA 681, 685 (1988).

usually not punishable by discharge but call for some penalty, such as a warning.

In cases of extremely serious offenses, arbitrators are more than willing to recognize the need for enforcing penalties that meet the seriousness of the offense.[37]

In the less serious cases, arbitrators continue to apply progressive discipline, exercise leniency, and modify disciplinary penalties imposed by management when there are mitigating circumstances that lead the arbitrator to conclude that the penalty is too severe.[38] The courts have also continued to uphold an arbitrator's consideration of mitigating factors in determining whether there is just cause for discharge unless the collective bargaining agreement clearly and unambiguously prohibits the arbitrator from doing so.[39] Courts will not hesitate in setting aside an arbitrator's decision, however, when the language of the collective bargaining agreement prohibits the arbitrator from fashioning remedies once "just cause" for an employer's action is found.[40] Moreover, in *Paperworkers v. Misco*, the Supreme Court reaffirmed that a reviewing court may vacate an arbitrator's decision when it contravenes a basic tenant of public policy that is "well defined and dominant," and ascertained under statutory law and legal precedents and not from general considerations of perceived public interest.[41] An arbitrator's award will be

---

[37]Burger Iron Co., 92 LA 1100, 1105 (Dworkin, 1987) (discharge for using or selling drugs on company property upheld because illegal activity); OK Grocery Co., 92 LA 441, 444 (Stoltenberg, 1989) (extorting money from fellow employees); Eastern Air Lines, 90 LA 272, 275 (Jedel, 1987) (unauthorized use of in-house computerized communication system to send messages disparaging of management, discrediting company, or objectionable to others); Safeway Stores, 89 LA 627, 629 (Staudohar, 1987) (suspension upheld for negligently selling alcohol to minors); American Welding & Mfg. Co., 89 LA 247, 252 (Dworkin, 1987) (theft); Consumer Plastics Corp., 88 LA 208, 211-214 (Garnholtz, 1987); Furr's, Inc., 88 LA 175, 178 (Blim, 1986); Goodyear Aerospace Corp., 86 LA 403 (Fullmer, 1985).

[38]MacMillan Bloedel Containers, 92 LA 592, 601 (Nicholas, 1989); Warren Assemblies, 92 LA 521, 523–524 (Roumell, 1989); Grinnell Corp., 92 LA 124, 126 (Kilroy, 1989); Lockheed Aircraft Serv., 90 LA 297, 298 (Kaufman, 1987); Furry Mach., 89 LA 739, 743-744 (Goldstein, 1987); Pennwalt Corp., 89 LA 585, 586-587 (Kanner, 1987); Whiteway Mfg. Co., 85 LA 144, 146 (Cloke, 1986); Hyatt Hotels Palo Alto, 85 LA 11, 16 (Oestrich, 1985); Tryco Mfg. Co., 83 LA 1131, 1137-1138 (Fitzsimmons, 1984); Southeastern Trailways, 82 LA 810, 813 (Craver, 1984); Great Midwest Mining Co., 82 LA 52, 55-56 (Mikrut, 1984).

[39]General Drivers, Warehousemen & Helpers Local 968 v. Sysco Food Servs., 838 F.2d 794, 127 LRRM 2925 (CA 5, 1988); Teamsters Local 330 v. Elgin Eby-Brown Co., 670 F. Supp. 1393, 127 LRRM 2950 (N.D. Ill., 1987); GSX Corp. of Mo. v. Teamsters Local 610, 658 F. Supp. 124, 127 LRRM 2391 (E.D. Mo., 1987); Industrial Mutual Ass'n v. Amalgamated Workers Local 383, 725 F.2d 406, 115 LRRM 2503, 2507 (CA 6, 1984); Hilton Int'l Co. v. Local 610, 600 F. Supp. 1446, 119 LRRM 2011 (D. Puerto Rico, 1985).

[40]Container Prods. v. Steelworkers, 873 F.2d 818, 131 LRRM 2623 (CA 5, 1989); Pennsylvania Liquor Control Bd. v. Independent State Stores Union, 553 A.2d 948 (Pa., 1989); Georgia Pac. Corp. v. Paperworkers Local 27, 864 F.2d 940, 130 LRRM 2208 (CA 1, 1988); S.D. Warren v. Paperworkers, 846 F.2d 827, 128 LRRM 2432 (CA 1, 1988); S.D. Warren v. Paperworkers, 845 F.2d 3, 128 LRRM 2175 (CA 1, 1988); Tootsie Roll Indus. v. Bakery Workers Local 1, 832 F.2d 81, 126 LRRM 2700 (CA 7, 1987); and Dobbs, Inc., v. Teamsters Local 614, 813 F.2d 85, 124 LRRM 2827 (CA 6, 1987), where the Sixth Circuit, applying plain-meaning rule, found arbitrator exceeded his authority by ordering reinstatement with back pay when contract plainly and unambiguously recognized employer's right to discharge employees for proper cause.

[41]Paperworkers v. Misco, Inc., 108 S.Ct. 364, 126 LRRM 3113 (1987); see also Gottesman & Vetter, "Enforceability of Awards: Public Policy Post-*Misco*," Proceedings of the 41st Annual Meeting of NAA, 75 (BNA Books, 1989); Gould, "Judicial Review of Legal Arbitration of Awards—30 Years of the Steelworkers Trilogy: The Aftermath of *AT&T* and *Misco*," 64 Notre Dame L. Rev. 463 (1989); Wayland, Stephens & Franklin, "*Misco*: Its Impact on Arbitration Awards," 39 Lab. L.J. 813 (1988).

vacated as conflicting with public policy only if a clear nexus exists between enforcement of the award and violation of public policy.[42] Whether an arbitrator's decision conflicts with public policy is to be narrowly construed.[43]

Most awards where penalties are modified involve a combination of mitigating circumstances. A recent study which examined the trends in arbitration awards involving discharge cases found that the prior work record of the grievant was the most commonly cited factor given consideration by arbitrators, with another frequently cited consideration being the motivation or reasoning behind management's action.[44]

Due Process and Procedural Requirements

Consideration of industrial due process as a component of just cause is still regarded as controversial by some commentators, but it is becoming widely accepted by arbitrators.[45]

Under due process, management must meet certain requirements, and where it fails to do so most arbitrators refuse to sustain the discharge or discipline assessed against the employee.

In one case where management failed to give an employee a chance to be heard, the arbitrator pointed out:

> A just cause proviso, standing alone, demands that certain minimal essentials of due process be observed. One at least of those minimum essentials is that the accused have an opportunity, before sentence is

---

[42]Russell Memorial Hosp. Ass'n v. Steelworkers, 720 F.2d 583, 132 LRRM 2642 (E.D. Mich., 1989) (court recognized public policy in ensuring safe and competent nursing care by vacating arbitrator's order reinstating nurse discharged for negligence); Delta Air Lines v. Air Line Pilots Ass'n, 861 F.2d 665, 130 LRRM 2014 (CA 11, 1988) (discharge of airline pilot who operated aircraft while intoxicated consistent with public policy in favor of airline safety); Iowa Elec. & Power Co. v. Electrical Workers (IBEW) Local 204, 834 F.2d 1424, 127 LRRM 2049 (CA 8, 1987) (public policy favoring strict observance of federally mandated safety regulations at nuclear power site).

[43]Stead Motors of Walnut Creek v. Machinists Lodge 1173, 886 F.2d 1200, 132 LRRM 2689 (CA 9, 1989) (state's general interest in safe motor vehicles did not form well-defined and dominant public policy necessary to bar reinstatement of negligent mechanic); Communications Workers v. Southeastern Elec. Coop., 882 F.2d 467, 132 LRRM 2381 (CA 10, 1989) (public policy did not preclude enforcement of arbitration award reinstating 19-year employee who sexually assaulted co-worker at home); U.S. Postal Serv. v. Letter Carriers, 839 F.2d 146, 127 LRRM 2593 (CA 3), cert. granted, 108 S.Ct. 1589, 128 LRRM 2144 (1988) (no adequate public policy in favor of protecting co-workers and customers from employee's violent conduct).

[44]Jennings, Sheffield & Wolter, "The Arbitration of Discharge Cases: A Fourth Year Perspective," 38 Lab. L.J. 33, 41 (1987).

[45]Arkansas Power & Light Co., 92 LA 144, 149–50 (Weisbrod, 1989) (grievant reinstated because employer violated employee's due process rights by denying him union representation during investigatory interview); King Co., 89 LA 681, 685 (Bard, 1987) (discharges overturned because employees not advised of their Fifth Amendment *Miranda* rights); Adrian College, 89 LA 857, 861 (Ellmann, 1987) (employer failed to make fair investigation); Hogler, "Just Cause, Judicial Review, and Industrial Justice: An Arbitral Critique," 40 Lab. L.J. 281 (1989); McPherson, "The Evolving Concept of Just Cause: Carroll R. Daugherty and the Requirement of Disciplinary Due Process," 38 Lab. L.J. 387, 390 (1987); DeVry Inst. of Technology, 87 LA 1149, 1157 (Berman, 1986); Kaiser Aluminum & Chem. Corp., 87 LA 236, 243-244 (Feldman, 1986); Sun Valley Bus Lines, 87 LA 195, 198 (D'Spain, 1986); McCartney's Inc., 84 LA 799, 803-804 (Nelson, 1985); Associated Grocers of Colo., 82 LA 414, 418-420 (Smith, 1984); but see Beatrice/Hunt-Wesson, 89 LA 710, 715-716 (Bickner, 1987) (employer's failure to hear grievant's explanation prior to suspension did not violate industrial due process where grievant had ample opportunity to explain his position at first grievance meeting).

carried out, to be heard in his own defense. * * * It is the *process,* not the *result* which is at issue.[46]

As a result, Arbitrator Wallace B. Nelson refused to sustain the employee's discharge.[47]

In another case, management failed to conduct a reasonable inquiry or investigation before assessing punishment. Refusing to sustain the employee's discharge, Arbitrator John J. Mikrut, Jr., noted:

> [I]t is well established in labor arbitration that prior to assessing discipline, management, except in the most obvious and heinous of situations * * * must conduct a fair and impartial investigation of the incident and that a sufficient quantum of evidence or proof must be adduced by the accusing party in order to establish the guilt of the charged party.[48]

In a third instance, management did not give the employee the opportunity to question his accuser. As Arbitrator Samuel S. Kates noted:

> It is improper for the company to rely upon the written statement of an employee without presenting his personal testimony, if his presence is requested by the union and if the party relying on the written statement has the power to have him appear at the hearing.[49]

Arbitrators will, in many cases, refuse to uphold management's action where it failed to fulfill some procedural requirement specified by the agreement.[50] If, however, an arbitrator feels the company has complied with the spirit of the procedural requirement and the employee was not adversely affected by management's failure to comply, the company's action may be deemed sufficient.[51] Arbitrators have, in a few cases, refused to disturb management's decision even though the company failed to comply with even the spirit of the requirement.[52]

---

[46]McCartney's Inc., 84 LA 799, 804 (Nelson, 1985).

[47]Id. Also see Adrian College, 89 LA 857, 861 (Ellmann, 1987); Singer Co., 85 LA 152, 155 (Yarowsky, 1985); Otero County Hosp., 85 LA 98, 106 (Finston, 1984) (citing Elkouris); but see Beatrice/Hunt-Wesson, 89 LA 710, 715 (Bickner, 1987); Roadmaster Corp., 89 LA 126, 129 (Doering, 1987) (failure to provide grievant with details concerning discharge in letter did not, by itself, warrant vacating discharge).

[48]Great Midwest Mining Corp., 82 LA 52, 55 (1984). See also MacMillan Bloedel Containers, 92 LA 593, 600 (Nicholas, 1989); Misco, Inc., 89 LA 137, 143 (Fox, 1983); Kidde, Inc., 86 LA 681, 682 (Dunn, 1985); Lee Dodge, 84 LA 1073, 1077 (Chandler, 1985).

[49]Marion Power Shovel Div., 82 LA 1014, 1016 (1984); but see Snapper Power Equip., 89 LA 501, 505–506 (Weston, 1987).

[50]Polysar, Inc., 91 LA 482, 484 (Strasshofer, 1988); Warehouse Distrib. Centers, 90 LA 979, 983 (Weiss, 1987); Adrian College, 89 LA 857, 861 (Ellmann, 1987); Gold Kist, Inc., 89 LA 66, 70 (Byars, 1987); Kidde, Inc., 86 LA 681, 682 (Dunn, 1985).

[51]Union Oil Co. of Cal., 91 LA 1206, 1208 (Klein, 1988) (to overturn employer's action on procedural grounds, proof must exist that grievant was denied fair consideration of his case due to procedural error. Discipline sustained, but employer ordered to pay union's arbitration costs since union was forced to arbitrate because of procedural defect); Roadmaster Corp., 89 LA 126, 129 (Doering, 1987); Intermountain Rural Elec. Ass'n, 86 LA 540, 543 (Watkins, 1985); Shamrock Indus., 84 LA 1203, 1206-1207 (Reynolds, 1985).

[52]Metro Pittsburgh Pub. Broadcasting, 89 LA 934, 936 (Talarico, 1987) (failure to provide contractually required two-week notice did not invalidate discharge of probationary employee); Safeway Stores, 89 LA 627, 630 (Staudohar, 1987); Amax Coal Co., 85 LA 225, 228 (Kilroy, 1985) (where there was no prejudice to either grievant or union); Bogalusa Community Medical Center, 84 LA 978, 982 (Nicholas, 1985); Spaug & Co., 84 LA 342, 346 (Joseph, 1985) (where grievant's suspension was for medical rather than disciplinary reasons); Phoenix Prods. Co., 82 LA 172, 174 (Imes, 1983) (decided under particular facts of case).

An exception is developing to the application of industrial due process when an employee is discharged under a "last chance agreement." These agreements are being used more frequently by employers and arbitrators to allow employees with serious discipline problems, particularly in the areas of drug and alcohol abuse, to continue their employment provided certain defined conditions are met.[53] When considering whether there is just cause for discharge under such agreements, arbitrators do not apply the same due process considerations or procedural protections as under a normal discharge or disciplinary matter.[54] According to Arbitrator William Daniel:

> Arbitrators encourage such progressive programs of salvage and rehabilitation by strict enforcement of such "last chance agreements" in accordance with the terms which the parties, including the employee, have been willing to accept. However harsh or strict such terms and even though the arbitrator might well regard such conditions as unfair, that cannot be his concern.[55]

The arbitrator did note, however, that such agreements do have some limitations, and that neither the union nor the employee can, by the terms of the agreement, be deprived of access to the grievance and arbitration procedure.[56]

In *Taracorp Industries*,[57] the NLRB, overruling its prior decisions, held the appropriate remedy for a *Weingarten*[58] violation is a cease and desist order if the employee was suspended or discharged "for cause." On the same day the Board held that the term "for cause" meant if discipline was imposed for some reason other than an employee's concerted activities.[59] The Board later did not require reinstatement where an employee was discharged on the basis of information obtained in violation of his "*Weingarten* rights"; the rationale was that the employee was discharged "for cause."[60]

Post-*Taracorp* arbitration decisions have not specifically mentioned the change in Board policy. Instead, arbitrators continue to address the situations under traditional *Weingarten* standards. In one case the arbitrator found that a written reprimand rather than discharge was the appropriate penalty for destruction of company prop-

---

[53]Southern Cal. Permanente Medical Group, 92 LA 41, 46 (Richman, 1989); S.E. Rykoff & Co., 90 LA 233, 237 (Angelo, 1987); TRW, Inc., 90 LA 31, 35 (Graham, 1987).

[54]Sorg Paper Co., 89 LA 1237, 1241 (Dworkin, 1987).

[55]Kaydon Corp., 89 LA 377, 379 (1987).

[56]Id. at 379.

[57]273 NLRB 221, 117 LRRM 1497 (1984).

[58]NLRB v. J. Weingarten Inc., 95 S.Ct. 959, 88 LRRM 2689 (1975).

[59]Southwestern Bell Tel. Co., 273 NLRB 663, 118 LRRM 1087 (1984).

[60]Greyhound Lines, 273 NLRB 1443, 118 LRRM 1199 (1985). See also Fischel, "Self, Others and Section 7: Mutualism and Protected Activities Under the National Labor Relations Act," 89 Colum. L. Rev. 789 (1989); Orkin & Schmoyer, "*Weingarten*: Rights, Remedies, and the Arbitration Process," 40 Lab. L.J. 594-602 (1989); Procopio, "A *Weingarten* Update," 37 Lab. L.J. 340, 346-347 (1986); Hogler, "*Taracorp* and Remedies for *Weingarten* Violations: The Evolution of Industrial Due Process," 37 Lab L.J. 403 (1986).

erty where the employee was denied union representation.[61] Likewise, another arbitrator ordered reinstatement of an employee discharged for theft where it was determined that the employee was not given the opportunity to have a union representative present when confronted by an alleged eyewitness.[62] In contrast, one arbitrator refused to set aside the discharge of an employee found sleeping on the job while working under a last-chance agreement, where the employee was denied his *Weingarten* right to union representation.[63] The employer was required to give the employee one month's pay because of the *Weingarten* violation.

Arbitrators, however, have always been more flexible than the Board in the remedies they impose to correct procedural violations.[64] It therefore remains to be seen whether the change in the Board's position will have any appreciable effect on arbitrator's views toward modifying penalties when union representation is denied.

Postdischarge Conduct or Charges

When deciding whether the penalty imposed by management is proper, the general rule is that an arbitrator will consider only the facts known to the employer at the time of the decision to discipline. Postdischarge conduct is considered irrelevant.[65] There is, however, a growing tendency to consider postdischarge treatment as a mitigating factor in considering the propriety of discharges where drug and alcohol addiction is involved.[66] Arbitrators who recognize this exception treat alcoholism and drug addiction as illnesses over which the employee has no control. The misconduct is considered the consequence of the employee's illness.[67] Other arbitrators have extended the exception to cases involving certain forms of mental illness.[68] Arbitrators who recognize the exception consider all the circum-

---

[61]Transitank Car Corp., 84 LA 1112, 1114 (Sartain, 1985). See also Arkansas Power & Light Co., 92 LA 144, 149 (Weisbrod, 1989) (arbitrator concurred with many arbitrators who hold employers to higher standard than strict requirements of *Weingarten* and who require union representation whether or not employee has knowledge to demand representation); Southern Cal. Gas Co., 89 LA 393, 397 (Alleyne, 1987) (discharge overturned where employer improperly failed to provide union representation at interview that resulted in decision to test employee for drug use after employee requested such test).

[62]Bake Rite Rolls, 90 LA 1133 (DiLauro, 1988).

[63]Maui Pineapple Co., 86 LA 907 (Tsukiyama, 1986).

[64]Hill & Sinicropi, Remedies in Arbitration, 91-96 (BNA Books, 1981); Fleming, The Labor Arbitration Process, 139–140 (U. of Ill. Press, 1967).

[65]Fairweather, Practice and Procedure in Labor Arbitration, 2d ed., 303-306 (BNA Books, 1983); Paperworkers v. Misco, Inc., 108 S.Ct. 364, 371, 126 LRRM 3113, 3117 n.8 (1987).

[66]Ashland Petroleum Co., 90 LA 681, 687 (Volz, 1988); Northwest Airlines, 89 LA 943 (Nicolau, Chm., 1984), aff'd, 808 F.2d 76, 124 LRRM 2300 (D.C. Cir., 1987), cert. denied, 108 S.Ct. 1751, 128 LRRM 2296 (1988) (reinstating airline pilot discharged for consuming alcoholic beverages within 24 hours of flight who was found to be an alcoholic and who offered postdischarge evidence of his progress in rehabilitation); but see Duquesne Light Co., 92 LA 907, 910-911 (Sergent, 1989).

[67]Northwest Airlines, 89 LA 943, 952–953 (Nicolau, Chm., 1984); Youngstown Hosp. Ass'n, 82 LA 31, 34-35 (Miller, 1983).

[68]Duquesne Light Co., 90 LA 696, 700 (Probst, 1988); General Tel. Co. of Ind., 90 LA 689, 694-696 (Goldstein, 1988) (discussion of issue, but arbitrator finds insufficient basis for reinstating employee discharged for voyeurism who received postdischarge therapy).

stances of the postdischarge treatment and review each one on a case-by-case basis.[69]

Double Jeopardy

Where management unduly delays in the assignment or enforcement of discipline, arbitrators have applied the double jeopardy concept. As Arbitrator Herbert M. Berman stated: "[I]t is a denial of procedural due process and just cause to hold a charge over an employee's head indefinitely and to revive it whenever corroborating or substantiating evidence might eventually surface."[70] Conversely, another arbitrator held that an employer did not waive its right to impose discipline by failing to act for more than six months where the employer was participating in a police investigation and had agreed to take no action against its employees until the police matter was completed.[71]

In many instances the double jeopardy concept is not applicable, as discipline imposed on the employee may not be final. One arbitrator held that management properly discharged several employees for fighting after first suspending them, pending investigation, and giving them a memorandum to inform them that further incidents between them would result in firing. The union's claim of double jeopardy could not be supported as the memo was not discipline, and it was not perceived by either grievant as such.[72]

Grievant's Past Record

Where a letter of intent that became part of the contract specified that records of disciplinary action in an employee's personnel file should be removed two years after issuance, provided there was no intervening disciplinary action, the arbitrator found that discharge was too severe, since he could not consider these prior records, and the present record of disciplinary action was not sufficient.[73] Another arbitrator held that the employer could not use disciplinary warnings incurred during the probationary period.[74]

Yet another arbitrator held that an employee's absentee record prior to a previous arbitration of his earlier discharge could not be considered in determining the propriety of the second discharge because the first arbitrator "wiped the slate clean."[75] In a similar case,

---

[69]Shell Oil Co., 90 LA 286 (McDermott, 1988); S.E. Rykoff & Co., 90 LA 233, 235 (Angelo, 1987).

[70]DeVry Inst. of Technology, 87 LA 1149, 1157 (1986).

[71]Zenith Elec. Corp., 90 LA 881, 884-885 (Patterson, 1987).

[72]Montgomery Ward & Co., 84 LA 905, 906 (Wilcox, 1985); see also Joerns Healthcare, 92 LA 694, 696-697 (Kessler, 1989).

[73]Calgon Carbon Corp., 88 LA 347, 349 (Tharp, 1987). See also Bethlehem Steel Corp., 92 LA 857, 860 (Witt, 1988); Southern Cal. Permanente Medical Group, 92 LA 41, 45 (Richman, 1989); City of Rochester, 82 LA 217, 220 (Lawson, 1984).

[74]Trailways Computer Transit, 92 LA 503, 506 (Marcus, 1989).

[75]American Brass Co., 88 LA 161 (Fullmer, 1986).

however, an arbitrator permitted an employer to consider an employee's 20-year work record despite a provision in the parties' bargaining agreement that discipline was "wiped-clean" after one year. The employer considered the employee's entire work history to determine the existence of mitigating circumstances that would justify leniency.[76] Conversely, when an agreement expressly restricts an arbitrator from considering mitigating factors in discharge situations, courts will not hesitate in setting aside arbitral decisions to the contrary.[77]

Length of Service With Company

When arbitrators review employee discharges, long-term service with the company, especially if blameless, may be a mitigating factor.[78] However, in one case, the arbitrator found just cause existed, under a rule prohibiting sexual harassment, for discharge of a union steward. The employer had a practice of discharging both employees and management personnel found to have violated the rule, and the steward's 32 years of service and unblemished record did not excuse his conduct.[79]

Knowledge of Rules; Warnings

Where suspension or discharge is a possible penalty for violation of a rule, the rule must be reasonable, consistently applied and enforced, and widely disseminated. Unless the conduct proscribed is so clearly wrong that it need not be specifically referenced, an arbitrator will usually refuse to sustain a grievance where management did not

---

[76]Babcock & Wilcox Co., 90 LA 607, 610-611 (Ruben, 1987).

[77]Georgia-Pac. Corp. v. Paperworkers Local 27, 864 F.2d 940, 130 LRRM 2208 (CA 1, 1988); Pennsylvania Liquor Control Bd. v. Independent State Stores Union, 553 A.2d 948 (Pa., 1989).

[78]Rohm & Haas Texas, 92 LA 850, 856 (Allen, 1989) (14-year employee with good record reinstated where operational errors were attributed to new job classification); S.E. Rykoff & Co., 90 LA 233, 235 (Angelo, 1987) (15-year work record without prior discipline); Climate Control, 89 LA 1062, 1064 (long service was only mitigating factor); Weyerhauser Co., 88 LA 270 (Kapsch, 1987); Consolidation Coal Co., 85 LA 506, 511 (Hon, 1985) (17-year employee reinstated with 20-day suspension); Victory Mkts., 84 LA 354, 357 (Sabghir, 1985) (14-year employee discharged for incompetence reinstated without back pay to lower level position because of his length of service); Pepco, 83 LA 449, 453 (Kaplan, 1984) (unblemished 21-year record of service a mitigating factor); Fisher Foods, 82 LA 505, 512 (Abrams, 1984) (discharged employee with 11 years of seniority and no prior discipline reinstated without back pay); Southwest Detroit Hosp., 82 LA 491, 492 (Ellmann, 1984) (discharge converted to two-month suspension for nine-year employee who was considered a "relatively long term employee"); City of Burlington, 82 LA 21, 24 (Kubie, 1984) (discharge of employee with "over thirteen years apparently blameless service" reduced to five-day suspension). But see Safeway Stores, 84 LA 910, 915 (discharge for dishonesty upheld even though grievants were long-term employees).

[79]Schlage Lock Co., 88 LA 75 (Wyman, 1986). See also Can-Tex Indus., 90 LA 1230, 1231 (Shearer, 1988) (discharge of 21-year employee with good record upheld where employee sexually harassed co-worker despite warning); Babcock & Wilcox Co., 90 LA 606, 610 (Ruben, 1987) (despite 20-year service record arbitrator sustained discharge for poor workmanship); Standard Oil Co., 89 LA 1155, 1158 (Feldman, 1987) (arbitrator upheld discharge of long-term employee who pleaded guilty to drug trafficking).

give an employee adequate notice.[80] If an employee has previously been warned of unsatisfactory conduct, discipline is proper.[81] However, where management fails to give prior warnings, arbitrators will often refuse to sustain disciplinary action taken, especially discharge.[82]

Lax Enforcement of Rules

Discharge for tardiness in reporting to a work station was improper where there was no notice that the rule, which had not been enforced for four years, was going to be enforced.[83]

Unequal or Discriminatory Treatment

Arbitrators will refuse to sustain or will reduce disciplinary penalties where rules and regulations are not enforced consistently, unless reasonable basis exists for variation in assessing punishment.[84] Variations in penalties will be allowed where reasonable

---

[80]Bayshore Concrete Prods. Co., 92 LA 311, 316 (Hart, 1989); Fairmont Mining Co., 91 LA 930, 932 (Hunter, 1988); Donaldson Mining Co., 91 LA 471, 476 (Zobrak, 1988) (verbal policy, unwritten and unpublished, simply does not rise to level of policy that can bind employees; company cannot demand compliance with policy that has not been communicated to affected employees, nor can employees be disciplined for violating policy they do not know exists); Menasha Corp., 90 LA 427, 430 (Clark, 1987); Foote & Davies, 88 LA 125, 127-128 (Wahl, 1986); Warner Jewelry Case Co., 87 LA 160 (Atleson, 1986) (notice and warning that violation of company work rule is grounds for discharge must be made clear to employee in order to sustain discharge); Canteen Corp., 86 LA 378, 383 (Hilgert, 1986) ("This arbitrator has always maintained that company management must be held to a high standard of basic considerations and conduct (which many arbitrators have used) in order to interpret or apply a just cause provision in a labor agreement. One of the most fundamental considerations of all is whether or not an employee is under clear notice that the behavior which was expected would lead to a certain type of penalty."); Stauffer Chem. Co., 83 LA 332, 336 (Blum, 1984).

[81]Food Barn Stores, 92 LA 1199, 1203 (Belcher, 1989); Hughes Aircraft Co., 92 LA 635, 636-637 (Richman, 1989); Service Am. Corp., 92 LA 241, 245-246 (Murphy, 1988); Goodyear Tire & Rubber, 92 LA 91, 96 (Dworkin, 1988); Jim Walter Resources, 90 LA 367, 369 (Nicholas, 1987); Pittsburgh Press Club, 89 LA 826, 830 (Stoltenberg, 1987); General Tel. of Cal., 89 LA 867, 870-872 (Collins, 1987) (discussing decisions of other arbitrators); Augusta Newsprint Co., 89 LA 725, 726 (King, 1987); Texas City Ref., 83 LA 923, 926 (King, 1984), where the arbitrator stated that it is absolutely essential for employees to know what is required of them, but in this case the grievant did have adequate notice and thus the discipline was proper.

[82]Binswanger Glass Co., 92 LA 1153, 1156 (Nicholas, 1989); Georgia-Pac. Corp., 89 LA 1080, 1082 (Nicholas, 1987); Sanford Corp., 89 LA 968, 972 (Weis, 1987) (discharge of employee who refused to take drug test reduced because employer failed to warn of grave consequences of disobedience); Adrian College, 89 LA 857, 861 (Ellmann, 1987); Peoples' Gas, Light & Coke Co., 89 LA 786, 794 (Smith, 1987); Food Mktg. Corp., 88 LA 98, 102-103 (Doering, 1986); Bumper Works, 87 LA 586, 588 (Schwartz, 1986); Federal Mogul Corp., 86 LA 225, 231 (Blinn, 1985); General Tel. Co., 86 LA 138, 141 (Maxwell, 1985); Empire Tractor & Equip. Co., 85 LA 345, 351 (Koven, 1985).

[83]See Great Plains Bag Corp., 83 LA 1281, 1285 (Laybourne, 1984); but see Southern Cal. Edison, 89 LA 1129, 1136 (Collins, 1987) (lax enforcement of reimbursement request program not sufficient to make rule unenforceable; employee properly discharged for falsifying expense account).

[84]Peabody Coal Co., 92 LA 658, 660 (Hewitt, 1989); MacMillan Bloedel Containers, 92 LA 592 (Nicholas, 1989); Worcester Quality Foods, 90 LA 1305, 1309-10 (Rocha, 1988); Beth Energy Mines, 90 LA 1111, 1114 (Feldman, 1988); Marion Gen. Hosp., 90 LA 735, 739 (Curry, 1988); Kable Printing Co., 89 LA 314, 319 (Mikrut, 1987); Joe Wheeler Elec. Coop., 89 LA 51, 57 (Yancy, 1987); Navistar Int'l Corp., 88 LA 179, 182 (Archer, 1986); Nuodex Inc., 87 LA 256 (Millious, 1986); General Bag Corp., 86 LA 739, 741 (Klein, 1985); Stedman Mach. Co., 85 LA 631, 635 (Keenan, 1985); Solar Turbines Inc., 85 LA 525, 529 (Kaufman, 1985); Apex Int'l Alloys, 82 LA 747, 751 (Wright, 1984); ACF Indus., 82 LA 459, 463 (Maniscalco, 1984).

basis exists even though disparate treatment is charged.[85]

Where illicit strikes or slowdowns are involved, management may vary discipline according to degree of fault.[86]

Arbitral Remedies in Discharge and Discipline Cases

Arbitrators continue to use similar remedies when modifying or overruling managerial actions in discharge and discipline cases. The commonly used remedies are found in many of the cases listed in the present Chapter's Table of Offenses.

Some variations in arbitral remedies are:

a. Loss of seniority.[87]

b. Loss of other benefits under the agreement.[88]

c. Probation[89] or final warning.[90]

d. Reinstatement conditioned upon some special act or promise by employee.[91]

---

[85]S.B. Thomas, 92 LA 1055, 1057-58 (Chandler, 1989) (Prohibition against disparate treatment only requires like treatment under like circumstances. These circumstances include nature of offense, degree of fault, and mitigating or aggravating circumstances.); P.D.I., Inc., 91 LA 21, 24-25 (Dworkin, 1988); Nottawa Gardens Corp., 90 LA 24, 27 (Bendixen, 1987); Southern Gas & Elec. Co., 90 LA 1311, 1314 (Dilts, 1988) (finding different penalties for same offense was justified because employees had different disciplinary records); Northwest Airlines, 89 LA 943, 953 (Nicolau, chm., 1984) (Different treatment is not necessarily disparate treatment. Arbitrators have long held that circumstances must be considered and that a wide range of factors—length of service, prior work record, degree of culpability—can properly be taken into account. Indeed, if those factors are not taken into account and "equal" treatment is imposed, that in itself might be disparate.); Central Ohio Transit Auth., 88 LA 628, 632 (Seinsheimer, 1987); Potomac Elec. Power Co., 88 LA 290, 295 (Feigenbaum, 1986); Eastern Airlines, 88 LA 223, 226-227 (Dworkin, 1986); Inter-Pack Corp., 87 LA 1232, 1236 (Brown, 1986); Dresser Indus., 86 LA 1307, 1311 (Taylor, 1986); Phoenix Prods. Co., 82 LA 172, 174 (Imes, 1983); see also Excel Corp., 89 LA 1275, 1280 (McDermott, 1987).

[86]Continental Can Co., 86 LA 11, 15-16 (Hunter, 1985); Schnadig Corp., 85 LA 692 (Seidman, 1985).

[87]City of Massillon, Ohio, 92 LA 1303 (Elkin, 1989); City of Tampa, 92 LA 256 (Rains, 1989); Cincinnati Gas & Elec. Co., 90 LA 841 (Katz, 1988); Burton Mfg. Co., 82 LA 1228 (Holley, Jr., 1984).

[88]City of Massillon, Ohio, 92 LA 1303 (Elkins, 1989); Binswanger Glass Co., 92 LA 1153 (Nicholas, Jr., 1989); Rustco Prods. Co., 92 LA 1048 (Watkins, 1989); City of Tampa, 92 LA 256 (Rains, 1989); Meyer Prods., 91 LA 690 (Dworkin, 1988); Sahara Coal Co., 89 LA 1257 (O'Grady, 1987); Northwest Airlines, 89 LA 943 (Nicolau, 1984); Mare Island Naval Shipyard, 89 LA 861 (Wilcox, 1987); Delta Air Lines, 89 LA 408 (Kahn, 1987); Georgia-Pacific Corp., 88 LA 244 (Byars, 1987); Philips Indus., 87 LA 1122 (Rezler, 1986); Olin Corp., 86 LA 1096 (Seidman, 1986); G. Heileman Brewing Co., 83 LA 829 (Hilgert, 1984); American Packaging Corp., 83 LA 369 (Laybourne, 1984); Burton Mfg. Co., 82 LA 1228 (Holly, Jr., 1984).

[89]Duquesne Light Co., 90 LA 696 (Probst, 1988) (6-months probation); Board of Supervisors, 90 LA 469 (Riker, 1988) (1-year probation); S.E. Rykoff & Co., 90 LA 233 (Angelo, 1987) (1-year probation); Sanford Corp., 89 LA 968 (Wies, 1987) (1-year probation); Phillips Indus., Inc., 87 LA 1122 (Rezler, 1986) (6-months probation); Lull Eng'g Co., 85 LA 579 (Kramer, 1985) (90-days probation); Saucelito Ranch, 85 LA 279 (D'Spain, 1985) (1-year probation).

[90]G.T.E. Fla., 92 LA 1090 (Cohen, 1989); U.C. Agric. Prod. Co., 89 LA 432 (Anderson, 1987); University of Cincinnati, 89 LA 388 (Wren, 1987); Internal Revenue Serv., 89 LA 59 (Gallagher, 1987); U.S. Plywood Corp., 88 LA 275 (Mathews, 1986); Food Mkt. Corp., 88 LA 98 (Doering, 1986); Lockheed Corp., 83 LA 1018 (Taylor, 1984); Pittsburgh Testing Laboratory, 83 LA 159 (Herrick, 1984).

[91]Rustco Prods. Co., 92 LA 1048 (Watkins, 1989) (employee to complete a program of counseling in race relations at his own expense); United Technologies Carrier, 92 LA 829 (Williams, 1989) (express willingness to participate in EAP for 6 months); Bay Area Rapid Transit Dist., 92 LA 444 (Koven, 1989) (subject to daily drug testing); Federal Bureau of Prisons, 91 LA 276 (Statham, 1988) (employee to offer official and personal apology for his racial comment

e. Reinstatement conditioned upon proof of mental or physical fitness.[92]

f. Reinstatement conditioned upon the employee's not holding union office.[93]

g. Reinstated to a different job.[94]

h. Other variations in remedies.[95]

---

and to thank fellow employee for his restraint and control during incident); Ashland Petroleum Co. 90 LA 681 (Volz, 1988), grievant to remain drug free and continue rehabilitation); U.S. Postal Serv., 89 LA 1269 (Talmadge, 1985) (attend Gamblers Anonymous meetings and not gamble); Climate Control, 89 LA 1062 (Cromwell, 1987) (employee resigning from second job within 2 weeks); Iowa State Penitentiary, 89 LA 956 (Hill, Jr., 1987) (grievant ordered to continue regular attendance at AA meetings for 12 months); S.C. Elec. & Gas Co., 89 LA 845 (Boals, 1987) (subject to grievant's cooperation in EAP); TRW, Inc., 89 LA 31 (Graham, 1987) (reinstatement conditioned upon employee signing "last chance" agreement); Weyerhaeuser Co., 88 LA 270 (Kapsch, Sr., 1987) (employee pursue proper medical treatment); Morgan Adhesives Co., 87 LA 1039 (Abrams, 1986) (continue to attend AA meetings and maintain absenteeism below plant average); Lever Bros. Co., Inc., 87 LA 260 (Traynor, 1986) (consult with psychiatrist, be evaluated, submit to treatment); Smith Meter, Inc., 86 LA 1009 (Creo, 1986) (no more than 160 hours of time off and return to work physical); Kenneth City, 85 LA 819 (Seidman, 1985) (personal apology); Mazza Cheese Co., 84 LA 947 (LaCugna, 1985) (hand write letter of apology to president of company expressing gratitude for opportunity to work at company; hand write letter to president of union expressing appreciation for efforts in his defense).

[92]Firestone Tire & Rubber Co., 93 LA 381 (Cohen, 1989); Delta-Macon Brick & Tile Co., 92 LA 837 (O'Grady, 1989); Westinghouse Elec. Corp., 91 LA 685 (Talarico, 1988); Pacific Bell, 91 LA 653 (Kaufman, 1988); S.E. Rykoff & Co., 90 LA 233 (Angelo, 1987); U.C. Agric. Prods. Co., 89 LA 432 (Anderson, 1987); Alton Packaging Corp., 83 LA 1318 (Talent, 1984).

[93]Devon Apparel, Inc., 85 LA 645 (Rock, 1985).

[94]Sanford Corp., 89 LA 968 (Wies, 1987); Weyerhaeuser Co., 88 LA 270 (Kapsch, Sr., 1987); Social Sec. Admin., 84 LA 1100 (Weinstein, 1985).

[95]Rustco Prods. Co., 92 LA 1048 (Watkins, 1989) (employer may bar employee driver from bidding route that would require delivery to customer where employee used racial epithet and vulgar language on dock); Rohm & Haas Tex., 92 LA 850 (Allen, Jr., 1989) (employee can be promoted only at the sole discretion of management); Cincinnati Gas & Elec. Co., 90 LA 841 (Katz, 1988) (no opportunity to be promoted to any job with significant customer contact); Boise Cascade Corp., 90 LA 791 (Nicholas, Jr., 1988) (company directed to allow grievant to engage in drug rehabilitation and to reinstate him when completed); City of Pomona, 90 LA 457 (Rule, 1988) (remand to grievance procedure); U.S. Postal Serv. 89 LA 1269 (Talmadge, 1985) (60-day medical leave of absence); Peoples' Gas Light & Coke Co., 89 LA 786 (Smith, 1987) (parties to negotiate "reinstatement agreement"); Morton Thiokol, Inc., 89 LA 572 (Nicholas, Jr., 1987) (to qualify for back pay, grievant must submit affidavit to company disclosing all income received during his interim discharge period); Northwest Airlines, 89 LA 268 (Flagler, 1987) (employer may withhold grievant from flight assignments and offer grievant option of referral to chemical dependency diagnosis, or termination); Kansas Power & Light Co., 87 LA 867 (Belcher, 1986) (amount of back pay to be reduced if grievant did not earnestly seek other employment during period of termination to mitigate damages); Nuodex, Inc., 87 LA 256 (Millious, 1986) (grievant to submit medical report); Harbor Furniture Mfg. Co., 85 LA 359 (Richman, 1985) (employee reinstated with 85% back pay).

Table of Offenses

The following table is classified according to the type of conduct which prompted the industrial discipline in order to make selected cases quickly available.

Offense	*Discharge Upheld*	*Lesser Penalty Upheld (as assessed by employer)*	*Penalty Reduced by Arbitrator*	*No Penalty Permitted*
Absenteeism	92 LA 1289 Nolan	92 LA 994 Dilts	91 LA 653 Kaufman	92 LA 837 O'Grady
	92 LA 634 Richman	89 LA 80 Nicholas	90 LA 1305 Rocha, Jr.	92 LA 124 Kilroy
	91 LA 1206 Klein, J.	88 LA 447 Witney	90 LA 469 Riker	91 LA 1237 Kilroy
	91 LA 339 McDermott	87 LA 863 Dworkin	90 LA 423 Cohen, H.	91 LA 231 Weiss
	91 LA 154 Sharpe	86 LA 1064 Krislov	90 LA 233 Angelo	90 LA 427 Clark
	90 LA 286 McDermott	86 LA 417 Feldman	90 LA 31 Graham	89 LA 66 Byars
	89 LA 1316 Baron	86 LA 211 Feldman	89 LA 1221 Duda	88 LA 610 Heinsz
	88 LA 343 Rothschild, P.	83 LA 923 King, O.	89 LA 1062 Cromwell	87 LA 589 Christopher
	88 LA 223 Dworkin	83 LA 398 Boner	89 LA 388 Wren	87 LA 586 Schwartz
	88 LA 23 Weiss	82 LA 665 Seinsheimer	89 LA 122 Handsaker	86 LA 864 Beilstein
	87 LA 975 Flannagan		88 LA 347 Tharp	85 LA 971 Creo
	87 LA 691 DiLauro		88 LA 275 Mathews	85 LA 921 Mikrut
	87 LA 236 Feldman		88 LA 270 Kapsch, Sr.	85 LA 29 Gunderson
	87 LA 83 Morgan		88 LA 161 Fullmer	84 LA 1008 Probst
	86 LA 1277 Williams, C.		88 LA 98 Doering	84 LA 986 Valtin
			87 LA 1039 Abrams	84 LA 613 Cloke
	86 LA 1050 Hockenberry		87 LA 972 Johnson	84 LA 393 Kubie
	86 LA 786 Sacks		87 LA 867 Belcher	83 LA 1186 Speroff
	86 LA 686 Daniel		87 LA 260 Traynor	82 LA 652 Duda
	86 LA 673 Petersen		87 LA 256 Millious	82 LA 36 Speroff
	86 LA 601 Bognanno		87 LA 214 Allen	
	86 LA 451 Feldman		86 LA 1263 Jacobowski	
	86 LA 393 Dunn		86 LA 1009	

Offense	*Discharge Upheld*	*Lesser Penalty Upheld (as assessed by employer)*	*Penalty Reduced by Arbitrator*	*No Penalty Permitted*
Absenteeism, cont'd	85 LA 769 LeBaron 85 LA 559 White, H. 85 LA 225 Kilroy 85 LA 212 Shieber 84 LA 936 Milentz 84 LA 761 Bognanno 84 LA 451 Madden 84 LA 257 Gibson 83 LA 907 Katz 82 LA 735 Feldman 82 LA 497 Flannagan		Creo 86 LA 573 Traynor 86 LA 520 Byars 86 LA 120 Feldman 85 LA 359 Richman 84 LA 543 Feigenbaum 84 LA 459 Shieber 84 LA 447 Connors 83 LA 1318 Talent 83 LA 787 Allen	
Tardiness	93 LA 441 Dworkin 90 LA 131 Strasshofer 89 LA 1237 Dworkin 86 LA 1211 Miller, R. 86 LA 786 Sacks 84 LA 1058 Seidman 84 LA 936 Milentz	83 LA 337 Leach	89 LA 59 Gallagher 85 LA 411 Rothschild, P. 85 LA 279 D'Spain	91 LA 749 Clarke 87 LA 594 Helburn 84 LA 613 Cloke 83 LA 1281 Laybourne
Loafing	90 LA 1027 Wolff 89 LA 33 Seidman			91 LA 515 Mayer
Absence from Work	92 LA 793 Hockenberry 90 LA 1194 Dobry 90 LA 617 Daniel 89 LA 1150 Traynor 87 LA 1273 Murphy 87 LA 691 DiLauro	91 LA 1257 Bowers 91 LA 303 Kindig 86 LA 759 Chandler 85 LA 640 Thornell 82 LA 625 Hewitt	92 LA 691 Doering 91 LA 946 Dworkin 91 LA 727 Dworkin 91 LA 405 Williams, J. 91 LA 356 Byars 89 LA 804 Kaufman	93 LA 423 Bankston 93 LA 239 Schwartz 92 LA 1220 Curry, Jr. 92 LA 981 Cronin 92 LA 246 Gallagher 91 LA 1126 Kilroy

Offense	*Discharge Upheld*	*Lesser Penalty Upheld (as assessed by employer)*	*Penalty Reduced by Arbitrator*	*No Penalty Permitted*
	86 LA 786 Sacks		86 LA 1237 Abrams	91 LA 647 Concepcion
	86 LA 719 Brannen		86 LA 573 Traynor	91 LA 126 Hill, Jr.
	86 LA 686 Daniel		86 LA 486 Cohen, L.	90 LA 16 Volz
	85 LA 1003 High		85 LA 579 Kramer	89 LA 897 Koven
	83 LA 1165 Byars		84 LA 799 Nelson	89 LA 861 Wilcox
	83 LA 365 Shearer		82 LA 52 Mikrut	89 LA 739 Goldstein
			82 LA 21 Kubie	88 LA 337 Riker
				88 LA 167 Carter, A.
				86 LA 447 Daniel
				86 LA 225 Blinn
				85 LA 894 Concepcion
				85 LA 382 Rybolt
				84 LA 900 Thornell
				83 LA 1300 Lennard
				83 LA 1099 King, O.
				83 LA 281 Kelliher
Leaving Post (Includes early quitting)	90 LA 844 Lang	93 LA 450 Wilcox	92 LA 521 Roumell	92 LA 259 King, J.
	89 LA 985 O'Grady	92 LA 1055 Chandler	91 LA 1101 Volz	91 LA 1097 Talarico
	86 LA 929 Holman	91 LA 585 Yarowsky	91 LA 352 Frost	91 LA 234 Allen
	86 LA 451 Feldman	90 LA 856 Thompson	90 LA 1311 Dilts	90 LA 466 Lang
	83 LA 48 Mullin	90 LA 620 Poindexter	88 LA 145 Keefe	88 LA 118 McAlpin
	82 LA 1259 Seidman	83 LA 895 Fitzsimmons	87 LA 1122 Rezler	86 LA 1269 DiLauro
		82 LA 1090 Keenan	87 LA 357 Dworkin	86 LA 1032 Spilker
			87 LA 111 DiLauro	84 LA 1166 Duff, J.
			86 LA 545 Allen	82 LA 138 Ellmann, E.
			86 LA 144 Cloke	
			85 LA 443	

Offense	*Discharge Upheld*	*Lesser Penalty Upheld (as assessed by employer)*	*Penalty Reduced by Arbitrator*	*No Penalty Permitted*
Leaving Post (Includes early quitting) cont'd			Wyman 85 LA 359 Richman 85 LA 279 D'Spain	
Sleeping on Job	93 LA 505 Dworkin 90 LA 655 Kates 90 LA 516 Allen 86 LA 1211 Miller, R. 86 LA 907 Tsukiyama 86 LA 430 Cox	91 LA 30 Alleyne	93 LA 530 Cipolla 91 LA 443 Jacobowski 90 LA 1053 Runkel 88 LA 244 Byars 86 LA 1096 Seidman 86 LA 243 Sass 83 LA 159 Herrick	84 LA 400 Cohn 83 LA 468 Schedler
Assault and Fighting Among Employees	93 LA 580 Chandler 90 LA 837 Fullmer 90 LA 109 Flannagan 89 LA 1183 Madden 89 LA 501 Weston 87 LA 394 Feldman 84 LA 905 Wilcox 84 LA 134 Richman 83 LA 1172 Bickner 83 LA 253 Tsukiyama 81 LA 855 Kaufman	88 LA 157 Doering 87 LA 534 Krebs 82 LA 172 Imes	93 LA 189 Gentile 92 LA 1303 Elkin 92 LA 1107 Herring 92 LA 969 Dworkin 91 LA 957 Duda 91 LA 734 Miller, C. 91 LA 690 Dworkin 91 LA 685 Talarico 91 LA 185 Kanowitz 89 LA 432 Anderson 87 LA 1160 Clarke 86 LA 1197 Eisler 85 LA 859 Shanker 85 LA 631 Keenan 85 LA 525 Kaufman 84 LA 1289 Duda 84 LA 947 LaCugna	89 LA 427 Bard 89 LA 192 Yarowsky 83 LA 1172 Bickner 81 LA 158 Ray, D.

Offense	*Discharge Upheld*	*Lesser Penalty Upheld (as assessed by employer)*	*Penalty Reduced by Arbitrator*	*No Penalty Permitted*
			84 LA 367 Gibson	
			83 LA 829 Hilgert	
			83 LA 497 Richman	
			82 LA 1014 Kates	
			82 LA 747 Wright	
Horseplay	89 LA 297 DiLauro		91 LA 1402 Nathan	
			90 LA 783 Duda	
			90 LA 502 Wolff	
			88 LA 151 Mikrut	
Insubordination	92 LA 162 Clarke	92 LA 449 Mayer	93 LA 561 Strongin	93 LA 201 Crane
	92 LA 151 Hockenberry	92 LA 311 Hart	93 LA 520 Randall	92 LA 483 Dworkin
	91 LA 1129 Coyne	92 LA 265 Hilgert	93 LA 91 Rocha, Jr.	92 LA 127 Oestreich
	90 LA 462 Christopher	91 LA 987 Nolan	92 LA 1225 Girolamo	92 LA 97 Koven
	90 LA 373 Groshong	91 LA 909 Weiss	92 LA 367 Corbett	91 LA 895 Curry, Jr.
	89 LA 877 Handsaker	91 LA 697 Stephens	92 LA 3 Koven	91 LA 816 Nicholas
	89 LA 799 Brisco	90 LA 773 Baroni	91 LA 1049 Watkins	91 LA 73 DiLauro
	89 LA 333 Fogelberg	90 LA 479 Weiss	90 LA 1257 Tilbury	90 LA 1133 DiLauro
	89 LA 268 Flagler	89 LA 1252 Baroni	90 LA 1216 Babiskin	90 LA 1119 Staudohar
	89 LA 173 Hart	89 LA 361 DiLauro	90 LA 979 Weiss	90 LA 740 Ruben
	89 LA 16 Duda	87 LA 141 Zobrak	90 LA 696 Probst	90 LA 457 Rule
	88 LA 418 Scholtz	86 LA 832 O'Grady	89 LA 1257 O'Grady	89 LA 506 Wyman
	87 LA 1145 Cohen, S.	86 LA 180 Carson	89 LA 968 Wies	89 LA 398 Mikrut
	87 LA 1122 Rezler	85 LA 1162 Kulkis	89 LA 865 Duda	87 LA 51 Kapsch
	86 LA 1201 Alleyne	85 LA 89 Boyer	89 LA 572 Nicholas	86 LA 1168 Imes
	86 LA 1112 Richman	85 LA 70 White, J.	88 LA 475 Williams, J.	86 LA 874 Odom
	85 LA 1011 Kaufman	84 LA 770 Singer	88 LA 183 Belcher	86 LA 846 Gentile
	85 LA 667	84 LA 734		86 LA 532

Offense	*Discharge Upheld*	*Lesser Penalty Upheld (as assessed by employer)*	*Penalty Reduced by Arbitrator*	*No Penalty Permitted*
Insubordination	Smedley	Nemaizer	86 LA 378	Cooley
cont'd	84 LA 693	84 LA 418	Hilgert	86 LA 345
	Cantor	Bowers	86 LA 232	Vause
	82 LA 358	84 LA 201	Duff, J.	85 LA 1179
	Draznin	Storey	86 LA 171	White, J.
	82 LA 306	82 LA 1202	Draznin	85 LA 716
	Williams, C.	Rothstein	86 LA 144	Nathan
	82 LA 12	82 LA 1161	Cloke	85 LA 575
	Fitzsimmons	Nicholas	86 LA 75	Bolte
	81 LA 158	82 LA 1020	Wies	84 LA 1112
	Ray, D.	Groshong	85 LA 1185	Sartain
			Gallagher	83 LA 1300
			85 LA 819	Lennard
			Seidman	83 LA 1099
			85 LA 207	King
			Kelliher	83 LA 1096
			84 LA 1073	Thornell
			Chandler	83 LA 1029
			84 LA 886	Kilroy
			Eisele	
			83 LA 1018	
			Taylor	
			83 LA 966	
			Jacobowski	
			83 LA 369	
			Laybourne	
			83 LA 98	
			Finston	
			82 LA 1228	
			Holley	
			82 LA 1032	
			Miller, C.	
			82 LA 761	
			Zack	
			82 LA 360	
			Denson	
			82 LA 313	
			Bressler	
Racial Slur	88 LA 391	91 LA 957	92 LA 256	
	Ipavec	Duda	Rains	
	87 LA 394	89 LA 198	91 LA 276	
	Feldman	Concepcion	Statham	
		89 LA 27	83 LA 829	
		Goldstein	Hilgert	
Threat or Assault	90 LA 1137		92 LA 871	88 LA 547
of Management	Jensen		Roumell	Baron
Representative	90 LA 634		92 LA 340	
	Ross		Kaufman	
	89 LA 1201		91 LA 550	
	Hayford		Brown	
	87 LA 59		85 LA 645	
	Borland		Rock	

Offense	*Discharge Upheld*	*Lesser Penalty Upheld (as assessed by employer)*	*Penalty Reduced by Arbitrator*	*No Penalty Permitted*
	84 LA 1166 Duff, J. 83 LA 1197 Yaney		82 LA 1228 Holley	
Abusive Language to Supervision	88 LA 512 Strasshofer 88 LA 418 Scholtz 85 LA 1011 Kaufman	84 LA 860 Weiss 84 LA 591 Strongin 82 LA 1017 Modjeska, A.	92 LA 521 Roumell 92 LA 28 Allen, Jr. 87 LA 877 Daniel 84 LA 1100 Weinstein 84 LA 124 Nicholas 83 LA 1018 Taylor 83 LA 966 Jacobowski 82 LA 1228 Holley 82 LA 1032 Miller, C.	91 LA 905 Nicholas 91 LA 482 Strasshofer 90 LA 1302 Odom 86 LA 874 Odom
Profane or Abusive Language (Not toward supervision)	91 LA 451 McCurdy 90 LA 662 Sacks 90 LA 387 Stephens 86 LA 654 Adelson	92 LA 1048 Watkins 92 LA 433 Belshaw 91 LA 335 Craver 90 LA 111 Feldman	91 LA 920 Ellmann, E. 91 LA 21 Dworkin 90 LA 1206 Fitzsimmons 86 LA 681 Dunn 84 LA 947 LaCugna	93 LA 345 Flannagan 93 LA 24 Canestraight 90 LA 1176 Valentine 88 LA 547 Baron
Falsifying Employment Application	93 LA 124 Gentile 91 LA 1193 Ross 91 LA 951 Sergent 90 LA 497 Talarico 89 LA 762 King, J. 86 LA 480 Mikrut 85 LA 834 Williams, J. 85 LA 643 Brisco 83 LA 1265 Cantor 81 LA 158 Ray, D.		93 LA 381 Cohen, L. 91 LA 588 Howell	

Offense	*Discharge Upheld*	*Lesser Penalty Upheld (as assessed by employer)*	*Penalty Reduced by Arbitrator*	*No Penalty Permitted*
Falsifying Company Records (Including time records, production)	91 LA 951 Sergent 88 LA 804 King, J. 87 LA 500 Klein, J. 86 LA 999 Galambos 82 LA 1283 Watkins 82 LA 604 Hanes	86 LA 1156 Oestreich	90 LA 297 Kaufman 87 LA 160 Atleson 85 LA 279 D'Spain 83 LA 418 Feigenbaum 82 LA 810 Craver 82 LA 28 Nolan	91 LA 647 Concepcion 84 LA 600 Armstrong 82 LA 647 Maxwell
Disloyalty to Government (Security risk)	No Cases			
Theft	92 LA 241 Murphy 91 LA 845 Concepcion 91 LA 681 McKee 90 LA 112 Massey 89 LA 1138 Grinstead 89 LA 710 Bickner 89 LA 247 Dworkin 87 LA 182 Woolf 86 LA 877 Stoltenberg 85 LA 991 Bocken 84 LA 910 Staudhofer 84 LA 586 Penfield 83 LA 261 Odom 83 LA 127 Seidman 83 LA 27 Griffin 82 LA 409 Maniscalco 82 LA 136 Darrow		92 LA 813 Seidman 92 LA 515 Erbs 92 LA 144 Weisbrod 90 LA 841 Katz 88 LA 587 Wolff 87 LA 403 Darrow 87 LA 160 Atleson 86 LA 270 Berger 85 LA 1001 Jones, H. 84 LA 868 Keefe 84 LA 384 Darrow 84 LA 80 Wright 83 LA 983 Jacobowski 83 LA 845 Rothstein 82 LA 810 Craver 82 LA 505 Abrams 82 LA 414 Smith, J. 82 LA 76 Feldesman	87 LA 441 Collins 85 LA 435 Alsher 84 LA 620 Stephens 82 LA 1128 Kossoff

Offense	*Discharge Upheld*	*Lesser Penalty Upheld (as assessed by employer)*	*Penalty Reduced by Arbitrator*	*No Penalty Permitted*
Dishonesty	90 LA 1027 Wolff, A. 88 LA 265 Ipavec 88 LA 175 Blum 86 LA 673 Petersen 86 LA 59 Bell 85 LA 643 Brisco 84 LA 910 Staudohar 83 LA 48 Mullin 82 LA 1238 Watkins 82 LA 604 Hanes 82 LA 445 Kapsch		91 LA 351 Cohen, L. 89 LA 258 Ipavec 87 LA 793 Vernon 86 LA 633 Hannan 86 LA 531 Tharp 86 LA 195 Darrow 85 LA 827 Statham 83 LA 870 Talent 82 LA 491 Ellmann, W. 82 LA 309 Chandler	87 LA 572 Hockenberry 82 LA 647 Daughton 82 LA 642 Maxwell
Disloyalty to Employer (Includes competing with employer, conflict of interests)	87 LA 1140 Darrow 84 LA 1315 Abrams 84 LA 743 Taylor 82 LA 1259 Seidman	85 LA 286 Bognanno 84 LA 860 Weiss 84 LA 583 Penfield 82 LA 1039 Johnston 82 LA 880 Schedler	87 LA 1129 Duda 83 LA 487 Seidman	88 LA 337 Riker 86 LA 274 Rothschild, D. 83 LA 163 Seidman
Moonlighting (Excluding competing with employer)			90 LA 16 Volz 89 LA 1062 Cromwell	92 LA 408 Hilgert
Unsatisfactory Performance (Includes incompetence, low productivity, and poor or improper job performance)	91 LA 1014 Chandler 91 LA 824 Grimes 91 LA 593 Koven 91 LA 286 Craver 90 LA 570 Clifford 89 LA 867 Collins 87 LA 1136 Yarowsky	87 LA 844 Stoltenberg 87 LA 534 Krebs 87 LA 318 Seltzer 86 LA 263 Gould 85 LA 889 Brisco 84 LA 710 Oestreich 83 LA 900 Kanzer	92 LA 1153 Nicholas 92 LA 850 Allen 91 LA 1087 Duff 89 LA 853 Madden 87 LA 793 Vernon 87 LA 678 O'Grady 87 LA 273 Allen	92 LA 862 Singer 90 LA 761 Schwartz 89 LA 857 Ellmann, E. 88 LA 323 Kindig 88 LA 204 Dworkin 87 LA 586 Schwartz 87 LA 568 Clarke

Offense	*Discharge Upheld*	*Lesser Penalty Upheld (as assessed by employer)*	*Penalty Reduced by Arbitrator*	*No Penalty Permitted*
Unsatisfactory Performance cont'd	87 LA 989 Armstrong	83 LA 318 Leahy	86 LA 1197 Eisler	87 LA 217 Cohen, H.
	86 LA 1253 Liberman	83 LA 276 Roomkin	86 LA 1017 Duda	86 LA 1003 Hockenberry
	86 LA 854 Flannagan	83 LA 224 Gentile	86 LA 739 Klein, L.	86 LA 475 Bendixsen
	86 LA 597 Hannan		86 LA 681 Dunn	85 LA 152 Yarowsky
	86 LA 536 Watkins		84 LA 978 Nicholas	85 LA 58 House
	85 LA 805 Bowers		84 LA 354 Sabghir	84 LA 627 Marlatt
	85 LA 769 LeBaron		84 LA 248 Jacobowski	83 LA 776 Creo
	85 LA 468 Foster		84 LA 230 Hayford	83 LA 583 Hedges
	84 LA 496 Feldman		84 LA 89 Mittelman	83 LA 521 Morgan
	84 LA 443 Sacks		83 LA 1033 Singer	83 LA 462 Storey
	83 LA 1024 Denson		83 LA 533 Wren	83 LA 453 Draznin
	83 LA 945 Mikrut		83 LA 369 Laybourne	83 LA 287 Abrams
	83 LA 538 Roumell		83 LA 332 Blum	83 LA 279 Daughton
	83 LA 424 Meyers		83 LA 323 Yaney	83 LA 273 Corbett
	83 LA 179 Bognanno		83 LA 319 Leahy	83 LA 182 Maxwell
	82 LA 1186 Allen		83 LA 159 Herrick	82 LA 1024 Fish
	82 LA 921 Madden		83 LA 98 Finston	82 LA 950 Kanzer
	82 LA 895 Kelliher		82 LA 391 Madden	82 LA 198 Ray, D.
	82 LA 714 Seidman		82 LA 386 Daniel	82 LA 164 Stix
	82 LA 657 Yaney		82 LA 229 Roberts, T.	82 LA 1 Woy
	82 LA 597 Concepcion		82 LA 217 Lawson	81 LA 158 Ray, D.
	82 LA 518 Dworkin		82 LA 105 Belcher	
	82 LA 256 Hauck			
Refusal to Accept Job Assignment	89 LA 283 Sinicropi	92 LA 265 Hilgert	92 LA 951 Bickner	92 LA 433 Belshaw
	87 LA 889 Schwartz	84 LA 770 Singer	87 LA 1002 Volz	87 LA 1057 Gundermann
	87 LA 537 Gentile	82 LA 1161 Nicholas	84 LA 1073 Chandler	87 LA 559 Kates
	86 LA 1201 Alleyne			85 LA 1179 White, J.

Offense	*Discharge Upheld*	*Lesser Penalty Upheld (as assessed by employer)*	*Penalty Reduced by Arbitrator*	*No Penalty Permitted*
	82 LA 306 Williams, C.			85 LA 657 Flagler 83 LA 1029 Kilroy 83 LA 574 Koven
Refusal to Work Overtime	89 LA 985 O'Grady 85 LA 1059 Talarico 85 LA 1017 Nitka 85 LA 787 Canestraight 84 LA 1254 Seidman	86 LA 1137 Seidman 86 LA 832 O'Grady 85 LA 567 Penfield 85 LA 89 Boyer 83 LA 605 Millious	92 LA 367 Corbett 87 LA 318 Seltzer 86 LA 378 Hilgert 83 LA 1131 Fitzsimmons 83 LA 644 Jacobowski	92 LA 1295 Feldman 92 LA 483 Dworkin 91 LA 816 Nicholas 86 LA 11 Hunter 84 LA 1085 Newmark
Negligence	91 LA 1284 Hunter 86 LA 597 Hannan 86 LA 536 Watkins 85 LA 805 Bowers 85 LA 468 Foster 82 LA 597 Concepcion 82 LA 518 Dworkin	92 LA 1143 Borland 92 LA 709 Crane 86 LA 854 Flannagan 85 LA 889 Brisco 84 LA 710 Oestreich	90 LA 354 Levak 88 LA 323 Kindig 87 LA 318 Seltzer 86 LA 739 Klein, L. 85 LA 506 Hoh 84 LA 978 Nicholas 84 LA 248 Jacobowski 83 LA 900 Kanzer 82 LA 229 Roberts, T.	90 LA 1061 Fullmer 86 LA 1003 Hockenberry 83 LA 521 Morgan 83 LA 287 Abrams 83 LA 279 Daughton 83 LA 182 Maxwell 82 LA 1 Woy
Damage to or Loss of Machine or Materials	88 LA 773 Belcher 88 LA 175 Blum 85 LA 594 Garnholz 85 LA 468 Foster 82 LA 895 Kelliher 82 LA 136 Darrow	83 LA 318 Leahy	90 LA 354 Levak 86 LA 1260 Armstrong 86 LA 390 Kates 85 LA 506 Hoh 84 LA 1112 Sartain 83 LA 1033 Singer 83 LA 900 Kanzer 83 LA 559 Grohsmeyer 83 LA 533 Wren 83 LA 318 Leahy	85 LA 58 House 83 LA 776 Creo 83 LA 462 Storey 83 LA 273 Corbett

Offense	*Discharge Upheld*	*Lesser Penalty Upheld (as assessed by employer)*	*Penalty Reduced by Arbitrator*	*No Penalty Permitted*
Prohibited Strike	90 LA 24 Bendixsen 85 LA 1017 Nitka	86 LA 622 Smith, C. 85 LA 692 Seidman 82 LA 226 Jones, D.	89 LA 1257 O'Grady 85 LA 692 Seidman	84 LA 185 Feldman
Misconduct During Strike	92 LA 578 Dunn 89 LA 126 Doering 87 LA 394 Feldman 87 LA 99 Feldman 84 LA 919 Cerone 83 LA 608 Guild 83 LA 501 Chandler		90 LA 502 Wolff 87 LA 188 Gibson 87 LA 103 Duda 84 LA 367 Gibson 83 LA 487 Seidman	83 LA 327 Hewitt
Refusal to Cross Picket Line (Usually another union's picket line)				89 LA 1227 Hogler 84 LA 5 Kienast
Union Activities	90 LA 463 Christopher 90 LA 96 Kilroy 88 LA 563 Madden 83 LA 116 Neas	91 LA 1324 Goldstein 90 LA 486 Marlatt 89 LA 5 Daniel 87 LA 1042 Imundo 87 LA 318 Seltzer 86 LA 1301 Vause	91 LA 1317 Volz 88 LA 145 Keefe 86 LA 293 Ipavec 83 LA 369 Laybourne	92 LA 76 McDermott 92 LA 46 Holley 91 LA 525 Collins 91 LA 435 Shieber 91 LA 311 Weiss 91 LA 131 Rothschild, D 90 LA 1065 Cohen, G. 90 LA 928 Jennings 90 LA 466 Lang 89 LA 232 Roumell 89 LA 151 Goetz 87 LA 619 Ellmann, W. 87 LA 51 Kapsch 86 LA 11 Hunter 83 LA 281 Kelliher

Offense	*Discharge Upheld*	*Lesser Penalty Upheld (as assessed by employer)*	*Penalty Reduced by Arbitrator*	*No Penalty Permitted*
Slowdown	84 LA 1315 Abrams		89 LA 880 Ross	89 LA 232 Roumell
			83 LA 552 Concepcion	
Possession or Use of Intoxicants	92 LA 793 Hockenberry	88 LA 44 Robinson	92 LA 609 Roumell	92 LA 96 Koven
	92 LA 780 Roumell	88 LA 36 Roumell	89 LA 1001 Allen	91 LA 841 Richard
	92 LA 726 Chumley		89 LA 956 Hill	91 LA 539 Marcus
	92 LA 91 Dworkin		89 LA 943 Nicolau	91 LA 512 Gunderson
	91 LA 544 Howell		89 LA 786 Smith, C.	90 LA 1161 Caraway
	91 LA 431 Cohen, G.		89 LA 572 Nicholas	90 LA 701 Byars
	90 LA 960 Draznin		89 LA 409 Kahn	90 LA 579 Sutliff
	90 LA 625 Allen		89 LA 268 Flagler	90 LA 27 Yarowsky
	90 LA 579 Sutliff		88 LA 941 Heinsz	89 LA 617 Berger
	90 LA 573 Crane		88 LA 937 Ipavec	89 LA 492 Jedel
	90 LA 460 Daniel		88 LA 781 Morgan	88 LA 1049 Lewis
	90 LA 399 Oestreich		88 LA 703 Ross	88 LA 441 Strasshofer
	90 LA 286 McDermott		88 LA 275 Mathews	86 LA 1174 Ellmann, E.
	89 LA 1275 McDermott		88 LA 183 Belcher	85 LA 1127 Coyne
	89 LA 838 High		88 LA 179 Archer	
	89 LA 621 Flagler		88 LA 125 Wahl	
	89 LA 99 Ross		88 LA 96 Doering	
	88 LA 457 Wolff		87 LA 973 Johnson	
	88 LA 340 Strasshofer		87 LA 972 Neyland	
	88 LA 214 Feldman		86 LA 497 D'Spain	
	88 LA 208 Garnholz		86 LA 75 Wies	
	86 LA 891 Ferguson		83 LA 211 Hewitt	
	86 LA 686 Daniel		82 LA 31 Miller, C.	
	86 LA 540 Watkins		81 LA 1083 Hill	
	86 LA 430 Cox			

Offense	*Discharge Upheld*	*Lesser Penalty Upheld (as assessed by employer)*	*Penalty Reduced by Arbitrator*	*No Penalty Permitted*
Possession or Use of Intoxicants cont'd	85 LA 542 King, O.			
	82 LA 861 Roberts, R.			
	82 LA 420 Murphy			
	81 LA 733 Wright			
	81 LA 630 Fogelberg			
	81 LA 449 Hewitt			
	81 LA 344 Hanes			
	81 LA 318 Nelson			
	81 LA 243 Everitt			
Possession or Use of Drugs	92 LA 1100 Dworkin	92 LA 471 McDermott	92 LA 829 Williams	92 LA 995 Concepcion
	92 LA 1033 Abrams	90 LA 105 Hart	92 LA 444 Koven	92 LA 777 Nicholas
	92 LA 937 Seidman	89 LA 795 Flannagan	91 LA 158 Nicholas	92 LA 592 Nicholas
	92 LA 907 Sergent	87 LA 297 Boner	90 LA 979 Weiss	92 LA 374 Nicolau
	91 LA 1353 Petersen	81 LA 497 Roberts, R.	90 LA 791 Nicholas	91 LA 1105 Berkeley
	91 LA 1193 Ross		90 LA 681 Volz	91 LA 993 Fullmer
	91 LA 1129 Coyne		90 LA 657 Jedel	91 LA 137 Huffcut
	91 LA 400 Allen		90 LA 457 Rule	90 LA 1225 Schwartz
	91 LA 363 Yarowsky		90 LA 347 Duff, J.	90 LA 1161 Caraway
	91 LA 213 Goldstein		89 LA 1257 O'Grady	90 LA 815 Hockenberry
	91 LA 6 Ables		89 LA 1001 Allen	90 LA 578 Sutliff
	90 LA 881 Patterson		89 LA 968 Wies	90 LA 341 Boals
	90 LA 578 Sutliff		89 LA 845 Boals	90 LA 189 Goldstein
	90 LA 497 Talarico		89 LA 786 Smith, C.	90 LA 55 Levin
	90 LA 367 Nicholas		89 LA 688 Gwiazda	90 LA 38 Concepcion
	90 LA 286 McDermott		89 LA 585 Kanner	89 LA 1280 DiLauro
	90 LA 154 Riker		89 LA 314 Mikrut	89 LA 1265 Weisbrod

Offense	*Discharge Upheld*	*Lesser Penalty Upheld (as assessed by employer)*	*Penalty Reduced by Arbitrator*	*No Penalty Permitted*
	89 LA 1275 McDermott		88 LA 749 Koven	89 LA 1196 Draznin
	89 LA 1193 Ahern		88 LA 528 McKay	89 LA 1087 Wolk
	89 LA 1159 Milentz		88 LA 463 Wren	89 LA 973 Speroff
	89 LA 1076 Wright		88 LA 366 Nathan	89 LA 925 McIntosh
	89 LA 877 Handsaker		88 LA 194 Koven	89 LA 398 Mikrut
	89 LA 716 Grimes		88 LA 51 Weiss	89 LA 393 Alleyne
	89 LA 587 Katz		87 LA 1261 Jewett	89 LA 265 Sloan
	89 LA 544 Brisco		87 LA 1160 Clarke	89 LA 137 Fox
	89 LA 436 Allen		87 LA 1145 Cohen, S.	88 LA 1001 Heinsz
	89 LA 377 Daniel		87 LA 1039 Abrams	88 LA 91 Rothschild, D.
	89 LA 375 Seidman		87 LA 1010 D'Spain	87 LA 543 Berns
	89 LA 333 Fogelberg		87 LA 737 Caraway	87 LA 441 Collins
	89 LA 209 Brisco		87 LA 478 Howell	87 LA 313 Schubert
	89 LA 129 Baroni		87 LA 473 Nicholas	86 LA 1026 Nicholas
	89 LA 1 Doering		87 LA 111 DiLauro	86 LA 1023 Warns, M.
	88 LA 1031 Tripp		82 LA 360 Denson	86 LA 411 Clarke
	88 LA 1010 Weisenberger			86 LA 182 Levin
	88 LA 633 Murphy			83 LA 580 Canestraight
	88 LA 628 Seinsheimer			82 LA 6 Edes
	88 LA 521 Allen			
	88 LA 425 Baroni			
	88 LA 386 Kindig			
	88 LA 290 Feigenbaum			
	88 LA 51 Rothschild, D.			
	87 LA 1300 Thornell			

Offense	*Discharge Upheld*	*Lesser Penalty Upheld (as assessed by employer)*	*Penalty Reduced by Arbitrator*	*No Penalty Permitted*
Possession or Use of Drugs cont'd	87 LA 1062 Concepcion 87 LA 994 Feldman 87 LA 953 Lipson 87 LA 826 Volz 87 LA 800 Byars 87 LA 743 Allen 87 LA 729 Hoh 87 LA 719 Rothstein 87 LA 224 Cooper 86 LA 1307 Taylor 86 LA 1211 Miller, R. 86 LA 403 Fullmer 86 LA 1 Miller, R. 85 LA 542 King, O. 85 LA 407 Whyte 83 LA 270 Ives 82 LA 558 Mikrut 82 LA 150 Bernhardt 82 LA 112 Thornell 81 LA 174 Darrow			
Distribution of Drugs	92 LA 1100 Dworkin 90 LA 881 Patterson 89 LA 1155 Feldman 89 LA 1 Doering 81 LA 695 Aronin 81 LA 174 Darrow		92 LA 41 Richman 89 LA 688 Gwiazda	92 LA 669 Jewett

Offense	*Discharge Upheld*	*Lesser Penalty Upheld (as assessed by employer)*	*Penalty Reduced by Arbitrator*	*No Penalty Permitted*
Obscene or Immoral Conduct	90 LA 689 Goldstein 88 LA 791 Vause 88 LA 75 Wyman 86 LA 1253 Liberman 84 LA 363 Keefe 82 LA 1017 Modjeska, A. 82 LA 921 Madden 82 LA 640 Daughton 82 LA 493 Jason 81 LA 722 Miller, M. 81 LA 99 VanWart	84 LA 240 Nicholas	86 LA 1017 Duda 83 LA 449 Kaplan	91 LA 1244 Eagle 91 LA 920 Ellmann, E. 88 LA 547 Baron 82 LA 747 Wright
Gambling			89 LA 1265 Talmadge 83 LA 593 Kulkis	
Attachment or Garnishment of Wages	83 LA 998 Richman		82 LA 1004 Laybourne	89 LA 1302 Talarico
Abusing Customers (Includes abuse of public agency clientele)	89 LA 826 Stoltenberg 83 LA 424 Meyers 82 LA 1186 Allen 81 LA 1112 Westbrook 81 LA 722 Miller, M.	89 LA 11 Gallagher 86 LA 1301 Vause 83 LA 224 Gentile	89 LA 1247 Kaufman 86 LA 249 Gallagher 83 LA 449 Kaplan	87 LA 195 D'Spain 83 LA 24 Marlatt 82 LA 217 Lawson 82 LA 198 Ray, D.
Abusing Students, Patients, or Inmates	86 LA 597 Hannan 83 LA 44 Lipson 81 LA 306 Lewis	92 LA 833 Gentile 91 LA 451 McCurdy 90 LA 333 Imes 89 LA 1166 Borland	82 LA 1179 Kossoff	
Sexual Harassment	90 LA 1230 Shearer 89 LA 41 Eisler	91 LA 1391 Duda 90 LA 478 Duda	92 LA 1090 Cohen, C. 91 LA 1097 Talarico	92 LA 653 Cohen, G. 89 LA 80 Nicholas

Offense	*Discharge Upheld*	*Lesser Penalty Upheld (as assessed by employer)*	*Penalty Reduced by Arbitrator*	*No Penalty Permitted*
Sexual Harassment cont'd	88 LA 791 Vause	89 LA 27 Goldstein	90 LA 783 Duda	87 LA 1149 Berman
	88 LA 75 Wyman	89 LA 11 Gallagher	89 LA 427 Bard	87 LA 697 D'Spain
	87 LA 405 Yarowsky	87 LA 844 Stoltenberg	86 LA 1017 Duda	86 LA 254 Sass
	86 LA 1253 Liberman		86 LA 249 Gallagher	83 LA 824 Kapsch
	85 LA 246 Feldman		85 LA 11 Oestreich	82 LA 25 Dallas
	84 LA 915 Gray		83 LA 570 Ellmann, E.	81 LA 730 Stonehouse
	82 LA 921 Madden			
	82 LA 640 Daughton			
	81 LA 687 Taylor			

Chapter 16

Safety and Health

The notion of "reasonableness" continues to pervade arbitration decisions on safety and health matters. Emerging issues include no-smoking rules and the appearance of AIDS in the workplace.

Management Rights and Obligations in Safety and Health Matters

Many safety and health arbitrations arise in the context of contractual safety provisions. They may involve demands for the eradication or amelioration of a hazard or additional compensation.

In one case, an employer was not obliged to provide air conditioned mobile equipment since the equipment had not been recommended by a mine safety committee, which was contractually empowered to inspect and report conditions endangering the miners' lives and safety.[1] In another, an employer was found not to have violated a health and safety clause where the premises showed no evidence of bare wires or filth, obvious tripping or electrical hazards, or serious overcrowding; the offices were fairly well lit, and the restrooms fairly well equipped.[2] On the other hand, an employer was found to have violated a provision of a contract's safety code where a supervisor had assigned an untrained worker to operate heavy equipment, but no monetary award was assessed by the arbitrator.[3]

Under a contract covering prison guards, which obligated the employer to notify the union of any inmates who were known to have or medically suspected of having a communicable disease, an arbitrator found that the prison had breached the contract in failing to divulge the names of those whose tests were positive for the AIDS

[1]Brownies Creek Collieries, 83 LA 919 (Chapman, 1984).
[2]U.S. Steel Corp., 88 LA 240 (Petersen, 1986).
[3]A.E. Staley Mfg. Co., 85 LA 880 (Kates, 1985).

virus. He directed the parties to negotiate procedures to protect the guards who worked with the AIDS-positive prisoners.[4]

In another case, an arbitrator ruled that a nursing home could not discharge an employee with AIDS, but could put him on a medical leave until he no longer had a communicable disease, although the arbitrator acknowledged that absent a "medical breakthrough" the employee would never be reemployed.[5]

An employer was deemed to have met its duty to bargain over safety in connection with a layoff of firefighters when it told the union of the planned layoff, met to discuss it, and sought information.[6]

Despite a union's complaint that supervisors acting as firebosses led to many mine safety citations, Arbitrator Michael E. Zobrak found that he lacked authority to assign "fireboss" positions to the bargaining unit.[7] Several arbitrators have upheld staffing reductions despite safety challenges where there is no indication that the reduction in force would create unsafe working conditions.[8]

One arbitrator has held that an employer could unilaterally impose fitness evaluations pursuant to its right to establish reasonable rules to ensure employee health and safety.[9] However, another arbitrator found that an employer had violated senior crane operators' contractual bidding rights in its efforts to implement a new unilateral safety policy.[10]

Under a contract clause providing for environmental differential and hazardous duty pay, an employer was ordered to pay extra compensation to employees exposed to asbestos.[11] Arbitrator William G. Haemmel found that painters were entitled to contractual environmental pay for cleaning and spray painting the top of three aircraft hangars "under the worst conditions within recent memory."[12]

In one case an arbitrator denied differential pay to a vehicle operator who transported infectious waste (including blood and urine specimens and used syringes) but mandated certain extra safety measures.[13] In other cases, one arbitrator found that a unilateral rule limiting safety premium pay to "actual time worked while dressed out in full anti-radioactive contamination clothing" was unreasonable,[14] while another determined that, in light of past practice and a contract provision for one shift's pay, a company need only pay a safety committee for one day although their inspection took two.[15] Employees who left work in a group because of smoke in their below-ground mining

---

[4]Delaware Dep't of Corrections, 86 LA 849 (Gill, 1986).
[5]Nursing Home, 88 LA 681 (Sedwick, 1987).
[6]Airport Auth. of Washoe County, 86 LA 237 (Christopher, 1985).
[7]Donaldson Mining Co., 89 LA 188 (1987).
[8]City of Laredo, 91 LA 381 (McDermott, 1988); San Francisco Gen. Hosp., 90 LA 1293 (Winograd, 1988); Western Fuel Oil Co., 89 LA 772 (Kaufman, 1987).
[9]Mason & Hanger, 92 LA 131 (McKee, 1989).
[10]Lockheed Space Operations Co., 91 LA 457 (Richard, 1988).
[11]Veterans Admin. Medical Center, 86 LA 698 (Eisler, 1986).
[12]Marine Corps Air Station, 82 LA 563, 568 (1984).
[13]Naval Medical Clinic, 90 LA 137 (Rothschild, 1987).
[14]Pan Am World Servs., 91 LA 859 (Finston, 1988).
[15]Peabody-Eastern Coal, 90 LA 1248 (Volz, 1988).

area and did not assert an individual safety right as the contract required were not entitled to reporting pay.[16]

In reviewing the composition of a joint employer-union safety and health committee, an arbitrator held that the union was empowered to appoint members to the committee and to its subcommittee on accident review and that the employees were entitled to union representation at accident review committee meetings.[17]

A contract that established a joint safety committee did not preclude departmental safety committees where the latter did not interfere with the former and the employer bore the duty of providing a safe workplace.[18]

Without reference to any contract clause, an arbitrator found that crossing an American Agricultural Movement picket line would have presented an immediate hazard to longshoremen's health and safety.[19] Another arbitrator overturned the suspensions of employees who refused to cross a picket line, claiming that to do so was unsafe.[20]

OSHA Considerations

An employer's argument raising OSHA regulations as a defense to a grievance that it had awarded overtime in violation of the contract was rejected. Arbitrator Duane L. Traynor noted:

> It seems to this Arbitrator that where grievant was qualified and contractually entitled to the overtime, it could have been offered to him with appropriate equipment as it was to the laborer and the OSHA regulations would have been complied with. While the Company's concern for the safety of its employees is laudatory it cannot violate the Contract, particularly where not to do so would not violate government regulations.[21]

In a case where an employer had been cited by OSHA for excessive noise in the workplace, the employer was upheld in conducting hearing tests of employees pursuant to a consent order between OSHA and the employer. The arbitrator ruled that employees who came to work one-half hour early to take such tests were not entitled to overtime.[22]

Another arbitrator ruled that an employer did not have the right to insist that employees sign a document attesting that they had been trained to handle certain hazardous chemicals when the employees had a good faith doubt that the training met OSHA requirements. However, he emphasized that under such circumstances employees should sign under protest and then grieve.[23]

---

[16]Buffalo Mining Co., 90 LA 939 (Feldman, 1988).
[17]City of Great Falls, 88 LA 396 (McCurdy, 1986).
[18]John Morrell & Co., 92 LA 1071 (Murphy, 1989).
[19]Pacific Maritime Ass'n, 86 LA 1248 (Sutliff, 1986).
[20]West Penn Power Co., 89 LA 1227 (Hogler, 1987).
[21]A.E. Staley Mfg. Co., 86 LA 627, 632 (1986).
[22]Pabst Brewing Co., 88 LA 656 (1987).
[23]James B. Beam Distilling Co., 90 LA 740 (Ruben, 1988).

Employee Obligations in Safety Matters

An employer could require that employees pay 50 percent of the cost of one pair of safety shoes up to a $25 maximum under a contract mandating that the company provide "all tools, safety goggles, hard hats and gloves that it requires to be used."[24]

Safety Rules

No-smoking rules in the workplace have been the subject of a number of arbitration cases. Fourteen arbitrators upheld company implementation of such rules[25] while two overturned them, directing the parties, in one case, to negotiate a smoking policy and, in the other, to place the matter before a joint safety committee.[26] Explaining that he drew his authority solely from the agreement, which covers only bargaining unit employees, one arbitrator held that he had no jurisdiction to determine whether the restricted-smoking rule should apply to nonunit employees.[27] Another arbitrator found that an employer had not violated a contractual provision mandating a safe and healthful work environment when it declined to provide a smoke-free environment for a worker who was allergic to smoke.[28]

An arbitrator found a contract violation in a rule requiring a medical evaluation for respirator users, because the joint health and safety committee had not passed on the rule and the OSHA standard on which the employer relied was not mandatory.[29] Another arbitrator substantially upheld a rule that respirator users must be clean shaven or buy their own respirators which would permit a proper seal with a beard.[30] In another decision, an arbitrator upheld a rule restricting the playing of radios in a power plant.[31]

However, another arbitrator modified a company rule banning radio use to allow radios with earphones (Walkman), with certain restrictions.[32]

---

[24]Sky Top Sunroofs, 89 LA 547 (Newmark, 1987).

[25]Wyandot Inc., 92 LA 457 (Imundo, 1989); Honeywell, Inc., 92 LA 181 (Lennard, 1989); Acorn Bldg. Components, 92 LA 68 (Roumell, 1988); Methodist Hosp., 91 LA 969 (Reynolds, 1988); J.R. Simplot Co., 91 LA 375 (McCurdy, 1988); Dayton Newspapers, 91 LA 201 (Kindig, 1988); Michigan Bell Tel., 90 LA 1186 (Howlett, 1988); Des Moines Register, 90 LA 777 (Gallagher, 1988); Worthington Foods, 89 LA 1069 (McIntosh, 1987); Lennox Indus., 89 LA 1065 (Gibson, 1987); Ohio Dep't of Health, 89 LA 937 (Cohen, 1987); Morelite Equip. Co., 88 LA 777 (Stoltenberg, 1987); National Pen & Pencil Co., 87 LA 1081 (Nicholas, 1986); Snap-On Tools Corp., 87 LA 785 (Berman, 1986).

[26]In Dental Command, 83 LA 529 (Allen, 1984), the employer had no general uniform "established policy" for all dental clinics. In H-N Advertising & Display Co., 88 LA 329 (Heekin, 1986), the employer had improperly imposed a no-smoking rule without using the processes of the joint safety committee.

[27]Snap-On Tools Corp., 87 LA 785 (Berman, 1986).

[28]County of Santa Clara, 88 LA 489 (Koven, 1986).

[29]Sohio Oil Co., 92 LA 201 (Strasshofer, 1988).

[30]Mississippi Power & Light Co., 92 LA 1161 (Taylor, 1989).

[31]Southern Ind. Gas & Elec. Co., 88 LA 132 (Franke, 1986).

[32]Creative Prods., 89 LA 777 (McDonald, 1987).

Safety rules must be publicized and consistently enforced or arbitrators will not uphold them. Thus a reprimand for failure to wear a seat belt was overturned where the rule requiring fastened seat belts had been previously unenforced for 20 years.[33] If an employer wishes to begin enforcing a dormant rule, it must publicize its intent to do so and set forth penalties for noncompliance.[34] An arbitrator reduced a written warning to an oral warning in a case where an employee violated a safety rule by neglecting to wear a rain jacket while working on top of a caustic soda rail car, finding that the employer had not adequately informed the workers of penalties for breaking safety rules.[35]

Refusal to Obey Orders—The Safety Exception

Arbitrators continue to recognize the safety exception to the "work now—grieve later" doctrine. They generally apply a reasonable person approach to analyzing the situation.[36]

An arbitrator overturned a three-day suspension of a control room operator who did not finish removing ash from inside a hopper after a slab of ash fell on him, but hastily exited the hopper door exclaiming (according to his testimony), "I'm going to the office and find out if I am supposed to be buried alive or get three days off."[37] Arbitrator Samuel S. Kates ruled that the grievant "reacted as a reasonable person would under the circumstances in failing to return inside the hopper to complete the ash removal work."[38]

Another arbitrator overturned discipline of an acting crew chief for stopping gravity defueling of a helicopter where the operation would have been unsafe; he sustained discipline, however, for failure to notify supervision that the procedure had been stopped.[39] An employee, on light duty less than 24 hours after a work-related accident, was justified in refusing to check operating equipment in a low-visibility basement; Arbitrator John F. White noted that the "combination of circumstances was more than enough to cause a reasonable person to fear for his or her safety."[40] An employee who demanded to see a safety committeeman after he activated a breaker by touching a high-voltage plug with his leg acted reasonably and "in good faith," and should not have been suspended.[41]

---

[33]U.S. Army Corps of Eng'rs, 86 LA 939 (O'Grady, 1986).

[34]Id. at 942.

[35]Stauffer Chem. Co., 83 LA 332 (Blum, 1984).

[36]Amoco Oil Co., 87 LA 889 (Schwartz, 1986); Beth Energy Mines, 87 LA 577 (Hewitt, 1986); Indianapolis Power & Light Co., 87 LA 559 (Kates, 1986); Minnesota Mining & Mfg. Co., 85 LA 1179 (White, 1985); U.S. Army Armor Center & Fort Knox, 82 LA 464 (Wren, 1984).

[37]See Indianapolis Power & Light Co., 87 LA 559, 560 (1986).

[38]Id. at 562.

[39]See U.S. Army Armor Center & Fort Knox, 82 LA 464 (Wren, 1984).

[40]See Minnesota Mining & Mfg. Co., 85 LA 1179, 1182 (1985).

[41]Beth Energy Mines, 87 LA 577 (Hewitt, 1986).

Arbitrator Allen D. Schwartz upheld the dismissal of refinery workers who balked at performing a routine asbestos removal job, noting that "[t]he safety exception is not applicable—obedience did not involve an unusual or abnormal safety hazard once the right safety equipment was supplied. Under the facts and circumstances, a reasonable person would not have feared for his life."[42] Another arbitrator reduced a discharge to a reinstatement without back pay where an employee refused to wear an organic vapor mask.[43] The grievant had a history of insubordination, but she insisted that the mask made her feel dizzy and asked for substitute work. Arbitrator James C. Duff observed that wearing the mask "did not pose any major hazard to her health, so she could not invoke that exception to the fundamental work now, grieve later principle."[44]

An arbitrator upheld the suspension of an employee who walked off the job saying his assignment was "too hard"; the arbitrator concluded that there was no safety hazard, or, if one did exist, it was corrected before the employee left.[45] Another arbitrator overturned the discharge of an employee who, after two attempts in inclement weather, refused to clean a "cyclone" on a high roof with no catwalk or railing.[46]

Discharge of an employee who refused to load 28 pounds of parts was upheld where the arbitrator concluded the employee had no reasonable belief he would injure himself.[47] Relying on a contract provision which embodied the "safety exception," an arbitrator ordered a state agency to stop requiring employees to transport 150-200 pounds of documents as they reasonably feared serious injury.[48]

Arbitrators insist that employees make their safety concerns clear. Under a contract which required an employee to notify his supervisor of the specific physical conditions he believed in good faith were abnormally hazardous, an arbitrator found that the grievant had no safety defense because he had not complied with that contractual procedure.[49] In another case, an arbitrator upheld the five-day suspension of an employee who refused to temporarily transfer to another machine but failed to explain to the company that her refusal was based upon her high blood pressure and the fact that the machine was not in an air conditioned area.[50] However, a rule that required union safety and health inspectors and visitors to a coal mine to execute a release and a waiver of liability was held to be unreasonable.[51]

---

[42]See Amoco Oil Co., 87 LA 889, 894 (1986).
[43]Roemer Indus., 86 LA 232 (1986).
[44]Id. at 234.
[45]Northern Automatic Elec. Foundry, 90 LA 620 (Poindexter, 1987).
[46]Leland Oil Mill, 91 LA 905 (Nicholas, 1988).
[47]Lancaster Electro Plating, 93 LA 203 (Bressler, 1989).
[48]Vermont Dep't of Motor Vehicles, 90 LA 677 (McHugh, 1988).
[49]Peabody Coal Co., 87 LA 1002 (Volz, 1986).
[50]Morton Thiokol Inc., 88 LA 254 (Finan, 1987) (leaving steam boiler to do temporary painting).
[51]Utah Power & Light Co., 88 LA 310 (Feldman, 1986); General Indus., 82 LA 1161 (Nicholas, 1984).

The Statutory Picture: OSHA, NLRA § 7, LMRA § 502

Since the Supreme Court's 1980 *Whirlpool* decision,[52] the federal courts have continued to protect the right of an employee who refuses to perform work where that refusal is based upon a "reasonable apprehension of death or serious injury coupled with a reasonable belief that no less drastic alternative is available."[53] In a case decided by the Tenth Circuit, U.S. Court of Appeals, an employee who worked as a cement finisher refused to go up in a gondola because of repeated problems with the gondola and scaffolding and the employer's cavalier approach to safety issues. The court found that the employee had a "reasonable and good faith belief that the gondola was both defective and hazardous and that riding in it would present an imminent risk of serious bodily injury or death."[54]

The Supreme Court addressed similar issues pursuant to an unfair labor practice charge filed under § 7 of the National Labor Relations Act in its *City Disposal Systems* decision.[55] Following that decision by the Court, the NLRB has considered several cases where employees have refused to perform work because of alleged unsafe conditions. Where an employee seeks to invoke a contractual right by refusing to perform work he in good faith believes to be unsafe, he is engaged in protected concerted activity, and any discipline for refusal to perform the work is in violation of § 7 of the NLRA.[56] Similarly, where an employee complains to a safety committee provided for pursuant to the terms of a collective bargaining agreement, even though he acted alone in his complaints, his invocation of a contractual right, to complain to the safety committee, provides protection under the NLRA.[57]

The Courts of Appeals have struggled with NLRB standards regarding safety issues raised in good faith by individuals pursuant to labor agreements. For example, in one case the Second Circuit reversed the NLRB's finding that the employer did not discriminate against an employee when it refused to rehire him in the mistaken belief that he had filed a complaint with OSHA.[58] The court remanded the case to the NLRB for reevaluation under the new legal standard arising from *Meyers I*.[59] On remand, the NLRB found that a single

---

[52]Whirlpool Corp. v. Marshall, 100 S.Ct. 883, 8 OSHC 1001 (1980) (upholding 29 CFR 1977.12(b)(2)).

[53]Id.

[54]Donovan v. Hahner, Foreman & Harness Inc., 736 F.2d 1421, 1428 (CA 10, 1984).

[55]NLRB v. City Disposal Sys., 104 S.Ct. 1505, 115 LRRM 3193 (1984).

[56]Union Elec. Co., 275 NLRB 389, 119 LRRM 1160 (1985).

[57]Wabash Alloys Inc., 282 NLRB 391, 124 LRRM 1393 (1986). See also Bechtel Power Corp., 277 NLRB 882, 120 LRRM 1291 (1985) (employee's good faith complaint about noxious fumes was protected).

[58]Ewing v. NLRB, 732 F.2d 1117, 116 LRRM 2050 (CA 2, 1984).

[59]Meyers Indus., Inc., 268 NLRB 493, 115 LRRM 1025 (1984). The NLRB's *Meyers I* standard required a demonstrable link with group action before an individual act could be deemed "concerted" and therefore intended to involve the provisions of a collective bargaining agreement. Such activity is "concerted" only if "engaged in with or on the authority of other employees."

employee's assertion of a statutory employment right was too remotely related to collective acts to constitute "concerted activity." This ruling was also appealed, resulting in a second remand by the Second Circuit based on the absence of a definitive agency decision.[60]

Rejecting the Second Circuit's suggested approach, the NLRB adhered to the *Meyers* standard.[61] This ruling was again appealed in *Ewing III*[62] and *Prill II*;[63] the Second Circuit and the District of Columbia Circuit affirmed the *Meyers II* ruling, reluctantly concluding that it constituted a reasonable interpretation of the NLRA.

As a result, at least one Court of Appeals has refused to rule that a purely unilateral safety complaint may be concerted activity protected by § 7 of the NLRA.[64]

Compatibility of Award With Employee Rights Under Statute

The NLRB has generally continued to apply a subjective "good faith belief" test to determine whether the actions of the employee are reasonable. Thus, so long as the employee holds a "good faith honest belief" that the job assigned is unsafe, it does not matter whether the employee turns out to have been correct.[65] On the other hand, arbitrators in general continue to apply an objective "reasonable person similarly situated" test. In one case, an arbitrator upheld the discipline of an employee even though he found that the employee was motivated by a good faith fear that the work was dangerous. At the hearing, the company established that under the circumstances the conditions were reasonable and safe and of a commonplace type at foundries.[66] In another case, an arbitrator disallowed the suspension of an employee who was assigned a task well outside the scope of his normal duties and where another employee had been injured performing similar work. Arbitrator Samuel S. Kates concluded that the employee "acted as a reasonable person would have acted under the circumstances."[67] It remains to be seen whether the NLRB, pursuant to *Spielberg*,[68] will defer to the decision of an arbitrator upholding discipline on the basis of the reasonable person test and not the Board's traditional subjective test.

---

[60]Ewing v. NLRB, 768 F.2d 51, 56, 119 LRRM 3273 (CA 2, 1985) (Ewing II). The Second Circuit suggested that it would be reasonable for the NLRB to hold that individual invocation of a statutory right was sufficiently related to group action to warrant protection under the NLRA.

[61]Meyers Indus., Inc., 281 NLRB 882, 123 LRRM 1137 (1986) (Meyers II).

[62]Ewing v. NLRB, 861 F.2d 353, 129 LRRM 2853 (CA 2, 1988).

[63]Prill v. NLRB, 835 F.2d 1481, 127 LRRM 2415 (D.C. Cir., 1987).

[64]LaBuhn v. Bulkmatic Transp. Co., 865 F.2d 119, 123, 130 LRRM 2301 (CA 7, 1988) (holding that claim of retaliation for complaining about unsafe working conditions was not preempted by § 301 of the Labor Management Relations Act pursuant to Lingle v. Norge Div. of Magic Chef, 108 S.Ct. 1877, 128 LRRM 2521 (1988).

[65]Bechtel Power Corp., 277 NLRB 882, 120 LRRM 1291 (1985).

[66]U.S. Pipe & Foundry Co., 84 LA 770 (Singer, 1985).

[67]Indianapolis Power & Light Co., 87 LA 559 (1986).

[68]Spielberg Mfg. Co., 112 NLRB 1080, 36 LRRM 1152 (1955).

At least one Court of Appeals has held that the NLRB abused its discretion in deferring to a joint management-labor panel award which reduced a parcel delivery service employee's discharge to a ten-day suspension for refusing to obey a supervisor's order to tap his horn when stopping to make residential deliveries, where state law prohibited horn honking unless necessary for safety.[69]

Employee Complaints of Specific Hazards

Employee complaints about safety hazards typically require arbitrators to consider whether the complained-of condition amounts to an unsafe working condition or merely an uncomfortable or displeasurable work environment. In one case where employees repeatedly complained of uncleanliness, poor air quality, and an unsafe physical plant, the arbitrator found that although the employees' offices and work areas were not as clean as their supervisors' offices, there was nothing unsafe or unhealthy, especially in the context of an office in a steel production plant.[70]

However, where the employee's health was in jeopardy, an arbitrator reduced the discharge of an employee to a suspension based on a refusal to work a double shift due to fatigue. While it was determined that the employer had an obligation not to force overtime on employees who are physically unable to perform, the employee also had an obligation to clearly communicate legitimate health concerns to her foreman.[71]

In another case, an arbitrator found no contract violation by the employer, despite a dispatcher's strong allergic reaction to smoke at the workplace and the employer's refusal to promulgate a no-smoking rule. No other employee had complained of the level of smoke, and the health department tests established that the dispatch room air quality exceeded building code standards.[72]

Physical or Mental Condition as a Safety Hazard

Arbitrators have continued to consider the physical and mental condition of co-workers in evaluating whether a safety hazard is present. Thus, it was found that a junior employee acted properly in refusing to ride with another driver whom he had recently seen have an apparent "seizure" while in driving status. The senior driver had in

---

[69]Garcia v. NLRB, 785 F.2d 807, 121 LRRM 3349 (CA 9, 1986).

[70]U.S. Steel Corp., 88 LA 240 (Petersen, 1986).

[71]Kaiser Aluminum & Chem. Corp., 92 LA 37 (Corbett, 1989).

[72]County of Santa Clara, 88 LA 489 (Koven, 1986); see also Brownies Creek Collieries, 83 LA 919 (Chapman, 1984), where the union sought to require air conditioning in bulldozers, graders, and drilling equipment, because the heat and dust allegedly created hazardous working conditions. The arbitrator found that the working conditions were far less than ideal but were not necessarily hazardous.

fact merely reacted to a bee sting, but the company had made no effort to explain the situation to the junior employee, and the junior employee had reason to believe that by riding with the other driver his life was in jeopardy.[73]

Arbitrators have shown a sensitivity to employee refusals to work based on legitimate physical or mental limitations. For example, an employer may have an obligation to transfer an employee with a legitimate disability, such as epilepsy, to a work area which accommodates the disability for safety reasons.[74]

However, refusals to work based on working conditions reasonably foreseeable as part of the nature of the work are not generally upheld.[75] Under certain circumstances, employers may have no obligation to reassign an employee with a physical or mental condition which creates a potential hazard at a particular job. In one case, an employer was justified in discharging a probationary employee from a position involving tasks on platforms, catwalks, and ladders after he admitted that he suffered from a fear of heights.[76]

Management Action: Transfer, Demotion, Layoff, Leave of Absence, or Termination

Arbitrators have continued to evaluate closely the nature of an employee's work assignment to determine the appropriate management response to injured employees whose return to work might jeopardize that employee or others. For example, a company did not have to reinstate an employee to his old job because to do so would be a hazard to the employee and to others. However, under the terms of the contract, the employer was required to reinstate the employee to a less strenuous available job where he would not be a hazard to himself or other employees.[77] Similarly, an employee with a serious eye injury, which resulted in a loss of depth perception, created a hazard to other employees and thus the employee could not be reinstated.[78]

Management actions taken for the safety and health of the work force or third parties, such as a smoking ban or relieving an employee with a contagious disease from work, have also been upheld by arbitrators.[79] Arbitrators have upheld discharges based on violations of rules against horseplay which result in injuries to co-employees.[80]

---

[73]Hoover Universal, 82 LA 569 (Cabe, 1984).

[74]Weirton Steel Corp., 89 LA 201 (Sherman, 1987).

[75]Northern Automatic Elec. Foundry, 90 LA 620 (Poindexter, 1987).

[76]Pacific Power & Light Co., 89 LA 283 (Sinicropi, 1987).

[77]Manufacturing Co., 82 LA 614 (Ray, 1984).

[78]U.S. Steel Corp., 82 LA 913 (Tripp, 1984) (medical evidence indicated employee had lost ability to judge speed and direction of molten metal slag found in production process. Without such ability, employee posed a serious risk to his co-workers).

[79]Wyandot, Inc., 92 LA 457 (Imundo, 1989); Des Moines Register & Tribune Co., 90 LA 777 (Gallagher, 1988); Mercy Convalescent Center, 90 LA 405 (O'Grady, 1988). Arbitrators are increasingly faced with employer actions taken in response to employees suffering from AIDS. Nursing Home, 88 LA 81 (Sedwick, 1987).

[80]Muskin, Inc., 89 LA 297 (DiLauro, 1987).

A requirement that employees inform their supervisors of their use of prescription drugs has also been upheld as a reasonable action to ensure a safe work environment, provided that the rule applies only to medications that affect performance and all information provided is kept confidential.[81] Many of these decisions uphold discharges for drug and alcohol abuse, and drug and alcohol urine testing, particularly in safety intensive industries.[82] By contrast, some arbitrators have refused to permit employers to engage in drug or alcohol testing where the employer has no basis for suspecting such abuse is occurring.[83] In addition, arbitrators have upheld the legitimacy of staffing reductions where there is no indication that the reduction in force would create unsafe working conditions per se.[84]

Protecting the Employee Himself

Arbitrators continue to uphold employee refusals to work based on legitimate safety considerations.[85] In some cases, arbitrators have upheld the decisions of employers not to reinstate employees whose injuries create potential hazard to themselves, even though the employees were willing to accept the risk. One arbitrator refused to require the reinstatement of an employee with a serious back injury, whose job required lifting, where to do so created a safety hazard to the employee himself. The arbitrator also found that the claim of discrimination on the basis of a handicap was irrelevant because in fact the employee could not safely be returned to his job.[86]

Another arbitrator upheld a company's decision to deny reemployment to an employee who had been out of work for two years due to a serious lung injury caused by chlorine gas. Examination of medical evidence showed that the employee still suffered from a pulmonary problem and that the working conditions would subject the employee again to chlorine gas, which could cause a serious re-injury.[87]

The transfer of a cement truck driver to yardwork was upheld where the employee had suffered three epileptic seizures within one and a half years after sustaining brain injury.[88]

---

[81]Texas Utils. Elec. Co., 90 LA 625 (Allen, 1988).

[82]Bowman Transp., 90 LA 347 (Duff, 1987); Shell Oil Co., 90 LA 286 (McDermott, 1988); Ashland Oil, 89 LA 795 (Flannagan, 1987). However, the failure of an employer to notify employees of the consequences of refusing a drug test may serve to reduce the discipline imposed. Sanford Corp., 89 LA 968 (Wies, 1987).

[83]Vulcan Materials Co., 90 LA 1161 (Caraway, 1988).

[84]San Francisco Gen. Hosp., 90 LA 1293 (Winograd, 1988); Western Fuel Oil Co., 89 LA 772 (Kaufman, 1987).

[85]West Penn Power Co., 89 LA 1227 (Hogler, 1987) (inherently dangerous nature of assignment, which involved moving power lines during picketing, justified refusal).

[86]Griffin Pipe Prods. Co., 87 LA 283 (Yarowsky, 1986).

[87]Mead Corp., 86 LA 201 (Ipavec, 1985); see also Peabody Coal Co., 84 LA 511 (Duda, 1985) (employee with large abdominal hernia had a physical impairment which made him a hazard to himself).

[88]Lone Star Indus., 88 LA 879 (Berger, 1987).

However, another arbitrator found that an employee who had an arm injury had to be given at least a trial period at her old job to determine whether she could perform the job. The company had a practice of providing such "trial" periods, and the medical evidence did not establish that the employee was a hazard to herself if she returned to her job.[89]

[89]Firestone Tire & Rubber Co., 88 LA 217 (Cohen, 1986).

Chapter 17

Employee Rights and Benefits

Vacations

Vacation benefits are a product of the labor agreement and any right the employee may have arises strictly from the contract.[1]

Arbitrators have recognized the twofold nature of the vacation benefit: time off from work, and pay.[2] The duality of the benefit has surfaced in grievances asserting an employee's claim to vacation without pay after having received vacation pay while on layoff. One arbitrator concluded that it was implicit in the contract language that once a laid-off employee had been paid vacation pay, the employee had taken the vacation for which he received pay.[3] The arbitrator found that the past practice of the parties dictated the denial of additional time off without pay after the employee returned to work. However, a second arbitrator noted that employees who received vacation pay while on layoff were unable to even visit friends and relatives during their layoff because of the reporting requirements for unemployment compensation eligibility. He found the past practice of the parties supported additional time off without pay after the employees returned to work.[4]

Scheduling Vacations

Vacation provisions in collective bargaining agreements generally provide that seniority will prevail in vacation selection and scheduling.[5] The procedure for scheduling vacations is usually determined by contractual provisions or past practice. In one case

[1]The myriad issues relating to vacation benefits are analyzed in Abrams & Nolan, "The Common Law of the Labor Agreement: Vacations," 5 Indus. Rel. L.J. 603 (1983).

[2]See Arbitrator Hunter in Carrick Foodland, 87 LA 932, 934 (1986) (dictum).

[3]Koehring S. Plant, 82 LA 193, 196 (Alsher, 1984).

[4]Hess Oil, 87 LA 1109 (Eyraud, 1986).

[5]See Wellslee Coca-Cola Bottling Co., 86 LA 1165 (Spilker, 1986), and Commonwealth of Pa., 86 LA 1229 (Zirkel, 1985).

Arbitrator Richard John Miller found that the employer improperly implemented a rule requiring 72 hours notice and approval of a vacation request. Although the agreement gave the employer the right to schedule vacations, an established past practice continued over three contract terms had permitted employees to call in requests for vacation commencing on the same day or to make postabsence vacation requests for time already taken.[6] In another case, an arbitrator upheld a discharge for insubordination where an employee defied a direct order not to take a vacation at the time requested by the employee.[7]

Operational Needs—Generally, an employer may deny a request for vacation where the timing would be detrimental to its business needs. However, the employer has the "burden to substantiate denial of vacation requests as being reasonable in light of business needs."[8]

In some cases arbitrators have ruled against employers that establish blanket prohibitions of vacations during specified times. Although the collective agreements under consideration in two cases reserved discretion to the employers in scheduling vacations, the employers' blanket prohibitions of vacations during certain times of the year were rejected, since there was no evidence that complete bans were operationally required.[9] In a third case, however, an employer was permitted to schedule a vacation shutdown despite the fact that it had not "endeavored," in accordance with the contract, to allow vacations at the time requested by the employees. The arbitrator found that production and maintenance projects were at such low levels that rescheduling vacations as requested by the employees would have meant a layoff.[10]

Where an employee was unable to schedule his vacation during the year because the employer had reduced the complement of operators who could be on vacation at any one time too late for the employee to schedule his remaining vacation, the employer had to restore two weeks of vacation.[11]

Vacation Shutdown—An arbitrator held that an employee who was paid vacation pay for vacation time he took while on layoff was not entitled to take vacation without pay. Past practice was a controlling factor.[12]

An employer was permitted to change employees' vacation schedules to require the employees to take vacation during two one-week

[6]E.G. & G. Vactec, Inc., 89 LA 1108 (1987).

[7]Wilton Corp., 85 LA 667 (Smedley, 1985).

[8]Universal Eng'g, 90 LA 895, 898 (Roumell, 1988); also see Southern Cal. Permanente Medical Group, 90 LA 900 (Kaufman, 1988).

[9]Multimedia of Ohio, 87 LA 927 (Kindig, 1986); Supreme Life Ins. Co. of Am., 85 LA 997 (Cox, 1985).

[10]Deere & Co., 82 LA 1299 (Cox, 1984). See also Bethlehem Steel Corp., 85 LA 1130 (Sharnoff, 1985).

[11]Owens-Corning Fiberglass Corp., 82 LA 1156 (Mikrut, 1984). Cf. City of Lancaster, 87 LA 105 (Duda, 1986); Commonwealth of Pa., 86 LA 1229 (Zirkel, 1985); City of Pittsburgh, 84 LA 467 (Ipavec, 1985); Saginaw Mining Co., 83 LA 310 (Feldman, 1984).

[12]Koehring S. Plant, 82 LA 193 (Alsher, 1984).

shutdowns, since it gave them the required 60-day notice and the contract clearly stated that management had such a right provided it gave required notice.[13]

On the other hand, an employer's selection of a junior electrician to work through a vacation shutdown period was deemed improper since it was not in accordance with the past practice of selecting employees to work through this period on the basis of seniority in classification.[14]

Vacation Benefits: Deferred Wages or "Refresher"?

In order to determine the status of vacation benefits arbitrators usually turn to the contract and its bargaining history. It is well established in arbitration that an employee may be required to comply with a contractual requirement of minimum length of service to be eligible for vacation benefits.[15] Where a contract provided for overtime hours and premium for which vacation pay was regarded as time worked, an employer improperly charged the vacation of an employee to time off, thereby reducing paid overtime hours. The employer's claim of long-standing past practice was outweighed by the fact that the practice conflicted with the contractual provision.[16]

Are employees who cannot satisfy the contractual requirement of being active employees on a specified date entitled to vacation pay when their inability to maintain active status is controlled by the employer? One arbitrator applied a literal reading to a contract requirement related to an active employment requirement and ruled that employees' rights to vacation benefits, to which they would have been entitled if employed on January 1 of the following year, had not vested where the company was permanently closed on December 9.[17] However, Arbitrator J. Ross Hunter, Jr., held that employees who were terminated at midnight on December 31 were entitled to vacation pay, even though the contract required that they be on the payroll on the following January 1, because "the employees' service records at least 'touched' if they had not in fact 'hit' January 1."[18]

Layoff as Affecting Vacation Benefits

Several arbitrators have considered the effect of layoffs or other absences on the work eligibility requirement, or "continuous service"

---

[13]Bethlehem Steel Corp., 85 LA 1130 (Sharnoff, 1985); also see Deere & Co., 82 LA 1299 (Cox, 1984).

[14]Alabama By-Prods. Corp., 83 LA 1270 (Clarke, 1984). Cf. H.D. Hudson Mfg. Co., 84 LA 1141 (Gallagher, 1985).

[15]Southwest Airlines Co., 93 LA 543 (Fox, 1989).

[16]Hennepin County Sheriff's Dep't, 85 LA 425 (Jacobowski, 1985).

[17]Pollock Co., 87 LA 325 (Oberdank, 1986). See Marshalltown Instruments, 85 LA 123 (Thornell, 1985) (plant closure); Whirlpool Corp., 82 LA 686 (Allen, 1984) (layoff).

[18]Carrick Foodland, 87 LA 932, 936 (1986). Also see Arbitrator High in Celotex Corp., 88 LA 319 (1986) (employees who had worked enough hours to qualify for vacation when plant was shut down on February 27 were awarded vacation pay even though not on payroll on following May 31). See generally, Abrams & Nolan, "The Common Law of the Labor Agreement: Vacations," 5 Indus. Rel. L.J. 603 (1983).

reference, common to most contracts. The purpose of those two standards has been explained as follows:

> A work eligibility requirement is included in a vacation clause to ensure that an employee has actually worked for his vacation and thus has earned vacation pay as a form of deferred wages. By comparison, management will bargain for a "continuous service" reference to encourage long-term employee loyalty and discourage turnover.[19]

In one case, the contract provided that an employee's accrual of service for purposes of vacation and other benefits would be suspended during an "unpaid absence" exceeding 30 continuous calendar days. An arbitration board chaired by Arbitrator George W. Adams held that the employer properly considered the absence of an employee who had suffered an injury, for which she received workers' compensation benefits, as an "unpaid absence" and prorated her vacation benefit accordingly.[20] The decision was premised, in part, on the principle that vacation benefits are earned by working. In a second case, Arbitrator Llewellyn E. Slade held that when computing an employee's years of "continuous employment" for purposes of vacation benefits, an employer could not deduct periods of layoff so as to "move" the employee's anniversary date.[21] In addition to the "continuous employment" reference, the contract provided that an employee must work 60 percent or more of the total working days in a 12-month period to qualify for vacation pay. Arbitrator Slade concluded that to interpret the "continuous employment" language to permit the employer to deduct periods of layoff would be a "redundancy."[22]

A related issue considered in other cases is whether a discharged employee, subsequently reinstated through arbitration, receives vacation pay for the interval he is off from work. Where an employee was reinstated with back pay, he was awarded vacation pay for the hours he would have worked but for the discharge.[23] Where an employee was reinstated without back pay, he was denied vacation pay.[24]

Sick Leave as Affecting Vacation Benefits

A continuing issue in arbitration cases is the earning of vacation credits during time spent on sick leave. This issue depends on specific contract language, and its resolution depends on the particular collective bargaining agreement. In a recent decision, Arbitrator Sol M.

---

[19]Abrams & Nolan, at 614.

[20]Northwestern Gen. Hosp., 82 LA 697 (1984).

[21]Iowa Mold Tooling Co., 82 LA 469 (1984). See Eagle Iron Works, 85 LA 979 (Thornell, 1985). But see GTE Prods. Corp., 85 LA 754 (Millious, 1985) (time an employee is on involuntary layoff not included within "continuous service"), and Keystone Bakery, 82 LA 405 (Bolte, 1984) (to same effect).

[22]Iowa Mold Tooling Co., 82 LA 469, 472 (1984).

[23]Cowlitz Redi-Mix, 85 LA 745 (Boedecker, 1985).

[24]Parker White Metal Co., 86 LA 512 (Ipavec, 1985); Carling Nat'l Breweries, 84 LA 503 (Van Wart, 1985).

Yarowsky found that an employer should have taken into account, for vacation purposes, the time an employee spent on sick leave since the agreement based vacation entitlement on "employment," not on "work performed for wages."[25]

Under a contract providing that employees on vacation are not entitled to pay allowances under a sickness and accident disability plan, an employee was denied disability benefits arising from an accident that occurred at home after he had worked the regular shift and left the plant but before he commenced his regular three-week vacation, since the employee was considered to be "on vacation" after completion of the last scheduled shift.[26]

Holidays

An employer is not obligated to pay holiday pay to employees for holidays that occur after their termination as a result of plant closing, on the basis that terminated employees lose all rights under the contract other than those specifically granted to such employees.[27]

In another plant-closing situation, employees were held entitled to personal holiday pay where the contract provided the holiday should be taken when mutually agreed upon by the employee and the company; however, employees were not entitled to birthday holiday pay since the contract provided that such holiday was to be taken on the Monday following a birthday, and, therefore, the right had not vested at the time of the closing of the business.[28]

Work Requirements

Under certain circumstances, an employee may be deemed eligible for holiday pay even if he fails to work the days surrounding a holiday. In a case considered by Arbitrator Raymond R. Roberts, the bargaining agreement required employees to work the last scheduled workday before and the first scheduled workday after a holiday to qualify for holiday pay.[29] Certain exceptions to the work requirement were provided, but the arbitrator's award of holiday pay was based upon the definition of a scheduled workday as provided in the contract:

> ("The scheduled workday *of the employee* as used herein is the workday *designated by the Company* before and after such holiday, *and* on which

---

[25]Grundy Elec. Coop., 91 LA 440, 442 (1988); also see National-Standard Co., 92 LA 956 (Bittel, 1989) (contract required employee to work 1,040 hours in a year to be entitled to vacation pay); General Foods Mfg. Corp., 91 LA 1083 (Fox, 1988).

[26]Arco Pipe Line Co., 84 LA 907 (Nicholas, 1985).

[27]Container Gen. Corp., 85 LA 159 (McDermott, 1985); see also City of Brooklyn, Ohio, 85 LA 799 (Graham, 1985).

[28]Mahoning Sparkle Mkts., 91 LA 1366 (Sharpe, 1988).

[29]Penthouse Furniture Ltd., 81 LA 494 (1983). Also see Pennwalt Corp., 88 LA 769 (McDonald, 1987) (vacation merely changes employee's last scheduled shift before and first scheduled shift after holiday).

the employee is *directed by the Company* to appear *and* on which the employee works the *hours required by the Company.*")[30]

Arbitrator Roberts held that a scheduled workday under the parties' agreement was not only the one designated by the company but also the one the employee was directed by the company to appear. He found that the reasonable implication of being permitted by the company to leave the plant and go to a physician following a work-related injury was that the employee had not been directed to appear for work until released by his physician.

Part Day Absence or Tardiness on Surrounding Day

An arbitrator denied holiday pay to an employee who was nine minutes late for his scheduled shift the day following a holiday. While the contract permitted excused time off, up to a maximum of one hour, to be counted as time worked, the grievant, a 15-year employee, had failed to either call in or explain his reason for being late upon arriving at the plant.[31] Another arbitrator denied holiday pay to an employee who was injured on the job during his last scheduled workday preceding the holiday and was taken to the hospital for treatment. The employee returned to work with a doctor's release for "light duty," but he was informed there was none and was instructed to punch out and go home. In order to qualify for holiday pay, the contract required that the employee complete the full scheduled workday before and after the holiday. The arbitrator held that although his failure to work the entire shift was no fault of the employee's, he was not eligible for holiday pay.[32]

Holidays Falling During Layoff

An arbitrator sustained a grievance for holiday pay filed by employees who had worked up to the time of a seasonal layoff and who returned to work promptly thereafter.[33] The company had a long-established practice of not paying for holidays for employees laid off during the winter reduction in force, notwithstanding a provision in the contract that an employee would not be disqualified for holiday pay if the company decided that operations were not necessary on any of the days preceding or following a holiday. The company argued that the provision had become a part of the contract because other employers in the same industry had laid off employees on one or both days surrounding a holiday solely to avoid holiday pay. In sustaining the grievance awarding five paid holidays to laid-off employees, the arbitrator held that holiday pay is a monetary grant or employee

---

[30]Penthouse Furniture Ltd., 81 LA at 496 (emphasis added). See also Atlanta Wire Works, 93 LA 537 (Williams, 1989); but see Hospital Linen Serv. Facility, 92 LA 228 (Stoltenberg, 1989).
[31]Morton Thiokol, Inc., 91 LA 345 (Hoffmeister, 1988).
[32]Hospital Linen Serv. Facility, 92 LA 228 (Stoltenberg, 1989).
[33]R.A. Cullinan & Sons, 85 LA 162 (Newmark, 1985).

benefit that should be forfeited only by clear and unmistakable language.

In another case it was held that a layoff was not the type of absence specified in the contract which would disqualify an employee from the benefit of a personal holiday, since the word absence denotes circumstances over which the employee has control, when in fact the employer controls layoffs.[34]

Vacation or Leave as Affecting Holiday Pay

Employees who requested and were granted a vacation during a period which included a holiday were entitled to holiday pay even though they were placed on layoff prior to the start of their vacations.[35] Although the contract provided for pay for any holiday which fell during a vacation, it denied holiday pay during layoff "under any conditions." The arbitrator held that the employees were in a dual status, layoff and vacation, but since they had established the vacation status first, their primary status was that of vacationers, entitling them to holiday pay.[36] However, employees were not entitled to pay for a holiday which occurred during a two-week plant vacation shutdown where the grieving employees were not eligible for a vacation during the entire two-week period.[37] Another employee who by agreement received full pay during a military leave was held not entitled to eight hours additional pay for a holiday which occurred during the period. Instead he was credited for one additional day of military leave time.[38]

Where a disability income benefits plan failed to list receipt of holiday pay as precluding payment of disability benefits, an employer improperly denied payment of benefits to an employee during the time it paid him holiday pay, under a contract providing that employees in excused absences should be paid for holidays.[39]

An employee who elected to be placed in an accident and sick leave status, instead of remaining in a vacation status following an auto accident while on vacation, was properly denied holiday pay because she did not work her last scheduled day prior to the holiday and the contract did not provide holiday pay for anyone on accident and sick leave.[40] Another employee was denied holiday pay because of being on sick leave and receiving reduced rate-sick pay, even though the requirement of working pre- and post-holiday workdays could be excused because of sickness. The arbitrator held that the sickness exception applied only when the individual who was sick had been

---

[34]Louisiana-Pac. Corp., 86 LA 301 (Michelstetter, 1986).
[35]Pittsburgh Brewing Co., 88 LA 95 (Duff, 1986).
[36]Id. at 97, 98.
[37]Meyer Prods., 84 LA 767 (Laybourne, 1985).
[38]Capital Dist. Transit Sys., 88 LA 353 (La Manna, 1986).
[39]Bolens Corp., 83 LA 1286 (Wyman, 1984).
[40]Snap-On Tools Corp., 91 LA 1174 (Franke, 1988).

scheduled to work and, in this case, the employee was known to be on sick leave and had not been scheduled for any work.[41]

One arbitrator required payment of holiday pay to an employee who commenced two weeks vacation on Memorial Day, having worked the preceding Friday. The employee did not work the Monday following the end of his vacation but reported for work on Tuesday. The contract provided for holiday pay in addition to vacation pay when a recognized holiday occurred during an employee's scheduled vacation. The arbitrator held that the contractual provision required payment of holiday pay regardless of the "surrounding day" work requirements and the fact that the employee had failed to report to work on the Monday following his vacation.[42] Another arbitrator found an employee eligible for holiday pay who took a day of sick leave for which he was paid during his last regular scheduled shift before the holiday but who was neither excused nor presented a written doctor's excuse as required by the contract, due to the company's inconsistent application of this requirement in the past.[43]

Holiday Falling on Nonworkdays

The fact that grieving employees were scheduled to work 13 of 53 Saturdays during the year in question did not entitle them to premium pay, rather than straight-time pay, for a holiday that fell on a Saturday.[44] An employer who instituted a seven-day-per-week operation, which admittedly was intended to be cost-neutral to the employer and benefit-neutral to the employees, was required to pay holiday pay to employees who were not scheduled to work the holiday and to include nonworked holiday hours in their overtime computation, since this was the practice under the previous Monday-Friday operation.[45]

Strikes as Affecting Holiday Pay

Striking employees who did not return to work as scheduled on the day before a holiday because they were awaiting the local union's ratification of a strike settlement agreement were not excused from returning (excuse by the employer being the only exception in the contract) and, accordingly, were not entitled to holiday pay.[46]

Holiday pay was denied to an employee who provided timely notice of his election not to work on his birthday holiday because, following the notice, he and other employees engaged in a work stop-

---

[41]Dahlgren's, 92 LA 571 (Clifford, 1989).
[42]George E. Failing Co., 93 LA 598 (Fox, 1989).
[43]Atlanta Wire Works, 93 LA 537 (Williams, 1989).
[44]Consolidation Coal Co., 83 LA 367 (Feldman, 1984).
[45]Goodyear Tire & Rubber Co., 87 LA 1269 (Rubin, 1986).
[46]Safeway Stores, 85 LA 51 (Damon, 1985).

page which began before his last scheduled workday prior to his birthday and continued beyond his birthday.[47]

Loss of Holiday Pay as Penalty for Misconduct

Employees were found to be entitled to holiday pay where they worked their last scheduled workday preceding and the next scheduled workday following July 4 but clocked out and went home at their regular quitting time instead of working required overtime on July 3. The arbitrator found that, while some sort of disciplinary action was called for because of the employees' refusal to work required overtime, withholding of holiday pay was not available as a disciplinary option.[48]

Other Holiday Issues

Two recent cases examined the liability of retail grocery employers who opened their stores on holidays in violation of their respective bargaining agreements. In one case, the arbitrator noted that competitors of the employer—both union ones covered by similar restriction against holiday openings, and nonunion ones—had been open on New Year's Day, and that other competitors had announced openings for the New Year's Day on which the grievance arose.[49] The employer informed the union that five of its stores would be opened on New Year's Day 1986 and manned them with bargaining unit employees who volunteered and were paid premium pay. Finding that the union had taken reasonable steps to enforce the closure requirement among the employer's organized competition, the arbitrator declined to award punitive damages, was unable to find a basis for compensatory damages, and held that an award of profits made by the employer on New Year's Day 1986 would be inappropriate. The arbitrator did order the employer to cease and desist from opening any store on New Year's Day for the term of the agreement while the article requiring closure remained in effect.[50]

In the other case, which involved the same local union but a different employer, the union had unsuccessfully sought to enjoin the employer's opening of its stores on January 1, 1985, following the employer's refusal to submit to expedited arbitration.[51] The employer opened all 45 of its area stores for business, enlisting some employees involuntarily by inverse seniority since an insufficient number had volunteered. Only two of the employer's organized competition, whose contracts likewise prohibited opening on January 1, decided to open their stores and apparently only after hearing of the employer's plans.

---

[47]Consolidation Coal Co., 93 LA 473 (Seidman, 1989).
[48]Dillingham Mfg. Co., 91 LA 816 (Nicholas, 1988).
[49]Great Atl. & Pac. Tea Co., 88 LA 430 (Lipson, 1986).
[50]Id. at 432-435.
[51]Kroger Co., 85 LA 1198 (St. Antoine, 1985).

In sustaining the union's grievance, the arbitrator ordered the employer to cease and desist from opening on New Year's Days as long as the article prohibiting opening remained in effect and to make restitution of any profits actually realized on January 1, 1985, and directed the union to determine the disposition of any such funds recovered.[52]

Other holiday issues which have been the subject of recent decisions include the right of the employer to designate a particular day to be recognized as a holiday;[53] the basis for computation of holiday pay;[54] the withholding of pay for an unworked holiday during a strike;[55] and whether holiday pay is to be considered hours worked in determining whether an employee had been compelled to work an additional shift in violation of a letter of understanding between the employer and the union.[56]

Leaves of Absence

Where a contract provision required an employer to consult with the union before making any new rules, the arbitrator found that the employer could not unilaterally make significant change in a disability-pay claim form.[57]

Sick Leave

In order to protect itself against fraudulent sick pay claims, management has the right to require employees on medical leave to be evaluated by a company physician.[58]

Whether an absence from work should be classified as sick leave is a threshold determination in many situations. In one case, an employer discharged a 15-year employee, who was on leave as a result of a compensable occupational disease, under a contract provision that terminated seniority after an employee had been on sick leave for three years. The arbitrator found that under that particular provision, the discharge was inappropriate since the employee was not on "sick leave" when he was absent. In reaching this conclusion, Arbitrator Marlin M. Volz pointed out that "a forfeiture clause to terminate the seniority of a long-term employee must be clear and unambiguous."[59] The record showed that other provisions of the agreement did not support the employer's interpretation that a compensable occupa-

---

[52]Id. at 1200-1204.
[53]Retail Mkts. Co., 92 LA 1234 (Klein, 1989).
[54]Evanite Battery Separator, Inc., 90 LA 225 (Murphy, 1987).
[55]Akron Bd. of Educ., 92 LA 803 (Duda, 1989).
[56]Country Place Nursing Home, 90 LA 1316 (Duda, 1988).
[57]ITT Higbie Mfg. Co., 83 LA 394 (Edes, 1984).
[58]Caterpillar Tractor Co., 83 LA 226 (Smith, 1984).
[59]Lithonia Lighting Co., 85 LA 627, 630 (1985).

tional disease was sick leave under the provision calling for seniority termination. Arbitrator Volz provided the following analysis:

> The parties in other parts of their Agreement recognize a distinction between sickness and injury or accident and they recognize a distinction between compensable benefits under worker's compensation and benefits provided by sickness and accident insurance. And whenever they intend to have a contractual provision cover both injury and sickness, they have said so by using both terms. Here, an occupational disease found to be covered by worker's compensation equates with injuries which are job caused. They are different from sick or sickness as those words are used in their restrictive sense as it is found they were used in Section I (6) of Article 11.[60]

In another case, the definition of sick leave was limited by a 14-year practice of restricting application of the sick leave provision to employees who are hospitalized for illness.[61] An employee therefore was not entitled to sick pay for the day she was absent and under the doctor's care, yet not hospitalized.

Sick leave may also be denied where an employee fails to meet the criteria established in the agreement for the use of such leave. In one case, a teacher was considered by an ear specialist to have a permanent hearing loss in one ear and was advised by another physician not to teach. As a result, the teacher applied for a year of sick leave. In denying the leave, Arbitrator Clair V. Duff found that the specialist did not find the teacher was "unable to perform his duties" as required under the governing statute and that the other physician gave no professional reason to support his recommendation.[62] Other factors considered by the arbitrator were the facts that the employee had taught satisfactorily for some time in spite of the hearing problem and that sick leave would not improve the loss, which was permanent.

Arbitrators have recognized that medical documentation of illness provided by employees is often inadequate. Arbitrator William P. Daniel noted the following:

> The arbitrator agrees that, as here, often medical certification provided by an ill or injured employee leaves much to be desired. All too often, very informal prescription pad notes, sometimes stamped or signed by a nurse, are offered as proof. On the other hand, it must be remembered that extensive medical reports are expensive for an employee to obtain and time consuming for a physician. It is general practice that, unless there is some serious dispute, these forms will be used and accepted.[63]

A doctor's letter consisting of three sentences that did not specify an employee's illness was considered insufficient proof to substantiate sick leave for an extended period of time.[64]

Where a grievant's surgeon cleared him for light duty work, which the employer was prepared to provide, the employer reasonably

---

[60]Id. at 631.
[61]Sunrise Medical, 86 LA 798 (Redel, 1985).
[62]New Brighton Area School Dist., 84 LA 350 (1985).
[63]Toledo Dist. Bd. of Health, 92 LA 1262, 1266 (1989).
[64]Internal Revenue Serv., 85 LA 212 (Shieber, 1985).

relied upon the surgeon's statement, rather than the contrary opinion of grievant's later-acquired physician that grievant would be "temporarily totally disabled" for a period of three or four months.[65]

However, an employer improperly refused to pay sickness and accident benefits to an employee who missed a doctor's appointment where the disability was verified by the doctor two days later.[66] On the other hand, a school board was found to have violated the parties' agreement when it unilaterally adopted a "Highly Contagious Diseases Policy" permitting it to place employees on compulsory sick or health leave upon determination that they posed a serious threat to the health and welfare of others. Recognizing that arbitrators have consistently upheld an employer's right to place an employee on leave of absence for health or medical reasons in order to assure the safety of the employees or other personnel or to maintain efficiency of operations, Arbitrator Fred Witney found that the leave policy involved in this instance was directed at AIDS, which had not been demonstrated to affect a teacher's ability to perform teaching duties or to constitute a danger to others.[67]

In some situations, the sick leave "benefit" may be initiated by the employer rather than the employee. In one case, an arbitrator found that the employer acted properly within the contractual provision in placing a teacher on sick leave after she was examined by a psychiatrist who made recommendations against her returning to teaching responsibilities.[68]

Some sick leave plans require a waiting period, that is, days without pay, before sick leave pay becomes available. In one case, the agreement provided the "wait period" would not apply in situations involving an absence due to the same authenticated illness/injury of prolonged duration that required periodic treatment.[69] Another arbitrator found that an employee who missed work on three different occasions due to back problems came within the exception to the wait period. "Requiring periodic treatment" was interpreted by the arbitrator to include an illness that requires treatment as need occurs.

Another arbitrator held that after the waiting-day requirement was met, an employer must pay sick leave benefits even though this resulted in paying the employee for hours in excess of the 40-hour guaranteed workweek.[70] Nothing in the contract language tied payment of sick leave benefit to the pay for the guaranteed workweek.

At times, the question of sick leave abuse is a central issue in arbitration. In one recent case, Arbitrator Marvin Hill, Jr., found insufficient evidence to establish sick leave abuse by an employee, who after calling in sick on two successive days, was shopping for a vaporizer

---

[65]Beatrice/Hunt Wesson, 92 LA 383, 390 (Brisco, 1989).
[66]Lever Bros. Co., 85 LA 995 (Thornell, 1985).
[67]Cook County Bd. of Educ., 89 LA 521, 527–528 (1987).
[68]Boces, First Supervisory Dist., Erie County, N.Y., 82 LA 1269, 1272 (Sabghir, 1984); also see County of Becker, 93 LA 673 (Neigh, 1989); ITT Higbie Mfg. Co., 85 LA 859 (Shanker, 1985).
[69]Monsanto Indus. Chems., 85 LA 113 (Grinstead, 1985).
[70]Certified Grocers of Cal., Ltd., 85 LA 414 (Sabo, 1985).

during the evening of the second day. The arbitrator noted that there was no evidence that the grievant was not ill on the day in question and the employer did not have a "24-hour stay-at-home rule."[71]

In considering the responsibility of a successor employer for sick leave that accrued under the term of employment with a predecessor, Arbitrator Ronald F. Talarico found that under the particular facts of the case the successor employer had made clear to the union that it would not be responsible for vacation benefits earned and accrued prior to the change in ownership.[72] The union acquiesced to this position by failing to take any action, and the specific issue of accrued sick leave did not arise until some time later. Nevertheless, the arbitrator found that the issues of sick leave and vacation are "reasonably identical" and that the successor employer was not liable for the previously accrued sick leave.

In a case where the parties' agreement based seniority on "continuous service," Arbitrator Howard M. Bard determined that seniority should accrue "only during periods of active service or availability for active service." However, he further determined that absence during sick leave is not a termination of employment, but rather a temporary absence, the right to which "inures to the employment relationship in general." Therefore, Arbitrator Bard concluded that seniority should continue to accrue during sick leave periods absent a showing by the employer that the parties' intent was otherwise.[73]

Discharge was found too harsh a penalty for an employee whose excessive, sporadic absenteeism had been caused by drug abuse, where the employee had, subsequent to his discharge, successfully completed the in-patient portion of a rehabilitation program and was responsibly and reliably in the process of participating in the outpatient phase. However, sick pay benefits were not awarded because there was no showing that grievant had been admitted for treatment to a company-approved facility, as required by the sick leave provisions of the collective bargaining agreement.[74]

Maternity or Maternity-Related Leave

In *California Federal Savings & Loan Association v. Guerra,* the U.S. Supreme Court held that the 1978 Pregnancy Discrimination Act does not prohibit preferential treatment for pregnancy.[75] The Court upheld a California statute which requires employers to provide

---

[71]Central Ill. Pub. Serv. Co., 91 LA 126 (1988). Also see County of Appanoose, 92 LA 246 (Gallagher, 1989) (employer failed to prove that grievant's pattern of sick leave indicated fraudulent use of such leave); and Straits Steel & Wire, 91 LA 1058 (Elkin, 1988) (discipline reduced for employee who altered physician's excuse where physician inadvertently wrote excuse for one day instead of two).

[72]Servicecare, Inc., 82 LA 590, 592-593 (1984). Also see City of Crystal, 89 LA 531, 537 (Bard, 1987); Ashland Petroleum Co., 90 LA 681 (Volz, 1988).

[73]City of Crystal, 89 LA 531, 537 (1987).

[74]Ashland Petroleum Co., 90 LA 681 (Volz, 1988).

[75]107 S.Ct. 683, 42 FEP 1073 (1987); the maternity leave issue has been the focus of recent legislation among the several states. See, e.g., Tenn. Code Ann. § 50-1-501 et seq.

female employees an unpaid pregnancy disability leave of up to four months and to reinstate these employees when they return to work. The Court found that the California statute, which provided women with a benefit not applicable to men, does not conflict with Title VII of the Civil Rights Act, as amended by the 1978 Pregnancy Discrimination Act; it reasoned that the legislative history of the Pregnancy Discrimination Act shows that the amendment was intended to be "a floor beneath which pregnancy disability benefits may not drop—not a ceiling above which they may not rise."[76] The Act was designed to eliminate discrimination against pregnancy, not to prohibit preferential treatment.

After interpreting the parties' agreement, which based seniority on "continuous service," to permit the accrual of seniority during sick leave, Arbitrator Howard M. Bard determined that both state and federal law compelled the conclusion that seniority accrual should be permitted during leave related to illness or disability during pregnancy, citing the Minnesota Human Rights Act, Minn. Stat. § 363.03, Subd. 1(5) and Title VII of the Civil Rights Act as amended by the Pregnancy Discrimination Act of 1978, 42 U.S.C. § 2000(e)(k). However, he further determined that neither the contract nor legal considerations precluded the tolling of seniority during an open-ended leave for child nurturing.[77]

Generally, a period of leave for purposes of maternal bonding with an infant will not be allowed unless authorized by law such as the California statute described above, or by the agreement. Arbitrator Arthur Berkeley held that a school properly denied a teacher's request for paid leave for an employee who wanted to stay home to bond with her newborn infant where the agency regulations interpreting the leave provision restricted the use of leave to medically established incapacitation.[78]

Leave for Union Business

Arbitrator Marlin M. Volz recently set aside a unilaterally adopted policy statement which placed undue limitations on the right to be away from work for union business set forth in the collective bargaining agreement. However, he observed that the term "union activities" is not unlimited, and that arbitrators must determine whether, under the facts and circumstances of each case, "the nature of the particular activity is an appropriate basis for absence." He further stated:

> Arbitrators apply the twin concepts of reasonableness and undue burden as limitations upon requests for leaves of absence for Union activities.* * * What these two concepts essentially mean, when con-

---

[76]Ibid.
[77]City of Crystal, 89 LA 531, 537 (1987).
[78]Defense Dep't Dependents School, 89 LA 105 (1987).

strued together with [an article requiring] regularity of attendance, is that if the activity in question reasonably can be done on off-duty time without encroaching on work hours, it should be done then. In such case the need of the Company for his or her services exceeds the need to be absent from work which, boiled down, is what "undue burden" means. Replacing an absent employee ordinarily places a burden upon management and added expense whenever overtime is involved. The concept of reasonableness requires accommodation on both sides.[79]

Arbitrator Neil M. Gundermann has stated that in determining which activities constitute official union business, arbitrators generally give "wide latitude to the unions," but suggests the following guidelines:

> A review of arbitral authority regarding the issue of what constitutes official Union business suggests that arbitrators generally give wide latitude to the unions in making such determinations. Generally, official union business falls within two broad areas: the first area includes those activities performed by the union as the bargaining representatives for the employees; a second and broader area includes those activities which the union performs on behalf of itself as an entity. The latter activities include such things as organizing (Walker Manufacturing, 42 LA 632), political activity (Consolidation Coal Co., 84 LA 1042), and bargaining in another plant (Hurd Millwork, 58 LA 523).[80]

Attendance at a workers' compensation proceeding was found to fall into a third category, namely "activity on behalf of bargaining union employees not arising out of the bargaining relationship," on grounds that eligibility for workers' compensation is established by statute, not by the parties, and is therefore a "peripheral" benefit to the union and its members. However, Arbitrator Marlin M. Volz held that under the 1988 National Coal Agreement, an employee responding to a call to be interviewed by a Workers' Compensation Fund investigator could be considered engaged in a union activity since the parties, having dealt with job-related injuries in the health and safety provision of that Agreement, "do not depend upon state or federal laws alone to require [the] employer to maintain workers' compensation: they direct that it be done."[81]

While arbitrators have held that leave for "union business" does not encompass union political activity, Arbitrator Marvin J. Feldman stated in a recent case that the "modern labor law of this country" requires a different conclusion, namely that "union activities* * * do not mean some, those that are liked, those that involve non-political activity, but rather it means *all* union activity."[82] And Arbitrator R. Douglas Collins, in determining that participation in school board election activities constituted "normal business activity," observed:

> In the public sector, political activity is interwoven with bargaining activity as public employee unions seek to influence the legislative

---

[79]Sharples Coal Co., 91 LA 1317, 1322 (1988), citing Arbitrator Hoh's decision in 84-12-85-12 between Consolidation Burning Star No. 5 Mine and UMWA Local 2216.

[80]Consolidated Foods, 88 LA 1148, 1152-1153 (1987). Also see City of San Antonio, Tex., 92 LA 76 (McDermott, 1989); Texas Utils. Generating Co., 86 LA 1108 (Nicholas, 1986).

[81]Sharples Coal Co., 91 LA 1317, 1322 (1988).

[82]Consolidation Coal Co., 84 LA 1042, 1044 (1985) (emphasis in original).

bodies which control their fate at the bargaining table. Whether one views this as proper or wise, it is undeniably part of normal union business in the public sector.[83]

Attendance at an arbitration hearing has been found to be a union activity.[84] In addition, to carry out the representation function, arbitrators have held that a reasonable time must be provided for both preparation and delivery of representation services. Thus, Arbitrator Howard V. Finston found that a "reasonable period of time" provision for union representation encompassed adequate time to prepare a post-hearing brief in an arbitration case.[85]

Where a union official had been on unpaid leave of absence for nine years prior to the plant closing, Arbitrator Charles A. Askin held that according to the agreement, accrual of his severance pay during the leave period had been suspended, but not forfeited altogether. The official was entitled to receive contractual severance pay benefits accrued prior to his leave of absence.[86]

Funeral Leave

Employees were held entitled to bereavement pay for taking their scheduled working days of Saturday and Sunday as part of their bereavement leave, under a contract provision granting pay for "working days off" for bereavement, even though the company alleged a past practice of not granting bereavement pay when funeral leave fell on Saturday or Sunday.[87] However, in three cases where the contract provided for "consecutive" days off, the arbitrators interpreted "consecutive" to mean calendar, and not scheduled, work days.[88]

In some instances arbitrators have inclined to a rather strict construction of the provision specifying relationship requirement. The death of a niece's daughter did not trigger bereavement benefits;[89] the term "grandparent" did not include the wife's grandmother;[90] and the definition of a spouse did not include a man the grievant had lived with for 25 years.[91]

And finally, one arbitrator refused to extend a funeral leave provision listing "brother, sister, brother-in-law [and] sister-in-law"

---

[83]Orange Unified School Dist., 91 LA 525, 529 (1988) (holding also that attendance at arraignment of school board members and officials on charges of misappropriation of public funds and willful misconduct was within union's "normal business activities" since indictment related to district's financial condition and ability to pay employees).

[84]Sharples Coal Co., 91 LA 1317, 1323 (Volz, 1988). Compare Youngstown Vindicator Printing Co., 88 LA 17 (Cohen, 1986) (no reasonable inference could be drawn that attendance at arbitration hearings was contemplated by parties when negotiating leave clause).

[85]Immigration & Naturalization Serv., El Paso Border Patrol Sector, 91 LA 713 (1988).

[86]Fleming Foods of Cal., 90 LA 1071 (1988).

[87]Hussman Corp., 84 LA 137 (Roberts, 1983).

[88]Gulf Printing Co., 92 LA 893 (King, 1989); Consolidation Coal Co., 89 LA 179 (Wren, 1987); Blue Grass Cooperage Co., 89 LA 385 (Sergent, 1987).

[89]Lawrence Bros., 86 LA 1132 (Gibson, 1986).

[90]Town of Danie, 83 LA 1153 (Kanzer, 1984).

[91]Derby Cab Mfg. Co., 87 LA 1042 (Imundo, 1986).

to a stepsister, distinguishing cases in which arbitrators found that the step-relative "stood in place" of the employee's predeceased natural sister or lived in the same household as the grievant or grievant's parents when they were growing up.[92] While another arbitrator, relying upon dictionary definitions and state law and noting the absence of any qualifications such as "immediate family," held that the term "brother" included a half-brother without regard to whether he and the employee could be considered a "family unit."[93]

Leave for "Personal Business"

Where no specific criteria are spelled out for granting personal leave, the question posed is whether the employer's denial of the leave was unreasonable or arbitrary.[94] However, where the contract specifically stated that personal leave "may not be taken contiguous to a holiday," the arbitrator refused to find unreasonable the employer's denial of a personal leave for days missed after a holiday due to snow emergency conditions.[95]

"Moonlighting" and Outside Business Interest

Interestingly, the absence of a contractual provision prohibiting "moonlighting" activities does not bar an employer's disciplinary action in this area. As Arbitrator Mario F. Bognanno recently emphasized:

> Labor agreements must be read in a reasonable manner and to reflect a sense of fair dealing and good faith. Thus, labor agreements lacking in extensive express prohibitions or constraints will be read to implicitly contain certain clauses. Within the employment relationship the quid pro quo for employment and subsequent wages is the duty of loyalty and an agreement not to compete with the Employer's business. These obligations are, in the opinion of the undersigned, so fundamental to the employment relationship that they need not be expressly stated.[96]

In finding overly broad a city's requirement that a construction inspector and his spouse cease selling real estate within the city because of potential conflicts of interest, Arbitrator William P. Daniel observed as follows:

> The application, in an individual case, of the conflict of interest policy requires the city to be ready to make reasonable accommodations to

---

[92]Ashley Community Schools, 89 LA 1285 (McDonald, 1987).

[93]Hartman Elec. Mfg., 92 LA 253 (Rybolt, 1989).

[94]See DeBourgh Mfg. Co., 90 LA 471 (Flagler, 1987) (refusal to grant personal leave to employee with car trouble found unreasonable); Westinghouse Elec. Corp., Westinghouse Materials Co. Div., 89 LA 1150 (Traynor, 1987) (denial of incarcerated employee's request for extended leave of absence not arbitrary or capricious); U.S. Dep't of the Navy, 88 LA 1269 (Nolan, 1987) (employer did not act arbitrarily by deciding to remain open during hurricane and announcing liberal leave policy rather than granting administrative leave); Hennepin Technical Centers, Dist. 287, 86 LA 1293 (Kapsch, 1986) (denial of employee's request for leave to attend a school's grandparents' day function found arbitrary).

[95]Community Unit School Dist. No. 303, 88 LA 1159 (Goldstein, 1987).

[96]Country Club Mkts., 85 LA 286, 289 (1985).

preserve the employee's job rights and for the employee to be prepared to accept reasonable restrictions to preserve the integrity of the public service, even for just appearance's sake.[97]

In a case where the contract provided for an employee's termination if he "without the consent of the Company engages in employment with another employer or organization while on leave of absence," Arbitrator Marlin M. Volz observed as follows:

> The decisions are not in harmony as to whether [the term "another"] includes working for oneself. They are, however, in agreement that the usual prohibition against working while on leave of absence does not apply to the continuation of work which the employee had been doing during off hours on a part-time basis before leave was granted, commonly referred to as "moonlighting," provided that the nature of the work is not inconsistent with treatment of his or her injury or sickness and would not prolong the period of leave.* * *[98]

Personal Appearance: Hair and Clothes

The Employer's "Image"

Dress and grooming policies imposed upon employees by employers continue to be the subject of arbitration. In a recent case, Arbitrator Marshall Ross found no cause to discipline a grocery store clerk for his hair style which was in accord with current men's style, where grievant's appearance had not changed substantially in two years, he had cut his hair three times in an effort to comply with the company's rule, and the two-toned appearance of his hair was caused naturally by sun bleaching. Arbitrator Ross pointed out that management must provide evidence of "the grooming's negative impact on customers because of the contractual requirement that employees can only be disciplined for just cause," and in this case there was no evidence of any customer objection.[99]

In another case, an arbitrator reversed the discharge of a grievant who was terminated for not removing his hard hat that had a lewd message where the employer had no rule or policy concerning any writing on hard hats and many co-workers continued to wear hard hats with equally lewd or suggestive messages.[100]

In a case involving a public employer, an arbitrator found that a change in the dress code to require the wearing of ties and jackets was

---

[97]City of Rochester Hills, 90 LA 237, 242 (1987).

[98]Alcan Aluminum Corp., 90 LA 16, 19 (1987). And see Foster Food Prods., 88 LA 337 (Riker, 1986) (provision providing for termination if employee "accepts work at another job, or at any other company, while on a leave of absence" did not preclude grievant's working while on worker's compensation leave in absence of evidence that leave was fraudulently obtained).

[99]Lucky Stores, 91 LA 624, 628 (1988); but see Alpha Beta Co., 93 LA 855 (Horowitz, 1989) (where current style haircut was found to be inappropriate under "good grooming" rule which is entitled to "considerable deference" for store located in small farming community).

[100]Armco, Inc., 93 LA 561 (Strongin, 1989).

a change in "working conditions" and was, therefore, subject to the "meet and confer" process of the collective bargaining agreement.[101]

Safety and Health Considerations

Safety and health considerations can be valid reasons for an employer to place restrictions on dress, hair, or beards. In a recent case, the arbitrator upheld the discharge of an 11-year employee who on four separate occasions refused to shave off his beard for an annual respirator fit test. The arbitrator noted that respiratory policy which required shaving was negotiated with the union and was legitimately related to the safety program.[102]

Accommodation of Employee Religious Beliefs

The conflict between workplace policies and required religious observances of employees was reviewed once more by the U.S. Supreme Court in 1986 in *Ansonia Board of Education v. Philbrook*.[103] The employee, a high school instructor, was unable to pursue his employment on certain holy days designated by the church to which he belonged. The Board of Education, which employed the instructor, maintained a detailed, rigid policy with respect to paid leaves of absence. Under the collective bargaining agreement, up to three days annually could be authorized as leave for observance of mandatory religious holidays. In addition, up to three days per year could be used for necessary personal business. Use of these personal days, however, had to be limited to purposes other than those for which the contract provided specific leave periods. Other such leaves were listed in the contract for illness, death in the family, weddings, and acting as a delegate to certain conventions. The employee's observances of holy days usually amounted to six days per year, but only the first three days could be paid under the leave policy. The Board of Education in no way threatened the instructor with a loss of employment. However, he was seeking a greater degree of accommodation in order to avoid the loss of pay for unauthorized religious leaves.

The Supreme Court ruled that Title VII of the Civil Rights Act of 1964 as amended does not require an employer to implement an accommodation plan which is most beneficial to the employee as long as the employer avoids undue hardship. The Court observed that the "undue hardship" consideration comes into play only when the employer is unable to offer any reasonable accommodation. In this case, the leave policy itself was offered by the employer as reasonable accommodation to the employee's required religious observances. Additionally, the Court conceded that such an accommodation plan

---

[101]County of Riverside, 92 LA 1242 (Gentile, 1989).
[102]Central Contra Costa County Sanitation Dist., 93 LA 801 (Silver, 1989).
[103]107 S.Ct. 367, 42 FEP 359 (1986).

would generally be reasonable. However, unpaid leave is not a reasonable accommodation if paid leaves are available for every purpose except religious purposes, since such an arrangement would be discriminatory and clearly unreasonable. The Court held that the development of additional facts concerning the administration of the agreement was necessary to make a determination of the reasonableness of the accommodation. Accordingly, the case was remanded to the District Court.

Arbitrators have applied the standards set out in the *Philbrook* case. Arbitrator Joseph F. Gentile discussed the "reasonable/accommodation/undue hardship" test established by *Philbrook* and a prior Supreme Court decision.[104] In applying the test in a particular arbitration, Arbitrator Gentile found an employer improperly discharged a grocery store cashier for refusing on religious grounds to sell state lottery tickets. Although her retention in the same position without ticket-selling duties would constitute an undue hardship on operations, the employer should have explored some other accommodation, such as transfer to another position.

When attempting to accommodate the religious beliefs of an employee, an employer must also avoid discriminating against other employees. One Seventh-Day Adventist successfully challenged management's policy requiring the employees to recruit their own replacement for mandatory Saturday work as being in violation of the overtime distribution provisions of the bargaining agreement.[105]

The issue of whether the accommodation offered was reasonable is reached only after determining that the employee's action was truly based upon religion. A Jehovah's Witness, who refused to sell lottery tickets, was found to be motivated by a sincerely held religious conviction and not merely a personal philosophical preference, despite the fact that another Jehovah's Witness in the same workplace had agreed to perform subject duties while maintaining his religious faith.[106] On the other hand, a Catholic employee who refused work on Good Friday was properly subject to disciplinary penalties, since neither attendance at religious services, nor avoidance of work on Good Friday, was found to be a religious obligation. The arbitrator held that the griev-

---

[104]Lucky Stores, 88 LA 841 (1987) (discussing Ansonia Bd. of Educ. v. Philbrook, 107 S.Ct. 367, 42 FEP Cases 359 (1986), and Trans World Airlines v. Hardison, 97 S.Ct. 2264, 14 FEP Cases 1697 (1977)); also see Helburn & Hill, "The Arbitration of Religious Practice Grievances," 39 Arb. J. 3 (1984).

[105]United States Playing Card Co., 87 LA 937 (Duda, 1986).

[106]Lucky Stores, 88 LA 841 (Gentile, 1987). In this case testimony was received from an elder in grievant's congregation indicating that selling lottery tickets was not clearly prohibited by their religion. Many parts of scripture could be consulted by an individual seeking guidance. In the final analysis, however, a person's choice of action would have to be based upon their "God-given conscience," and two Jehovah's Witnesses may reach different decisions regarding the moral correctness of selling lottery tickets. The arbitrator, in deciding not to become an arbiter of varying scriptural interpretations, relied upon Thomas v. Review Bd., Ind. Employment Sec. Div., 101 S.Ct. 1425, 25 FEP Cases 629 (1981). The grievant's sincerity in her religious convictions was sufficient in this case.

ant's decision to attend services was a matter of religious preference rather than obligation.[107]

Protection Against Sexual Harassment

The law is still developing regarding the conditions under which sexual harassment constitutes a type of sex discrimination prohibited by Title VII of the Civil Rights Act of 1964. The Equal Employment Opportunity Commission and the lower federal courts have recognized two distinct types of sexual harassment—"quid pro quo" harassment and "hostile environment" harassment. The former occurs when an employment benefit or continuing employment is expressly or implicitly conditioned on an employee's acquiescence to the sexual advances or sexual conduct of another person, usually a supervisor or manager. Hostile-environment sexual harassment occurs when an employee is subjected to a pattern of unwelcome sexually related conduct in the workplace that creates a hostile, intimidating, or offensive work environment.[108]

In *Meritor Savings Bank v. Vinson*, the Supreme Court for the first time recognized the hostile-environment theory of sexual harassment.[109] In that case the Court held that Title VII protects employees from discriminatory intimidation, ridicule, and insult, even though such conduct does not result in any economic loss to the employee. Although the Court's recognition of hostile-environment sexual harassment did not mark a new development in the law, the publicity surrounding its decision has brought this form of discrimination to the attention of the general public and may result in increased claims in the future.

In the arbitration context, the issue of sexual harassment generally continues to arise in the form of grievances challenging the discharge or discipline of an employee for misconduct based in whole or in part upon alleged sexual harassment of another employee rather

---

[107]Bronx-Lebanon Hosp. Center, 90 LA 1216 (Babiskin, 1988).

[108]For cases illustrating the distinctions and requirements for establishing a Title VII violation of quid pro quo sexual harassment or hostile environment sexual harassment, see Jones v. Flagship Int'l, 793 F.2d 714, 41 FEP Cases 358 (CA 5, 1986) (sexual advances by a supervisor on three occasions and a sexually offensive decoration at an office party did not create a pervasive atmosphere of sexually hostile conduct); Downes v. Federal Aviation Admin., 775 F.2d 288 (Fed. Cir. 1985) (sporadic instances of offensive behavior over a three-year period did not constitute an illegal pattern of sexual harassment) and Henson v. City of Dundee, 682 F.2d 897, 29 FEP Cases 787 (CA 11, 1982) (court distinguished between quid pro quo sexual harassment and hostile environment sexual harassment); Broderick v. Ruder, 685 F. Supp. 1269, 46 FEP Cases 1272 (D.D.C. 1988) (conduct of consentual sexual relationships between three male office managers and certain female employees, which resulted in promotions and benefits to females, constituted illegal sexually hostile environment although not involving plaintiff personally); Priest v. Rotary, 634 F. Supp. 571, 40 FEP Cases 208 (N.D. Cal., 1986) (conduct of male employer who grabbed a female employee, touched intimate parts of her body, tried to kiss her, rubbed his body against hers, picked her up, and carried her across the room constituted illegal sexual harassment). For EEOC Policy Guidelines on Sexual Harassment, see 29 C.F.R. § 1604.11.

[109]106 S.Ct. 2399, 40 FEP Cases 1822 (1986); see Monat & Gomez, "Sexual Harassment: The Impact of *Meritor Savings Bank v. Vinson* on Grievances and Arbitration Decisions," 41 Arb. J. 24 (1986).

than from complaints of alleged victims of sexual harassment. Many arbitrators have upheld discharge or discipline imposed by an employer for conduct which constitutes sexual harassment under the descriptions noted above.[110] In one case, an arbitrator upheld the discharge of a chief union steward, with an unblemished 32-year work record, for allegedly leaving an anonymous note in a female co-employee's locker, which stated she was sleeping with her boss, and mailing a similar anonymous letter to the co-employee's husband.[111] Citing the *Vinson* case, the arbitrator determined that the grievant's conduct was based upon a vendetta against the co-employee, that the vehicle used to carry out the vendetta was sex, and that the vendetta constituted sexual harassment causing a hostile or offensive working environment.[112]

In some cases, arbitrators found misconduct constituting sexual harassment but held that the penalty assessed by the employer was inappropriate because of mitigating factors or because the employer failed to properly investigate the sexual harassment complaint, failed to give the grievant adequate notice of the prohibition, or failed to give the grievant an opportunity to defend himself before discipline was imposed.[113]

---

[110]For cases upholding discharge, see Arbitrator Shearer in Can-Tex Indus., 90 LA 1230 (1988) (grievant persistently made crude advances to female co-worker and frequently grabbed at her breasts); Vause in Tampa Elec. Co., 88 LA 971 (1986) (grievant used crude, explicit language in describing to married female co-worker his sexual fantasies about her despite her rejection of his advancements in the past); Lieberman in Porter Equip. Co., 86 LA 1253 (1986) (grievant pulled the hand of a female co-worker and forced her to touch his exposed sex organ—evidence established that co-employee suffered an intense emotional reaction); Feldman in Rockwell Int'l Co., 85 LA 246 (1985) (grievant touched the bodies of three female co-workers without any authorization and used body language that made the women uncomfortable); Gray in New Indus. Techniques, 84 LA 915 (1985) (offensive touching of female co-worker); Allen in Nabisco Foods Co., 82 LA 1186 (1984) (grievant made sexual propositions and other forms of customer abuse for several years at retail stores in many locations to which he delivered company products in spite of repeated warnings about such behavior); Madden in United Elec. Supply Co., 82 LA 921 (1984) (grievant made persistent and continued advances to several female co-workers which created an offensive working environment).

[111]Schlage Lock Co., 88 LA 75 (Wyman, 1986).

[112]Id. at 78-79. In so holding, Arbitrator Wyman identified four types of sexual harassment: verbal, physical, written, and visual (which includes indecent exposure and distribution of pornographic pictures).

[113]See Arbitrator Cohen in GTE Fla., 92 LA 1090 (1989) (discharge too severe for male employee who physically removed female employee of subcontractor from a ladder, bent her backwards over a desk, and put his face near the woman's neck in a nuzzling fashion); Wilmoth in Boys Mkts., 88 LA 1304 (1987) (discharge too severe for employee who allegedly moved his finger in upward movement between buttocks of female co-worker, since "mainstream of arbitral thinking" calls for a less severe penalty); Duda in Sugardale Foods, 86 LA 1017 (1986) (discharge reduced to long-term suspension where grievant hovered around a female co-employee for 10 minutes in a semi-dark room, briefly touched employee, and obviously made her uncomfortable and nervous—discipline reduced where employee handbook did not address sexual harassment specifically); Gallagher in County of Ramsey, 86 LA 249 (1986) (discharge of guidance counselor for sexual comments to client was too severe since lesser discipline than discharge is sufficient to prevent repetition of conduct); Oestreich in Hyatt Hotels Palo Alto, 85 LA 11 (1985) (discharge of employee for exposing himself to female co-employee during working hours reduced to 15-day suspension where employer failed to show that grievant could not be rehabilitated, grievant was not co-employee's supervisor, grievant received no warning about likely consequences of his misconduct, and employer did not have clear sexual harassment policy that had been reasonably disseminated); Arbitrator Ellmann in Meijer, Inc., 83 LA 570 (1984) (penalty of discharge was too severe for employee who admittedly embraced fellow employee and gave "little bit of a hump motion" where incident may have been provoked by fellow employee and grievant had a good work record).

In some other cases, no penalty was permitted against an employee charged with sexual harassment because of the particular circumstances or because the burden of proof had not been met.[114] Finally, in one case, allegations of sexual harassment were successfully used as a defense where the grievant was discharged for threatening a co-worker with bodily harm.[115]

With the growing body of reported arbitration decisions involving sexual harassment, various important substantive and evidentiary issues relating specifically to sexual harassment have arisen.[116] First, the burden of proof placed upon an employer who has discharged an employee for sexual harassment is unclear. Some arbitrators treat cases involving discipline for sexual harassment similar to any other case involving discipline for misconduct and, without specifically mentioning a burden of proof, appear to require the employer to establish sexual harassment merely by a preponderance of the evidence.[117] However, other arbitrators have stated that an employer must prove that the disciplined employee engaged in sexual harassment by "clear and convincing evidence."[118] Finally, some arbitrators require that an employer prove "beyond a reasonable doubt" that the grievant engaged in sexual harassment.[119] In justifying this stricter standard, Arbitrator John F. Sass stated:

> The charge of sexual harassment clearly involves an accusation of moral turpitude. * * * The charges * * * also carry enormous social stigma. * * * [I]t is not overly dramatic to say, as another witness said, that the Grievant's very life is on the line. All that he is: his marriage; his relationship with his children; * * *; his standing in the community; his relationships with other employees—all of this is on the line. In such case, the company has the burden of proving, *beyond a reasonable doubt*,

---

[114]See DeVry Inst. of Technology, 87 LA 1149 (Berman, 1986) (grievant improperly terminated for alleged sexual harassment that took place before he received a written warning after a prior offense that subsequent substantiated allegations of sexual harassment would result in discharge); Kidde, Inc., 86 LA 681 (Dunn, 1985) (grievant improperly suspended without adequate notice and without any opportunity to defend himself); King Soopers, Inc., 86 LA 254 (Sass, 1985); Washington Scientific Indus., 83 LA 824 (Kapsch, 1984) (grievant improperly discharged for attempting to shake a female co-employee whom he perceived as being "down" by telling her that he did not think that she would even enjoy sex—grievant's comment was neither obscene nor abusive in the context in which it was uttered).

[115]United Indus., 88 LA 547 (Baron, 1986). In that case, the arbitrator determined that grievant had made threat because he was upset about his marital troubles and because threatened co-employee had repeatedly provoked him by engaging in conduct amounting to sexual harassment, including making lewd remarks and gestures implying that grievant was a homosexual. See also EZ Communications, 91 LA 1097 (Talarico, 1988) (female radio newscaster terminated for flagrant neglect of duty after walking off job successfully proved that two-year campaign of outrageous, lewd on-air remarks directed at her constituted hostile work environment that justified her actions).

[116]See Monat & Gomez, "Decisional Standards Used by Arbitrators in Sexual Harassment Cases," 37 Lab. L.J. 712 (1986); and Nelson, "Sexual Harassment, Title VII, and Labor Arbitration," 40 Arb. J. 55 (1985).

[117]Heublein, 88 LA 1292 (Ellmann, 1987); Porter Equip. Co., 86 LA 1253 (Lieberman, 1986); New Indus. Techniques, 84 LA 915 (Gray, 1985); Veterans Admin. Medical Center, 82 LA 25 (Dallas, 1984). For a case in which preponderance of evidence is mentioned as a standard, see Veterans Admin. Medical Center, 87 LA 405 (Yarowsky, 1986).

[118]Clover Park School Dist., 89 LA 76 (Boedecker, 1987); Sugardale Foods, 86 LA 1017, 1020 (Duda, 1986); Washington Scientific Indus., 83 LA 824, 828 (Kapsch, 1984).

[119]King Soopers, Inc., 86 LA 254, 258 (Sass, 1985); Hyatt Hotels Palo Alto, 85 LA 11, 15 (Oestreich, 1985).

that the Grievant is guilty of the conduct he is charged with. Once this is done, the company still must establish that the conduct provides just and sufficient cause for the discipline that is imposed in the case.[120]

After sexual harassment has been established, other important issues are the factors an arbitrator will consider in determining the seriousness of the sexual harassment and the propriety of the penalty imposed by the employer. Arbitrator Herbert Oestreich has adopted five areas of inquiry in evaluating this issue:

(1) Did the employer have a sexual harassment policy at the time the incident(s) occurred? Was it written? Was it specific enough to make employees understand what constitutes sexual harassment and what the consequences of the infractions of this policy would be? Was the sexual harassment policy adequately disseminated to employees?

(2) Does the employer have an effective vehicle for employees to bring complaints of sexual harassment to the attention of management? Is the work environment such that it discourages employees from making formal or informal complaints?

(3) Did management know, or should it have known, of the sexual harassment practice(s) that occurred?

(4) Was the sexual harassment committed by a supervisor of the harassed employee or a person on whom the employee was dependent for employment, work assignment, promotion, performance ratings, and/or salary increases?

(5) What is the *personal* relationship between the person accused of sexual harassment and the person(s) considered to be the "victim(s)"?[121]

A unique evidentiary question that has arisen in arbitrations involving employees disciplined for conduct constituting sexual harassment is the relevance of allegations of past sexual harassment by the grievant against other individuals. Such evidence has been considered relevant by one arbitrator to the extent that the prior conduct established a pattern of conduct that was consistent with the accusations of the current sexual harassment victim.[122] However, in another case, an arbitrator found that the employer had improperly considered prior incidents of alleged sexual harassment in determining that the grievant was guilty of the current charges.[123]

In a recent case, an arbitrator held that an employee was improperly suspended for allegedly making a false claim of sexual harassment by a co-worker, where the grievant, who had previously been raped, may have exaggerated one claim and inaccurately stated the other but did not intentionally mean to deceive or defraud.[124]

Fraternization, Intermarriage of Employees, Employment of Relatives, Married Employees

Grievances continue to arise from management rules prohibiting fraternization among employees, intermarriage of employees,

[120]King Soopers, Inc., 86 LA 254, 258 (1985).

[121]Hyatt Hotels Palo Alto, 85 LA 11, 15 (1985). For additional cases see Cohen in GTE Fla., 92 LA 1090 (1989); Duda in Onio Dep't of Transp., 90 LA 783 (1988).

[122]King Soopers, Inc., 86 LA 254, 255 (Sass, 1985).

[123]Kidde, Inc., 86 LA 681, 683 (Dunn, 1985).

[124]Defense Mapping Agency, 92 LA 653 (Cohen, 1989).

employment of relatives, and employment after marriage of certain employees. In a recent case, a rule that prohibited spouses from working for the same supervisor was held by an arbitrator to be unenforceable where the employer had failed to inform its employees or its supervisors of the rule.[125] The arbitrator agreed with the employer that such a policy was reasonable under the circumstances but refused to enforce the policy where it had not previously been disseminated.[126]

In another case, pursuant to a policy in an internal management document that was not incorporated into the applicable collective bargaining agreement, an employer discharged an employee who married a co-employee.[127] The arbitrator refused to rule on the validity of the rule on its face because it existed separate from the agreement, but he held that there was no just cause for the discharge in this case because the grievant and his spouse had worked for the company for six and seven years, respectively, and the company had had adequate time to determine that the employees were capable, had no attendance problems, and were loyal to the company.[128]

In another case an arbitrator found that the hiring of a county sheriff's daughter constituted a violation of a county ordinance prohibiting a county officer from supervising or participating in decisions relating to certain relatives.[129]

In a nepotism case, an arbitrator upheld the discharge of a seven and one-half year employee with a good record. The grievant was terminated when the employer learned that the grievant's uncle had been in its workforce since before the grievant's hiring.[130] A different result was reached in a case involving first cousins by marriage, where the arbitrator ruled that this relationship was outside the scope of the antinepotism rule.[131]

Privacy, Dignity, and Peace of Mind

Employees continue to challenge various management rules on the grounds that the rules invade their right of privacy or infringe upon their dignity or peace of mind. The observations of some arbitrators in recent cases in regard to claimed rights of privacy, dignity, and peace of mind are noted below in the setting of the particular situations to which they apply.

Disclosure of Information to Employer

An arbitrator determined that an employer had the right to issue a rule requiring laid-off employees to put their telephone numbers on

---

[125]Duquesne Light Co., 87 LA 420 (Hannan, 1986).

[126]Ibid. For a case in which a reasonable antinepotism rule was properly disseminated to employees, see Electrical Workers (IBEW), 90 LA 383 (O'Grady, 1987).

[127]Distribution Center of Columbus, 83 LA 163 (Seidman, 1984).

[128]Id. at 164, 165.

[129]County of Riverside, 86 LA 903 (Gentile, 1985).

[130]Florida Power & Light, 90 LA 195 (Holliday, 1987).

[131]Camp Lejeune Marine Corps Base, 90 LA 1126 (Nigro, 1988).

the back of their time cards, under a contractual notification process, but could not state that failure to observe the rule would result in a reprimand, since the consequences of failing to comply were unclear.[132] The arbitrator also determined that the employer had a right to require injured individuals to report the injury to a foreman because of the employer's obligation to timely initiate procedures under the applicable workers' compensation statute. However, the arbitrator held it was unreasonable for the employer to imply that a failure to immediately report the injury could result in the loss of workers' compensation benefits.

Another arbitrator found it was not an invasion of privacy, or a violation of the Privacy Act, to require an employee attempting to check out a government-owned tool to state his social security number.[133]

Checking Out

An arbitrator upheld a discharge where a company rule required employees to fill out time cards noting the time they were not producing—mainly during periods when they were engaged in union business or taking a restroom break.[134] The arbitrator determined that the company had properly discharged an employee who failed to comply with this rule, where the rule was instituted because of a productivity problem, and the employee had been previously disciplined for taking excessive restroom breaks, and where it was undisputed that the grievant had spent more than 30 minutes in the restroom on certain days, despite a contractual lunch period and two 10-minute breaks granted to employees each day for personal matters.

Inspecting Employee Lockers, Purses, or Briefcases

In several cases, arbitrators have evaluated the propriety of an employer's search of employees' lunch boxes, tool boxes, and other personal articles.[135] In one case an arbitrator stated that discipline imposed for refusing to submit to a search is proper only when the order is reasonable and when the employee understands both the order and the consequences for refusing to obey the order.[136] In a private-sector case, an arbitrator held that the standard used in determining the reasonableness of such an order is not the same as the standard applicable to the Constitution's Fourth Amendment prohibition of unreasonable searches and seizures—namely, probable

---

[132]Tinker Air Force Base, 86 LA 1249 (Nelson, 1986).
[133]Trojan Luggage Co., 81 LA 409, 414, 415 (Lane, 1983).
[134]ARA Mfg. Co., 85 LA 549, 551, 552 (Heinsz, 1985).
[135]Pacific Sw. Air Lines, 87 LA 701 (Rothschild, 1986); Kawneer Co., 86 LA 297 (Alexander, 1985); Daniel Int'l Corp., 83 LA 1096 (Thornell, 1984); Kraft, Inc., 82 LA 360 (Denson, 1984); Shell Oil Co., 81 LA 1205 (Brisco, 1983).
[136]Kraft, Inc., 82 LA 360, 364 (Denson, 1984).

cause.[137] However, even in private-sector cases, arbitrators have considered the motivation for the search and the circumstances under which it was conducted.[138] In so doing, arbitrators have looked to how a search was conducted and have balanced the legitimate interests of the employer with the personal dignity of the employee.[139]

In a case concerning an employee's expectation of privacy with respect to the contents of his tool box, an arbitrator found that it was the past practice of the company to open the boxes either to remove tools needed for other employees or to protect against theft.[140] However, because of increased theft, the company had recently required employees to purchase their own locks. The arbitrator held that this requirement had endowed the tool boxes with a half-private and a half-company characterization that gave the employees an increased expectation of privacy.[141] Consequently, since there was no express rule allowing the employer to search the boxes, the employer could search them only if it had a reasonable basis for believing that a violation of a promulgated and published rule of conduct had occurred.[142]

Use of Personal Radios

Where a company has a stated policy restricting the use of radios to certain times and areas, and such policy has been in effect for at least 12 years, even though the company has been lax in enforcing the restrictions, a plant manager was held to have properly issued a memorandum reaffirming the company's policy restricting radio use. The arbitrator found there was no dispute about management's right in this regard by virtue of the contract, and the sporadic nonuse of a management right did not amount to a relinquishment of such right. Thus the issuance of the memorandum was held to be an appropriate exercise of management's right to direct its working forces.[143]

Where a radio provided background music for nuclear plant control operators for 15 years, and both the union and the employer viewed its presence as beneficial, the practice was held to be a "binding" past practice, and the employer was held not to have the right to unilaterally remove the radio from the control room even though its removal was in response to "strong suggestions" and "urging" from

---

[137]Kawneer Co., 86 LA 297, 300 (Alexander, 1985).

[138]Kraft, Inc., 82 LA 360 (Denson, 1984); Shell Oil Co., 81 LA 1205 (Brisco, 1983).

[139]Ibid.

[140]Kawneer Co., 86 LA 297, 300, 301 (Alexander, 1985).

[141]Id. at 301.

[142]Id. at 301. Because there was a reasonable basis to search tool box in this case—namely, a company rule prohibited gambling—and grievant had been observed by a supervisor exchanging currency with another employee for a small piece of paper that was suspected to be a lottery ticket—arbitrator held that search was not improper. See also Lake Park of Oakland, 83 LA 27 (Griffin, 1984), where the arbitrator upheld the discharge of an employee for refusing to permit a search of her purse after she had clocked out, the search having been attempted in response to recent incidents of missing food items.

[143]Southern Ind. Gas & Elec. Co., 88 LA 132 (Franke, 1986).

the Nuclear Regulatory Commission.[144] In a recent case, however, an arbitrator held that although the employees' use of personal radios on the shop floor was a long-standing privilege protected by contract, the employer's rule limiting employees to "Walkman" radios with ear phones was valid since the company had moved to a new, larger facility and there were traffic safety concerns. The arbitrator concluded that the "continual use of radios is not conducive to the work environment" and, as a result, "the prohibition against radios is reasonably related to the work product of the company."[145]

Dangerous Weapons on Company Property

Discharge was not warranted for an employee who participated in picketing the employer's premises with a sheathed hunting knife on his belt where it was reasonable to infer that employees at a shipyard were accustomed to seeing sheathed knives on fellow employees, and the striker's mode of dress, unaccompanied by threatening gestures, did not reasonably tend to coerce nonstriking employees.[146]

However, discharge was found to be proper where a striking employee carried a gun in the vicinity of the plant entrance used by nonstriking employees. The Board determined that this type of conduct was the type of misconduct that would reasonably tend to coerce or intimidate nonstriking employees in the exercise of their § 7 rights.[147]

The discharge of an employee was found to be proper where a loaded .22 caliber pistol was discovered in the employee's pickup truck in the company parking lot. Although the employee had not fired the weapon or threatened anyone with it, the employer's rule against possession of firearms was consistently enforced and sufficiently communicated to the employee, and was justified by the potential threat to the life and health of the employees.[148]

Company Liability for Employee's Damaged or Stolen Property

In determining whether an employer may be held liable for an employee's lost or stolen property (usually tools), an arbitrator will generally look to the collective bargaining agreement to determine the parties' intent. Absent specific contract language indicating employer liability in these situations, most arbitrators have found that an employer is not obligated to reimburse its employees for lost or stolen property.

[144]Northern States Power Co., 87 LA 1077 (Fogelberg, 1986).
[145]Creative Prods., 89 LA 777, 780 (McDonald, 1987).
[146]Newport News Shipbldg. Co. v. NLRB, 738 F.2d 1404, 116 LRRM 3042 (CA 4, 1984).
[147]KECO Indus., 276 NLRB 1469, 120 LRRM 1269 (1985).
[148]Goodyear Aerospace Corp., 86 LA 403 (Fullmer, 1985).

Even where an employee was required to furnish his own tools as a condition of employment, and removing the tools from company property was impractical due to the weight of the tool box and the time it took to check them out of the plant, Arbitrator Barbara Bridgewater held that an employer was not required to reimburse one of its employees for personal tools that were stolen after they were left at the plant overnight. Arbitrator Bridgewater found "no specific mutually agreed to contract language" indicating a "clear contractual intent" that the employer indemnify its employees for lost or stolen tools.[149] In this particular case, the arbitrator stated that she did not have to balance the equities between the employee's transportation difficulties and the adequacy of plant security because the contract had a provision restraining her from adding to the scope or terms of the contract.[150]

In another case, an arbitrator denied a grievance seeking reimbursement for stolen tools where the tools were under the almost exclusive control of the employee at the workplace, the union had proposed and then dropped a tool-theft insurance provision during contract negotiations, and where one prior instance of reimbursement did not constitute a binding past practice.[151]

Some arbitrators have held that where bargaining agreements do not specifically require an employer to indemnify employees for lost or stolen tools, grievances for reimbursements are nonarbitrable, even if an employer provides a steel locker for maintenance employees who are required to furnish their own tools as a condition of employment.[152] However, where the contract provides for an allowance for "maintenance of personal tools of employees," a grievance seeking reimbursement for stolen tools has been held to be arbitrable.[153]

Where a contract specified the employer had a duty to strive to eliminate industrial accidents or illness, an arbitrator limited the employer's obligation to protecting the person of the employee rather than his property. The arbitrator also relied upon the fact that the union had twice before failed in its attempts in past negotiations to include in the contract provisions requiring the company to replace lost tools.[154]

---

[149]Transamerica Delaval Inc., 85 LA 321, 324, 325 (Bridgewater, 1985).

[150]Id. at 325. See also San Bernardino School Dist., 90 LA 214 (Collins, 1987) (grievance seeking reimbursement for theft of car stolen from school parking lot is denied where contract limits district's obligation to losses from "malicious acts" and where all claims related to vehicle theft have been consistently denied); Grocers Baking Co., 83 LA 376 (McDonald, 1984) (fact that employee was required to furnish tools as condition of employment does not change ultimate responsibility concerning reimbursement if loss takes place under circumstances described in contract).

[151]Niagara Frontier Transit Metro, 90 LA 1171 (Fullmer, 1988). Also see Southern Clay, 92 LA 731 (Odom, 1989) (where employee was not entitled to reimbursement since his tool box was not locked at time of theft).

[152]Reyco Indus., 85 LA 1034 (Newmark, 1985) (where grievance held nonarbitrable absent relevant contract language).

[153]Niagara Frontier Transit Metro, 90 LA 1171 (Fullmer, 1988).

[154]Owens-Corning Fiberglass Corp., 85 LA 305 (Madden, 1985).

Union Bulletin Boards

Many agreements contain clauses specifying the types of notices a union may post on an employer's property and the location at which they may be posted. Such clauses usually limit union postings to "official union business" such as notices of union meetings, elections, social activities, and the like.[155]

Absent such specific contract language defining proper posting procedures, past practice will usually dictate the propriety of what may be posted. Issues have been arbitrated, however, where clear and unambiguous contract language specifies the types of notices allowed to be posted but a long-standing past practice has allowed bulletin board postings beyond those covered by the language of the contract. In such a case, an arbitrator held that when past practice conflicts with contract language regarding bulletin boards, even where the employer may have been lax in enforcing the provisions of the agreement over the years, the clear and unambiguous language of the contract will prevail absent "very strong proof" that the parties have mutually agreed to the past practice.[156]

Another problem that often arises with respect to union bulletin boards are those notices that are allowed to be posted under the terms of the contract but cause disruptive behavior among employees. Where this situation has occurred the NLRB has held that absent evidence of special circumstances showing that the posting caused employee behavior which amounts to a serious threat to discipline in the workplace, the union will be permitted to keep the notice posted. Chairman Donald L. Dotson, however, disagreed with his colleagues, holding that the company had the right to "prevent the deleterious consequences the posting might reasonably be expected to produce under the circumstances."[157] He stated that where a notice was likely to provoke confrontation, the company should not have to wait until an actual confrontation or breakdown of discipline has already occurred before special circumstances warranting the prohibition of the posting are deemed to be present.[158]

In a recent case, Arbitrator Elliott H. Goldstein allowed the employer to unilaterally relocate a bulletin board where the contract required that the union be provided one bulletin board in the department, but did not specify the location. The board often con-

---

[155]See U.S. Army, Soldier Support Center, 91 LA 1201 (Wolff, 1988), where contract language prohibited the posting of "any derogatory remarks" or "personal attacks on individuals"; Webb Furniture, 275 NLRB 1305, 120 LRRM 1034 (1985), where the Board found that the company violated § 8(a)(1) of the Act by disparately applying its no-posting rule to prohibit union posting while permitting nonunion-related postings; Roadway Express, 272 NLRB 895, 117 LRRM 1436 (1984).

[156]County of Hennepin, 84 LA 593 (Neigh, 1985).

[157]Southwestern Bell Tel. Co., 276 NLRB 1053, 120 LRRM 1145, 1147 (1985). See also Greyhound Food Mgmt., 87 LA 619 (Ellmann, 1985), where a posting was found to be legitimate union business even though it could be considered to be inflammatory.

[158]120 LRRM at 1146. Cf. Mobil Oil Corp., 87 LA 837 (Koven, 1986), and Dalfort Corp., 85 LA 70 (White, 1985).

tained disloyal, critical, scatological, and obscene material and the employer felt that this material was inappropriate for public view, especially since the company had recently begun conducting tours for school children. The arbitrator held that such changed conditions overrode past practice and, therefore, the employer was allowed to move the board to a remote hallway corner on the edge of the department.[159]

Change in Time or Method of Pay

Arbitrators have agreed that unless restricted by contract, an employer may change the time of payment of wages. However, Arbitrator Raymond L. Hilgert held that an employer did not have the right to change from weekly to biweekly pay periods where the contract defined the payroll period as the "seven day period from 12:01 a.m. Sunday through midnight the following Saturday," and there was a long-standing past practice of paying employees weekly.[160] In this case, even though the company offered good business reasons as justification for the change, Arbitrator Hilgert found that its unilateral action was violative of the collective agreement and that any change in the pay period should come through the process of negotiations with the union.[161] More recently, a successor employer was found to have violated a local agreement by changing a 12-year practice of paying on a weekly basis. The arbitrator held that the union had given up seniority rights as a quid pro quo for the weekly pay schedule and the fact that the company no longer desired the benefits gained under the agreement was not determinative.[162]

In other cases, where the company changed the method of payment from cash or check to some other form of compensation, unless there was a contractual provision prohibiting the company from making such changes, or a past practice that was found to be binding on the company, arbitrators have generally permitted such unilateral action by an employer.[163]

---

[159]Copley Press, 91 LA 1324 (Goldstein, 1988).

[160]Creative Data Serv., 87 LA 962 (1986).

[161]Id. at 964. Arbitrator Hilgert found no merit in the company's contention that it did not in fact change the payroll period, it merely paid employees for two payroll periods in each paycheck rather than one.

[162]Arch of West Va., Inc., 90 LA 891 (Stoltenberg, 1988).

[163]See Stroehmann Bros., 268 NLRB 1360, 115 LRRM 1150 (1984), where the Board found that an employer had violated § 8(a)(5) and (1) of the Act by unilaterally changing the wages of its employees by granting a Christmas bonus consisting of food instead of money. Where the Christmas bonus was "consistently paid over a number of years" (in this case over 40 years), it became a term of employment even though it was not expressly provided for in the parties' agreement and, therefore, it could not be discontinued unless the union had notice and the opportunity to bargain about it. See also Pickands, Mather & Co., 87 LA 1071 (Garrett, 1986), where the arbitrator held that the unilateral requirement that all paychecks be directly deposited into employee-designated banks was improper; the practice of allowing certain employees to refuse to authorize direct deposit was a "benefit" for employees and should be protected as a local working condition.

Other Employee Rights and Benefits

Arbitrators have continued to determine the existence or coverage of a number of other types of rights and benefits that appear only sporadically in the reported cases. These miscellaneous rights and benefits vary greatly in subject matter and include topics such as free parking,[164] free tickets,[165] tuition reimbursement,[166] take-home vehicles,[167] bans or limitations on smoking,[168] use of refrigerators,[169] availability of hot showers,[170] and use of vending machines.[171] Like those discussed in other sections of this Chapter, these asserted rights and benefits are covered by the agreement or evolved from the practice of the parties.

---

[164]Social Security Admin., 85 LA 874 (Ellmann, 1985) (since contract provided for parking and to preserve prior benefits and practices, employer was required to continue to provide parking facilities without cost to employees); also see County of Wayne, 87 LA 134 (Daniel, 1986).

[165]Dallas Power & Light Co., 87 LA 415 (White, 1985) (employer was allowed to discontinue practice of providing free tickets to state fair).

[166]East Amwell Bd. of Educ., 86 LA 425 (Handsaker, 1985).

[167]Centel Business Sys., 88 LA 1301 (Nelson, 1987).

[168]J.R. Simplot Co., 91 LA 375 (McCurdy, 1988); Des Moines Register & Tribune Co., 90 LA 777 (Gallagher, 1988); Worthington Foods, 89 LA 1069 (McIntosh, 1987); Lennox Indus., 89 LA 1065 (Gibson, 1987); H-N Advertising & Display Co., 88 LA 1311 (Heekin, 1987); Morelite Equip. Co., 88 LA 777 (Stoltenberg, 1987); H-N Advertising & Display Co., 88 LA 329 (Heekin, 1986); National Pen & Pencil Co., 87 LA 1081 (Nicholas, 1986); Snap-On Tools Corp., 87 LA 785 (Berman, 1986).

[169]Homestake Mining Co., 90 LA 720 (Fogelberg, 1987).

[170]Monterey Coal Co., Mine No. 1, 89 LA 989 (Fullmer, 1987).

[171]Mechanical Prods., 91 LA 977 (Roumell, 1988).

Chapter 18

Standards in Arbitration of Interest Disputes

Prevailing Practice—Industry, Area, Industry-Area

In the absence of express statutory standards, comparability has been the principal criterion in the decisions reported in this Supplement.[1] Traditional factors such as cost-of-living, ability to pay, and wage patterns have become points of reference in evaluating various governmental units.

Some statutes, in addition to setting out the factors to be weighed in determining which of two final offers will be incorporated into the parties' next collective bargaining agreement, direct the arbitrator to also consider "such other factors * * * which are normally or traditionally taken into consideration."[2]

Where the arbitrator relies on the prevailing practice in other communities, or goes outside the immediate work force, for a basis of determination, it is known as "external comparison." By contrast, "internal comparison" involves an examination of the employer's treatment of its other employees. Applying the internal-comparison standard to determine the appropriate health insurance package, Arbitrator Mario F. Bognanno explained:

> [B]ecause of risk pooling, economies of scale and the lack of quality data about the coverage, contribution levels and the costs of health insurance benefits to external communities, most Arbitrators give heavy weight to evidence about the instant Employer's internal structure of health insurance coverage/contributions as opposed to what external practices are in these areas. Clearly, one cannot expect the Employer to offer a different health insurance package to each of its different work groups. By pooling risk and by "spreading" costs, the individual Employer can

[1]City of Farmington, 85 LA 460 (Bognanno, 1985); City of Newark, 86 LA 149 (Duda, 1985); Sioux County Bd. of Supervisors, 87 LA 552 (Dilts, 1986).

[2]Deerfield Community School Dist., 93 LA 316, 319 (Michelstetter, 1988).

buy insurance protection at a far more reasonable price. Hence, in the health area the comparison focus shifts from the "external" to the "internal." This conclusion applies to dental insurance as well.[3]

In construction industry disputes, standards often referred to for determining wage rates include special training required; hazards of the craft; productivity data; cost-of-living index; effect of weather; economic trends and outlook for the geographic area (including growth or decline in population, industry, wages, employment, and inflation); and nonunion competition.[4]

In newspaper industry disputes, comparisons of operations in comparable cities across the nation are used to determine the prevailing practice in that industry.[5]

As noted in the Fourth Edition, determining which cities are "comparable" for purposes of arbitrable resolution of a dispute between a city and its police officers has been made on the basis of the following factors: (1) proximity to a large city; (2) population; (3) size of the police force; and (4) size of the police department budget.[6] Another factor is the union status of the police department.[7] Thus one arbitrator selected the cities to be used as the comparison group, then computed the mean, or average, value of the settlements reached by those cities' unionized police departments, determined it to represent a wage increase of 4.5 percent, and applied that percentage uniformly across the parties' wage schedule.

Selection of the "appropriate comparability group" from among 25 counties offered by the parties for purposes of resolving percentage wage increase and medical insurance contribution issues has been made on the basis of three standards of comparability. They include close geographic proximity; population and its density; and union representation. In identifying those standards, Arbitrator David A. Dilts explained:

> [A] close geographic proximity may signal certain shared characteristics such as climate, avenues of transportation*** and possibly socio-political values of the population.*** [L]abor markets tend to have geographic boundaries.*** [W]hat occurs in other counties within this range may be expected to affect the ability of Sioux County to employ or retain workers and may affect the nature of the duties of secondary road employees.
>
> ***[C]ounties with metropolitan areas will typically have a larger tax base, and may have greater diversity of industry***. Population therefore may be an important determinant of whether a county is

[3]City of Farmington, 85 LA at 464 (1985). Also see Birmingham Bd. of Educ., 86 LA 462 (Frost, 1985), and Zia Corp., 87 LA 28 (Dunn, 1986).

[4]Houston Insulation Contractors Ass'n, 84 LA 1245 (Williams, 1985).

[5]In Newark Morning Ledger Co. v. Newark Typographical Union Local 103, 797 F.2d 162, 123 LRRM 2283 (CA 3, 1986), the annual wage increases in the contract were tied to those received by comparable employees of daily newspapers in New York City. The court found that the arbitrator's award did not draw its essence from the agreement when he claimed that it was impossible to figure the average increase of three New York papers when only one of them granted an increase.

[6]See Chapter 18 of the Fourth Edition, p. 809, n.23.

[7]City of Farmington, 85 LA 460, 464 (Bognanno, 1985).

comparable *** with respect not only to ability to pay but also to the nature of duties required of secondary road employees.

Employees represented by a union have an effective vehicle by which to present their views on *** salary and fringe benefits ***. Employees without such representation cannot be said to be similarly situated***.[8]

The terms of employment of public-sector employees may not always be compared with those of other public sector employees. The decision may be legislatively determined. As one arbitration board observed:

In its deliberations and decision-making, the board has been circumscribed by a number of constraints, two of them imposed by Acts of Congress***.

With regard to the first of the constraints *** it has [been] directed in two separate provisions of the Postal Reorganization Act (sections 101(c) and 1003(a)) that compensation paid to Postal Service officers and employees is to be "comparable to the rates and types of compensation paid in the private sector of the economy of the United States" and that they are to receive "compensation and benefits paid for comparable levels of work in the private sector of the economy."[9]

Where the task involves setting the proper wage rate for newly created positions, other considerations may arise. An initial determination may be whether a "new department" or "new work" has in fact been created. Concluding that a new or changed job had been established, an arbitration board described its task as follows:

The more difficult question is how can an arbitration board decide whether the rates set by the Company are appropriate or fair ***.

[T]he labor contract has provided no standard to guide the board, and *** therefore an implied standard should be applied *** [to be fair and consistent, and not to be arbitrary, capricious, or discriminatory, in setting the wage rates].

***Interest arbitration *** requires the arbitrator to set the rates that the negotiators couldn't agree on. Perhaps the most accepted method of proof *** is to have industrial engineer types study the jobs on the basis of skill, effort, responsibility and working conditions. This is usually done by awarding points to each of the elements of the job based on a nationally recognized manual. Each side presents its expert with differing evaluations; the arbitrator makes the decision based on this kind of evidence.

Another method of proof in interest arbitration is to compare the jobs with the same jobs for other employers***.

A third method is to try to fit the new jobs into an existing scale based on written job descriptions and verbal testimony as to the actual day to day activities of the jobs being compared***.[10]

---

[8]Sioux County Bd. of Supervisors, 87 LA 552, 555 (1986).

[9]U.S. Postal Serv., 83 LA 1120, 1122 (Volz, Chm., 1985). Compare D.C. Office of Labor Relations, 84 LA 809 (Rothschild, Chm., 1985), involving a District of Columbia statute which provided that: "Compensation shall be competitive with that provided to other public sector employees having comparable duties, responsibilities, qualifications, and working conditions by occupational groups."

[10]West Penn Power Co., 86 LA 1217, 1225 (Lubow, Chm., 1986).

The prevailing practice standard has been applied to define a contract term,[11] determine what percentage an employer should pay toward health care coverage of its employees' dependents,[12] establish the composition of a police department's board of promotion,[13] and an equity wage increase.[14]

Differentials and the "Minor" Standards

Skill and Training—Arbitrators have long recognized that wages should be to some extent responsive to the level of skill and experience required. An arbitration panel concluded that to make it possible for postal employees to be more readily rewarded, the wage spread between the employees with the most skill and experience and those with the least skill and experience had to be increased to provide greater career opportunities. As Chairman Clark Kerr of that arbitration panel stated:

> Congress, when it established the USPS in 1970, was very concerned with career opportunities. We find, however, that the wage structure has become very compressed since that date. This compression occurred primarily through across-the-board dollar increases over a period when the cost of living rose very rapidly. Today, the most skilled and long service employees receive only fifty percent more than the least skilled and newest hires. The wage structure that Congress had established had a spread of 150 percent.[15]

Geographic Differentials—Geographic differentials have been found appropriate.[16] Indeed, geographic differentials have been justified in the Postal Service based on legislative mandates requiring consideration of comparable rates and types of compensation paid in the private sector. In addition, prior and existing differentials between geographic areas brought about by voluntary collective bargaining have been considered as a precedent for maintaining geographic differentials in other areas such as wages.[17]

If There Is No Prevailing Practice

A party to interest arbitration will sometimes suggest its internal criteria for determining whether to deviate from prior negotiated wage patterns. In one case a county board set forth the following standards:

1. Ability to attract and retain qualified classification staff;
2. External worker comparisons;

---

[11]Kentucky Center for the Performing Arts, 89 LA 344 (Volz, 1987).
[12]City of Lake Worth, 91 LA 1408 (Weston, 1988).
[13]City of Swartz Creek, 90 LA 448 (Sugarman, Chm., 1988).
[14]Asplundh Tree Expert Co., 89 LA 183 (Allen, 1987).
[15]U.S. Postal Serv., 83 LA 1105, 1110-1111 (1984).
[16]U.S. Postal Serv., 83 LA 1120 (Volz, Chm., 1985), and U.S. Postal Serv., 87 LA 1233 (Peer, Member, dissenting, 1985). See also City of Lake Worth, 91 LA 1408 (Weston, 1988).
[17]U.S. Postal Serv., 83 LA at 1122-1123.

3. Employer's willingness to pay; and
4. Internal classification relationships.[18]

Standards in Public-Sector Disputes

Several surveys of public interest arbitration decisions have been conducted in recent years, and have arrived at similar, if not identical, findings regarding the standards interest arbitrators use. A survey of 995 police salary decisions revealed that the criteria arbitrators cited most often were salary comparability, ability to pay, and inflation/cost of living, in that order.[19] With regard to salary comparability, the arbitrators referred far more frequently to salaries in other police departments than to salaries in other comparison groups.[20] Interviews of interest arbitrators in Wisconsin disclosed that the arbitrators look first to internal wage-settlement patterns. If no clear pattern of percentage increases is observed, they next look at external comparability factors, followed by the cost of living and ability-to-pay criteria.[21] Another survey found that the criteria stressed by the parties are comparability, ability to pay, and cost of living, "although cost of living has been given less emphasis in recent years."[22]

One study explained why arbitrators do not emphasize the ability-to-pay criterion:

> The general conclusion [of the arbitrators interviewed] was that absent a specific ability-to-pay argument, the budget carried little weight on its own. * * * [T]he majority of arbitrators recognized the self-serving nature of such arguments. As one arbitrator noted, "any good city budget manager can manipulate the budget to look like the city can't afford anything—relying on this type of information is not bargaining."[23]

Nonetheless, when faced with serious, well-documented arguments about a public employer's financial condition, arbitrators will evaluate them, especially if the outcome hinges on the disposition of that issue. Most arbitrators will critically examine financial data presented to them, and raise questions about such matters as available funds and alternative priorities. An ability-to-pay argument is likely to carry the most weight when an employer can demonstrate that it has done everything in its power to overcome an adverse financial position, both absolutely and in relation to what comparable public employers have done. On the other hand, an arbitrator is more

---

[18] Hennepin County Medical Center, Medical Examiner/Security Unit, 88-1 ARB ¶ 8275 (Bognanno, 1988).
[19] Feuille & Schwochau, "The Decisions of Interest Arbitrators," 43 Arb. J. 28, 33 (1988).
[20] Ibid.
[21] Dell'omo, "Wage Disputes in Interest Arbitration: Arbitrators Weigh the Criteria," 44 Arb. J. 4, 8 (1989).
[22] Doherty, "Trends in Strikes and Interest Arbitration in the Public Sector," 37 Lab. L.J. 473, 474 (1986).
[23] Dell'omo, "Wage Disputes in Interest Arbitration: Arbitrators Weigh the Criteria," 44 Arb. J. 4, 10 (1989).

likely to rule in favor of a union if the employer has not made sufficient taxing efforts as measured against comparable communities.[24]

The State of Minnesota has passed a law introducing a new criterion for arbitrators to apply—comparable worth. The statute requires every political subdivision to "establish equitable compensation relationships between female-dominated, male-dominated, and balanced classes of employees."[25] In all interest arbitrations, arbitrators are to consider various "equitable compensation relationship standards," as well as "other standards appropriate to interest arbitration."[26]

This statute has been interpreted in several reported arbitral decisions. In one decision, the arbitrator adopted the public employer's position on wages because it took account of the statute, while the union's position did not.[27] In another decision, the arbitrator rejected the employer's position of no wage increase partly because of a comparable worth study.[28] The arbitrator said pay equity was only one factor to be considered, and that arbitrators could not "totally ignore historical comparisons, both external and internal."[29] Yet another arbitrator has ruled that the statute can be used "to decelerate the rates of increases for overcompensated employees while attempting to bring undercompensated employees to a more equitable relative position."[30]

Last Best Offer

Unlike the Postal Service award where the panel reached a middle ground on comparability data, a number of statutory schemes provide for "last best offer" as the only alternative to an award.

The District of Columbia Code required such arbitration upon the parties reaching impasse.[31] Unlike the Postal Service cases where the respective panels praised the parties for their previous efforts to resolve their outstanding issues, the conduct of the parties in this case was characterized as mutually acrimonious and resulted in the parties moving farther apart rather than nearer to agreement.

How much weight, if any, should be given to pre-impasse negotiations by the parties in determining which is the last best offer? Obviously, the conduct of the parties in the course of negotiations is measured by statutory criteria, past practice, and reasonable expecta-

---

[24]Krinsky, "Interest Arbitration and Ability to Pay: U.S. Public Sector Experience," Proceedings of the 41st Annual Meeting of NAA, 197-208 (BNA Books, 1989).

[25]Minn. Stat. § 471.992, Subd. 1.

[26]*Id.*, Subd. 2. Under Minn. Stat. § 471.995, a public employer must submit a report to the exclusive representatives of their employees which identifies "the female-dominated classes in the political subdivision for which compensation inequity exists, based on the comparable work value * * *."

[27]County of Carver, 91 LA 1222 (Kanatz, 1988).

[28]City of Blaine, 90 LA 549 (Perretti, 1988).

[29]*Id.* at 551.

[30]County of Kanabec, 93 LA 479, 482 (Ver Plueg, 1989).

[31]D.C. Office of Labor Relations, 84 LA 713 (Rothschild, Chm., 1985).

tions. Where demands, even unreasonable demands, are rationally connected to employee or employer interests, it can be assumed they are made in good faith. It is only where demands lack this legitimate interest on their face or by the conduct of the parties that bad faith requires they not be considered.[32] For instance, should any proposal previously withdrawn be permitted to be included into the party's last best offer?

Good faith standards are presumed in a last-and-best-offer approach. If not, the incentive to reach agreement item by item, word by word is lost and bargaining becomes a charade. The last-best offer process should be the arbitrator's final dressing of the corpus of the parties' agreement, not the creation of skeleton and flesh. Proposals withdrawn, or beyond the scope of required bargaining, should not be weighed in the balancing process of the last best offer.[33]

Where the issue presented is somewhere in that "gray area" between a mandatory and a permissive subject of bargaining, an examination of bargaining history and past practice is a more reliable gauge.[34] Where a labor organization has, by custom and practice, been allowed to bargain over what appear to be permissive bargaining subjects, and where proposals are made pursuant to this practice, they should not be excluded from the last-best-offer process.

On the merits, the panel found that the last best offer of the union satisfied relevant statutory criteria,[35] after defining the parties' respective burdens of proof:

> The Panel does not agree that it should impose the burden of proof on the Union by clear and convincing evidence to show a compelling

---

[32]Metro Council No. 23 v. Center Line, 115 LRRM 3610 (Mich. S.Ct., 1982).

[33]Fibreboard Paper Prods. Corp. v. NLRB, 85 S.Ct. 398, 57 LRRM 2609 (1964); First Nat'l Maintenance Corp. v. NLRB, 101 S.Ct. 2573, 107 LRRM 2705 (1981).

[34]D.C. Code § 1-618.2d:

Where deemed appropriate, impasse resolution machinery may be invoked by either party or on application to the Board. The choice of the form(s) of impasse resolution machinery to be utilized in a particular instance shall be the prerogative of the Board, after appropriate consultation with the interested parties. In considering the appropriate award for each impasse item to be resolved, any third party shall consider at least the following criteria:
(1) Existing laws and rules and regulations which bear on the item in dispute;
(2) Ability of the District to comply with the terms of the award;
(3) The need to protect and maintain the public health, safety and welfare; and
(4) The need to maintain personnel policies that are fair, reasonable and consistent with the objectives of this chapter.

[35]D.C. Code § 1-162.3:

(a) Compensation for all employees in the Career, Educational and the Excepted Services shall be fixed in accordance with the following policy:

(1) Compensation shall be competitive with that provided to other public sector employees having comparable duties, responsibilities, qualifications, and working conditions by occupational groups. For purposes of this paragraph compensation shall be deemed to be competitive if it falls reasonably within the range of compensation prevailing in the Washington, D.C. Standard Metropolitan Statistical Area (SMSA): Provided, that compensation levels may be examined for public and/or private employees outside the area and/or for federal government employees when necessary to establish a reasonably representative statistical basis for compensation comparisons, or when conditions in the local labor market require a larger sampling of prevailing compensation levels;

(2) Pay for the various occupations and groups of employees shall be the maximum extent practicable, interrelated and equal for substantially equal work;

(3) Differences in pay shall be maintained in keeping with differences in level of work and quality of performance***

> reason for departure from a traditional wage relationship or bargaining pattern in the instant case for a number of reasons. However, prior to stating them, the Panel wishes to clarify what is being rejected by it and what it wishes to preserve for its decision on the merits. The panel does not believe that last best offer arbitration imposes a burden of proof on the Union alone, even on issues as important as parity. The Panel believes last best offer arbitration imposes on both parties a burden to show by statute, by rule, and/or by traditional criteria that their final offer is best.[36]

In addition to defining comparability, the D.C. Code limited its application to "occupational groups of employees in other jurisdictions in the Washington Standard Metropolitan Statistical Area."[37] While exact comparisons cannot be made from SMSA statistics due to effective dates, increments, and variations in public-employee duties and responsibilities, some general conclusions can be made for comparing salaries, benefits, and revenues.

---

[36]D.C. Office of Labor Relations, 84 LA 809, 813 (Rothschild, Chm., 1985).
[37]Id. at 817.

Chapter 19

Arbitration's Place as an Industrial and Public-Employment Institution

Despite dire predictions and gloomy forecasts by many in the field, labor arbitration as an institution remains strong and vital to the labor-management relations of the United States. Fears that overlegalization and formalization of the labor arbitration process would lead to its demise have proven unfounded. Indeed, such formalization may have run its course.[1]

The increased use of interest arbitration, principally by governmental entities, together with the continued vitality of "rights" arbitration, is a cause for optimism about labor arbitration as an institution.[2] The publication of this supplement to *How Arbitration Works* by the Labor and Employment Law Section of the American Bar Association, together with the Bureau of National Affairs, Inc., is testimony to the vital nature of labor arbitration as an institution in the industrial and public-employment relations of this country.

The courts recognize that the successes of arbitration in the resolution of disputes have been due not so much to the arbitrators as to the arbitration process. Thus, Judge Harry T. Edwards explained in *Devine v. White*:

> The advantages of arbitration over litigation in personnel cases are attributable less to the characteristics of labor arbitrators than to the characteristics of the arbitration process. A principal characteristic of the common law of labor arbitration in the United States is judicial deference to arbitral decisions.[3]

---

[1]Nolan & Abrams, "The Future of Labor Arbitration," 37 Lab. L. J. 437, 439-440 (1986).

[2]A majority of states provide for arbitration of interest disputes. However, only a small percentage of the awards rendered in such arbitrations ever reach the reporting services. Therefore, the practitioner's perception of its use may be somewhat skewed. Doherty, "Trends and Strikes and Interest Arbitration in the Public Sector," 37 Lab. L. J. 473 (1986).

[3]697 F.2d 421, 112 LRRM 2374, 2384 (D.C. Cir.), affirmed, 711 F.2d 1082, 114 LRRM 2348 (D.C. Cir., 1983). If indeed the success of arbitration has been "judicial deference," as well as its finality and exclusivity, the recent decision of the U.S. Supreme Court in Lingle v. Norge Div. of Magic Chef, 108 S.Ct. 1877, 128 LRRM 2521 (1988), may, however, be cause for some concern. In *Lingle*,

And Judge Alvin B. Rubin added in *Teamsters Local 657 v. Stanley Structures*:

> When an employer and a union contract that all disputes and controversies that may arise between them shall be settled by arbitration, they do not simply substitute an arbiter for a judge. They adopt a different method of dispute resolution. They alter pretrial procedures, the method of trial, the standards for admissibility of evidence, and the method of rendering a decision, and they limit the scope of judicial review of the arbitration award.[4]

The prophecy of Frank and Edna Asper Elkouri in *How Arbitration Works* that arbitration would continue to be an exceedingly useful social and industrial institution, both in the private sector and in the public sector, has proven true in the 38 years following the 1952 publication of the first edition. Their second edition expressed confidence in the continued usefulness of arbitration in the private sector, but did not mention the public sector. This dimension was added in the third edition and reaffirmed in the fourth. We reiterate the same prophecy with the strong conviction that labor arbitration will continue in the future to be the vital social and industrial institution it has proven to be in the past half century.

---

the Court held that § 301 of the Labor Management Relations Act of 1947, 29 U.S.C. § 185, did not preempt a common law claim of retaliatory discharge. According to the Court,

> even if dispute resolution pursuant to a collective bargaining agreement, on the one hand, and state law, on the other, would require addressing the same set of facts, as long as the state law claims can be resolved without interpreting the agreement itself, the claim is "independent" of the agreement for Section 301 pre-emption purposes.

108 S.Ct. at 1883, 123 LRRM at 2525 (footnote omitted). See also Hanks v. General Motors Corp., 859 F.2d 67, 129 LRRM 2715 (CA 8, 1988); Nelson v. Lapeyrouse Grain Corp., 534 So. 2d 1085, 130 LRRM 2292 (Ala., 1988). But see Jackson v. Liquid Carbonic Corp., 863 F.2d 111, 130 LRRM 2143 (CA 1, 1988), cert. denied, 109 S.Ct. 3158, 131 LRRM 2528 (1989).

It is too early to tell the precise impact that *Lingle* and its progeny will have on arbitration as an institution.

[4]735 F.2d 903, 117 LRRM 2119, 2120 (CA 5, 1984).

BROWN, ANDREW, HALLENBECK,
SIGNORELLI & ZALLAR, P.A.
300 Alworth Building
Duluth, MN 55802

BROWN, ANDREW, HALLENBECK,
SIGNORELLI & ZALLAR, P.A.
300 Alworth Building
Duluth, MN 55802